The Foundations of Organizational Evil

The Foundations of Organizational Evil

Carole L. Jurkiewicz, Editor

Routledge
Taylor & Francis Group

LONDON AND NEW YORK

To Crosby and Spencer

First published 2012 by M.E. Sharpe

Published 2015 by Routledge
2 Park Square, Milton Park, Abingdon, Oxon OX14 4RN
711 Third Avenue, New York, NY 10017, USA

Routledge is an imprint of the Taylor & Francis Group, an informa business

Library of Congress Cataloging-in-Publication Data

The foundations of organizational evil / edited by Carole L. Jurkiewicz.
    p. cm.
Includes bibliographical references and index.
ISBN 978-0-7656-2558-8 (hbk. : alk. paper)— ISBN 978-0-7656-2559-5 (pbk. : alk. paper)
  1. Organizational behavior—Moral and ethical aspects. 2. Corporate culture—Moral and ethical aspects.
3. Good and evil. 4. Business ethics. 5. Organizational sociology. 6. Industrial sociology. I. Jurkiewicz,
Carole L., 1958–

HM791.F68 2012
302.3'5—dc23   2011030533

ISBN 13: 9780765625595 (pbk)
ISBN 13: 9780765625588 (hbk)

Contents

Foreword

Joseph Nowinski

If the events that have unfolded and rocked the world in recent years have taught us nothing else, they have taught us that organizations—corporate, government, even ecclesiastical—are, in fact, capable of acting in ways that can only be described as evil. How else to explain why hedge fund executives would be willing to bet (and make) money on a worldwide financial collapse? What alternative explanation accounts for banks' doling out billions in executive bonuses even as they slide into bankruptcy, taking their shareholders with them? What could one call it, other than evil, when corporations and government agencies conspire to flaunt safety regulations or willfully withhold information on dangerous products, leading to environmental catastrophes or the serious injury (or even death) of consumers? Finally, what can one call deliberate efforts by one of the world's foremost religions to systematically hide widespread sexual abuse of children by the very clergy it designates as its moral shepherds?

Until now, the dialogue about evil appears to have remained largely within the province of theology. To the extent that it has been conceptualized more broadly, it has been in the context of arguments that corporations as a group are collectively trying to "take over" American society. The present volume delves deeper than that, and therefore it breaks new ground by broadening the discussion and extending the very concept of evil. It examines, for example, the issue of whether evil can take hold and motivate not only an individual but an entire organization. In addition, it looks at how power within organizations can be used for good or evil. In the course of doing so, it inevitably confronts the thorny issue of defining evil. Is it, as traditional theology would suggest, something that is fundamentally personal? Can organizations, as well as individuals, reasonably be thought of as having a conscience? If so, how is it manifested? Does the concept of evil imply something more sinister than the idea of "ethical" practices? Is it truly evil or merely the inevitable fallout of competition, capitalism, or a desire for organizational survival that accounts for the events described above? Finally, how can those who work within an organizational structure (and are dependent on it) assess its "character," and what options do they have if they find it wanting?

This book asserts that organizational evil does exist. It is not a mere figment of the imagination or an exaggeration fomented by a disgruntled or cynical few. It involves something more than ethics, and it is not a necessary outcome of capitalism. Equally troubling, if unremedied, corporate evil has the potential to undermine the moral fiber of society.

The authors who contributed to this book have examined it from a variety of perspectives. No purview is overlooked as the contributors examine diverse social arenas, such as public administration, the law, and even academia. They write about the roots of corporate evil, its dynamics within organizations, how it is justified and defended, and even how it is rewarded. Readers will find this timely book engaging and thought-provoking. One hopes that it will mark the beginning of a long and much-needed conversation that spurs further research into a vital issue that for too long has lurked in the shadows of organizational literature.

Introduction

Carole L. Jurkiewicz

The slew of reprehensible corporate, government, and nonprofit activities witnessed over the past few years has highlighted the existence of organizational evil as a salient idea in the social psyche. Journalists have written about it, scholars have sought to understand it, and documentaries like *The Corporation and Enron: The Smartest Guys in the Room* have tried to illustrate the manifestations of evil in contemporary organizational life. The approach to organizational evil in the literature to date is either macro-level, as an entity separate from the individuals that comprise it, or presented as religiously based construct. To more fully develop the concept of organizational evil, it must be understood ontologically, conceptually weaving the interchange between evil individuals (the micro-level) who ultimately create an organizational environment that is evil and at the same time sustains evil through policy, culture, and manipulations of the social environment.

Understanding the nature of evil has long been a concern of philosophers, theologians, and scholars. The emphasis in this book represents a new conceptualization of organizational evil, one that goes beyond defining terms to applications and investigations of evil in practice. Key international scholars have contributed their perspectives and research on organizational evil, balanced by first-hand accounts by top professional executives, to this book. The chapters, which complement, extend, and sometimes contradict one another in the search for a clear rubric of organizational evil, are grouped into three parts: The Nature of Organizational Evil, Understanding Organizational Evil, and Faces of Organizational Evil. The overarching objectives of this edited volume are:

- to provide professionals, scholars, and students with a broad understanding of organizational evil, both from a conceptual and a practical vantage point.
- to provide a scientific paradigm for interdisciplinary research and theory.
- to offer a synthesis linking the divergent, interdisciplinary perspectives on evil into a cohesive whole and, in so doing, creating the seminal volume in this field of inquiry.
- to better understand the potential relationships between organizational evil and various aspects of organizational functioning.
- to integrate a philosophical and pragmatic understanding of organizational evil into a coherent approach to management and administration in the private, public, and nonprofit sectors.

In Part I, The Nature of Organizational Evil, the authors define and debate evil in the workplace, outline its origins, and discuss the psychological and structural foundations of its occurrence. How it is manifested, and why, is evoked through the application of theory to aspects of organizational life with which the reader will no doubt identify. In Part II, Understanding Organizational Evil, the mechanics of organizational evil both in the workplace and in the literature are viewed from a variety of new perspectives. Taking individual approaches, each chapter argues for a duality of evil as a concept and as an experience. Part III, Faces of Organizational Evil, examines evil in operation, how it evolves, what it looks like, and the impact it has on organizational life.

Collectively, *The Foundations of Organizational Evil* argues that the existence and maintenance of an evil organization is due to a complex interaction of individuals, organizations, and environmental factors. The popular belief that organizational evil continues to spread like a pernicious virus is not discounted here, and the outlook by some authors regarding the future of organizations and society is dim. Others point to the illusory nature of organizational evil, while those who acknowledge its existence offer some thoughts on stemming its growth. The book provides a wealth of theory and data for future research as well as a solid foundation for the development of a research paradigm that crosses many disciplines and all organizational sectors. In addition, the professional administrator, student, and consultant will find here the answers to why organizational evil evolves as it does, and hope on how it can be halted and, perhaps, reversed.

ACKNOWLEDGMENT

I am grateful to my graduate research assistant, Ms. Anna T. Trahan Stogner, who provided extraordinarily competent organizational assistance in the preparation of this book.

Part I

The Nature of Organizational Evil

1

Evil at Work

Carole L. Jurkiewicz and Dave Grossman

"Evil," like many four-letter words, has lost its shock value. Its meaning and impact has been diluted, and it is now used to characterize everything from mild rudeness to profound negativity. Because of this, the casualness with which the term "evil" is used has limited our ability to distinguish that which is truly, insidiously evil from that which is merely unethical. Any discussion of evil, thus, must start with a definition. "Organizational evil" is used here to signify the institutionalization of a set of principles whose purpose is knowingly to harm individuals, with disregard for consequences beyond those that would cause immediate repercussions to the evil-doer. Whereas unethical behavior is episodic and individualistic in nature, evil is systemic and embedded in the culture of the organization. Programs, policies, practices, reward systems, hiring and training, external and internal relations—all are designed with the intention to seek immediate advantage through the deliberate harm of others.

Organizational culture, whether positive or negative, develops over time as policies are reinforced, leaders model behavior (Dickson et al., 2001; Grojean et al., 2004), individuals are rewarded for behaviors, and the collective activities of organizational players cohere into an identity—an organizational personality. Emergent from the culture is a set of moral precepts, a corpus of moral principles that act as rules to constrain or facilitate behavior among organizational members—an ethic. The ethic of evil develops in the same way one of benevolence or benignity develops and shares the same level of cognitive complexity found in all organizations. This banality is arguably the most frightening aspect of evil. There is no one transformative moment to which we can point but, rather, an incremental shift from right to wrong that is barely perceptible on a day-to-day basis. It is difficult to recognize evil separate from an organization's history. If evil seeped into an organization suddenly, it, like all change initiatives, would likely be vigorously rejected. Certainly, some organizations are designed on a foundation of evil: sexual slavery, child pornography, nonprofit scams in the aftermath of crises, and so on. As a long-term shift in organizational culture, the realization that a seemingly legitimate organization has become evil is a sobering reality.

At what point does an organization become "evil"? When 100 percent of its policies and practices can be characterized by intentionally causing harm through self-advantage? 75 percent? 50 percent? Undoubtedly, the most notorious example of organizational evil, that is, Nazi Germany under Hitler's reign, while pervasively evil, retained some behaviors that

Figure 1.1   **The Dimensionality of Organizational Evil**

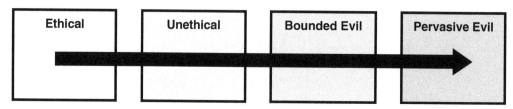

| Ethical | Unethical | Bounded Evil | Pervasive Evil |

- *Ethical*—Acting to achieve the greatest good for the greatest number; acting on principles that seek rights, justice, equality; eschewing personal gain for long-term societal benefit.
- *Unethical*—Episodically making decisions and acting in a manner that confers immediate individual advantage while disadvantaging the many; engaging in occasional deception and demonstrating lack of concerns for others.
- *Bounded Evil*—Individuals acting unethically a high proportion of the time yet most organizational policies and practices uphold principles of equality, rights, and justice.
- *Pervasive Evil*—An organizational culture that intentionally harms others to confer short-term organizational advantage as demonstrated through policies, practices, programs, and reward systems.

would be characterized as bounded evil, even if only in terms of pleasantries exchanged in the course of a day. And some organizations that are basically identifiable as bounded evil may have pervasively evil aspects, as this chapter discusses. "Bounded evil" and "pervasive evil" are thus, points on a continuum that extends from "ethical" at one end to "pervasively evil" at the other. Figure 1.1 illustrates the dimensions of individual versus organizational evils. An organization can be effectively categorized as evil when the majority of the policies, practices, programs, and reward systems that comprise its organizational culture intentionally cause harm to others, internal or external to the organization, as a means of obtaining a short-term organizational advantage. Recognizing and understanding this ethic of evil is important both in preventing its occurrence and in changing that which exists.

An evil organization, like all organizations, operates on a consistent set of principles that establish the acceptable and unacceptable norms of behavior within it. Just as gangs have a code of behavior (USDoJ, 2009), so, too, do the Mafia, genocidal regimes, and evil organizations. Kohlberg's (1976, 1981, 1985) widely regarded stage theory of moral development and ethical reasoning provides a foundation for understanding how a culture, whether evil or otherwise, develops and is sustained by individuals throughout the organization (McNeel, 1994; Rest, 1979). The theory posits a pyramid of six stages, ranging from the most elemental decision-making orientation in determining right from wrong, to the most complex. While the original research was focused on the individual level, it can be extrapolated to the organizational level as well being that organizations are defined as legal persons, as addressed later in this chapter. At the lowest level, Heteronomous Morality, Kohlberg exemplifies the most simplistic ethical reasoning as determining whether something is wrong or not based upon whether individuals think they are likely to get in trouble for it. Moving up a level to Individualism, Instrumental Purpose, and Exchange, ethical reasoning consists of following rules only when it is of immediate benefit to the individual, where people act to satisfy their own interests and needs and accept that others will do the same; the quid pro quo would be justified here. These first two stages are classified as egoist by Malloy and Agarwal (2008) in that the motivation is to avoid punishment and seek reward for an individual or a particular organizational unit; success is measured by short-term productivity and cost-effectiveness (Mayer et al., 1995). These two stages exemplify an ethic of evil if operationalized in the culture at the organizational level.

The third step in cognitive complexity is the stage in which individuals define what is right by living up to the expectations of those people closest to them, such as a family member, colleague, boss, or close friend. Characterized by demonstrating loyalty, gratitude, trust, and concern for others, this third stage is Mutual Interpersonal Expectations, Relationships, and Interpersonal Conformity. This level of ethical reasoning can sanction evil, assuming that the expectations of those closest to us are to gain advantage at all costs, or benevolence, depending upon the culture of the organization of which one is a part. Individuals entering an organization either adapt to the cultural expectations and act in ways for which they are rewarded or seek to reduce cognitive dissonance by leaving. The first three stages in Kohlberg's model are teleological in approach and justify all means to a particular end, a common thread in ethical violations and evil organizations, while the deontological perspective of stages four and five focus on the qualities intrinsic to the decisions themselves, an upholding of principles as the basis of organizational ethics.

The fourth stage, Social System and Conscience, is characterized by fulfilling the duties an individual has agreed to accept and upholding laws except under extreme circumstances, even where they conflict with social duties. Determining what is right here is also thinking through and choosing those actions that positively benefit society, the group, or the institution, extending the concept of benevolence beyond one's immediate personal affiliations to include the goal of group cohesion, public good, and mutual understanding divorced from egocentric motivation (Mayer et al., 1995). This, it could be argued, would be the basic level of movement from evil toward the ethical end of the continuum. The final stage, Universal Ethical Principles, is the culmination of the preceding stages but goes beyond them to establish principles that supersede laws, customs, and duties. These principles are "universalizable," meaning that they are thoughtfully considered on an individual basis, not something entered into lightly or adopted from a dogma or a person, and ones that the individual or organization wishes all humanity would share; they are absolute and inviolate (Jurkiewicz and Massey, 1998). These include universal principles of justice, respect for human rights and the dignity of the individual above all else. Given that less than 2 percent of the population attains the final stage, and that there exist only two verifiable methods by which individuals can achieve it (2002b), the vast majority of organizations have the potential to develop as systems that encourage and sustain evil by virtue of the stage level those in power perpetuate.

THE PSYCHOPATHOLOGY OF EVIL

In addition to an internally consistent system of ethical reasoning, albeit an evil or potentially evil system, an organization's culture can be characterized as evil based upon a

Figure 1.2 **Psychopathological Factors in Organizations**

- Callous unconcern for the feelings of others
- Incapacity to maintain enduring relationships
- Reckless disregard for the safety of others
- Deceitfulness: Repeated lying and conning others for profit or advantage
- Incapacity to experience guilt
- Failure to conform to social norms with respect to lawful behaviors

Source: Adapted from Bakan, 2004.

model of psychopathology (see Figure 1.2). An organization is recognized in the law as a person (Bakan, 2004) and thus can be seen as displaying cultural disorders, equivalent to personality disorders. As Bakan states (2004), the psychopathic nature of an organization is characterized by the attempt "to destroy your competition . . . you want to beat them one way or another . . . and you're not particularly concerned with what happens to the general public as long as they're buying your product" (2004, 56); "product" means an item, a political candidate, a policy initiative, or a nonprofit program. Yet while individuals are ethically multiplicative (Jurkiewicz, 2002a) and can compartmentalize evil, choosing to separate it from the rest of their lives or not, an organization is not similarly multidimensional. It is singularly self-focused and clearly exhibits elements of psychopathology (APA, 1994); this is as relevant for proprietary organizations as it is for nonprofits or public institutions. As Bakan writes, organizations are "irresponsible" in that exclusively seeking organizational goals puts individuals at risk. They are manipulative as they try to control "everything, including public opinion," and grandiose as they insist, "we're number one, we're the best." Lack of empathy and asocial tendencies are additional characteristics as "their behavior indicates they don't really concern themselves with their victims." Further, organizations "refuse to accept responsibility for their own actions and are unable to feel remorse; if (they) get caught breaking the law they pay big fines and . . . continue doing what they did before . . . in many cases the" profit or advantage obtained is worth substantially more than the fines imposed. Finally, organizations interact with others in a superficial manner; "their whole goal is to present themselves to the public in a way that is appealing . . . but in fact may not be representative of what the organization is really like." (Bakan 2004, 57)

The structure of many, if not most, organizations, according to Noam Chomsky (as quoted in Bakan, 2004, 69), is designed to exploit individuals for profit or advantage. Individuals thus become tools to be used to attain goals, a system of dehumanization that equates humans with a "piece of metal—you use it if you want, you throw it away if you don't." An organization's mandate, by law, is the pursuit of self-interest, whether product sales, political gain, or converting to nonprofit status to benefit from tax incentives and legal protections. Yet while an organization has the legal status of a person, it lacks a person's moral obligations. The individuals acting evilly on behalf of an organization are protected, for the most part, from legal prosecution as the organization is the entity of record; the consequence of this is that evil behavior is, in effect, rewarded, or at least not hindered, as the potential for an upside is high and that of a downside relatively low.

Figure 1.3   **The Narcissistic Organizational Personality Inventory**

The presence or absence of the factors below, either through an organization's communication materials or through their actions and decisions, indicates the degree to which an organization exhibits a narcissistic culture, or personality.

- If our organization were in charge of setting the rules, the world would be a much better place.
- We prefer it when our organization is the center of attention.
- We can act in whatever way we desire; we know what is best for us.
- We like to show off our power and assets and seek an attention-grabbing media presence.
- We will never be satisfied until we are the dominant organization (or political party).
- We think we are special and we are better than our competitors.
- It is easy to manipulate people into doing what you want.
- We will avail ourselves of opportunities to communicate our strengths and importance.
- We are extraordinary.
- We enjoy the ability to exercise control over our colleagues, clients, and competitors.

Source: Adapted by Twenge and Campbell, 2009, 20–21.

Efforts to reduce the regulation of and prevent the imposition of accountability standards for organizations are vigorous and measurable in terms of lobbying, political contribution, and public image campaigns. As Bakan (2004) points out, society would not tolerate the notion that individuals should regulate themselves and that laws against murder, rape, theft, and assault are thus unnecessary. Yet a substantial segment of society views as reasonable the idea that organizations, which have the potential for much more widespread harm than an individual acting alone, should be able to regulate themselves.

As organizations become further entrenched as the dominate force in society, their inherent view of individuals becomes more widely accepted: that of dehumanization, self-interest, and lack of empathy. This shift in sentiment is seen across industrialized cultures and has increased over time. As Adorno (2000) posits, individuals progressively acquire the ability to become detached from the consequences of their behavior; he views this reflective subjectivity of the individual to the organization as an evolutionary tactic for survival. After the public is dehumanized, any behavior becomes justifiable. By subjugating an individual's ethic to the organization's, the person succumbs to the compulsion of economic forces as a natural adaption to one's environment. Further, Adorno (2002) contends that society is moving more forcefully in the direction of organizational domination through molding of behavior via media manipulation, image management, and the industrial crafting of culture.

Evil at work is organizational narcissism. Just as narcissistic individuals need to sustain their self-image of perfection and importance by treating others as pawns in the effort to self-regulate, or the process of sustaining self-admiration (Twenge and Campbell, 2009), so, too, does an evil organization. The Narcissistic Personality Inventory, here adapted for organizations as depicted in Figure 1.3, is a key diagnostic tool in assessing an entity's degree of narcissism; as an organization is legally defined as person, the adaptation is a natural one. Concomitant with the increased incidence of narcissism in individuals (Twenge et al., 2008), organizations have moved in the direction of self-aggrandizement by seeking short-term advantage as a sustainable aspect of the workplace. Such a shift is attributable to the development of a culture, in all organizational sectors, that values systemic controls to advance immediate gains regardless of the consequences. Twenge and Campbell liken this cultural spread to a "pernicious virus" (2009, 37).

THE CULTURE OF EVIL

Organizational culture defined as evil develops in the same manner as an ethical one does. The founders establish, by intent or default, the basis of an organization's culture. The employees whom they hire are those who reinforce their beliefs; these employees are trained and rewarded for their adherence to these values; and as the organization succeeds, the employees feel an increasingly strong affiliation with these values and the systems that evolve from them (Andreoli and Lefkowitz, 2009; Schein, 1996). Traditions, customs, and implicit rules governing behavior emerge from this foundation as individuals build on what has led to success in the past. Culture serves a boundary-defining function as it distinguishes organizations from one another and communicates a sense of identity among employees. As employees identify with the organization, a stable social system develops that perpetuates the culture while, at the same time, being defined by it. The stronger the culture, the more deeply employees share the value system, the greater the employee commitment, and the more willing employees are to submit to behavioral controls imposed by the organization. The external manifestations of culture, which serve to strengthen employees' identification with the organization, include uniforms or identifiable forms of dress, specialized language such as acronyms, symbols such as logos or lapel pins, rituals, and stories told of organizational risk-takers who have become legends.

A powerful example of the strength of culture to create evil is one that results in having employees not only accept killing as a norm but celebrate those who excel at it. Grossman (2008, 2009) details how soldiers are trained to kill, how the organization systematically reinforces the shift in morals that allow one to accept killing as a normative behavior. Grossman cites the key literature on the power of authority in controlling individual behavior and the primary need of the individual to obey. The training protocol for and research into teaching soldiers to kill, against the natural and powerful resistance humans have toward killing each other, reveals some intriguing aspects of individual obedience to authority. The likelihood that a soldier will follow an order to kill is markedly enhanced by four factors: the proximity of the order-giver to the soldier; the soldier's subjective respect for the order-giver; the order-giver's clearly communicating the demand to kill; and the legitimacy of the order-giver to make such a demand. Within a highly vertical culture in which reporting relationships are clear and individuals are defined by their rank within the hierarchy, the obedience-demanding leader frames killing as an act of loyalty, in accordance with Kohlberg's model. Whereas many of us instinctively consider extreme action as part of a flight/fight response, soldiers are trained to inflict harm when ordered to do so, without the physiological urgency of a flight/fight event. Society deems lawful killing as necessary by soldiers, by law enforcement officers, and citizens in circumstances of self-defense. What is notable is the inculcation of a culture that requires an ethic to kill when ordered. Grossman (2008, 2009) explores the effect of killing on societal culture as a whole. This is the same process by which nonmilitary organizations demand evil behavior by their employees—the equivalent of a military "kill."

THE RULE OF ATROCITY EMPOWERMENT

Mass murder and execution, as well as organizational vengeance, can be sources of mass empowerment. It seemed as if a pact of evil had been made, developed, and thrived around the victimization of Jews by the Nazi SS (to select just one example), one that empowered its nation with an evil strength in exchange for its blood sacrifices. Each killing validated in blood the demon of Nazi racial superiority—thereby establishing a powerful pseudo speciation (categorizing a victim as an inferior species) based on moral distance, social distance, and cultural distance. Dyer's *War* (2006) contains a remarkable photograph of Japanese soldiers bayoneting Chinese prisoners: a seemingly endless line of prisoners on their knees in a deep ditch, hands bound behind their backs. Along the banks of the ditch stands an inimical line of Japanese soldiers with bayonets fixed on rifles. One by one the soldiers descend into the ditch and stab each prisoner with a bayonet as the prisoners hang their heads in dull acceptance and mute horror. The faces of those being bayoneted are contorted in agony, an expression mirrored in the faces of their executioners.

In executions, strong forces of moral distance, social distance, cultural distance, group absolution, close proximity, and obedience—demand that authority meld to compel the soldier to execute the kill, overcoming the forlorn forces of his natural and learned decency and his natural resistance to killing. Each soldier who actively or passively participates in such mass executions is faced with a stark choice: He can resist the incredibly powerful array of forces that call for him to kill, and be instantly denied by his nation, his leaders, and his friends and most likely be executed along with the other victims of the horror; or he can capitulate before the social and psychological forces that demand he kill and, in so doing, feel empowered.

The soldier who does kill must squelch that part of him that says that he is a murderer of women and children, a despicable beast who has done the unforgivable. He must deny the guilt within him and assure himself that the world is not mad, that his victims are lower than animals, that they are evil vermin, and that what his nation and his leaders have told him to do is right. He must force himself to believe that not only is this atrocity correct but it is proof that he is morally, socially, and culturally superior to those whom he has killed. It is the definitive act of denying others their humanity while affirming his own superiority; the soldier must actively suppress any dissonant thought that he has done wrong. Further, he must violently attack anyone or anything who would threaten these beliefs. His mental health is dependent upon his believing that what he has done is good and right, in accordance with the first three stages of Kohlberg's theory as detailed earlier. In effect, the blood of his victims binds and empowers him to even greater heights of killing and slaughter. When we realize that this same basic empowering process is what motivates organizational members to seek short-term advantage through fraud, lies, embezzlement, personal and environmental destruction, and even physical harm, it is sobering. The "kill" is the profit or advantage over one's competitor, client, citizen group, or constituency. This is the strength, the power, and the attraction of causing harm that has existed over millennia.

Twenge and Campbell (2009) document the rise and strength of antisocial behavior in American society. In the quest to attain media and reputational dominance, the narcissistic organization is much more likely to engage in aggressive and violent behavior. Lacking empathy and believing that their needs take precedence over those of individuals, evil organizations are significantly more likely to strike out against an individual or entity that offends them or tries to exercise control over them, whether a regulating agency or an individual whistleblower. If challenged, they become defensive, arrogant, and rude. They put up a vigorous and public fight in an effort to proclaim that no one person or entity has the power to tell them what to do, and they enjoy the public spectacle that ensues. For them, relationships are defined as advancing the glory of the organization, exploitation on behalf of organizational goals, and a commitment as long as it benefits the organization. The focus of individual value is exemplified; in the commonly used phrase, what have you done for me lately. In fact, individuals or organizations more prone to committing crimes and abuse are characterized as narcissistic, antisocial, and psychopathic, all elements that define the evil organization.

LEADER-TO-PEER BONDING

Those who command atrocities are powerfully bonded by blood and guilt to those who commit them, as well as to the cause, because only the success of their cause can ensure that they will not have to answer for their actions. In the case of totalitarian dictators, it is the secret police and other such Praetorian guard-type units that can be expected to fight for their leader and the cause to the bitter end. Nicolae Ceaușescu's state police in Romania, Hitler's SS units, Saddam Hussein's Republican Guard, and Muammar Gaddafi's loyalists are just a few examples of units bonded to their leaders by atrocity (members of the Mafia are another example). By ensuring that their men participate in atrocities, totalitarian leaders also ensure that for these minions there is no possibility of reconciliation with the enemy; they are inextricably linked to the fate of their leader. Trapped in their logic and their guilt, those who commit atrocities can see no alternatives to total victory or total defeat, in a great Götterdämmerung.

In the absence of a legitimate threat, leaders (whether national, organizational, or gang leaders) sometimes designate a scapegoat whose defilement and innocent "blood" empowers the killers and bonds them to their leaders. Traditionally, high-visibility weaker groups and minorities—such as Jews, African Americans, and the elderly—have filled this role. Women have also been defiled, debased, and dehumanized for the aggrandizement of others; throughout history, women have arguably been the greatest single group of victims of this empowerment process, which extends to discrimination and harassment in the workplace. Rape is a violent and important part of the process of dominating and dehumanizing the enemy; this process of mutual empowering and bonding at the expense of others is what occurs during gang rapes. In war, empowerment and bonding through gang rapes often occurs at the national level. The Nazi-Soviet conflict during World War II is a clear example of the vicious cycle in which both sides became completely invested in atrocity and rape. At the height of the atrocities, Soviet soldiers attacking Germany were told that they were not accountable for civil crimes committed in Germany and that personal property and German women were theirs by right; this is the same carte blanche German soldiers were given with respect to atrocities against Jews. The incidences of rape resulting from this kind of encouragement appear to have numbered in the millions. Cornelius Ryan (1995), in *The Last Battle,* estimated that a hundred thousand births after World War II resulted from rapes in Berlin alone.

In recent years, we have seen the use of rape as a political tool by all sides in the former Yugoslavia and among some Islamic fundamentalists using systematic gang rape to punish women who have violated sharia law. It is important to understand that gang rapes and gang or cult killings in times of peace and war are not "senseless violence." They are, rather, powerful acts of group bonding and criminal enabling that, quite often, have a hidden purpose of promoting the wealth, power, or vanity of a specific leader or cause, at the expense of the innocent. The same process occurs in gang rapes in high schools, of female journalists in countries such as Egypt, and in organizations as women and other minorities are marginalized, ridiculed, denied equal rights and benefits, and at times verbally and physically assaulted. The exercise of power (see Jurkiewicz and Brown, 2000b) to inflict abuse is violence regardless of the form of expression; the effect on the victim and society is the same.

THE COST OF KILLING

While soldiers are trained to kill through immersion in a culture that demands and rewards it, forcing them to overcome their natural disinclination to kill, when they leave their roles as soldiers to become civilians, there is no similar process of cultural reintegration. In the same manner, organizational members who have been systematically influenced and rewarded for committing evil acts in pursuit of organizational goals face a different reality after they exit the organization, and the psychological shift does not occur overnight. Just as a gradual shift occurs in moving individual behavior toward evil, whether in the military or a civilian organization, an incremental process is necessary to reacclimate them to a world in which killing, literally or figuratively, is neither lawful nor necessary. The result of this cultural clash is trauma (Grossman, 2008), which can have a variety of behavioral and psychological impacts. Depending upon the strength of an individual's identification with a culture of evil, as well as the degree of social support and acceptance s/he has when leaving that environment, responses can range from a relatively smooth rebound to recurrent bouts of post-traumatic stress disorder. It should be emphasized that the same severely disorienting process of shifting from an organization that demands evil to one that does not occurs in organizations all across sectors.

Another consequence of killing and equivalent reports of organizational egregiousness is the extent to which media violence facilitates violence in our society. Society communicates and reaffirms its culture using the same process as an organization. The behavioral standards exemplifying Kohlberg's first three stages of ethical reasoning predominate and teach us that egoism is to be celebrated and that the norms presented in the media are those by which we should judge and model our own behavior. As violence, lack of empathy, dehumanization of the individual, commercialization, and exemption from punishing consequences constitute the majority of cultural messages, these set the standard for societal behavior. This is especially true of children, as at least until the age of eight, they are unable to distinguish between commercials and reality, believing both to be equally factual (Bakan, 2004). Marketing to children is so successful that they are losing the ability to think for themselves, to be creative, or to make their own choices. The result is that children develop as consumers, and consumers of violence, from an early age, with the pervasive media creating a culture that encourages "very sophomoric behavior, irresponsible, hedonistic, egotistical, narcissistic behavior," to quote an advertising executive (Bakan, 2004, 126), as well as dehumanization of the individual and the value of an organization over any one person. This cultural development is one of the most noticeable aspects of the United States, as it is viewed by others through its own media as one populated by narcissists (Twenge and Campbell, 2009).

As a culture of evil grows in society, it in turn is facilitated by those who were trained by it, and thus the power of the culture is enhanced by every iteration.

CONCLUSION

Organizational culture exerts powerful influence over individual behavior, because of both the reward structure and humans' need to belong, but also significantly because the individual looks to those around him or her to determine what is right and what is wrong. Whether the message distinguishing right from wrong comes from an actual person or a media character, as long as the individual identifies with him/it, the power to exert control is the same. This need for affirmation determines not only work practices but ethical systems. Every culture develops an ethic, a set of morals and values that define it as separate from another organization and that tell employees what is acceptable and expected of them at work. An ethic is a definable aspect of an organization's culture, or personality, and can be characterized as evil when it embodies the elements as defined above. The impact of organizational evil on the individual as well as to society is profound, as it grows incrementally and becomes increasingly normalized over time.

The enunciation of these organizational and behavioral factors that lead to evil portend a dismal future. Yet the outcome is not predetermined. With action such a bleak future can be prevented; the segue toward evil, propelled by each decision that seeks short-term organizational advantage over the greater good, can be halted. The foils to the development of organizational evil are enforceable standards of accountability, transparency, and disclosure. This is inclusive of all sectors, as none can be depended upon to police themselves. Short of external monitoring, which is unlikely to be widely welcomed, organizations can establish self-monitoring processes to arrest the development of evil. Just as processes, programs, reward systems, training policies, and so on encourage evil, they can be used to create nonevil work environments. Rewarding behaviors that seek the greater good over advantage at all costs; creating a system in which whistleblowers are protected; providing open access to meetings and minutes; and promoting based upon a value system that attains organizational goals while protecting individuals and society are some of the approaches that could halt the development of organizational evil. Altering the laws so that individuals can be held legally and morally responsible for an organization and denying the organization the legal recognition of personhood is another important step. Placing effective controls on media output to ensure honesty, balanced perspectives from qualified sources, and being proactive in advocating societal values rather than feeding sensationalism to propel ratings is yet another.

Evil at work is not only dangerous from a moral perspective but moves us toward economic disadvantage as well. As individuals seek "me" time over time spent working, as the lure of fantasy over reality continues to grow and the motivation to achieve in the here and now declines in proportion, and as individuals and organizations seek instant fame over due diligence the economic impact translates into reduced national income. Lack of long-term sustainability, concern for short-term gains at the expense of long-term costs, and a culture of manipulation undercut organizational effectiveness in the long run. A loss of reputation, psychological, and economic instability have spurred the movement of proprietary organizations overseas, increased partisan politics, and diminished the ability of nonprofit organizations to raise funds. Given the impact on society, the concept of organizational evil needs to be extensively studied and deserves a more prominent focus in the literature. The consequences of organizational evil are insidious, and the solutions are difficult. Yet the choice of nonaction might prove the most problematic.

REFERENCES

Adorno, T. 2000. Cultural criticism and society. In *The Adorno Reader*, ed. Brian O'Connor, 195–210. Malden, MA: Blackwell.

———. 2002. *Problems of Moral Philosophy*, ed. Thomas Schroder, trans. Rodney Livingstone. Cambridge, UK: Polity Press.

American Psychiatric Association. 1994. *Diagnostic and Statistical Manual of Mental Disorders (DSM-IV)*, 4th ed. Washington, DC: American Psychiatric Association.

Andreoli, N., and J. Lefkowitz. 2009. Individual and organizational antecedents of misconduct in organizations. *Journal of Business Ethics*, 85, 3, 309–332.

Bakan, J. 2004. *The Corporation: The Pathological Pursuit of Profit and Power.* New York: Free Press.

Bero, B., and A. Kuhlman. 2010. Teaching ethics to engineers: Ethical decision making parallels the engineering design process. *Science and Engineering Ethics*. doi:10.1007/s11948-010-9213-7.

Blasi, A. 1980. Bridging moral cognition and moral action: A critical review of the literature. *Psychological Bulletin*, 88, 1, 1–45.

Bourdieu, P. 1990. *The Logic of Practice*, trans. Richard Nice. Stanford: Stanford University Press.

Bruce, G., and R. Edgington. 2008. Ethics education in MBA programs: Effectiveness and effects. *International Journal of Management and Marketing Research*, 1, 1, 49–70.

Dickson, M.W., D.B. Smith, M.W. Grojean, and M. Ehrhart. 2001. Ethical climate: The result of interactions between leadership, leader values, and follower values. *Leadership Quarterly*, 12, 1–21.

Dyer, G. 2006. *War: The Lethal Custom.* New York: Basic Books.

Foucault, M. 1984. On the genealogy of ethics: An overview of work in progress. In *The Foucault Reader*, ed. P. Rabinow, 340–372. New York: Pantheon.

Grojen, M.W., C.J. Resick, M.W. Dickson, and D.B. Smith. 2004. Leaders, values, and organizational climate: Examining leadership strategies for establishing an organizational climate regarding ethics. *Journal of Business Ethics*, 55, 3, 223–241.

Grossman, Dave. 2008. *On Combat: The Psychology and Physiology of Deadly Conflict in War and in Peace*. Millstadt, IL: Warrior Science Publications.

———. 2009. *On Killing*. New York: Back Bay Books/Little, Brown, and Company.

Hartman, L.P., and P.H. Werhane. 2009. A modular approach to business ethics integration: At the intersection of the stand-alone and the integrated approaches. *Journal of Business Ethics*, 90, 295–300. doi:10.1007/s10551-010-0427-z.

Hauser, M.D. 2006. *Moral Minds: How Nature Designed Our Universal Sense of Right and Wrong*. New York: HarperCollins.

Henle, C.P., R.A. Giacalone, and C.L. Jurkiewicz. 2005. The role of ethical ideology in workplace deviance. *Journal of Business Ethics*, 56, 219–230.

Hiltebeitel, K.M., and S.K. Jones. 1992. An assessment of ethics instruction in accounting education. *Journal of Business Ethics*, 11, 37–46.

Johnson, C.E. 2007. *Ethics in the Workplace: Tools and Tactics for Organizational Transformation*. Thousand Oaks, CA: Sage.

Jurkiewicz, C.L. 2002a. The phantom code of ethics and public sector reform. *Journal of Public Affairs and Issues*, 6, 3, 1–19.

———. 2002b. The influence of pedagogical style on students' level of ethical reasoning. *Journal of Public Affairs Education*, 8, 4, 263–274.

———. 2009. Political leadership, cultural ethics and recovery: Louisiana post-Katrina. *Public Organization Review*, 9, 4, 353–366.

———. 2010. The ethinomics of a leaking Louisiana. *Public Manager*, 39, 3, 38–41.

Jurkiewicz, C.L., and R.G. Brown. 2000a. Power corrupts absolutely . . . not. *Public Integrity*, 2, 3, 195–210.

———. 2000b. The P/E ratio that really counts. *Journal of Power and Ethics*, 1, 3, 172–195.

Jurkiewicz, C.L., and T.K. Massey, Jr. 1998. The influence of ethical reasoning on leader effectiveness: An empirical study of nonprofit executives. *Nonprofit Management and Leadership*, 9, 2, 173–186.

Kohlberg, L. 1976. Moral stages and moralization: The cognitive-developmental approach. In *Moral Development and Behavior*, ed. T. Lickona, 31–51. New York: Holt, Rinehart & Winston.

———. 1981. *Philosophy of Moral Development*. New York: Harper & Row.

———. 1985. A current statement on theoretical Issues. In *Lawrence Kohlberg: Consensus and Controversy*, ed. S. Modgil and C. Modgil, 485–546. Philadelphia: Falmer.

Loe, T.W., and W.A. Weeks. 2000. An experimental investigation of efforts to improve sales students' moral reasoning. *Journal of Personal Selling and Sales Management*, 20, 243–251.

Luthar, H.K., and R. Karri. 2005. Exposure to ethics education and the perception of linkage between organizational ethical behavior and business outcomes. *Journal of Business Ethics*, 61, 353–368.

Malloy, D.C., and J. Agarwal. 2008. Ethical climate in government and nonprofit sectors: Public policy implications for service delivery. *Journal of Business Ethics*, 94, 1, 3–21.

Mayer, R.C., J.H. Davis, and F.D. Schoorman. 1995. An integration model of organizational trust. *Academy of Management Review*, 20, 3, 709–735.

McNeel, S.P. 1994. College teaching and student moral development. In *Moral Development in the Professions: Psychology and Applied Ethics*, ed. J.R. Rest and D. Narvaez, 27–49. Hillsdale, NJ: Lawrence Erlbaum Associates.

Mill, J.S. 1863/2002. *Utilitarianism*. New York: Bobbs-Merrill.

Musick, D.W. 1999. Teaching medical ethics: A review of the literature from North American medical schools with emphasis on education. *Medicine, Health Care and Philosophy*, 2, 239–254.

O'Fallon, M.J., and K.D. Butterfield. 2005. A review of the empirical ethical decision-making literature: 1996–2003. *Journal of Business Ethics*, 59, 4, 375–413.

Pew Research Center. 2010. Distrust, discontent, anger and partisan rancor: The people and their government. April 18. http://pewresearch.org/pubs/1569/trust-in-government-distrust-discontent-anger-partisan-rancor/.

Piaget, J. 1965. *The Moral Judgement of the Child,* trans. M. Gabain. New York: Free Press.

Rest, J.R. 1979. *Development in Judging Moral Issues.* Minneapolis: University of Minnesota Press.

Ryan, C. 1995. *The Last Battle: The Classic History of the Battle of Berlin.* New York: Simon & Schuster.

Schein, E.H. 1996. Leadership and organizational culture. In *The Leader of the Future*, ed. F. Hesselbein, M. Goldsmith, and R. Beckhard, 59–69. San Francisco: Jossey-Bass.

Schmidt, F.L., and J.E. Hunter. 1998. The validity and utility of selection methods in personnel psychology: Practical and theoretical implications of 85 years of research findings. *Psychological Bulletin*, 124, 2, 262–274.

Schwitzgebel, E. 2009. Do ethics steal more books? *Philosophical Psychology*, 22, 711–725.

Talbot, S.E. 2000. *Partial Reason: Critical and Constructive Transformations of Ethics and Epistemology.* Westport, CT: Greenwood Press.

Thoma, S. 1994. Moral judgments and moral action. In *Moral Development in the Professions*, ed. J.R. Rest and D. Narvaez, 199–212. Hillsdale, NJ: Lawrence Erlbaum Associates.

Twenge, J.M., and W.K. Campbell. 2009. *The Narcissism Epidemic: Living in the Age of Entitlement.* New York: Free Press.

Twenge, J.M., S. Konrath, J.D. Foster, W.K. Campbell, and B.J. Bushman. 2008. Egos inflating over time: A cross-temporal meta-analysis of the narcissistic personality inventory. *Journal of Personality*, 76, 875–901.

United States Department of Justice (USDoJ). 2009. Drug and Gang Fast Facts. http://www.justice.gov/ndic/pubs11/13157/index.htm.

Vershoor, C.C. 2007. Work-life balance, superior's actions strongly influence ethical culture. *Strategic Finance*, 88, 13–16.

2

The Dynamics of Administrative Evil in Organizations

Guy B. Adams and Danny L. Balfour

"Evil" is not a widely used entry in the lexicon of the social sciences. Social scientists have long preferred to *describe* behavior, avoiding ethically loaded or judgmental rubrics—to say nothing of a word with a long tradition as a religious term. As Claudia Card notes:

> The denial of evil has become an important strand of twentieth-century secular Western culture. Some critics find evil a chimera, like Santa Claus or the tooth fairy, but a dangerous one that calls forth disturbing emotions, such as hatred, and leads to such disturbing projects as revenge. . . . Many reject the idea of evil because, like Nietzsche, they find it a *bad* idea. . . . Nietzsche's critique has helped engineer a shift from questions of what to do to prevent, reduce or redress evils to skeptical psychological questions about what inclines people to make judgments of evil in the first place, what functions such judgments have served. (2002, 28)

In *Unmasking Administrative Evil* (Adams and Balfour, 2009), we argued that evil is an essential concept for understanding the human condition and therefore is essential as well for understanding human action in organizational settings. We characterized evil as the actions of human beings that unjustly or needlessly inflict pain and suffering and death on other human beings (2009, 3).

There are many other useful definitions and characterizations of evil. Card defines evil as "foreseeable intolerable harm produced by culpable wrongdoing" (2002, 3). Ervin Staub offers another: "Evil is not a scientific concept with an agreed meaning, but the idea of evil is part of a broadly shared human cultural heritage. The essence of evil is the destruction of human beings. . . . By evil I mean *actions* that have such consequences" (1992, 25). Phillip Zimbardo suggests this definition: "Evil consists in intentionally behaving in ways that harm, abuse, demean, dehumanize or destroy innocent others—or using one's authority and systemic power to encourage or permit others to do so on your behalf" (2007, 5). Finally, Geddes emphasizes that:

> evil is relational. . . . For evil occurs between people: one or more persons do evil (and are thereby understood to be evil or connected to evil) and someone else, or some other group, suffers evil. As Paul Ricoeur (1995, 250) notes, "To do evil

is always, either directly or indirectly, to make someone else suffer. In its dialogic structure evil committed by someone finds its other half in the evil suffered by someone else." (2003, 105)

These definitions, while helpful, can be further refined. We proposed (Adams and Balfour, 2009, 11) a continuum of evil and wrongdoing, with horrible, mass eruptions of evil, such as the Holocaust and other, lesser instances of mass murder, at one extreme, and the "small" white lie, which is somewhat hurtful, at the other. Somewhere along this continuum, wrongdoing turns into evil. Staub notes: "Extreme destructiveness . . . is usually the last of many steps along a continuum of destruction" (1992, xi). Such a continuum is especially helpful in examining organizational dynamics in which seemingly innocuous acts of wrongdoing escalate into evil—both masked and unmasked.

ADMINISTRATIVE AND ORGANIZATIONAL EVIL

The culture of technical rationality (Vanderburg, 2005) as it pervades modern organizations has enabled a new form of evil that we call "administrative evil" and made it even more difficult to perceive. What distinguishes administrative evil from other forms of evil is that its consequences are masked within the ethos of technical rationality. Ordinary people might simply be acting appropriately in their organizational role, just doing what is expected of them while participating in what a critical observer (usually well after the fact) would call evil. Under conditions of what we term *moral inversion*, ordinary people can engage in acts of administrative evil—including the violation of basic human rights—while believing that what they are doing is not only procedurally correct but, in fact, good. Because administrative evil is typically masked, no one has to accept an overt invitation to commit an evil act, because such overt invitations are very rarely issued. Rather, the "invitation" to administrative evil might come in the form of an expert or technical role, couched in appropriate language, or it might even come packaged as a good and worthy project (moral inversion). In this context, organizational actors can violate human rights up to and including the very right to life without considering or realizing that their actions, and organizational outcomes, are destructive and sometimes catastrophically so.

People have always been able to delude themselves into thinking that their evil acts are not really so bad, and we have certainly had moral inversions in the past. Administrative evil, however, has three important differences: (1) in modern times, we have an inclination not to identity evil, an old concept that does not resonate with the technical-rational mindset; (2) modern, complex organizations, which diffuse and fragment information and individual responsibility and require the compartmentalized accomplishment of role expectations to perform work on a daily basis, have a strong influence; and (3) the culture of technical rationality has made moral inversions more likely. Our focus in this chapter is on the second difference: the organizational context of administrative evil.

Evil, then, occurs along another continuum: from acts that are committed in relative ignorance to those that are knowing and deliberate acts of evil, that is, what we characterize as masked and unmasked. Plato maintained that no one would knowingly commit an evil act; the fact that someone has done so demonstrates ignorance. Individuals and groups can engage in evil acts without recognizing the consequences of their behavior or when persuaded their actions are justified or serve the greater good. Administrative evil falls within this range of the continuum, where people engage in or contribute to acts of evil without recognizing that they are doing anything wrong.

INDIVIDUAL AND ORGANIZATION

Individualism, one of the core values of U.S. culture, hinders the perception and understanding of the group and organizational dynamics that underlie organizational evil (Zimbardo, 2007, 212). In our culture, we are inclined to assume that each individual's actions are freely and independently chosen. When we examine an individual's behavior in isolation or even in aggregate, as we often do, that notion can be reinforced. However, our culture's emphasis on individualism blinds us to group and organizational dynamics, which typically play a powerful role in shaping human behavior. It is an easy but important error to personalize evil in the form of the exceptional psychopath, such as a Charles Manson or a Jeffrey Dahmer (often without considering how that individual might be a product of our culture). We also tend to focus on particularly bad actors in organizations, such as Enron's Jeffrey Skilling or Charles Graner in the Abu Ghraib prison. This understanding of evil as arising from an individual's disposition—the default option in a society like ours that so highly values individualism—draws a cloak over social and organizational evil. As Zimbardo suggests (2007), situational and systemic factors are far more significant than we typically imagine. Thus, we focus here on group and organizational dynamics, which are crucial to understanding how evil and administrative evil occur in organizations.

Organizations, of course, are often the locus of both wrong-doing and evil (Darley, 1992, 1995, 1996). Indeed, they are the home base of administrative evil. Organizations can facilitate such activities both internally and externally. Internally, these acts would be inflicted on members of the organization, while externally, customers, clients, or citizens in various combinations would be the victims. Organizational evil can affect those both outside and inside the organization.

Modern organizations, as we have noted, are characterized by the diffusion of information and the fragmentation of responsibility. With diffuse and scattered information, literally no one in the organization might have a complete enough picture to adequately comprehend the destructive activity to try to reverse course. Those who have enough of a picture to perceive that something is wrong might well assume that higher management must be aware of the problem and has chosen to do nothing about it. With regard to responsibility, those in operational units might note a problem, or a part of a problem, but are likely inclined to understate it so as not to bring negative news to superiors. Not knowing may be replaced by "strategic ignorance," in which organizational actors might decide that pretending not to know is the safer approach.

The longer wrong-doing or evil activity persists, the more difficult it becomes to acknowledge it. The notion of "sunk costs," borrowed from economics, is descriptively helpful here. Each step along the way in which such activity is not halted becomes an additional commitment to that trajectory. This dynamic can be described as "successive ratification" (Darley, 1996). As a consequence, bringing such activity to a halt (to recall a product, ground a fleet, or fire a contractor, etc.) requires decisive action. One needs clear and overwhelming evidence to do so, for one can be certain that no thanks will be forthcoming. Allowing the existing processes (the status quo) to continue requires no action at all—momentum alone becomes a very powerful social force.

In some cases, a "turning point" is reached when administrative evil turns into evil, and those actively participating in it also become evil-doers (Darley, 1992). The mask is removed from administrative evil at this turning point. This is when people in the organization realize or discover that the organization has been engaged in actions destructive of human beings—in the more egregious cases, causing the death of innocent others. Occasionally, one can find cases of organizations in which people have knowingly engaged in harmful, destructive acts—that is, evil plain and simple, the unmasked version. More often, the activities that constitute the wrong-doing are thought of by the participants (or at least some of the participants) as benign or even beneficial. But now, at the turning point, the painful truth is seen.

At this point, personal guilt and shame—and organizational liability—are immediately present, because, in hindsight, most reasonable observers would say that someone should have known or done something about what was occurring. Since it is readily apparent that others are likely to react as though those involved should have known, relevant actors are likely to feel a level of guilt and shame commensurate with "knowingly" doing harm or evil. This, in turn, becomes a powerful psychological incentive to deny the harm or evil. If the wrong-doing or evil stems from management, such denial is likely to be read by those lower in the organization as sufficient guidance to collude in a cover up or lie. Apprehension over the potential loss of one's job is often sufficient incentive for such collusion.

While the psychological incentive to deny and cover up are clearly powerful, individuals in the organization have made a fundamental shift at the turning point from engaging in harmful or evil activities unknowingly to doing so knowingly. This has been termed the "evil turn" (Darley, 1996). It is evident that the incentives to cover up are socially powerful, if not indeed overwhelming, because it is widely known that a cover-up is highly unlikely to succeed and often results in the complete disclosure of the harmful or evil activities. Denial and cover-up are chosen in the face of knowing that they are unlikely to work. We see this same progression of dynamics at work in numerous organizational case examples, including those of the Dalkon Shield (Mintz, 1985), the American tobacco industry (Hurt and Robertson, 1998), the Goodrich corporation (Darley, 1996), NASA (Adams and Balfour, 2009), and Enron, WorldCom, and Blackwater (Adams and Balfour, 2010). Here we illustrate these dynamics in the case of the torture and abuse of detainees at Abu Ghraib prison in Iraq in 2003.[1]

TORTURE AND ABUSE AT ABU GHRAIB PRISON

Events and actions in the wake of September 11, 2001, over time created a partly tacit policy that essentially gave permission to engage in the torture and abuse of detainees at Abu Ghraib prison in Iraq, as well as other locations. The disturbing photographs of U.S. soldiers, who appeared to be gleefully humiliating, punching, and terrifying naked prisoners with dogs, indicated that things had gone terribly wrong at Abu Ghraib. The photograph of a hooded prisoner standing on a box connected to wires leading out of view has become an unfortunate and enduring symbol to the world of a superpower that appeared to have veered dangerously away from its espoused values. That photograph quickly appeared in downtown Teheran on a billboard with a message that was less than flattering to the United States.

The torture and abuse of detainees at the prison in Abu Ghraib and other locations, including Afghanistan and Guantánamo Bay, raised disturbing questions. Were these intentionally evil acts, committed by "a few bad apples" taking advantage of the situation to indulge in the power they wielded over the inmates? Or, were they cases of administrative evil, where the obvious evil of torture and abuse was masked from the perpetrators, including those who performed subsidiary and supportive functions? Were those who were brought to trial the only ones responsible for the abuse or are they scapegoats, deflecting attention from broader, systemic problems (see Zimbardo, 2007)? Even more fundamental is the question: Are torture and abuse always wrong (see Levinson, 2004; Rejali, 2007)? Could they perhaps be justified, at least in a carefully limited way, in the context of the "global war on terrorism" (GWOT) and the need for timely intelligence on potential terrorist attacks (see Mayer, 2005, 2008)?

In January 2002, the U.S. Department of Justice prepared a series of memoranda that argued that both the Taliban and al Qaeda could be considered as outside the Geneva Conventions, as "unlawful enemy combatants." During this same period, the U.S. State Department prepared memoranda arguing that whatever advantage might be gained in the war on terrorism by declaring the Geneva Conventions inapplicable would be more than outweighed by the disadvantages, including potential loss of the moral high ground accorded to the United States in the wake of 9/11. Alberto Gonzales, at the time White House counsel and later attorney general, advised President George W. Bush that he was persuaded by the Justice Department position. All of these communications were replete with references to a new paradigm of war, a different kind of war, or a global war on terrorism. There is inherent ambiguity in a new paradigm, and within that ambiguity is the potential for moral inversion. The memoranda discussed above represent attempts to clarify some of that inherent ambiguity. However, subsequent documents and events suggest that considerable ambiguity about the treatment and interrogation of detainees remained in the system and had the effect of giving the soldiers permission to torture and abuse detainees.

TAKING THE GLOVES OFF IN INTERROGATION POLICY AND PROCEDURE

In late 2002, the use of conventional interrogation techniques (that is, standard operating procedures as defined in Army Field Manual 34–52) at the Guantánamo Bay detention camp in Cuba had achieved about as much as they were going to. Some Guantánamo detainees effectively resisted interrogation methods, prompting authorities to request strengthened interrogation techniques in October 2002 (Strasser, 2004, 31). If additional usable intelligence were to come from the detainees, new techniques would have to be introduced, but would need to be duly authorized. Accordingly, Defense Secretary Donald Rumsfeld authorized the use of sixteen additional techniques beyond the standard Army doctrine in force at the time. By April 2003, these new techniques were mostly rescinded, and additional permissions were put in place in order to use the few of those techniques that remained. Most important, they were limited to use only at Guantánamo.

At Guantánamo, a number of approaches were tried after it was concluded that going by the Army book did not yield quick results. Psychologists and psychiatrists were brought in, hoping that their insights could lead to more effective techniques. Expert and seasoned interrogators from the Federal Bureau of Investigation (FBI) were also brought in. The FBI approach to interrogation is a more patient one that is premised on forging a relationship with the subject over time. It works very well, but it typically takes considerable time. According to Daniel Coleman, the senior FBI agent assigned to antiterrorism in the 1990s: "Brutalization doesn't work. We know that. Besides, you lose your soul" (Mayer, 2008, 119). The Bush administration, especially Vice President Dick Cheney and Defense Secretary Rumsfeld, was reacting to what it thought was a high probability of imminent future terrorist attacks, which created a high degree of urgency; the administration wanted immediate results—the phrase "the gloves are off" was repeated many times (Mayer, 2008). It appears that the impetus to permit torture, under the assumption that its use would yield actionable intelligence quickly, came from either the vice president (or his chief aide, David Addington) or the Central Intelligence Agency (CIA), although this is difficult to know with certainty (Mayer, 2008, 120).

The decision to turn to torture was a curious one (Sands, 2008). Torture not only was a poor choice on moral grounds but also was suspect on pragmatic grounds (Intelligence Science Board [ISB], 2006). A pragmatic assessment of torture does not provide a clear example of its effectiveness. As Jane Mayer notes:

> Scientific research on the efficacy of torture is extremely limited because of the moral and legal impediments to experimentation. Before endorsing physical and psychological abuse, the Bush administration did no empirical study. The policy seems to have been based on some combination of political preferences and intuitive belief about human nature. (2008, 134)

Indeed, a 2006 report by the Intelligence Science Board, under the auspices of the National Defense Intelligence College, found scant evidence to support the efficacy of torture and abuse as a means of gathering accurate, much less actionable, intelligence. Quite the contrary, as noted by John Wahlquist in that report: "Why, in the 21st century, with all our accumulated knowledge about how human beings think and interact and function, are we still repeating costly medieval mistakes?" (ISB, 2006, xxi).

On practical grounds, then, torture was a poor choice. Indeed, the Intelligence Science Board listed seven reasons not to engage in torture: Torture undermines international support for the struggle against terrorism; enhances danger to troops and others at risk of capture; entails legal problems for U.S. troops and officials; undercuts U.S. leadership on human rights; creates more enemies (terrorists); corrodes the integrity of the military; and displaces resources that could be better used elsewhere (2006, 13–15). Against the best available thinking on both moral and practical grounds, the United States chose the path of torture and abuse, first at Guantánamo Bay and in Afghanistan, and then in Iraq.

A BENIGHTED PRISON

The story of Abu Ghraib—a prison built by Saddam Hussein with a well-earned reputation for horrific torture and abuse—was one of chronically underresourced military police and military intelligence units, and a toxic mix of CIA, special operations, and contractor personnel, acting in the middle of a deadly insurgency. These units were faced with an extremely difficult and unfamiliar mission without clear procedural guidelines and under considerable pressure to produce actionable intelligence. Under the best of conditions, the running of a maximum-security prison is a high-risk operation that requires intensive oversight and professional staff. Firm rules and clear procedures are important control mechanisms, not just for the inmates but for the staff as well. Military prisons in the United States are staffed and operated by correctional specialists who are trained specifically for that mission. There are just enough correctional specialists in the force to secure existing fixed facilities. The number of correctional specialists in the active duty military force structure is really not intended to meet the needs of wartime requirements for detention operations. Thus, virtually all the units designed to deal with detainees existed in the reserve components.

Operations at Abu Ghraib took place in an environment that was inherently complex and dangerous. The fact that the soldiers had to deal with insurgent attacks on the compound in addition to the custody mission made it even more challenging. The 372nd Military Police Company, a reserve unit from Cumberland, Maryland, and its higher headquarters were trained, staffed, and equipped for an enemy prisoner of war mission, not for running a prison that housed a volatile mix of hostile insurgents, criminals, and some innocent bystanders simply caught up in extensive sweeps of suspect neighborhoods. Lest it be inferred that the abuses were excusable, there were a number of detention facilities in Iraq that managed to avoid the problems experienced at Abu Ghraib. Both the Schlesinger and Fay reports (Strasser, 2004) cited culpable deficiencies in command and control that extended from the lowest levels to the commander of the 800th Military Police Brigade, Brigadier General Janis Karpinski, as key contributing factors in the debacle. To help understand in a more direct way what happened on the night shift at Abu Ghraib, it is worth presenting a long summary of the case of Yasser, taken from a June 2008 report by the Physicians for Human Rights (in the text the U.S. personnel who participated in the torture and abuse of this detainee are in boldface):

> Yasser was arrested by **the U.S. military** on October 13, 2003. . . . [H]e was transferred to Abu Ghraib on October 15, 2003. According to Yasser, he was never informed of the reason for his arrest.

Upon arrival at Abu Ghraib, Yasser recalled that he was not forced to disrobe, although he felt "insulted" by the U.S. personnel as they "put their hands in my privates." He said he was forced to sit on the ground with other detainees for four hours and then to crawl on the ground with fellow detainees. **Three people** conducted the initial interrogation, during which Yasser was commanded to sit on the ground by an area near a putrid, dirty toilet. . . . When he was transferred to another section of Abu Ghraib he was told to "take off all [his] clothes." He followed the order but "kept the underwear [on]." The U.S. soldiers stripped him of his remaining clothing. . . . Yasser tearfully described that when he reached the top of the steps "the party began. . . . **They** started to put the [muzzle] of the rifle [and] the wood from the broom into [my anus]. **They** entered my privates from behind." He noted that **several other soldiers** and **civilians** were present, including an **interpreter with "a Lebanese accent."** . . .

Yasser reported that he did not receive any medical care while in the isolation cell. However, he stated, "**Doctors** . . . used to be included with the questioning. . . . Sometimes the dog[s] [bit] the prisoner, and [**the doctor**] gives the needle to the female soldier for stitching—I saw it."

Yasser was released from Abu Ghraib prison in February 2004 without charge.

Yasser suffered multiple forms of torture and abuse. The Taguba Report (Center for Public Integrity, 2004) detailed a long list of abuses inflicted on other detainees by military police personnel on Tiers 1A and 1B: breaking chemical lights and pouring the phosphoric liquid on detainees; threatening detainees with a 9mm pistol; pouring cold water on detainees; beating detainees with a broom handle and a chair; threatening males detainees with rape; sodomizing a detainee with a chemical light and perhaps a broomstick; using military working dogs to frighten and intimidate detainees; punching, slapping, and kicking detainees; jumping on their naked feet; videotaping and photographing naked male and female detainees; forcibly arranging detainees in various sexually explicit positions for photographing; forcing detainees to remove their clothing and keeping them naked for several days at a time; forcing naked male detainees to wear women's underwear and to masturbate while being photographed and videotaped; arranging naked detainees in a pile and then jumping on them; positioning a naked detainee on an MRE box, with a sandbag on his head, and attaching electrical wires to his fingers, toes, and penis as if in preparation for torture; placing a dog chain around a naked detainee's neck and having a female soldier pose for a picture; a male MP (military police) guard having sex with a female detainee; and taking photographs of dead Iraqi detainees. How these soldiers came to engage in such reprehensible activities offers considerable insight into the organizational dynamics of administrative evil.

INTELLIGENCE OPERATIONS IN IRAQ

The role of intelligence operations bears special mention. Counterinsurgency operations in Iraq, and indeed in the greater global war on terror, hinge on the collection, analysis, and timely dissemination of intelligence. Intelligence personnel were clearly under pressure to produce information that could be acted on to find weapons of mass destruction, quell the insurgency, and prevent terrorist attacks. Some of the pressure was self-induced, and some was undoubtedly created by a number of visits by senior officers, including one by the commander of the Guantánamo facility, Major General Geoffrey Miller. General Miller, whose military background was in artillery, not in detention or intelligence, was personally selected by Defense Secretary Rumsfeld to command the facility at Guantánamo Bay, after detainees failed to provide much usable intelligence during the first months. Miller was known as a commander who could make things happen. When the insurgency began to take hold in Iraq, Rumsfeld ordered Miller to take his Tiger team to Iraq because the gloves needed to come off there as well:

> Miller's concept was a change in policy that would place military intelligence officers in charge of prison operations in Iraq, blending the functions of interrogation and detention. Miller also recommended that interrogations be centralized at Abu Ghraib so that intelligence could be processed more efficiently. And in a break with traditional military doctrine, Miller advocated using ordinary military police officers who worked as guards in the prison to participate in the interrogation process, even though they had not been trained for this. The guards, he wrote, "must be actively engaged in setting the conditions for successful exploitation of the internees." Miller also recommended using military dogs for interrogation. (Mayer, 2008, 241)

Because of decisions made during the drawdown of the Army after the end of the cold war, there were too few linguists and human intelligence operatives to meet the demand. There was a critical shortage not only of experienced and well-trained interrogators but of interpreters as well. Civilian contractors, some with dubious expertise, provided almost half the interrogators at Abu Ghraib and were involved in more than a third of the abuses (Schooner, 2005). The Schlesinger Report indicated that the Joint Interrogation and Debriefing Center was cobbled together from six different units (Strasser, 2004, 71). Intelligence personnel involved in interrogations were implicated in a number of excesses. Specialist Charles Graner Jr., a military police officer and central figure in the abuses, steadfastly maintained at his court-martial that he was just following orders—that he was encouraged to soften up inmates for interrogation.

BLURRING THE BOUNDARIES

Obviously, the military police mission of providing custody and control became enmeshed with the mission of producing actionable intelligence. This was deliberately done at Guantánamo Bay and migrated to Iraq under the auspices of General Miller. Techniques that may have been authorized at one time or another at Guantánamo and those used in Afghanistan (apparently by CIA personnel and perhaps by special operations personnel)—including the use of stress positions, removal of clothing, isolation, and sleep deprivation—found their way to Iraq (Strasser, 2004, 72). The commanding general in Iraq at that time, Ricardo Sanchez, authorized Miller's program in a memo on September 14, 2003 (Zimbardo, 2007, 412).

The line between the permissible and the prohibited was blurred by varying legal opinions, the lack of clearly established written procedures, and a perceived need to adapt to a new paradigm of warfare in which the enemy did not adhere to the established rules of land warfare (Mayer, 2008). Rule and procedure ambiguity can provide beneficial space for flexibility and creativity when individuals have a clear sense of professional ethics and a well-grounded moral compass. Without ethical and moral anchors and in the absence of clear procedural guidelines or solid supervision, some MPs at Abu Ghraib increasingly moved from passive observers and reporters of detainee conduct to active participants in the process of breaking inmates down for interrogation purposes. It was an inappropriate function for which they were ill-suited on multiple levels. The prison was under the tactical control of a military intelligence brigade, and the collection of intelligence clearly trumped what would be recognized as good practices of custody and control in the field of corrections.

The Fay Report observed that the CIA conducted unilateral detention and interrogation operations at Abu Ghraib that contributed to abuse and a lack of accountability (Strasser, 2004, 111). The Schlesinger Report also noted that the CIA was allowed to conduct its interrogations separately and "under different rules" (Strasser, 2004, 75). Both reports noted the existence of unregistered "ghost" detainees that complicated prisoner reporting processes, apart from violating inspection and reporting protocols with the International Red Cross. Neither report addressed the specific interrogation tactics used by the CIA (often referred to as OGA—"other government agency") and focused instead on the absence of a memorandum of agreement between the military command and the CIA. Civilian contractors may well have been in an even more ambiguous situation. The extent to which CIA tactics influenced the conduct of interrogations by military intelligence personnel is not clear, but the existence of such influence remains an obvious possibility. Accounts of the death of an Iraqi general in November 2003 during interrogation by CIA personnel, their hired Iraqi mercenaries, and an Army interrogator in Qain suggest that this was indeed a toxic mix (White, 2005).

The torture and abuse inflicted on Iraqi prisoners in Tier I at Abu Ghraib fit the clear definition of evil as acts of knowing and deliberate infliction of pain and suffering on other human beings (even if these soldiers thought they were "just following orders"). The moral inversion of reducing all detainees at Abu Ghraib and elsewhere to "terrorists" allowed many personnel to rationalize their actions as acceptable and justified. For examples of administrative evil in which people can "engage in acts of evil without being aware that they are in fact doing anything wrong" and be "acting appropriately in their organizational role," we must look to those guards and interrogators—and their officers—who did not participate directly in the abuse but ignored what they saw or failed to act on it and to the myriad other personnel who interacted with the detention and intelligence systems (Zimbardo, 2007, 395–396). Clearly, a number of doctors and other health workers observed suspicious injuries or evidence of abuse (Physicians for Human Rights, 2008) but did not report it to authorities. They may have remained within the bounds of professional practice by recording the injuries in medical records, but did not raise the alarm on the abusers to those empowered to stop the abuse. Thus we see an important aspect of administrative evil: Actions viewed as appropriate in the professional role are viewed as morally questionable in retrospect. We are left to wonder how much sooner the evil might have been unmasked had the medical workers not only recorded the injuries but reported them through their chain of command. Other groups also chose not to "see" the torture and abuse that they had witnessed (Zimbardo, 2007).

MAKING SENSE OF THE SENSELESS

Our choice in the wake of 9/11 to redefine the rules of war to fit a new paradigm of war—the global war on terrorism—set off the extensive paper trail of memos on torture. The United States crossed the threshold of overtly sanctioning torture and other abusive practices and walked down the road toward a moral inversion (Meyer, 2008; Pfiffner, 2009). This moral inversion created the permission that enabled the migration of practices and attitudes from Afghanistan to Guantánamo to Iraq. As in other historical examples of moral inversions and administrative evil, there was no overt paper trail or no explicit orders to torture anyone, but permission was given that said in essence: Because these terrorists are so thoroughly bad, we are justified in approaching this war differently from all other wars and in redefining the rules accordingly.

With all these elements combined in an unholy mix, one almost had a field replication of the Stanford Prison Experiment (Zimbardo, 2007), and, indeed, a number of individuals responded to the invitation to sadism that is irresistible to the handful of thugs who are always available and waiting in the wings. There were also presumably well-intentioned people who found themselves drawn in both passively and actively based on the social-psychological cues embedded in the situation.

One possible explanation centers on the individual dispositions of those who were directly involved. This is the default account when we attempt to explain evil that occurs in organizations. The simplest one is that the perpetrators were a "few bad apples," who committed crimes on their own with no one else responsible for their heinous acts. In effect, this is the explanation, or theory-in-use, behind the trials and convictions of Spc. Charles Graner and others. The trials do not seek to assign responsibility or account-ability beyond the scope of the accusations of prisoner abuse by an individual (nor is it typically their role to do so).

Whether Graner and others followed orders is a separate issue. All that the trials focus on is whether the abuses (and conspiracy to abuse) occurred and whether they were illegal acts. Whatever the outcome of an individual trial, questions remain about which other factors may have been involved. As all the investigations note, commanding officers in the chain of command claimed that no orders were given to torture prisoners. At the same time, the low-ranking personnel accused of abuse in the prisons claimed that they "were just following orders" and could not be expected to disobey directives from their superiors in a wartime situation. Although some have stated that they felt uncomfortable about some of the acts in which they participated, they also believed that they were doing what was expected of them. In the end, this explanation sounds much more like the processes that lead to administrative evil (diffusion of responsibility, strategic ignorance, successive ratification, and the "evil turn") than a convincing justification for what was done in the name of national security.

ADMINISTRATIVE EVIL IN ORGANIZATIONS

The Stanford Prison Experiment (Zimbardo, 2007) suggests that the social and psychological dynamics at Abu Ghraib carried with them the potential for abuse, yet it does not fully fit the specifics of the situation. Unlike in the Stanford experiments, the guards did not act in an isolated and controlled environment but were part of a larger organizational structure and political environment. They interacted regularly with all sorts of personnel both directly and indirectly involved with the prisoners. They were in a remarkably chaotic environment, were by and large poorly prepared and trained for their roles, and were faced with both enormous danger and ambiguity. But, most important, as in the Stanford Prison Experiment, permission to torture and abuse was available to those who chose to accept it.

In his ground-breaking book, *The Destruction of the European Jews*, Raul Hilberg observed that a consensus in favor of and the practice of mass murder coalesced among German bureaucrats in a manner that "was not so much a product of laws and commands as it was a matter of spirit, of shared comprehension, of consonance and synchronization" (2003, 55). In another study of mid-level bureaucrats and the Holocaust, Christopher Browning describes this process in some detail as he also found that direct orders were not needed for key functionaries to understand the direction that policy was to take:

> Instead, new signals and directions were given at the center, and with a ripple effect, these new signals set in motions waves that radiated outward . . . with the situations they found themselves in and the contacts they made, these three bureaucrats could not help but feel the ripples and be affected by the changing atmosphere and course of events. These were not stupid or inept people; they could read the signals, perceive what was expected of them, and adjust their behavior accordingly. . . . It was their receptivity to such signals, and the speed with which they aligned themselves to the new policy, that allowed the Final Solution to emerge with so little internal friction and so little formal coordination. (Browning, 1992, 141–142)

If something as horrific and systematic as the Holocaust could be perpetrated based as much on a common understanding and permission to test moral boundaries as upon direct orders, it should not be difficult to imagine how the torture and abuse of detainees in Iraq and elsewhere occurred, with otherwise unacceptable behaviors substituting for ambiguous, standard operating procedures. Although the Holocaust was far, far worse than anything that happened during the U.S. occupation of Iraq, it has been amply demonstrated that Americans were not immune to the types of social and organizational conditions that made it possible and even permissible to violate the boundaries of morality and human decency, in at least some cases, without believing that they were doing anything wrong.

It would be naive to assume that the "few bad apples" acted alone and that others in the system did not share and support the torture and abuse as they went about their routines and did their jobs. Before and surrounding overt acts of evil, there are many more and much less obviously evil organizational activities that lead to and support the worst forms of human behavior. Moreover, without these instances of masked evil, the more overt and unmasked acts are less likely to occur (Staub, 1992, 20–21). The apparent willingness and comfort level with taking photos and being photographed while abusing prisoners seems to reflect the "normalcy" of the acts within the context of at least the night shift on Tiers 1A and 1B at Abu Ghraib (and is hauntingly similar to photos of atrocities sent home by SS personnel in World War II). Instead, we find a high stress situation, in which the expectation was to extract usable intelligence from detainees in order to help their comrades suppress a growing insurgency, find weapons of mass destruction, and prevent acts of terrorism. In this context, the power of group dynamics, social structures, and organizational ambiguities can be readily seen.

The normal inhibitions that might have prevented those who perpetrated the abuses from doing these evil deeds may have been further weakened by the shared belief that the prisoners were somehow less than human and that getting information out of them was more important than protecting their rights and dignity as human beings. For example, in an interview with the BBC on June 15, 2004, Brig. General Janis Karpinski stated that she was told by General Miller that the Iraqi prisoners "are like dogs and if you allow them to believe at any point that they are more than a dog then you've lost control of them." Just as anti-Semitism was central to the attitudes of those who implemented the policy of mass murder in the Holocaust, the torture and abuse at Abu Ghraib and elsewhere were facilitated by an atmosphere that dehumanized the detainees. These detainees, with their ambiguous legal status, were in effect seen as a "surplus population," as terrorists living outside (and undeserving of) the protections of society and state (Rubenstein, 1983; Sandel, 2009). And when organizational dynamics combine with a tendency to dehumanize or demonize a vulnerable group, the stage is set for the mask of administrative evil. Abu Ghraib serves well as an example of the dynamics of administrative evil in organizations.

CONCLUSION

In considerations of eruptions of evil throughout our history it is commonplace to assume, as Stanley Milgram (1974) initially did, that such acts emanate from a unique context, such as the complex and threatening environment of Abu Ghraib prison. We want to believe that they occur at a particular historical moment and within a specific culture or situation. Although this is clearly true, at least in part, it also allows a deception: The effect of understanding eruptions of evil as historical aberrations is that we safely wall them off from our own time and space and from ordinary people in ordinary times. A lack of attention to what we believe is a vitally important concept can be explained by this understandable, yet unfortunate, tendency to lament acts of administrative evil while dismissing them as temporary and isolated aberrations or deviations from proper administrative behavior and rational public policy.

As compliance accounts of human behavior suggest, social structures and organizational roles are far more powerful in shaping our behavior than we typically think. Within a culture of technical rationality, a model of professionalism that drives out ethics and moral reasoning offers all too fertile soil for administrative evil to emerge. Professionals and citizens alike would do well to consider not only that acts of administrative evil require modern organizations, but also the extent to which modern management is in part founded on and sustained by systematic dehumanization, exploitation, and even extermination. To the extent that this is true, and we believe that it is, we must remake our ethical foundation into one that unmasks and confronts the reality of administrative evil.

NOTE

1. Dr. George E. Reed, formerly on the faculty at the U.S. Army War College and now at the University of San Diego, was a full partner in our initial research on the events in Abu Ghraib prison and co-author of our 2006 article in *Public Administration Review*, which won the Marshall Dimock award for best lead article. We appreciate his willingness to let us use parts of this research in this chapter.

REFERENCES

Adams, G.B., and D.L. Balfour. 2009. *Unmasking Administrative Evil*, 3d ed. Armonk, NY: M.E. Sharpe.
———. 2010. Market-based government and the decline of organizational ethics. *Administration and Society*, 42, 615–637.
Browning, C. 1992. *The Path to Genocide*. Cambridge: Cambridge University Press.
Card, C. 2002. *The Atrocity Paradigm: A Theory of Evil*. New York: Oxford University Press.
Center for Public Integrity. 2004. The Taguba report. http://projects.publicintegrity.org/docs/AbuGhraib/Taguba_Report.pdf.
Darley, J.M. 1992. Social organization for the production of evil. *Psychological Inquiry*, 3, 199–218.
———. 1995. Constructive and destructive obedience: A taxonomy of principal-agent relationships. *Journal of Social Issues*, 51, 3, 125–154.
———. 1996. How organizations socialize individuals into evildoing. In *Codes of Conduct: Behavioral Research into Business Ethics,* ed. D.M. Messick and A.E. Tenbrunsel, 266–287. New York: Russell Sage Foundation.
Geddes, J.L. 2003. Banal evil and useless knowledge: Hannah Arendt and Charlotte Delbo on evil after the Holocaust. *Hypatia*, 18, 104–115.
Hilberg, R. 2003. *The Destruction of the European Jews*, 3d ed. New York: Holmes & Meier.
Hurt, R.D., and C.R. Robertson. 1998. Prying open the door to the tobacco industry's secrets about nicotine. *Journal of the American Medical Association*, 280, 13, 1173–1205.
Intelligence Science Board [ISB]. 2006. Educing Information: Interrogation: Science and Art—Foundations for the Future. Report. National Defense Intelligence College, Washington, DC.
Levinson, S., ed. 2004. *Torture: A Collection*. New York: Oxford University Press.
Mayer, J. 2005. Outsourcing terror. *New Yorker*, February 14, 1–14.
———. 2008. *The Dark Side: The Inside Story of How the War on Terror Turned into a War on American Ideals*. New York: Doubleday.

Milgram, S. 1974. *Obedience to Authority.* New York: Harper and Row.

Mintz, M. 1985. *At Any Cost: Corporate Greed, Women, and the Dalkon Shield.* New York: Pantheon.

Pfiffner, J.P. 2009. *Torture as Public Policy.* Boulder, CO: Paradigm Press.

Physicians for Human Rights. 2008. *Broken Laws, Broken Lives: Medical Evidence of Torture by U.S. Personnel and Its Impact.* Cambridge, MA.

Rejali, D. 2007. *Torture and Democracy.* Princeton: Princeton University Press.

Ricoeur, P. 1995. Intellectual autobiography. In *The Philosophy of Paul Ricoeur*, vol. 22, ed. Lewis Edwin Hahn, 222–256. Chicago: Open Court.

Rubenstein, R.L. 1983. *The Age of Triage: Fear and Hope in an Overcrowded World.* Boston: Beacon Press.

Sandel, M.J. 2009. *Justice: What's the Right Thing to Do?* New York: Farrar, Straus and Giroux.

Sands, P. 2008. *Torture Team: Rumsfeld's Memo and the Betrayal of American Values.* New York: Palgrave Macmillan.

Schooner, S.L. 2005. Contractor atrocities at Abu Ghraib: Compromised accountability in a streamlined, outsourced government. *Stanford Law and Policy Review*, 2, 45–67.

Staub, E. 1992. *The Roots of Evil: The Origins of Genocide and Other Group Violence.* New York: Cambridge University Press.

Strasser, S., ed. 2004. *The Abu Ghraib Investigations.* New York: PublicAffairs.

Vanderburg, W.H. 2005. *Living in the Labyrinth of Technology.* Toronto: University of Toronto Press.

White, J. 2005. Documents tell of brutal improvisation by GIs. *Washington Post*, August 3, A01.

Zimbardo, P. 2007. *The Lucifer Effect: Understanding How Good People Turn Evil.* New York: Random House.

3

Machiavellians and Organizational Evil

Barbara Oakley

As is the case with pornography, most people believe that they know evil when they see it. It seems distinct: Dictionaries define evil as "morally wrong; causing harm or injury." The implication is that the "evil" act or person is beyond the pale—a fib, for example, may be bad but is not generally thought to be evil. A psychopath who laughs as he rapes and kills a pregnant woman in front of her bound and horrified five-year-old child would be judged by most as evil. To gain perspective on how evil fits into the greater scheme of things, we might think of a Likert scale anchored by "saintly" at one end and "evil" at the other. The religious connotations of the endpoints—"saintly," "evil"—emphasize our emotional investment in the judgment. Behaviors at those extremes seem fairly easy to recognize.

But *organizational* evil is more difficult to identify. For one thing, while we normally would not call an individual with whom we had a moral disagreement "evil," it can be easy and natural to use that label for a faceless organization. In fact, depending on what a person finds morally unacceptable, many organizations could be labeled as evil. A stalwart environmentalist, for example, might think that automobile manufacturing companies are intrinsically evil (Manes, 1990). But an executive in one of those companies might believe that his corporation provides a valuable product and service to society and likewise believe that the often corrupt unions with which he deals are evil by their very nature (remember Jimmy Hoffa and the Teamsters? [Bernstein, 2007; Kennedy, 1994]). Ultimately, then, various organizational entities might be considered by some to have aspects of "organizational evil."

Other organizations, according to an impartial observer, arguably do not even pretend to be on the "saintly" end of the scale—at least toward those outside the organization: the Ku Klux Klan, street gangs, the Mafia, the Taliban—although, of course, each of these groups is intended to benefit at least some of those within the organization.

Governments, through their unwieldy size and the necessity of interacting with other governments, perforce can be perceived as evil: One person's idea of strict immigration control can be another's idea of a police state. In addition, the Internal Revenue Service and the Transportation Security Administration are only partly tongue-in-cheek perceived as plumbing the depths of hell. But in some cases, such as Germany under the Nazi regime, the horrific Soviet purges, or the Great Leap Forward in China, governments can become truly and obviously evil. (Obvious, that is, to everyone but the country's rulers at the time and to those who, for ideological reasons, prefer to look the other way.) Political scientist Rudolph Rummel, who has studied mass murders committed by governments, observes: "The closer to absolute power, the more a regime's disposition to murder one's subjects or foreigners multiplies" (1999, vii)—the very definition of "organizational evil."

Although most wide-scale murders that took place in the twentieth century were perpetrated at the hands of atheist governments (most prominently including the regimes of Mao in China, Stalin in the Soviet Union, and Pol Pot in Cambodia), religions can also be organizations that, wittingly or not, inflict, encourage, or promote what amounts to evil in terms of causing harm and destroying lives. Although religious organizations can provide meaning for many, they can also provide havens for others who ruin lives, as with the pedophile priests of the Catholic Church or Islamist suicide bombers. Alternatively, religious tendencies can manifest in organizational fashion as ruinous cults, as with the Reverend Jim Jones and his followers who drank the lethal Kool-Aid in Jonestown. Ultimately, however, it is clear that religion or lack thereof is not necessarily a causal factor in what we might consider "evil" done by organizations.

The only organizations that might appear not to contain elements of organizational evil are those devoted to philanthropy. But much recent press has been devoted to detailing how even perfectly well-intended philanthropy can go awry—worsening the very situations it is meant to improve and potentially causing great harm (Easterly, 2006; Kennedy, 2005; LeBor, 2006; Moyo, 2009). Good intentions, it seems, do not necessarily make for good outcomes. In fact, as a recent book, *Pathological Altruism*, makes clear, good intentions—or at least a semblance of good intentions—often enables behavior that causes great harm (Oakley et al., 2011). This is especially true when these good intentions are carried out by an organization, with a legitimacy and power dwarfing that of any single individual.

With all these observations and caveats in mind, organizational evil might then be best defined as "harm or injury done by an organization under the cloak of some greater beneficial cause." It is "behavior that, if engaged in by an individual, would be recognizable as morally wrong."

Apparently benevolent organizations, large or small, can and do have the same problems with causing harm or injury as those organizations that might more readily be recognizable as "bad." Thus, benevolent atheistic or religiously founded governments, along with unions, professional organizations, and universities, can be just as guilty of causing deep-rooted harm as organizations such as corporations that are not ostensibly benevolent. In fact, the same professors who are quick to point at business as the epitome of organizational evil often turn a blind eye to the multitudinous problems of the university system, which include imposing Sisyphean debt-loads on students that are impossible to escape through bankruptcy, professor indifference, research fraud, and occasional downright wicked office politics and administrations (Asquith, 2006; Cahn, 2010; Kiyosaki, 1995; Westhues, 1998). Universities also serve as bastions for seemingly well-intentioned professional organizations, for example, the American Psychological Association and the American Sociological Association, which have deep-rooted problems related in part to their insular academic nature (Brannigan, 2004; Carlat, 2010; Cole, 2001; Cummings and O'Donohue, 2009; Tierney, 2011; Wright and Cummings, 2005).

Figure 3.1   **Evil Can Occur Both External and Internal to the Organization**

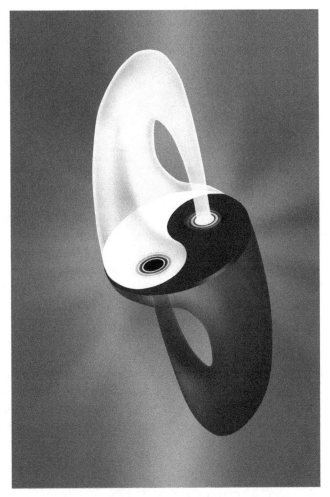

Organizational evil never appears to occur on its own. As shown symbolically here, it always seems coupled in some way with those whose intentions are genuinely benevolent.

One framework for understanding organizational evil of all these different types and degrees is shown in Figure 3.2. Evil can occur both inside and outside an organization. One example within an organization is the intentionally corrupt, inept leadership of Enron's Andrew Fastow, who went out of his way to ruin the careers of those who opposed him. But Enron was also externally evil by continuing a ruthless Ponzi scheme that defrauded thousands of investors (Brenner, 2002; McLean and Elkind, 2003).

Figure 3.2 is admittedly flawed—virtually every organization has good and bad aspects and intended as well as unintended actions that can have both good and bad—or even evil—consequences. Thus, one could argue about the placement of some of the examples or the appropriateness of the categories. (For example, was the enormously corrupt oil-for-

Figure 3.2   **A Framework for Understanding Organizational Evil**

		Evil toward others outside the organization is	
		Intended	Unintended
Evil within the organization is	Intended	Nazi Germany, Soviet Purges, Enron, UN (oil-for-food), Jim Jones's "People's Temple" cult	Corrupt leadership within a nominally altruistic organization (e.g., Texas Southern University, unions), petty office dictator
	Unintended	KKK, Mafia	Philanthropic organizations that worsen the situation they were meant to resolve

Note: Judgment is presumed to be made by a relatively impartial external observer.

food program by the United Nations, which dwarfed Enron's scale [LeBor, 2006; Rosett, 2005], intended to be evil both for people inside and outside the UN? In a different vein, is *intentional* evil worse than unintentional evil if the latter causes more harm?)

Yet, much as engineering and scientific models are admittedly flawed, a framework like the one outlined in Figure 3.2 is still useful in giving us new perspectives. This figure helps organize thinking about organizational evil not only on a larger scale—as in Pol Pot's Cambodia—but also on a smaller scale, as in the case of the petty office dictator who ruins the lives of those under his purview (Sutton, 1994) or the state legislator who uses his authority as the head of a powerful committee to ruin the lives of those who oppose him (Morgan and Reynolds, 1997, 129–136).

In essence, an organization often appears to begin its way down the road to being "evil" when it is led by a Machiavellian who guides the organization in service of the Machiavellian himself and toward that which the Machiavellian and his minions and followers believe is beneficial. These Machiavellian-oriented goals are generally quite different from those that other individuals, outside the sway of the Machiavellian, believe to be beneficial.

JOEL BAKAN'S *THE CORPORATION* AND ITS PROBLEMATIC THESIS

At first glance, it might seem that Joel Bakan's attack on corporations fits into this argument about the evil done by organizations. Bakan's *The Corporation: The Pathological Pursuit of Profit and Power* (2004) makes the case that corporations are, in essence, psychopaths. This concept has become a dominant theme in academic discussions involving organizational evil. Such a conception might sound helpful, but this kind of singular aim and oversimplified thesis diverts us from the scattered, often hidden harm done in and by organizations. It makes it far too easy to label and blame one kind of organization and miss what is really happening in many different venues.

Bakan established his "corporation as psychopath" meme through a number of mechanisms. First, he provided a veneer of scientific respectability by citing an expert in psychopathy, Robert Hare, who asserts that corporations show a close match between their institutional characteristics and Hare's checklist of psychopathic traits. Left out of Bakan's analysis was that Hare personally receives royalties each time his checklist is used—thus, it was to Hare's financial advantage to get a credulous academician with no scientific training, like Bakan, to tout Hare's checklist even in a situation where it clearly had no scientific applicability. (One might have come up with equally convincing conclusions by applying Hare's checklist to a cantaloupe, which, much like the corporation, is "unable to feel genuine concern for others in any context.") Recently Hare himself has come under fire for his self-serving, litigious attitudes toward criticism of his checklist, which has fundamental problems (Carey 2010; Skeem and Cooke 2010).

Bakan's credulous attitude regarding any theme or scheme that supports the thesis of his book is apparent elsewhere. For example, he earnestly accepted marketing CEO Jonathon Ressler's word that undercover marketing "is happening everywhere" (Bakan 2004, 32). Bakan seemed unaware that Ressler's own role as the originator of undercover marketing might be why Ressler states the technique is everywhere. Six years after Bakan's book was first published, Ressler's primary marketing mechanism seemed to be a poorly worded online pdf stating that he can't really describe what he does. ("We like to say if you talk, as soon as I talk about a client, like I'm pressing the self-destruct button. However, on the overt stuff, I mean we work with very big companies, we work with small companies . . . So I mean we kind of really run the gambit (*sic*)" [Ressler].) Seven years after publication of Bakan's book, Ressler's firm appears defunct.

To support his "corporation as psychopath" thesis, Bakan also deftly rewrites history, for example, making Ford's battle to protect his assets from the Dodge brothers through chicanery with Ford stock look like a battle where Ford was trying to protect his workers. (See Pitrone 1989 for a discussion of the real motivations involved.) Bakan goes on to tar corporations by association with fascist regimes—ignoring the clear association of labor unions with communist regimes that, as mentioned, have been responsible for far more deaths in the past century than fascist regimes (Cochran, 1977; Conquest, 1990; Hyman, 1971; Keeran, 1980; Rummel, 1994, 1999; Volkogonov, 1994). Indeed, Bakan's one-dimensional analysis ignores the very real evils of excessive government control that have been manifested continuously in both communist and fascist regimes over the past century. One cannot help but wonder what some of the 20 million purged by Soviet Communists, Holocaust victims, or those trapped in the death camp of North Korea (as opposed to the corporatized world of South Korea) would have made of Bakan's approving characterization of Chomsky's thoughts: "Whatever one thinks of governments, they're to some extent publicly accountable, to a limited extent. Corporations are to a zero extent" (Bakan, 2004, 152).

Corporations, in other words, are hardly the only self-interested entities. Virtually every organization has self-interests, including professional organizations, unions, academic institutions, religious groups, branches of government, and political parties. These self-interests often have little to do with the public interest—regardless of the organizations' proclamations to the contrary. Attempts to reform long-standing public school disaster areas like Washington, DC, and Detroit, for example, have often foundered in the face of determined resistance from teachers' unions. Teachers might have the interest of students and the public at heart but, in many instances, their own professional organization clearly does not (Greenhut, 2009; Lieberman, 1997; Moo, 1999; Paige, 2007).

Bakan also associates corporations with corruption, even as he ignores the long-standing association of unions with equivalent corruption, including racketeering, embezzlement, fraud, theft, linkages to organized crime, and murder (Coombs and Cebula, 2011; Jacobs, 2006; Methvin, 1998; Moldea, 1992). One recent study identified twenty-five separate categories of significant union corruption and found that

> among these embezzlement remains the most common, but kickbacks and mal-feasance with respect to pension plan management are of much greater financial concern. Peculation associated with gaining and maintaining high union office together with the bloated perks and emoluments that obtain thereto fuel internal corruption without diminishing the practice of extortion, bribery, conspiracy, sell-ing labor peace, licensing loose contracts, selling job access, and other traditional external corrupt practices. (Thieblot, 2006)

Beyond unions, examples abound of organizations that look "uncorporate-like" but suf-fer from the same weaknesses as corporations. *Unhinged: The Trouble with Psychiatry—A Doctor's Revelations About a Profession in Crisis* describes how psychiatry has largely forsaken the practice of talk therapy in favor of the more lucrative practice of simply prescribing drugs, with a host of deeply troubling consequences (Carlat, 2010). *Profession and Monopoly: A Study of Medicine in the United States and Great Britain* describes how the American Medical Association has helped limit the supply of physicians and inflated the cost of medical care in the United States (Berlant, 1975). *The United Way Scandal: An Insider's Account of What Went Wrong and Why* describes the roots of the nonprofit scandal involving United Way CEO William Aramony's criminal activities (Glaser, 1994). Worse yet, Congress exempts itself from its own legislation—members cannot be found guilty of insider trading, for example, because they are exempt from insider trading laws (Cramer, 1988; Mullins, McGinty, and Zweig, 2010). The list of similar seemingly enlightened and beneficial organizations that ignore their ultimately deleterious effects on society through self-serving support of their own members—particularly support of their own leaders—is virtually endless. It should also be noted that Bakan avoids discussion of the benefits of the increased regulation he promotes in his book to his own legal profession—in other words, Bakan is hardly a disinterested observer. A recent detailed analysis has, in fact, shown that judges make rulings that promote complexity in the law and favor lawyers and the legal profession over the interests of the public (Barton 2010).

Part of the problem regarding Bakan's arguments against corporations in general, as opposed to specific corrupt firms, is his confusion with regard to Machiavellian leader-ship, which he implies exists broadly in the corporate world. Corporate leaders such as Warren Buffett—and thousands of less heralded but no less hard-working CEOs—are serving the public as a whole by providing quality services, even as they legitimately and modestly serve their shareholders and themselves. Leaders such as Enron's Ken Lay and Jeffrey Skilling, by contrast, squandered the livelihoods of shareholders as they were serving themselves. One could similarly point at Jimmy Hoffa's corrupt, self-serving leadership of the International Brotherhood of Teamsters; James Bakker's plundering of the profits from his PTL ministries (he owned six luxurious homes, complete with gold-plated bathroom fixtures and an air-conditioned doghouse) (*Time,* 1987); and Texas Southern University's unethical president Priscilla Slade. (One regent was "in awe over Slade's lifestyle and asked how she could afford the expensive artwork, furnishings and manicured lawns. 'Girl, the university is paying for it,' Slade is said to have replied" [Asquith, 2006].)

It is not that corporations cannot be "evil"; rather, there is an extraordinary difference between corporations such as Warren Buffett's Berkshire Hathaway and Ken Lay and Jeffrey Skilling's Enron. A real understanding of organizational evil of any type must clearly go far deeper than Bakan's credulous and simplistic analysis. Moreover, any understanding of organizational evil requires each of us to stop imagining that the problem is "out there," that it can't be happening in *my* organization, just because we are in love with our own organization and our own good causes.

THE ROLE OF MACHIAVELLIANS IN ORGANIZATIONAL EVIL

In virtually all types of organizational evil, four elements seem to be present: Machiavellian[1] leaders (Berlin, 1955; Oakley, 2007, 280–81); fear, particularly among those at lower rungs of the social hierarchy; obedience to authority; and, finally, altruism and pathologies of altruism that allow such leaders to ascend to their role (Oakley et al., 2011). This chapter focuses on Machiavellian behavior, although the other elements also creep into the discussion.

If one thing has become clear over the millennia, it is that leaders with Machiavellian tendencies can wreak havoc (Oakley, 2007). The higher the Machiavellian rises in an organizational structure, and the larger that structure, the more harm can be caused. Machiavellians are found in small numbers in *any* social structure, particularly those with opportunities for power, control, money, or prestige, including:

- academia
- the arts
- business
- the legal system
- the media
- the military
- nongovernmental agencies and not-for-profits
- politics and government
- religious institutions
- unions

We must then clearly focus not on the shape, size, or intentions of an organization as a whole but on understanding the personal characteristics of Machiavellians who play leadership roles within organizations. This chapter highlights some of what we know about Machiavellians through discussion and exploration of aspects of clinical and subclinical borderline personality disorder. This is not to say that Machiavellians necessarily suffer from subclinical borderline personality disorder. We do not know enough from a neuroscientific perspective to make such a claim, and, in any case, the coming decades will provide a far more comprehensive understanding of the various syndromes involved in Machiavellianism, including psychopathy, narcissism, and emotional lability. But a discussion of Machiavellian characteristics through the lens of clinical and subclinical borderline personality disorder—a disease increasingly recognized as having neurological underpinnings—can provide profound insight into the distinctive elements of the behavior (Oakley, 2007).

It is difficult to do empirical studies to determine the percentage of Machiavellian individuals in any given social structure and how their distribution might vary by level within the hierarchy. Surveys—the mainstay of psychological research—are useless in the face of self-serving Machiavellians who are more likely than others to skip the thankless job of actually filling out the survey and who are, by definition, unlikely to answer honestly. A reasonable hypothesis, however, is that the higher one climbs in any given social structure, the higher the percentage of Machiavellians—that is, successfully sinister individuals who are able to mask their self-serving tendencies when necessary so as to attain their sought-after positions of power.

The reasoning behind this hypothesis is as follows. People often want to rise in any social structure because there are advantages for doing so, including prestige, power, and money. Some individuals rise because they are naturally talented—the straight-arrow business leader, for example, who spearheads his team through many a late night to a successful product launch. However, others rise because they are willing to lie, cheat, and misrepresent themselves and their intentions—such as the boss who blames all mistakes on his underlings even as he takes credit for their work and ideas. (In other words, there are two ways to rise to the top: One is to be the cream, while the other is to be the scum [Oakley, 2007, 31].) Moreover, as discussed below, a natural inclination of Machiavellians is to achieve power and control. It stands to reason that those who are willing to use subterfuge to enhance their standing will often rise higher or faster than one might expect in any social system given their level of talent (thus perhaps providing a foundation for parts of the Peter Principle [Peter and Hull, 1994]).

For the purposes of this chapter, a Machiavellian is defined as a person who is superficially charming and friendly but is capable of extraordinary acts of deceit for control or personal gain. Reflecting more deeply, a Machiavellian is perhaps best characterized as

> a person whose narcissism combines with subtle cognitive and emotional disturbances in such a fashion as to make him believe that achieving his own desires, and his alone, is a genuinely beneficial—even altruistic—activity. Since the Machiavellian gives more emotional weight to his own importance than to that of anyone or anything else, achieving the growth of his preeminence by any means possible is always justified in his own mind. The subtle cognitive and emotional disturbances of Machiavellians mean they can make judgments that dispassionate observers

would regard as unfair or irrational. At the same time, however, the Machiavellian's unusual ability to charm, manipulate, and threaten can coerce others into ignoring their conscience and treading a darker path. (Oakley, 2007, 409)

EVOLUTIONARY PERSPECTIVES

Evolutionary psychologists have long been plagued by a lack of general theory to guide studies of inherently manipulative, deceitful, and often malign individuals who are a small part of virtually every human social group. David Sloan Wilson, whose perceptive studies, along with those of John McHoskey, have formed a high point of work in the area, has succinctly summarized the lack of a general theory of Machiavellianism:

the majority of Machiavellianism studies do not appear to be guided by any theoretical framework at all. . . . In fact, interest in the very subject of Machiavellianism appears to have waned among psychologists, with the number of publications per annum peaking in 1982. Recent textbooks either do not discuss Machiavellianism at all or provide a short paragraph that reads like an obituary, a description of something that happened in the history of psychology, unconnected to any ongoing conceptual theme. This is a pity because Machiavellianism does represent a fundamental theme, the tension that exists between exploitive and prosocial behaviors in real life. One does not need to be an evolutionary biologist to recognize that this is an important topic that should be guided by a predictive theoretical framework of some sort. (Wilson, Near, and Miller, 1996, 295)

In looking for "a predictive theoretical framework," we can turn to the work done in psychology cataloging traits and clusters of traits that comprise dysfunctional and sometimes dangerous personalities. When we turn to the official manual used for this purpose, the *Diagnostic and Statistical Manual of Mental Disorders* (soon to be published in its fifth edition, the *DSM-5*), we find that the traits we are looking for, these "Machiavellian" traits, are scattered among various disorders. Figure 3.3 reveals how seemingly different psychological disorders can often share many common traits—only a few differences can earn the disorder a new name. The "set" (disorder) boundaries are, in some sense, arbitrarily chosen within a continuum of characteristics. In general, psychological definition and diagnosis constructs are based loosely upon arbitrary symptom-related dimensional axes (Kim and Tyrer, 2010). It is hoped that the *DSM-5* will help provide a better framework for analysis, although any nosological system inevitably unveils new vistas even as it masks others.

BORDERLINE PERSONALITY AND COMMONLY CO-OCCURRING DISORDERS

Borderline personality disorder (BPD) is thought to occur in approximately 1–2 percent of the population (Torgersen, Kringlen, and Cramer, 2001). It is the most common per-

Figure 3.3 **How Different Psychological Disorders Share Many Common Traits**

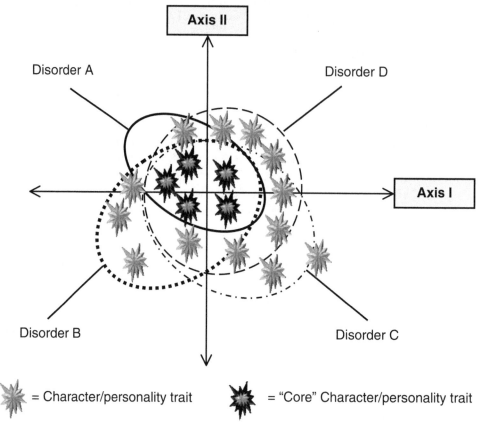

= Character/personality trait   = "Core" Character/personality trait

An illustration of the "fuzzy" nature of personality disorder diagnosis. The definition and diagnosis constructs are based loosely upon arbitrary symptom-related dimensional axes. The choice of axes determine the degree of separation/identification of each trait; possibly re-plotting would more clearly delineate clusters of traits. The "set" (disorder) boundaries are arbitrarily chosen within a continuum of characteristics. Disorder definitions are in many cases symptom-based, not neurologically based. (Illustration courtesy Brian Sangeorzan.)

sonality disorder in clinical settings, affecting 10 percent of all psychiatric outpatients and 15–20 percent of inpatients (Widiger and Francis, 1989). It is reasonable to assume the disorder occurs worldwide (Ikuta et al., 1994; Moriya et al., 1993; Nathan, 1994; Swenson, 2000; Zheng et al., 2002), although some social protective factors may minimize occurrence of BPD in more traditional societies (Miller, 1996; Paris, 1996). The categorical description of BPD in the current edition of the *DSM* (*DSM-IV*) is in Figure 3.4. A number of researchers have noted common traits of BPD that are not included in the *DSM-IV* description—these additional traits are listed in Figure 3.5.

Understanding of the neuroscientific correlates of BPD has grown tremendously in recent years (Crowell, Beauchaine, and Linehan, 2009; Dell'Osso et al., 2010; Harari

Figure 3.4 **DSM-IV Diagnostic Criteria for Borderline Personality Disorder**

1. Frantic efforts to avoid real or imagined abandonment. Note: Do not include suicidal or self-mutilating behavior covered in Criterion 5.
2. A pattern of unstable and intense interpersonal relationships characterized by alternating between extremes of idealization and devaluation. [This also includes the concept of "splitting," where a person is either "good" or "evil," with nothing in-between.]
3. Identity disturbance: markedly and persistently unstable self-image or sense of self.
4. Impulsivity in at least two areas that are potentially self-damaging (e.g., spending, sex, substance abuse, shoplifting, reckless driving, binge eating). Note: Do not include suicidal or self-mutilating behavior covered in (5).
5. Recurrent suicidal behavior, gestures, or threats, or self-mutilating behavior.
6. Affective instability due to a marked reactivity of mood (e.g., intense episodic dysphoria, irritability, or anxiety usually lasting a few hours and only rarely more than a few days). [Dysphoria is the opposite of euphoria; it is a mixture of depression, anxiety, rage, and despair.]
7. Chronic feelings of emptiness.
8. Inappropriate, intense anger or difficulty controlling anger (e.g., frequent displays of temper, constant anger, recurrent physical fights).
9. Transient, stress-related paranoid ideation or severe dissociative symptoms.

Figure 3.5 **Traits Not Necessarily Noted in the DSM-IV** (which are believed by BPD researchers to also be common to the disorder)

1. Pervasive shame
2. Undefined boundaries
3. Control issues
4. Lack of object constancy
5. Interpersonal sensitivity
6. Situational competence
7. Narcissistic demands
8. Manipulation
9. Extreme Defense Mechanisms
   a. Denial
   b. Rationalization
   c. Splitting
   d. Projection
   e. Continual blame and criticism of others
   f. Domination through threats
   g. Verbal assaults
   h. Abusive expectations
   i. Unpredictable responses
   j. Gaslighting (denying the perceptions of others about events and conversations)
   k. Deliberate creation of constant arguments and conflict
   l. Placement of individuals in no-win situations

et al., 2010; Mauchnik and Schmahl, 2010). Both genetics and environment, through differing paths, appear to play a role in the development of the disorder (Steele and Siever, 2010). The genes and alleles implicated in BPD clearly have varying degrees of overlap with the many emotional disorders that often co-occur with BPD and personal quirks of those without BPD but with, for example, traits such as a hair-trigger temper (Distel et al., 2008; Gunderson and Lyons-Ruth, 2008; Rosenthal et al., 2008).

BPD does not appear to be a single-locus trait or even be affected by only a few loci but, rather, may be due to conditions created by a confluence of multiple, at least partially independently inherited genes (Livesley and Jang, 2008). The combination of these genes, along with environmental factors, can lead to mild or pronounced versions of the disorder. Thus, having one or both parents with the disorder would not guarantee the disorder would be inherited but, rather, would lead to an increased degree of predisposition to the disorder or its subclinical manifestations. Some or many borderline traits could also appear, due to organic brain dysfunction in the same areas thought to be affected by the genetics of the disorder, for example, the dorsolateral prefrontal region of the brain or the amygdala.

It is important to point out that strides are being made in the development of therapies that have proven to improve the lives of those with BPD. Although BPD may be in part genetically based, genetics do not absolutely predetermine how each individual will act. A decision by some of those with the disorder to participate in, for example, dialectical behavior therapy, can reduce, although not necessarily eliminate, dysfunctional behaviors (Bateman and Fonagy, 2010; Paris, 2009).

High-Functioning Borderlines

"High-functioning" borderlines are individuals who exhibit an indication of some or even many of the nine traits that characterize BPD in the *DSM-IV*, yet who have never seen a physician for emotional difficulties and therefore avoid a psychiatric label.* These individuals can also mask problematic behavior when necessary. It is perhaps helpful at this juncture to describe the characteristics of high-functioning borderlines as perceived by "normal" people—not clinicians or academicians—surrounding the borderlines (see Figure 3.6).

The current *DSM-IV* categorical approach to analyzing borderline personality disorder can mask the relationship between low-functioning, clinically diagnosed borderlines and high-functioning, but undiagnosed borderlines, or "borderline borderlines" (those with substantial borderline traits, even if they do not necessarily meet the subjective "clinically significant" *DSM-IV* standards for the disorder). This relationship is clearer when a dimensional approach is used to quantify borderline traits (a sample dimensional approach is presented in Figure 3.7).

Indeed, it appears high-functioning borderlines have scarcely been studied (Posner et al., 2002), although research by Adrian Raine related to white-collar criminals provides insight in this area (Gao and Raine, 2010). Interestingly, it appears that white-collar criminals might exhibit stronger cognitive control on some tasks than ordinary individuals (Banich et al., 2009). One Italian study revealed traits of borderline personality disorder and antisocial personality disorder in a small percentage of 747 students (Fossati et al., 2004). (The precise percentage was not given, as the focus of the study was on the individual traits rather than the diagnoses.) This supports the idea that individuals in the

---

*In this chapter I follow the example of borderline expert Jerold Kreisman and others who, for the sake of clarity and efficiency, refer to individuals by their diagnosis. Thus, "borderline" is shorthand for someone who exhibits symptoms consistent with the *DSM-IV* diagnosis of borderline personality disorder (Kreisman and Straus, 2004).

Figure 3.6 **Common Characteristics of High-functioning Borderlines**

1. Make untrue accusations (lie).
2. Act verbally abusive toward people they know very well, while putting on a charming front for others. Can switch from one mode to the other in seconds.
3. Change their wants and opinions quickly so that it is impossible to keep the borderline happy. Have frightening, unpredictable rages that make no logical sense.
4. Are extremely manipulative; anything that others do or say may be twisted around and used against them. Put others in no-win situations. Will act in what seems like extreme or controlling manners to get their own needs met.
5. Can insist so convincingly on their version of reality, whatever the contrary evidence, that other individuals are left with the feeling they are living in a fantasy world. ("Welcome to Oz" is the title of a listserv devoted to non-BPs attempting to deal with borderlines in their lives.)
6. Blame others for actions that are not the others' fault. Project their own unpleasant traits, behaviors, or feelings by attributing them (often in an accusing way) to someone else. Unwilling to admit to a mistake.
7. Act competent and controlled in some situations but extremely out of control in others.
8. Their relationships appear to be more about power and control than kindness and caring. They will cut some people out of their life over issues that seem trivial or overblown. Contrarily, will not let other individuals escape from their control (as by divorce or refusal to continue a friendship), and will take extraordinary measures to maintain the relationship, often exhibiting paranoid, aggressive or clingy behavior in the process.
9. Black-and-white thinking: views others as either all good or all bad, with nothing in between. Can flip easily from one state regarding a person to another. Often somewhat or very paranoid about the motives of others.
10. Change their opinions depending on who they are with if necessary to charm a potentially useful individual.
11. Take undeserved credit for others' efforts.
12. Feel ignored when they are not the focus of attention, and feel they can never get enough love, affection, or attention. Do or say inappropriate things to keep the focus on them when they feel ignored.
13. Deny the effects of their behavior on others and deny their behavior is problematic.

Figure 3.7 **Characteristics of BPD Defined Using a Dimensional Approach**

1. Poorly regulated emotions
2. Impulsivity
3. Impaired perception and reasoning
4. Markedly disturbed relationships

general population may possess symptoms of the disorders without necessarily having been diagnosed.

One study found that most borderlines do not appear different from normal individuals on tasks of executive functioning or memory and that the introduction of emotional stimuli did not impair performance (Sprock et al., 2000). High-functioning borderlines can maintain a seemingly normal, or even highly valued, position in society (Mason and Kreger, 1998, 48). These successful, outgoing, popular individuals might show their dark side only to people whom they know very well (Friedel, 2004, 189–90). Many nonborderlines seeing therapists in relation to their issues with an individual with suspected borderline personality disorder have related that even their therapists refused to believe them when they described the out-of-control behavior (BPD Central, 2001).

Figure 3.8   **Characteristics Important for Manipulative, Controlling Personalities**

1. A relative lack of affect in interpersonal relationships. Views others as objects to be manipulated rather than as individuals with whom one has empathy.
2. A lack of concern with conventional morality. Lying, cheating, and other forms of deceit are acceptable.
3. A lack of gross psychopathology.
4. Low ideological commitment. More involved in tactics for achieving possible ends than in an inflexible striving for an ultimate idealistic goal.

MACHIAVELLIANISM AND BORDERLINE PERSONALITY DISORDER

Christie and Geis used the list given in Figure 3.8, as well as the discussions in Machiavelli's *The Prince*, to guide them in developing a definition of and test for Machiavellian personalities (Christie and Geis, 1970). Their work resulted in the Mach-IV, the oldest, most well-known and broadly used test for Machiavellianism. The test was developed to measure how formal and informal power is used by organizational leaders to control or manipulate others (McHoskey, Worzel, and Szyarto, 1998).

The Hidden Nature of Machiavellianism in Those with Subclinical Borderline Personality Disorder

At first glance, and even after careful study, it would appear that psychopathy would relate best to Machiavellianism (McHoskey, Worzel, and Szyarto, 1998). However, psychopaths, at least under Robert Hare's popular conception of the disorder, tend to be so physically aggressive, irresponsible, unreliable, and incapable of forming, or even imitating, lasting personal commitments that they either become incarcerated at a relatively early age, or remain at lower levels in the social hierarchy (Mealey, 1995). The question of whether some seeming aspects of psychopathy, for example, physical aggressiveness, might simply be due to the way the disorder has been conceptualized has recently been explored in a controversial study (Cooke, Michie, and Skeem, 2007; Skeem and Cooke, 2010). However, another possible way of parsing the behavior may relate to those with subclinical aspects of BPD. One reason the Machiavellian-borderline connection was not made earlier might relate to the *DSM-IV* (Figure 3.4) description of BPD, which makes it difficult to see that traits found in those with the disorder can manifest as Machiavellian behavior. Relevant literature on BPD is often written in clinical, dispassionate tones that give little hint of the emotional impact that borderline behavior can cause in others. For example, a borderline might unconsciously revise facts to fit her feelings and emotions, so that her perception of events is different from others. However, others see the borderline as a liar—an obvious point that is left out of research studies.

It should be kept in mind that all categorical approaches are simply reductive attempts to classify extraordinarily complex neurological processes. Recent research reveals, for example, that borderlines appear to have problems with the cognitive, as opposed to the affective (emotional) aspects of empathy, which might explain the social interactions of

Figure 3.9 **Linking BPD with Machiavellian Traits**

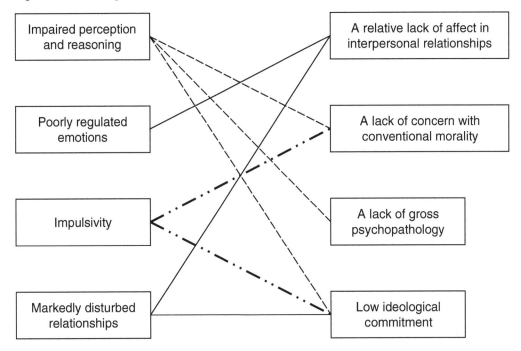

Relationship between dimensional traits for borderline personality disorder and Machiavellian traits as outlined by Christie and Geis.

Note: The different lines do not represent anything except to clarify which lines go to which box.

borderlines or subclinical borderlines that sometimes appear to grow from genuine feelings of empathy and care (Harari et al., 2010).

Overall, it should be clear that there is broad overlap between subclinical borderline and Machiavellian behavior patterns. The relationship can be seen by corresponding the four dimensional traits thought to be characteristic of BPD with the set of four prototypical Machiavellian traits developed by Christie and Geis (1970; Figure 3.9).

Nonborderline responses to borderline-like behavior are often characterized by bewilderment. Borderline-like behavior can seem so willfully malevolent that individuals simply do not know how to respond. One psychiatrist, writing before BPD became broadly known, characterized much of the borderline-like behavior he observed as "evil" (Klose, 1995; Peck, 1983).

McHoskey's Work in Relating Machiavellianism to Other Personality Disorders

John McHoskey (2001) used the Personality Diagnostic Questionnaire-4+ (PDQ-4+) (Hyler, 1997; Hyler et al., 1988) as a dimensional measure of the personality disorders included in the *DSM-IV* with a sample of 287 student respondents. Scores on the PDQ-4+

Table 3.1

Correlation between Machiavellianism (Mach-IV scores) and various DSM-IV Personality Disorders as assessed by the Personality Diagnostic Questionnaire-4+ (PDQ-4+) for *n* = 287 respondents

PDQ-4+ measure	R (Mach)
PDQ-4+ total score	0.44***
Cluster A: odd or eccentric	
Total cluster score	0.36***
Paranoid	0.36***
Schizoid	0.23***
Schizotypal	0.20**
Cluster B: dramatic, emotional or erratic	
Total cluster score	0.42***
Antisocial	0.33***
Antisocial Behavior	0.20**
Borderline	0.40***
Impulsivity	0.39***
Histrionic	0.13*
Narcissistic	0.22***
Cluster C: anxious or fearful	
Total cluster score	0.17**
Avoidant	0.18**
Dependent	0.15*
Obsessive-compulsive	0.03
Provisional personality disorders	
Depressive	0.23***
Negativistic	0.38***

Source: Summarized from McHoskey, 2001.
*p < 0.05; **p < 0.01; ***p < 0.001 (all two-tailed).

were correlated with scores on the Mach-IV test (Christie and Geis, 1970). An abbreviated version of McHoskey's findings is presented in Table 3.1. Borderline personality shows the strongest correlation of any *DSM-IV* disorder with Machiavellianism, 0.40. One of the four dimensional traits defining BPD, impulsivity, has a similarly high correlation, 0.39. Frequent BPD codisorders—paranoid and narcissistic—correlate at 0.36 and 0.22, respectively, while antisocial personality disorder, which shares some traits with BPD and is often considered a BPD codisorder (Grilo, Sanislow, and McGlashan, 2002; Zanarini et al., 1998), correlates at 0.33.

McHoskey's 2001 study puts into perspective McHoskey's own earlier work linking Machiavellianism to psychopathy (McHoskey, Worzel, and Szyarto, 1998). A correlation is present between psychopathy (antisocial personality) and Machiavellianism, but it may relate to an underlying correlation between antisocial personality and BPD (Leichsenring, Kunst, and Hoyer, 2003). (Paris writes: "If it were not inconsistent with clinical tradition, we could have described a single gender-neutral disorder that covers the present ground traversed by the criteria for ASPD and BPD" [1997].) Paris also points out that comorbidity in the personality disorders "have used clinical populations in which patients with antisocial personality are relatively rare. The comorbidity between ASPD and BPD in these clinical samples is only about 10 percent to 15 percent, but it might be higher in community samples" (1997, 240) This observation is borne out in Fossatti et al.'s borderline and antisocial personality disorder (ASPD) studies in a large nonclinical population of 747 university students. Correlation between BPD and ASPD in the sample was 0.37 (Fossati et al., 2004). Moreover, secondary psychopathy, with its strong association with anxiety and emotional disturbance, shares many traits with BPD (Fossati et al., 2004; Kiehl et al., 2004; Lykken, 1996; Mealey, 1995).

Although BPD had the highest correlation to Machiavellianism of any individual personality disorder or trait, a 0.40 correlation still indicates some divergence between borderline and Machiavellian traits. This may relate in part to Mach-IV questions such as: "The world would be in much better shape than it is if people acted upon basic ethical principles," and "One should take action only when sure it is morally right." A borderline might very well answer "yes" to such questions, because through dissociation, a borderline often *believes* he or she is acting ethically, whether or not that is actually the case from another's perspective.

EVOLUTIONARY ADVANTAGES OF BORDERLINE PERSONALITY AND RELATED CODISORDERS

This section is perhaps best prefaced by repeating George William's perceptive statement:

> One of the strengths of scientific inquiry is that it can progress with any mixture of empiricism, intuition, and formal theory that suits the convenience of the investigator. Many sciences develop for a time as exercises in description and empirical generalization. Only later do they acquire reasoned connections within themselves and with other branches of knowledge. (Tooby and Cosmides, 1992, 19)

Abundant evidence exists that what are often thought to be hereditary disorders in reality may have developed as a way of coping with adverse various environmental factors, as, for example, the wide variety of genetic "defects" associated with living in areas where malaria exerts a high selective effect (Nesse and Williams, 1996). It is thus plausible that a widespread syndrome such as that of BPD and its subclinical manifestations might have benefits that allowed for survival or at least continued reproduction under certain conditions. The actual percentage of those with the syndrome, although small, might vary from one society to another and between different social hierarchies. (High versus low social hierarchies, in particular, have seemed to vary with something akin to a predator-prey relationship in some periods of recorded history, possibly due to the animosity that the "successful sinister" can engender [MacMullen, 1988, 85].)[2] Much as the incidence of those who are left-handed appears to vary, increasing where hand-to-hand combat is common despite the fact that they are, on average, smaller and lighter than those who are right handed (Faurie and Raymond, 2005), perhaps there are environments, for example, the highly populated areas made possible by the agricultural revolution, in which borderline-like behavior provides reproductive advantages (Cosmides and Tooby, 1992; Kenrick and Simpson, 1997;

Tooby and Cosmides, 1990a, 1990b). It has been shown that competition increases the use of antisocial and Machiavellian strategies (Christie and Geis, 1970). Increased antisocial behavior has also been associated with high population density, an indirect form of competition (Ellis, 1988; Mealey, 1995; Robins, Tipp, and Przybeck, 1991; U.S. Department of Justice, 1993; Wachs, 1992; Wilson and Herrnstein, 1985).

It is hypothesized here that many borderline traits that appear pathological, and that are uncomfortable or even emotionally difficult for nonborderlines to deal with, can be valuable in enabling borderlines to work their way into, or retain, positions of power and control or serve other evolutionarily valuable purposes (Brüne, Ghiassi, and Ribbert, 2010; Molina et al., 2009). Like viruses and parasites interacting with the human immune system, people can trick others into discomfort to further their own purposes.

Real World Data

Preeminent psychiatrist Theodore Millon (2004) has emphasized the critical importance of staying close to the data provided by real people in a broad array of contexts when analyzing mental function and dysfunction. So it is reasonable to begin this section by relating the experiences of a psychiatrist specializing in the treatment of patients with borderline personality who was himself intimidated and manipulated by a borderline in a fashion that was beneficial to the borderline. Here is psychiatrist Robert Friedel, writing of his youthful experiences with his sister Denise, who was afflicted with BPD:

> I was cleaning my golf clubs in preparation for the spring, but one was missing. I looked everywhere in the house—no club. Denise walked by, so I asked her if she had seen it. She calmly said yes, she had broken it in two and thrown the pieces into the snow behind the house. It seemed we had argued over something a few weeks earlier, and she had done it then. At first, I thought she was taunting me. She knew how hard I had worked and saved to buy those clubs. Surely no one would do such a thing, not even Denise. . . . Later, when the snow melted and I found the broken club, I realized that something was truly different about Denise, *and that it was probably best not to provoke her in any way, for any reason.* (Friedel, 2004, 24; emphasis added)

Such a story supports Randolph Nesse's point: "Individuals gain a huge ability to influence others if they can convince others that they will, in a specified future situation, act in ways that will not then be in their best interests" (Nesse, 2000). Scaring others, as Denise shows, is an effective technique to control of the actions of others.

However, despite the clear success of such emotionally based strategies, much past research into Machiavellian behavior has focused on obtaining algorithms, such as the tit-for-tat strategy in the game of prisoner's dilemma (Axelrod, 1984), that provide a rationale for deceitful behavior. Some references have taken tit-for-tat further to include being able to abandon a group and other permutations on the theme (Boyd and Lorberbaum, 1987; Dugatkin, 1992). Many models and explanations have also been developed to describe the rise of altruistic and cooperative behavior (Boyd et al., 2003; Nesse, 2000;

Simon, 1990; Wright, 1994). But this chapter is based on the idea that, rather than logical or rational strategies, it is the wealth of emotional strategies inherent in BPD that are the mark of true Machiavellianism, and these strategies can lead to profound, reoccurring social success (Nesse, 1990).

Specific Examples of the Manipulative Power of Borderline Traits and Common Codisorders to Achieve Dominance

Many examples of borderline-like strategies that lead to dominance and control could be given from anonymous patients described in the research literature. But such examples do not often show that such strategies can be successfully used to achieve high positions of status and control in conventional society. Therefore, some of the examples presented below are chosen from the behavior of well-known or even notorious pathological and nonpathological leaders and individuals who displayed borderline-like traits and the traits of frequent borderline codisorders to successfully manipulate the behavior of surrounding individuals.

Emotional Lability

Emotional lability refers to emotional manipulation by borderlines to keep the people around them off balance and at a disadvantage in dealing with them. Engaging in such manipulation was part of the behavior that enabled former General Electric CEO Jack Welch to achieve acclaim as one of the business greats of the twentieth century. As Welch's biographer Christopher Byron recounts:

> once Welch discovered that edgy, unpredictable behavior was something for which . . . people had simply no frame of reference, he had their number. It was as if the veil of mystery had suddenly fallen away, and he understood the rules of the game. . . . To get people's attention, do the unexpected; don't hold your temper, *use* it. Be quick, be smart, keep everyone off balance. (2004, 51)

Mao Zedong employed many BPD traits, including emotional liability, to his advantage in his rise to power. (Unlike Welch, Mao is thought by a definitive biographer to have had BPD [Terrill, 1998].) "Getting upset is one of my weapons," he once confided to his personal physician, Dr. Zhisui Li (1994, 180). As Andrew Nathan writes in the foreword to Dr. Li's memoirs:

> The real Mao could hardly have been more different from the benevolent sage-king portrayed in the authorized memoirs and poster portraits that circulate in China today. To be sure, on first meeting he could be charming, sympathetic, and casual, setting his visitor at ease to talk freely. But he drew on psychological reserves of anger and contempt to control his followers, manipulating his moods with frightening effect. Relying on the Confucian unwillingness of those around him to confront their

superior, he humiliated subordinates and rivals. He undertook self-criticism only to goad others to flatter him, surrounding himself with a culture of abasement. . . . He understood human suffering chiefly as a way to control people. In politics and personal life alike, he discarded those for whom he had no present use, just as coolly calling them back when he wanted them, if they were still alive. (1994, viii)

Reliance on Transitional Objects

Many borderline traits can be similarly analyzed for their advantageous evolutionary effects. For example, the inability of many borderlines to let go of others who make efforts to extricate themselves (called "reliance on transitional objects") results in borderline behavior ranging from death threats against the person who to is trying to leave to declarations of undying love to suicide threats. Such actions, although seemingly pathological, could have a sound evolutionary value. As the song goes, "And if you can't be with the one you love, honey, love the one you're with" (Stills, 1970). The confusing nature of borderline interactions with others is perhaps best summarized by psychiatrist Jerold Kreisman's aptly titled book: *I Hate You, Don't Leave Me: Understanding the Borderline Personality*. Borderlines who keep the ones they are with, by whatever means, would be far more likely to reproduce with them.

Projection

Borderline inability to accept blame and ability to deflect criticism by deflecting it onto others appears to shield the borderline from a tendency to second-guess their actions. Such second-guessing, in fact, can often cripple more empathetic or thoughtful individuals. Sincere and convincing protestations by a borderline-like individual that, for example, the police at a crime scene were actually the ones who were somehow at fault can lead to a quagmire of doubt in jurors, even in the face of other compelling evidence of an accused perpetrator's guilt (Simpson, 1995). Borderline traits such as projection—deflecting all blame onto others—can be particularly valuable for attaining and retaining leadership positions, notwithstanding the obvious affiliated drawback of inability to make change when change is really needed.

Black-and-White Thinking

The black-and-white thinking typical of borderlines often involves their idealizing an individual, who consequently basks in the attention and limitless focus. After borderlines' focus and attention change from positive to negative, often as a result of a minor slight or perceived slight, those individuals will often do almost anything to regain that attention. This consciously or unconsciously provides the borderline with an excellent means of control. Numerous spouses of borderlines have commented on Web sites and in books that the desire to return to the center of the borderline's mesmerizing attention is a major factor in their love for the borderline and desire to remain in the relationship.

The flip side is that the borderline's demonizing of that individual for slight "transgressions" serves as a warning to others that they, too, might fall out of favor, with obvious attendant consequences if they do not conform to the borderline's wishes.

Dissociation

Possibly one of the most evolutionarily successful borderline strategies, at the same time perhaps the most bothersome to nonborderlines, is the ability of borderlines to seemingly revise their memories and perception of reality to suit their needs. Whatever the neurological mechanism by which this takes place, it appears to provide an effective method for confusing and outwitting others, again providing for a highly effective means of manipulation and control. Research has revealed that an unrealistic, essentially irrational view of the world can sometimes be advantageous (Nesse, 1999; Taylor and Brown 1988, 1994). It is thus plausible that the skewed perspective of borderlines is similarly an adaptation that can at times be beneficial.

In his perceptive memoirs, *Son of a Grifter*, Kent Walker tellingly describes how his mother, the notorious conwoman Sante Kimes, spent two decades in a globetrotting orgy of criminal behavior, torching houses, defrauding friends, crashing White House parties, stealing fur coats, and cuckolding her husbands. In the end, she and her younger son, Kenny, were both convicted of the savage murder of the millionaire heiress Irene Silverman in New York City. Walker writes:

> Who can beat a lie detector test? . . . Mom would have [had] no trouble fooling a machine. I've seen her walk into parties filled with little clumps of people who each know her under a different alias. Instead of fleeing in panic, she works the room, remembering what fake name she used with each mark, never slipping, never breaking a sweat. A few electrodes and straps on her arms wouldn't faze her. But it's too easy to say her skill comes from the sangfroid of a grifter. Her gift for lying comes from passionate conviction. She never blinks or stutters in the midst of the most ornate fibs, because she believes what she's saying without reservation. A good liar always starts with a germ of truth and builds from there: that's Mom. She can't distinguish between what's real and what's she's invented, which makes her preternaturally persuasive. (Walker and Schone, 2001, 1–2)

Taking Advantage of Trust

Borderlines, like ultimate con artists, take advantage of the inherent desire of others to give the benefit of the doubt. Indeed, some people are so trusting, so congenitally unable to face the possibility of deception, that it is almost impossible for them to believe that others could have different motives. Perhaps the "emotional module,"[3] or sets of neural circuits related to this activity, are such that it is difficult for them to detect malign motives—particularly when the con artists themselves believe (at least momentarily) what they are saying (Baron Cohen, 2011; Cosmides and Tooby, 1992; Homant and Kennedy,

2011; McGrath and Oakley, 2011; Oakley, Knafo, and McGrath, 2011; Riby, Bruce, and Jawaid, 2011; Turvey, 2011; Zahn-Waxler and Van Hulle, 2011). In some sense, these trusting individuals may be rather like Darwin's finches on the far reaches of the Galapagos, which, having little or no experience with land predators, will stand stupidly and stare as their fellow birds are caught and killed (Weiner, 1995). Actually, evolutionary theory might predict that women who remained committed even to a painfully abusive spouse would have children, whereas those who tried to leave might have been killed or had less opportunity to have children. This would select, willy-nilly, for *Women Who Love Too Much,* the title of a once-popular bestseller (Norwood, 1990). (A number of other books display the same sentiment toward women; there appear to be few books describing a male equivalent of the phenomenon.)

An alternative or ancillary explanation for why extraordinarily "nice" people seem to remain in relationships with borderlines may be that the borderline consciously or unconsciously trains them to be nice. In the classic Skinner-box experiments, a rat trained to press a lever to get a treat will quickly stop pressing the lever if the treats stop coming. However, if treats are handed out at random intervals, it takes a very long time for the lever-pressing behavior to cease. Likewise, if a borderline at least occasionally responds to helpful behavior with showers of thanks and praise, it may continue to generate even more helpful, hopeful behavior in those so inclined. This would explain anecdotal comments that seem to indicate that some children of those with BPD, or those who have been in long-term relationships with those who show characteristics of the disorder, are almost too kind.

Narcissism

Narcissism can be a co-occurring syndrome with BPD (Ronningstam, 1996). Surprisingly, little solid medical research has been conducted on narcissism (Fan et al., 2010). This is in sharp contrast with the wealth of such studies available on other important emotional disorders such as BPD, schizophrenia, or bipolar disorder. Whatever the neurological underpinnings, however, a narcissistic component, at least insofar as it related to ambition (Posner and Ware, 2000),[4] seems to be present in many individuals, pathological or not, who have obtained high social status. Thus some degree of narcissism/ambition would be useful on an evolutionary basis. Correlation with Machiavellianism and narcissism has been noted (McHoskey, 1995). A correlation, of course, implies that the relationship between Machiavellianism/borderline and narcissism/ambition is not absolute. Unlike CEOs Martha Stewart or "Chainsaw Al" Dunlap, some men and women with many borderline-like traits are perfectly content with low-status jobs.

Paranoia

Paranoia, another co-occurring syndrome with BPD, can be a useful evolutionary trait in less obvious ways. Severe, unwarranted paranoia may seem counterproductive, but in social situations, it can lead to "forced teaming": the artificial creation of a team that can induce others to do what they normally would not do (De Becker, 1999). As conwoman

Sante Kimes would tell her son Kent: "Those sons of bitches are trying to kill us." Kimes's absolute belief in this statement, no matter how irrational, was often enough to get her son to come to her aid (Walker and Schone, 2001, 13).

Possible Advantages of Machiavellian Parenting and Machiavellian Children

A Machiavellian parent or parents would, virtually by definition, not be good nurturers for their offspring. There is evidence that diagnosed (that is, generally low-functioning) borderlines appear to have lower reproductive rates, although studies on this have taken place when contraceptives and abortion were easily available, unlike all other evolutionary periods (Weiss et al., 1996). However, it is interesting to consider that Machiavellians might interact differently with their own children than toward other people. Perhaps, for example, a Machiavellian parent would be more willing to view his or her child as a narcissistic self-extension. This might explain the occasional odd legal spectacle of parents who show no empathy toward a victim, insisting despite overwhelming evidence to the contrary in their son's innocence in the course of gruesome murder trials. It also might explain the phenomenon of abandonment mixed with indulgence seen in some children of wealthy parents (Stone, 1983). Yet, although the phenomenon of BPD in children is not well understood (Dávila, 2007; Meekings and O'Brien, 2004), it is clear that borderline-type behavior in a family setting with multiple children would lead parental focus to be diverted to the borderline child. The phenomenon of the borderline-like child (but not their other children) being appeased by parents to avoid explosive temper tantrums is frequently described in Web site postings. At the other side of the sociological spectrum, one African study revealed that infants with "difficult" temperaments fared better than those with "easy" dispositions during famine (De Vries, 1984).[5]

Borderline Personality Disorder: Disorder or Adaptation?

From an evolutionary perspective, BPD might not be a disorder but, rather, an evolutionarily successful strategy that can lead to social advantage at the expense of "normal" people. Those who have the disorder might be correct in insisting that there is nothing wrong with them, even though their behavior might be destroying the emotional lives of those around them. And the very real difficulty that psychologists and psychiatrists have had in treating those with BPD—to the point that many therapists refuse to handle such patients—might simply be evidence that the disorder is a manifestation of something that is a successful part of human evolution. So, BPD might be underpinned by a broad range of genetic structures. However, some evidence indicates that BPD can become more pronounced in those with alcohol or other drug addictions (Dulit et al., 1990; Hatzitaskos et al., 1999; Mason and Kreger, 1998; Miller et al., 1993), thus, what are currently perceived as the more severely dysfunctional aspects of BPD may not have been as common in previous evolutionary periods.

Some readers might make the mistake of believing that to say some dysfunctional personality traits might be evolutionarily advantageous for the individual involved is to find these characteristics in some way desirable. This is far from the case and would, in fact, be analogous to finding sickle-cell anemia desirable because it allows some to be protected against malaria.

Emotion is much more ancient than logic or reason. In fact, emotions have played an important role in the survival of species. No lesser a light than Darwin predicted that the physiological basis for emotion would be conserved throughout evolution. Indeed, opiate receptors have been found in the brains of all vertebrates, from hagfish to humans. Insects and other invertebrates have also been shown to have opiate receptors (Pert, 1997, 134). It is plausible that, in the evolutionary periods related to the development of the portions of the brain related to rational thought and speech, the emotional system of borderlines has evolved in such a way as to occasionally hijack or mold conscious thought processes so as to better control a surrounding environment filled with fellow humans.

REASONS FOR DIFFICULTIES IN STUDYING PATHOLOGICAL LEADERS

Too Narrow a Focus

A theory of Machiavellianism related to pathological leaders—the heart of organizational evil of virtually all forms—has been difficult to develop for a wide variety of reasons. First is the stance of many social psychology researchers that an individual can be declared symptomatic of a mental disorder only after long and careful analysis of the individual in question, preferably with extensive personal interviews. This hesitation to engage in analysis at a distance arose for good reason: A 1964 Republican presidential candidate, Barry Goldwater, received several hundred glib psychiatric assessments, with the consequence that it is now considered unethical for psychotherapists to diagnose someone they have not interviewed or studied intensively (Goleman, 1991). The result of this thoughtful and careful approach is that few analysts have extensively studied more than a few pathological leaders. Individual analysts generally focus on trees—not the forest.

It would appear, then, that a study of common pathologies of aberrant leaders would best be conducted through meta-analysis. But the meta-approach remains elusive: The commonly used diagnoses, which are based on categories, rather than dimensions, can easily lead to different labels for similar behavior. For example, where one analyst might diagnose borderline with a codisorder of narcissism, another might diagnose antisocial personality or psychopathy, and yet another an utterly nonstandard term such as "political paranoia."

A Natural Tendency to Study Convenient Subjects

Machiavellianism in general has also been difficult to study because, despite the emphasis on a finding of subjective "clinical significance" (American Psychiatric Association, 2000, 8) to determine whether a person has a personality disorder, clinicians generally analyze only individuals who are either so psychologically disordered that they are involuntarily hospitalized or who voluntarily come in for treatment. This leaves unexamined a wealth of clearly dysfunctional (at least to others who interact closely with them), highly Machiavellian individuals who would never present themselves for analysis or diagnosis, because their disorder itself renders them incapable of recognizing or acknowledging their dysfunctional behavior. Moreover, a highly successful Machiavellian brought before a clinician, for example, during marital divorce proceedings, can appear friendly, helpful, and rational—completely masking certain aspects of their behavior. The *DSM-IV-R* states that when a clinician is making a clinical diagnosis, "Reliance on information from family members and other third parties (in addition to the individual) regarding the individual's performance is often necessary." But in practice, what clinician could effectively interview the subordinates of a Machiavellian supervisor who emotionally and even physically abused his staff? The subordinates would be loath to speak the truth about a supervisor who had so much control over their lives.

Congenial Double-Speak

On those less common occasions when Machiavellian individuals *are* analyzed, psychological terminology is predisposed toward understandably nonjudgmental terms and descriptions of the behavior in question. For example, what in normal usage might be referred to as "lying" might be referred to clinically as "dissociation"; what people might refer to (in more polite terms) as "being a jerk" might be termed "affective instability due to marked reactivity of mood"; and the uncanny, chameleon-like ability of some Machiavellians to charm their supervisors might be referred to as a "markedly and persistently unstable self-image or sense of self."

The Threat of Litigation

In addition, researchers avoid examining dysfunctional public and private figures because of the threat of litigation. For example, convicted felon and *über*-homemaker Martha Stewart filed a $10 million lawsuit against the *National Enquirer* after the magazine published an article by a nationally renowned expert on BPD that described how Stewart's many reported pathological traits dovetailed with those of BPD. Stewart is thought to have filed the suit, one of the few she ever filed, over concern that being tagged with a personality disorder diagnosis might complicate her efforts at taking her company public (Byron, 2002, 309, 314–15, 345–51). Few academicians have the deep pockets to risk the wrath of Stewart or any other current major business, political, or religious figure for the sake of a journal article analyzing and labeling dysfunctional behavior patterns.

Reluctance to make in-depth psychological analysis of current public figures is particularly distressing because of the frustrating wealth of data often made available by journalists in modern Western countries about the personal lives of major public figures. Although Cambodia's Pol Pot, for example, called for destroying documentation related to the killing of many of those who knew him in his formative years (Chandler, 1999), the Reverend Jesse Jackson has a mass of well-documented facts available about alleged activities such as massive defrauding of the federal government, financial ties to third world dictators, and lurid private life—discussion of which he is quick to litigate (Timmerman, 2001). Litigation thus may serve something of the same function in modern democratic countries as political suppression in totalitarian regimes.*

Confusion and Silence from Those Surrounding a BPD-Like Leader

It is very difficult for any leader, borderline or not, to make it to the top of a social hierarchy without making some enemies. Subordinate to any leader are many who are colloquially referred to as "butt-kissers" and "back-stabbers," many of whom might show traits of subclinical BPD themselves. Recent research has shown that collecting accurate data in this kind of environment is problematic at best. As mentioned earlier, even normal people surrounding a borderline-like person are often kept from revealing horrific yet confidential information to which they are privy for fear of retaliation. This can contribute to a relative "cone of silence" about the individual in question. Biographers are often reduced to talking to individuals who are once or twice removed from the person in question or attempting to put the pieces together from scattered documentation (Gross, 2003).

Personal Safety Issues

Personal safety issues also play a role in the investigation of Machiavellian leaders and organizational evil. For example, one of Church of Scientology founder L. Ron Hubbard's policies was that

> all perceived enemies are "fair game" and subject to being "tricked, sued or lied to or destroyed." Those who criticize the church—journalists, doctors, lawyers and even judges—often find themselves engulfed in litigation, stalked by private eyes, framed for fictional crimes, beaten up or threatened with death. Psychologist Margaret Singer, 69, an outspoken Scientology critic and professor at the University of California, Berkeley, [traveled] regularly under an assumed name to avoid harassment. (Behar, 1991)

RETHINKING THE PATHOLOGY OF ABERRANT LEADERS

The Confusing Aspects of Scales of Control and Disjointed "Boutique" Labels

As the discussion related to evolutionary advantages shows, BPD and related codisorder traits can clearly assist individuals in ascending to high positions within a given social

---

*This statement comes from the author's personal experiences working as a Russian translator on Soviet trawlers during the early 1980s; the comparison is thus based on personal experiences in both modern democratic regimes such as the United States and West Germany, as well as an in-depth experience in a totalitarian regime.

group. The question is, if this is the case, why haven't more pathological leaders, past and present, been diagnosed as having subclinical aspects of the disorder? Or should they be? After all, it hardly seems possible that, for example, the matronly local president of Mothers Against Drunk Drivers who has just been accused of embezzling funds could have anything in common with pathological leaders who terrorize and kill millions. (When Hitler's secretary jokingly accused him of stealing her flashlight, he remarked: "I don't steal flashlights, I steal countries" [Redlich, 1998, 334].)

In fact, however, it seems that when Machiavellians reach positions of ultimate power in a large social group such as a country, the breadth of their control is so wide that their ability to manipulate, terrorize, and destroy often becomes orders of magnitude greater than anything they were previously capable of. This difference is so radical that analysts often miss the diagnostic possibility of BPD with a related codisorders, such as narcissism, paranoia, or obsessive compulsive disorder, or the often similar antisocial personality disorder (which is also sometimes thought to be a BPD codisorder [Stone, 2003]). Instead, they have frequently been reduced to inventing one-of-a-kind diagnoses or focusing on the borderline codisorder while missing the borderline diagnosis or using a diagnosis such as malignant narcissism even though virtually no medical studies support its usage (Glad, 2002; Kernberg, 1995; Post, 2003, 2004). (The fact that the term "malignant narcissism" can be used so freely with no medical studies to support its usage is a prominent example of how "the social sciences have largely kept themselves isolated from [the] crystallizing process of scientific integration" [Tooby and Cosmides, 1992, 21].)

Another fairly prominent term is "corporate psychopath," which relates to an attempt by psychologists Robert Hare and Paul Babiak to take Hare's work with psychopathic prisoners and extend it to explain Machiavellian behavior in the workplace (Babiak and Hare, 2006). Hare and Babiak's description of the corporate psychopath largely coincides with that of high-functioning borderlines. However, their research and findings do not display nuanced understanding of Machiavellians who appear to display real emotion and even undeniable compassion in situations where the display is clearly not "for show" (Byron, 2002).[6]

The drawback, of course, is that giving different labels to the same phenomenon— Machiavellian behavior in everyday life—makes it difficult to see important patterns. "Malignant narcissism," "corporate psychopath," and BPD with a codisorder of narcissism could be used to describe virtually identical behavior. And what is one to make of the hundreds of largely one-of-a-kind studies with key diagnoses or features such "Manichean sense of reality," "archaic narcissism," "mirror hungry," "personalized charismatic leader," or "political paranoia" (Miliora, 2004; Popper, 2000; Post, 1993a, 2004, 187; Robins and Post, 1997)? The short answer is: not much (Sokal, 1996).

To quote evolutionary psychologists John Tooby and Leda Cosmides:

> The recent wave of antiscientific sentiment spreading through the social sciences draws much of its appeal from [the] endemic failure [of the social sciences to produce intellectual discoveries, grand "laws," and validated theories to rival those of the rest of science]. This disconnection from the rest of science has left a hole in the

fabric of our organized knowledge of the world where the human sciences should be. After more than a century, the social sciences are still adrift, with an enormous mass of half-digested observations, a not inconsiderable body of empirical generalizations, and a contradictory stew of ungrounded, middle-level theories expressed in a babel of incommensurate technical lexicons. This is accompanied by a growing malaise, so that the single largest trend is toward rejecting the scientific enterprise as it applies to humans.

We suggest that this lack of progress, this "failure to thrive," has been caused by the failure of the social sciences to explore or accept their logical connections to the rest of the body of science—that is, to causally locate their objects of study inside the larger network of scientific knowledge. (1992, 23)

That statement, written nearly two decades ago, still holds true today (Carlat, 2010; Cole, 2001; Cummings and O'Donohue, 2009; Wright and Cummings, 2005).

Overall, it should be compellingly clear that the many different labels, often one of a kind, provided by psychologists and biographers of pathological leaders have confused and dissipated psychological and psychiatric research in this important area. Moreover, scientific advances related to many salient areas, such as genetics and neurochemistry, and intriguing results from rapidly advancing fields, such as that of medical imaging, have not been connected with the study of aberrant leaders—a critical aspect in understanding organizational evil. In this age of global terrorism, researchers would be well advised to re-establish work in the field based on the vast amount of clearly appropriate research available on borderline personality and co-occurring disorders as well as related disorders.

The Confounding Nature of Intelligence and Memory

It should be emphasized that seemingly irrational borderline/Machiavellian motivations and traits, deeply embedded in one's emotional underpinnings, may be decoupled in important ways from reason, logic, and intelligence (Johnson et al., 2003; Matthews, Roberts, and Zeidner, 2004; Posner et al., 2003). Misunderstanding of this point has been deeply confusing for researchers. It takes certain characteristics to climb to the top of the social ladder as a leader, whether the leader has a "normal" or borderline emotional outlook. Many top leaders, including remarkable individuals such as Warren Buffett, Jack Welch, and Bill Gates as well as political leaders such as Franklin Delano Roosevelt and Mohandas K. Gandhi, possess or possessed keen intelligence and remarkable memories (Roosevelt's own family members were often apparently "floored" by his memory [Lash, 1964, 149; Willner, 1984, 144–146]). Statistically speaking, at least a few such leaders would also be expected to display some or many of the characteristics of BPD with various codisorders. Emotionally aberrant leaders from all walks of life, including former Hollinger CEO Conrad Black, Martha Stewart, former Enron CEO Jeffrey Skilling, dreaded *capo di tutti i capi* Totò Riina (Robb, 1996, 112–113), and many other dysfunctional leaders each possesses or possessed a good or even great intellect as well as eidetic memories—it is these skills as much as borderline-like traits and no small amount of luck that propelled the individuals to the top of their social hierarchy.

In general, people associate remarkable memory with remarkable intelligence, although the two qualities are not necessarily linked (Oberauer et al., 2005). Thus, for example, the Indonesian dictator Sukarno, who possessed an extraordinary memory:

> acquired a reservoir of miscellaneous knowledge, items of which were strategically and seemingly spontaneously retrieved in order to impress. To the common people and even to others, Sukarno sounded like a very learned man. His speeches were sprinkled with allusions and quotations, not only from the various ethnic traditions of Indonesia but also from foreign and Western source, often in the language of these sources. In one frequently reprinted speech, for example, he quoted Ernest Renan, Otto Bauer, Sun Yat-sen, Gandhi, and Jean Jaurès, and in a national day address he developed an extended metaphor from Dante's *Divine Comedy*. Those who were close to him or in frequent contact with him still recall his fabulous memory with awe. He had a particularly impressive ploy of addressing by name someone he had met only once many years earlier and making a specific reference to that meeting. (Willner, 1984, 146)

Mussolini used his similarly prodigious memory to fool people into thinking that he had an exceptionally wide knowledge of science and philosophy. In reality his knowledge was often limited to what he happened to skim a few pages of but could recite practically verbatim. Castro, Hitler, and Stalin possessed similar abilities (Montefiore, 2004; Willner, 1984, 144–146).

A description of Jeffrey Skilling sheds light on the phenomenon of decoupled emotion, memory, and reason:

> Skilling thrived on confrontation and had a perfect command of the minutiae of deals. In interviews he could stun financial writers with his grasp of details, but that same superiority made corporate meetings enervating for his colleagues. His vision was messianic. . . . From the beginning, colleagues say, Skilling's pattern was to scapegoat others without leaving a trail that could lead back to him. In meetings that Ken Lay chaired, Skilling was often silent, letting Lay believe that he was completely in control. But at other times Skilling could be very volatile. . . . He would often blurt out astonishing remarks in public—he once, famously, called a stock analyst an asshole during a conference call—and the public-relations staff worried each time he gave an interview. (Brenner, 2002)

It was Skilling's charismatic, typically borderline-like ability to convince listeners that he was creating a new vision for business, rather than recycling a de facto pyramid scheme, that led whistleblower Sherron Watkins to openly declare during meetings: "This is a circle jerk." But the other listeners were swept into agreement. Unsurprisingly, Skilling's Harvard professor Chip Bupp, who declared Skilling possibly the single best student he had ever had, was bewildered by Skilling's duplicity. "I can't believe he did not know what was going on, yet I can't believe Jeff would lie. . . . [The partnerships are] a clear black-and-white conflict of interest. Holy smokes!" (Brenner, 2002).

Enron's top ranks were filled with individuals like Skilling who displayed clear borderline-like characteristics (Brenner, 2002). Failed Machiavellian leaders from K-Mart (Turner, 2003) to Dennis Kozlowski's Tyco (Byron, 2004) to Nazi Germany and the Soviet Union have displayed a propensity for selecting self-similar Machiavellian partners or underlings, with dismal results. If only a capacity for ruthlessness were not sometimes necessary and useful for any discipline in which competition is stiff, including business, politics, music, and film, it might be easier to spot and deter borderlines before their talents took them perilously close to the top. (Stalin, in fact, was Lenin's right-hand man precisely *because* of his ruthlessness in carrying out Lenin's desires [Montefiore, 2004].) Recent research has shown that individuals who share certain personality traits, even certain sets of genes, have a preference for being together (Fowler et al., 2011; McPherson et al., 2001).

A balanced analysis of borderline-like traits must also include the occasional constructive attributes of such behavior. For example, despite the fact that many former friends of Martha Stewart describe her as a psychopath, Stewart single-handedly created a billion-dollar empire from nothing. Her selfish, relentless desire for riches created job opportunities for thousands.[7] By contrast, Hitler's constructive rebuilding of Germany after World War I laid the groundwork for public acceptance of the Final Solution.

The Confusion Caused by "Now You See It, Now You Don't" Behavior

Among many other confounding factors, it is the borderline and related codisorders' "now-you-see it, now-you-don't" mixture of charm and malevolence that confuses researchers, making them grab for a one-of-a-kind label rather than noticing the underlying commonality of the borderline syndrome, regardless of the various codisorders. Such chameleon-like behavior was shown by Idi Amin, the butcher of Uganda, who could appear "uncomplicated, unaffected, kindly, and affable," so that many who were acquainted with him could not believe he possessed another side to his personality even when confronted with the evidence (Post, 1993b, 29). David Koresh, the charismatic leader of the Branch Davidian religious sect in Waco whose compound was raided by agents of the Bureau of Alcohol, Tobacco, and Firearms (BATF) after accusations that he had engaged in massive child abuse, was known for his severe psychological abuse of his followers. Yet he could be a friendly sort who sent beer and pizza as housewarming presents to the BATF agents stationed to watch the compound from across the road—bonhomie that started a fountain of conspiracy theories spiraling around the theme that "Koresh was misunderstood and wronged" (Kick and Metzger, 2002).

Slobodan Milošević, "the Butcher of the Balkans," serenaded U.S. negotiators during the 1995 peace negotiations in Dayton, Ohio. He also "drank Johnnie Walker Scotch, cursed in colorful American epithets, waxed eloquent about his love of New York and American coffee, and became misty eyed when difficult compromises were reached.

Milošević conveyed the impression—seconded by the U.S. negotiator, Ambassador Richard Holbrooke—of a leader with whom the United States could reason and negotiate" (Post, 2004, 179).

Hitler has been diagnosed by hundreds of authors and analysts with dozens of disorders hypothesized to have caused his behavior, including bipolar disorder, histrionic personality disorder, paranoia, syphilis, encephalitis, drug addiction, megalomania, "enfeebled and unformed self," "charisma," and "a constitutional left-side weakness that allowed his right cerebral hemisphere to exert a strong influence on his thought and behavior" (Hummel, 1975; L. Langer, 1999; W. Langer, 1972; Martindale, Hasenfus, and Hines, 1976; Muslin, 1992; Redlich, 1998; Rosenbaum, 1999; Sleigh, 1966). But a reading of virtually any biography of Hitler reveals an overwhelming number of borderline characteristics. In fact, it was Hitler's charming, charismatic ability to switch from monster to savior at will, so characteristic of those with subclinical BPD, that researchers have found perhaps most bewildering. It is interesting to note that the otherwise meticulously researched 1998 volume *Hitler: Diagnosis of a Destructive Prophet,* by Fritz Redlich (1998), a practicing psychiatrist with extensive access to the Führer's medical records, contemptuously concluded that Hitler did not suffer from BPD by citing numerous obsolete publications, including some forty and fifty years old. Redlich finally diagnosed Hitler as a "destructive and paranoid prophet," another in a series of dozens of "boutique" labels that, if nothing else, gives the researcher the visceral thrill of naming his or her own syndrome.

The Problem of the Soapbox

One of the few captured pathological leaders to have been confronted with the consequences of his actions is Serbian former dictator Slobodan Milošević." Several years' worth of trial transcripts reveal Milošević displaying the typical, uncanny ability of a borderline to insist on his version of reality, sophistically arguing against any contrary evidence. As a result, coverage of Milošević's war crimes trial, rather than forcing Serbians to confront the brutality of the regime, has instead fueled Serbian nationalism (Goldsmith and Posner, 2005). Somewhat like the man who mistook his wife for a hat because of the inability of parts of his brain to cope with the special processing necessary to recognize facial features, the emotional system of borderlines might be "designed" by evolution with the ability to hijack or override some types of rational, conscious thought processes, to the unending bewilderment of others. Clearly a "fair and rational" approach to dealing with an individual who displays borderline characteristics that allows that person a "soapbox" can lead to unanticipated negative consequences.

An Example: Mary Baker Eddy

While in her mid-forties, Mary Baker Eddy overcame ill health and difficult personal circumstances to become a multimillionaire and founder of the Christian Science movement. She succeeded at both these endeavors though a woman at a time when society was dominated by men, the latter part of the nineteenth century. Mrs. Eddy provides an example of successfully using borderline-like strategies and traits to achieve goals. Only a brief description is given here. (The interested reader is referred to the several complete biographies available, although caution must be used because the Church of Christ, Scientist, has attempted to control the flow of information about the Church and Mrs. Eddy [Cather and Milmine, 1909/1993; Dakin, 1930; Dickey, 2002].)

Mary was "subject from infancy to convulsive attacks of a hysterical nature" such that, "between her nervous condition and her strong will, she quickly gained dominance over the otherwise well-ordered household" (Kramer, 2000, 37). She was very sensitive to the thoughts of people around her, which was thought to be in part responsible for her nagging illnesses, even as a child. Mrs. Eddy married three times and had one son whom she did not rear. There is some dispute over whether the son was taken from Mrs. Eddy or she willingly allowed him to leave as a child. Mary's father stated apropos the situation that Mary was like "an old ewe that won't own its lamb" (Kramer, 2000, 39).

Mrs. Eddy's charisma was remarkable. She was able to present herself to her followers as "the most gentle, courteous, and meek person you have ever met," "refinement itself," someone whose ring of sincerity left listeners spellbound, "the greatest benefactor to humanity that has lived since the time of Jesus." "God's chosen scribe," and as someone whose judgment was "as near to perfection as is possible in this world" (Kramer, 2000, 43). People with whom she stayed

> love to talk of her, and most of them are glad to have known her—even those who now say that the experience was a costly one. She was like a patch of color in those gray communities. She was never dull . . . and never commonplace. She never laid aside her regal air; never entered a room or left it like other people. There was something about her that continually excited and stimulated, and she gave people the feeling that a great deal was happening. (Cather and Milmine, 1909/1993, 122–123)

Behind the charisma, however, lay a dark side. Mrs. Eddy required perfect order and, in her later years, had a full-time staff of Christian Scientists living with her to take care of her house, assist her with her business responsibilities, and act as "spiritual body guards against the attacks of malicious animal magnetism (evil thought which could hurt and even kill a person)." It was difficult to find staff willing to follow Mrs. Eddy's orders implicitly and have their lives revolve completely around her and her absolutely precise way of doing things. Many of Mrs. Eddy's workers soon lost their joy and spiritual vision; she had difficulty maintaining a full staff (Kramer, 2000, 54–55).

However, Mrs. Eddy used projection to great effect, placing all blame for problems within her movement on others.

> Student defections or thoughts against Mrs. Eddy were always assumed to be the work of mesmerists and not the result of her own behavior. In the mass resignation of 1881, some of her most loyal students cited "frequent ebullitions of temper, love

of money, and the appearance of hypocrisy" as their reasons for leaving the Christian Scientist Association. Instead of examining her conduct which might have brought on these accusations, Mrs. Eddy blamed her students' dissatisfaction and defection on the work of aggressive mental suggestion emanating from a Mr. Howard.

She was often asked to move out soon after taking up residence in a home or boarding house, especially during the winter of 1879–1880. She blamed this misfortune on (a former admirer's) mesmerism against her, instead of considering whether her behavior or other circumstances might have caused the problem.

An autopsy showed that Mr. Eddy died of heart problems. Mrs. Eddy was shown the damaged heart but still announced that her husband had been murdered by mental arsenic poisoning. She even privately identified the mental assassin as Mr. Arens, one of her disaffected students.

She often experienced physical symptoms while trying to make important decisions related to the movement. Instead of recognizing the common signs of stress, she blamed her symptoms on the mesmerism of disaffected students working against the cause or on animal magnetism in general (Kramer, 2000, 59–60).

Mrs. Eddy had a habit of becoming close to a student and then experiencing an emotionally violent break with the person, turning him or her into an enemy (black-and-white thinking). In particular, she resented it if a student began to think for him or herself.

[S]he required of her students absolute and unquestioning conformity to her wishes: any other attitude of mind she considered dangerous. She often told [a follower who she resented for his popularity] that there was no such thing as devotion to the principle of revealed truth which did not include devotion to the revelator. "I am the Wisdom, and this revelation is mine," she would declare when a student questioned her decision. She loved to amaze and astonish; when her students ceased to "wonder," she was usually through with them. Each of her favorites gave her, as it were, a new lease of life; with each one her interest in everything quickened. . . . It was when Mrs. Eddy was weaving her spell around a new favorite that she was at her best, and it was then that she most believed in herself. But she could never stop with enchanting, merely. She must altogether absorb the new candidate; he must have nothing left in him which was not from her. If she came upon one insoluble atom hidden away anywhere in the marrow of his bones, she experienced a revulsion and flung him contemptuously aside. (Cather and Milmine, 1909/1993, 232, 382)

Those who have left the Christian Science religion have compared these techniques with those used for effective mind control in cults (Kramer, 2000, 58–59).

But it was Mary Baker Eddy's powers of dissociation that were to serve as a foundation for her new religion. In fact, "Christian Science tends to separate a person's mind and body in a form of mild, but almost constant, dissociation" (Kramer, 2000, 151). Mrs. Eddy believed that people are perfect, spiritual reflections of God, and so their true identity was purely spiritual. Therefore, a Christian Scientist does not, for example, think that his burned hand is not really burned. Instead, he understands that his true under-standing is purely spiritual, and so the burn is no longer manifested on his body and he is healed. Therefore, Mrs. Eddy believed that Christian Scientists should avoid any medical help and that directly confronting the evidence of the physical sense was the best way to overcome any physical problem, whether it be a broken arm, a burst appendix, or a child with a high fever. "She placed her students in an almost impossible dilemma—do not tackle what you are not ready for, but you will never learn Christian Science unless you follow its teachings exactly, taking a firm stand against medicine and materiality" (Kramer, 2000, 136). Among Mrs. Eddy's other magical, dissociated beliefs were that her students were responsible for virtually everything that went wrong, even conditions such as bad weather, and that she was the only one who could discern much of the animal magnetism that attacked the Church, its leader, and its workings.

Mrs. Eddy had a profound ability not only to disconnect from reality in this fashion but also to get others to buy into this alternative "nonreality."

> One of Mrs. Eddy's students lost two children under Christian Science treatment "with hardly a murmur." Calvin Frye, who served Mrs. Eddy for nearly twenty-eight years, lost interest in family ties and showed little concern upon losing his father and sister. When his father died four years after he began serving Mrs. Eddy, he made a brief appearance at the funeral. Frye did not acknowledge his sister's demise four years later. He ignored her death, the funeral, and his family's request for a little money to help with the burial. As [Willa] Cather puts it, "for him family ties no longer existed, and death had become merely a belief." (Kramer, 2000, 162)

Indeed, Mary Baker Eddy's evidence of borderline-like traits in the establishment of Christian Science should open doors to the examination of other organizations for similar effects of leaders with evidence of personality disorders.

MECHANISMS THROUGH WHICH AN ORGANIZATION MIGHT BECOME "EVIL"

As stated earlier, I believe an organization becomes evil when it comes to be led by a Machia-vellian who guides the organization toward service of the Machiavellian himself and toward that which the Machiavellian and his minions believe is beneficial. These Machiavellian-oriented goals are generally quite different from what other individuals, outside the sway of the Machiavellian, believe to be beneficial. Sometimes the Machiavellian's goals sound benign or expedient, as with Lenin's insistence on the necessity of the dictatorship of the proletariat in the Soviet Union or Enron CEO Jeffrey Skilling's insistence that "We don't need cops," when asked to explain why he was moving a manager who was beginning to question some of the transactions (Eichenwald, 2005, 250). But always—*always*—the Machiavellian's ultimate goal is the furtherance of his own self-serving aims.

An organization does not generally select for Machiavellians by virtue of its goals. Or, at least, not initially, unless the Machiavellian himself is creating the organization (as with Lenin and his creation of the communist party apparatus in the Soviet Union) Instead, Machiavellians target an organization because they realize the potential for power if they were to rise and make subtle and not-so-subtle shifts in the systems of checks and balances of the organization. These shifts place the Machiavellian and his supporters at a strategic advantage—changing the culture and focus of the organization into that which might be characterized as "evil."

Organizations are often, though not always, begun for good purposes by well-meaning people. Gradually, however, as the organization's power and influence become clear, its positions of power become attractive targets for those whose purposes are more self-centered. Machiavellians can rise in organizations through both legitimate prowess and through subterfuge. The ability to use subterfuge means that the Machiavellian can often rise higher than would ordinarily happen through sheer prowess alone. In any case, the higher the Machiavellian rises in the organization, the easier it becomes for them to place supporters in positions of power and to begin the subtle rewriting of rules and erasing of transparency that will further his own aims. (One can see these processes taking place, for example, in the card-check bill, which would effectively ban employee secret-ballot elections over unionization in the private sector and allow for union monopolies. Individuals could not bargain on their own behalf without the permission of union bosses [Lafer, 2007].)

How does a Machiavellian climb to the top of an organization? All the borderline-like traits outlined earlier—gaslighting, emotional lability, projection, black-and-white thinking, dissociation, narcissism, and paranoia—can play important roles in throwing adversaries off balance and gaining tactical advantage. (See Oakley, 2007, for a thorough discussion of these phenomena.) In addition, gullibility and narcissism by those whom the Machiavellian would fool also play important roles. Enron's malevolent, self-serving CFO Andrew Fastow, for example, could turn from tiger to pussycat in front of chairman Ken Lay. "It was like something out of a movie, with Fastow in the role of the obsequious yes-man," said Enron's head of corporate communications Mark Palmer [Eichenwald, 2005, 523]). Hitler, too, was a master at fooling gullible, self-important others who were susceptible to his stroking:

> To the sophisticated French ambassador, he appeared as "a well-balanced man, filled with experience and wisdom." An intellectual found him "charming," a person with "common sense" in the English sense. The British historian Arnold Toynbee came away from an interview thoroughly "convinced of his sincerity in desiring peace." The elegant and precise Anthony Eden was impressed by Hitler's "smart, almost elegant appearance" and found his command of diplomatic detail "masterful." (Waite, 1977, 435)

But, as previously mentioned, other decent traits underlie a Machiavellian's rise to power, most notably, native intelligence and a good memory.

The larger and more powerful the social structure, the more competition there is for leading roles in it. Machiavellians will be competing against honest brokers as well as other Machiavellians for positions of power. Of course, Machiavellian leaders with only a modicum of intelligence, memory skills, or industriousness can still rise to intermediate levels in any given social order. At these intermediate levels, although all rules cannot be rewritten, self-serving actions can still be taken that are damaging for the organization as a whole. In essence, then, even if the Machiavellian only reaches intermediate levels of management, pockets of organizational evil can be created.

The higher the Machiavellian climbs, the more likely it is that the Machiavellian can shift the organization's structure to benefit himself. This is done in a variety of ways, but primary mechanisms include:

- writing or rewriting the organization's rules so as to reduce or eliminate transparency, checks, and balances;
- compartmentalizing information and functions so that followers, employees, and outsiders are unable to see the full effect or scope of the organization's, and the Machiavellian's own, behavior;
- promoting, hiring, or otherwise assisting similarly Machiavellian individuals to positions where they can be of assistance to the Machiavellian leader;
- implementing strong mechanisms of punishment for those who disagree with the Machiavellian leader or his agenda, which induces paralyzing fear in many who might ordinarily oppose the Machiavellian and his agenda.

Using these strategies, virtually any organization can be put on a path toward organizational evil—evil, that is, for everyone except the Machiavellian(s) involved.

CONCLUSIONS

In this chapter, I have defined organizational evil as harm or injury done by an organization under the guise of some greater beneficial cause. It is behavior that, if engaged in by an individual, would be recognizable as morally wrong. It is my thesis that although an organization can become evil by many routes, this phenomenon occurs most commonly when the organization becomes led by a Machiavellian who guides the organization in service of his own interests and toward that which the Machiavellian and his minions believe is beneficial. Whatever statements the Machiavellian makes to the contrary, the Machiavellian's ultimate goals are always the furtherance of his own self-serving aims.

"Evil" organizations are characterized by a loss of transparency, checks, and balances as well as a compartmentalization of information and purpose that obscures a greater sense of the scope of the Machiavellian's influence and effects, for both those outside and within the organization. Machiavellians often affiliate with one another and can change the nature of any organization virtually overnight by promoting, hiring, and assisting other Machiavellians to rise to influential positions. All these actions allow the Machiavellian leader the ability to proceed with his self-serving agenda. The higher a Machiavellian rises, the greater his influence—reaching top leadership roles, however, allows the highest potential for compartmentalization, promotion of fellow Machiavellians, and reduction of rules meant to provide for transparency, checks, and balances. However, even if the Machiavellian only reaches intermediate levels of management in an organization, pockets of organizational evil can be created.

The correlation of aspects of what is currently known of BPD with Machiavellianism has been discussed at length. Many seemingly dysfunctional borderline-like traits that appear to have nothing to do with manipulation and control, such as impulsivity and black-and-white thinking, are shown to be advantageous in attaining or maintaining social status. The study of organizational evil through gaining an understanding of the role of Machiavellian leaders is a fruitful, vastly understudied area of research.

Hanna Arendt discussed the banality of evil, and the general tendency has long been to proclaim that the propensity for evil exists in everyone. Yet it is clear that, whatever the proximate mechanisms, some individuals have a far greater propensity for Machiavellian behavior than others, a factor that is of crucial importance in business, politics, religion, and other important societal and cultural enterprises. Organizational systems that do not provide for transparent checks and balances to mitigate the effects of Machiavellians are at risk of descent into organizational evil.

NOTES

The author thanks Drs. David Sloan Wilson, Kenneth Silk, Gabrielle Stryker, Mark White, Randolph Nesse, Richard Stamps, Brian Sangeorzan, and Gary Barber for insightful comments and discussion; and Craig Becker, Quinn Tyler Jackson, Ed White, Mark Leggett, and Lyndsey Adams for helpful suggestions. Audrey Perkins is sui generis as an editor and critic—her suggestions are greatly appreciated.

1. The conventional, current meaning of "Machiavellian" is "manipulative, cruel, and self-centered," entailing unethical practices that are justified in the development and defense of one's own power and success. In contrast, Machiavelli's original construct arguably held that leadership was ultimately to serve the needs of the common good rather than self-interest. Whatever Machiavelli's original intentions were, it is clear that there is a commonly encountered personality type that has induced people to appropriate Machiavelli's constructs. It is precisely this commonly encountered personality type that is the focus of this chapter.

2. Basil, who was born in Cappadocia in what is now Turkey about 329 C.E., wrote voluminously about his life and thoughts as he moved upward in the church to eventually become bishop of Caesarea. His description of what he must have had personal experience with is a telling witness to the effects of aggressive, ruthless, deceitful manipulators in the fourth century:

> then such a person recks not of time or space, will not wait his turn, but resembles the violence of a conflagration that seizes on everything and devours it. . . . Thus men who have arrived at some high degree of power derive from those they have already mastered the capacity for yet further injustice, reducing to slavery under their first victims those that remain. The superabundance of their wickedness serves to increase their power; for those who have suffered earlier supply aid to them under constraint, helping to work harm and injustice upon others. What neighbor, what abutter, what colleague is not swept off his feet? None can withstand the force of the rich man, everything bows to his sway and trembles at his rule. Anyone who has been hurt thinks more about how to avoid something worse than about how to protest in court against past ills. The rich man drives in his yoke of oxen, he plows and sows and harvests what is not his, and, if you protest, there are blows, if you complain, there are writs for assault, you are arrested, you will take up your lodging in jail. False accusers are a clever lot, able to bring your very life into danger. (MacMullen 1988, 85)

3. One might waggishly refer to this as the "Borderline Strategy" detector module, which would be abbreviated to BS detector.

4. Ambition has not been the focus of any set of definitive medical studies, but its presence appears to be real. Dr. Hans Münch, the only Auschwitz doctor acquitted by the Supreme National Tribunal in Kraków, attributed horrific camp doctor Josef Mengele's behavior to his driving ambition, along with the opportunities that Auschwitz presented. "Above all, I believe that he was doing this for himself, for his career. In the end, I believed that he would have killed his own mother if it would have helped him" (Posner and Ware, 1986). (This was a sentiment eerily echoed a comment made about Martha Stewart by her aunt.) The West German indictment concurred that it was blind ambition drove Mengele. Mengele, incidentally, lived incognito for some thirty years in South America after his escape from Nazi Germany. During this time, where he had nothing like his earlier degree of societal control, his interpersonal relationships and activities were marked by profound evidence of borderline traits.

5. Which cannot help but bring to mind comedian Bill Cosby's comment that parents aren't interested in *justice*—they're interested in *quiet*.

6. Take, for example, two contrasting images of Martha Stewart. After she published an open letter in *The New York Times* complaining that her neighbors were no longer friendly to her, one shop in her town posted a bulletin board where locals could vent. "Soon the bulletin board was festooned with notes: Of the time Stewart had cut to the head of the line at a tag sale, . . . had spoken rudely to a local merchant, . . . had failed to pay a bill." Later, biographer Christopher Bryant happened to mention to Stewart that he had seen her a few days earlier on a very low-rent program on public access cable TV and asked her why she had bothered with such a thing. "She looked at me somewhat perplexed and answered, 'They're nice people. They need help. Why shouldn't I?' " (Byron, 2002, 10).

7. As Stewart says, sneaking perilously close to the magical thinking sometimes thought to be characteristic of a borderline, "I can almost bend steel with my mind. I can bend anything if I try hard enough. I can make myself do almost anything" (Byron, 2002, 40).

REFERENCES

American Psychiatric Association. 2000. *Diagnostic and Statistical Manual of Mental Disorders,* 4th ed. Washington, DC.

Asquith, C. 2006. Trouble at Texas Southern. DiverseEducation.com, December 14. http://diverseeducation.com/artman/publish/article_6764.shtml.

Axelrod, R. 1984. *The Evolution of Cooperation.* New York: Basic Books.

Babiak, P., and R. Hare. 2006. *Snakes in Suits: When Psychopaths Go to Work.* New York: Harper-Collins.

Bakan, J. 2004. *The Corporation: The Pathological Pursuit of Profit and Power.* New York: Free Press.

Banich, M. T., Mackiewicz, K. L., Depue, B. E., Whitmer, A. J., Miller, G. A., & Heller, W. 2009. Cognitive control mechanisms, emotion and memory: A neural perspective with implications for psychopathology. *Neuroscience & Biobehavioral Reviews*, 33, 5, 613–630. doi: 10.1016/j.neubiorev.2008.09.010.

Baron Cohen, S. 2011. Autism, empathizing-systemizing (E-S) theory, and pathological altruism. In *Pathological Altruism*, ed. B. Oakley, A. Knafo, G. Madhavan, and D.S. Wilson, 345–348. New York: Oxford University Press.

Barton, B.H. 2010. *The Lawyer-Judge Bias in the American Legal System.* Cambridge, MA: Cambridge University Press.

Bateman, A., and P. Fonagy. 2010. Randomized controlled trial of outpatient mentalization-based treatment versus structured clinical management for borderline personality disorder. *Focus*, 8, 1, 55–65.

Behar, R. 1991. The thriving cult of greed and power: Ruined lives. Lost fortunes. Federal crimes. Scientology poses as a religion but is really a ruthless global scam-and aiming for the mainstream. *Time*, May 6, 137, 18, 50–58.

Berlant, J.L. 1975. *Profession and Monopoly: A Study of Medicine in the United States and Great Britain*. Berkeley: University of California Press.

Berlin, I. 1955. The originality of Machiavelli. In *Against the Current: Essays in the History of Ideas*, ed. I. Berlin, 25–79. Princeton: Princeton University Press.

Bernstein, L. 2007. Mobsters, unions, and feds: The Mafia and the American labor movement. *Labor: Studies in Working-Class History of the Americas*, 4, 139–141.

Boyd, R., H. Gintis, S. Bowles, and P.J. Richerson. 2003. Evolution of altruistic punishment. *Proceedings of the National Academy of Sciences*, 100, 6, 3531–3535.

Boyd, R., and J. Lorberbaum. 1987. No pure strategy is evolutionarily stable in the repeated Prisoner's Dilemma game. *Nature*, 327, 58–59.

BPD Central. 2001. Types of BPD, High Functioning, Low Functioning. http://www.bpdcentral.com/resources/basics/types.shtml.

Brannigan, A. 2004. *The Rise and Fall of Social Psychology: The Use and Misuse of the Experimental Method*. New York: Aldine de Gruyter.

Brenner, M. 2002. The Enron wars. *Vanity Fair*, April, 190.

Brüne, M., V. Ghiassi, and H. Ribbert. 2010. Does borderline personality disorder reflect the pathological extreme of an adaptive reproductive strategy? Insights and hypotheses from evolutionary life-history theory. *Clinical Neuropsychiatry*, 7, 1, 3–9.

Byron, C. 2002. *Martha, Inc.* New York: John Wiley & Sons.

———. 2004. *Testosterone, Inc.: Tales of CEOs Gone Wild*. Hoboken, NJ: John Wiley & Sons.

Cahn, S.M. 2010. *Saints and Scamps: Ethics in Academia, 25th Anniversary Edition*. Lanham, MD: Rowman & Littlefield.

Carey, B. 2010. Academic battle delays publication by 3 years. *New York Times,* June 11. http://www.nytimes.com/2010/06/12/health/12psych.html?_r=1.

Carlat, D. 2010. *Unhinged: The Trouble with Psychiatry: A Doctor's Revelations About a Profession in Crisis*. New York: Free Press.

Cather, W., and G. Milmine. 1909/1993. *The Life of Mary Baker G. Eddy and the History of Christian Science*. Lincoln: University of Nebraska Press.

Chandler, D.P. 1999. *Brother Number One: A Political Biography,* rev. ed. Boulder, CO: Westview Press.

Christie, R., and F.L. Geis. 1970. *Studies in Machiavellianism*. New York: Academic Press.

Cochran, B. 1977. *Labor and Communism: The Conflict That Shaped American Unions*. Princeton: Princeton University Press.

Cole, S., ed. 2001. *What's Wrong with Sociology?* New Brunswick, NJ: Transaction.

Conquest, R. 1990. *The Great Terror: A Reassessment*. New York: Oxford University Press.

Cooke, D.J., C. Michie, and J. Skeem. 2007. Understanding the structure of the Psychopathy Checklist-Revised: An exploration of methodological confusion. *British Journal of Psychiatry*, 190, 49, s39.

Coombs, C.K., and R. Cebula. 2011. The impact of union corruption on union membership. *Industrial Relations: A Journal of Economy and Society,* 50, 1, 131–148.

Cosmides, L., and J. Tooby. 1992. Cognitive adaptations for social exchange. In *The Adapted Mind*, ed. J. Barkow, L. Cosmides, and J. Toland, 163–228. New York: Oxford University Press.

Cramer, J. 1988. Above their own laws. *Time*, May 23. www.time.com/time/magazine/article/0,9171,967427,00.html.

Crowell, S.E., T.P. Beauchaine, and M.M. Linehan. 2009. A biosocial developmental model of borderline personality: Elaborating and extending Linehan's theory. *Psychological Bulletin,* 135, 3, 495.

Cummings, N.A., and W.T. O'Donohue. 2009. *Eleven Blunders That Cripple Psychotherapy in America: A Remedial Unblundering*. Boca Raton, FL: CRC Press.

Dakin, E.F. 1930. *Mrs. Eddy: The Biography of a Virginal Mind.* New York: Charles Scribner's Sons.

Dávila, W. 2007. Borderline children and young adults. *Avances en Salud Mental Relaciona* (Advances in relational mental health), 6, 1, 2.

De Becker, G. 1999. *The Gift of Fear: Survival Signals That Protect Us from Violence.* New York: Delta.

De Vries, M.W. 1984. Temperament and infant mortality among the Masai of East Africa. *American Journal of Psychiatry,* 141, 1189–1194.

Dell'Osso, B., H. Berlin, M. Serati, and A.C. Altamura. 2010. Neuropsychobiological aspects, comorbidity patterns and dimensional models in borderline personality disorder. *Neuropsychobiology,* 61, 4, 169–179.

Dickey, A.H. 2002. *Memoirs of Mary Baker Eddy.* Brookline, MA: Merrymount Press.

Distel, M.A., T.J. Trull, C.A. Derom, E.W. Thiery, M.A. Grimmer, N.G. Martin, G. Willemsen, and D.I. Boomsma. 2008. Heritability of borderline personality disorder features is similar across three countries. *Psychological Medicine,* 38, 9, 1219–1229.

Dugatkin, L.A. 1992. The evolution of the "con artist." *Ethology and Sociobiology,* 13, 161–169.

Dulit, R.A., M.R. Fyer, G.L. Haas, T. Sullivan, and A.J. Frances. 1990. Substance use in borderline personality disorder. *American Journal of Psychiatry,* 147, 8, 1002–1007.

Easterly, W. 2006. *The White Man's Burden: Why the West's Efforts to Aid the Rest Have Done So Much Ill and So Little Good.* New York: Penguin Press.

Eichenwald, K. 2005. *Conspiracy of Fools.* New York: Broadway Books.

Ellis, L. 1988. Criminal behavior and r/K selection: An extension of gene-based evolutionary theory. *Personality and Individual Differences,* 9, 4, 697–708.

Fan, Y., C. Wonneberger, B. Enzi, M. de Greck, C. Ulrich, C. Tempelmann, B. Bogerts, S. Doering, and G. Northoff. 2010. The narcissistic self and its psychological and neural correlates: an exploratory fMRI study. *Psychological Medicine,* 1–10. doi: 10.1017/S003329171000228X.

Faurie, C., and M. Raymond. 2005. Handedness, homicide and negative frequency-dependent selection. *Proceedings of the Royal Society: Biological Sciences,* 272, 25–28. http://rspb.royalsocietypublishing.org/content/272/1558/25.full.pdf.

Fossati, A., E.S. Barratt, I. Carretta, B. Leonardi, F. Grazioli, and C. Maffei. 2004. Predicting borderline and antisocial personality disorder features in nonclinical subjects using measures of impulsivity and aggressiveness. *Psychiatry Research,* 125, 2, 161–170.

Fowler, J.H., J.E. Settle, and N.A. Christakis. 2011. Correlated genotypes in friendship networks. *Proceedings of the National Academy of Sciences,* 108, 5, 1993–1997.

Friedel, R.O. 2004. *Borderline Personality Disorder Demystified.* New York: Marlowe & Company.

Gao, Y., & Raine, A. 2010. Successful and unsuccessful psychopaths: A neurobiological model. *Behavioral Sciences & the Law,* 194–210. doi: 10.1002/bsl.924.

Glad, B. 2002. Why tyrants go too far: Malignant narcissism and absolute power. *Political Psychology,* 23, 1, 1–36.

Glaser, J.S. 1994. *The United Way Scandal: An Insider's Account of What Went Wrong and Why.* New York: Wiley.

Goldsmith, J.L., and E.A. Posner. 2005. *The Limits of International Law.* New York: Oxford University Press.

Goleman, D. 1991. Experts differ on dissecting leaders' psyches from afar. *New York Times,* January 29, C1.

Greenhut, S. 2009. *Plunder: How Public Employee Unions are Raiding Treasuries, Controlling Our Lives and Bankrupting the Nation.* Santa Ana, CA: Forum Press.

Grilo, C.M., C.A. Sanislow, and T.H. McGlashan. 2002. Co-occurrence of *DSM-IV* personality disorders with borderline personality disorder. *Journal of Nervous & Mental Disease,* 190, 8, 552–553.

Gross, M. 2003. *Genuine Authentic: The Real Life of Ralph Lauren.* New York: HarperCollins.

Gunderson, J.G., and K. Lyons-Ruth. 2008. BPD's interpersonal hypersensitivity phenotype: A gene-environment-developmental model. *Journal of Personality Disorders,* 22, 1, 22–41.

Harari, H., Shamay-Tsoory, S. G., Ravid, M., & Levkovitz, Y. 2010. Double dissociation between cognitive and affective empathy in borderline personality disorder. *Psychiatry Research,* 175, 3, 277–279. doi: 10.1016/j.psychres.2009.03.002.

Hatzitaskos, P., C.R. Soldatos, A. Kokkevi, and C.N. Stefanis. 1999. Substance abuse patterns and their association with psychopathology and type of hostility in male patients with borderline and antisocial personality disorder. *Comprehensive Psychiatry,* 40, 4, 278–282.

Homant, R., and D. Kennedy. 2011. Does no good deed go unpunished? The victimology of altruism. In *Pathological Altruism,* ed. B. Oakley, A. Knafo, G. Madhavan, and D.S. Wilson, 193–206. New York: Oxford University Press.

Hummel, R.P. 1975. Psychology of charismatic followers. *Psychological Reports,* 37, 3, 759–770.

Hyler, S.E. 1997. PDQ-4 and PDQ-4+ instructions for use. Unpublished manuscript. New York State Psychiatric Institute, New York.

Hyler, S.E., R.O. Rieder, J.B. Williams, R.L. Spitzer, J. Hendler, and M. Lyons. 1988. The personality diagnostic questionnaire: development and preliminary results. *Journal of Personality Disorders,* 2, 229–237.

Hyman, R. 1971. *Marxism and the Sociology of Trade Unionism.* London: Pluto Press.

Ikuta, N., M.C. Zanarini, K. Minakawa, Y. Miyake, N. Moriya, and A. Nishizono-Maher. 1994. Comparison of American and Japanese outpatients with borderline personality disorder. *Comprehensive Psychiatry,* 35, 5, 382–385.

Jacobs, J.B. 2006. *Mobsters, Unions, and Feds: The Mafia and the American Labor Movement.* New York: New York University Press.

Johnson, P.A., R.A. Hurley, C. Benkelfat, S.C. Herpertz, and K.H. Taber. 2003. Understanding emotion regulation in borderline personality disorder: Contributions of neuroimaging. *Journal of Neuropsychiatry and Clinical Neurosciences,* 15, 4, 397–402.

Keeran, R. 1980. *The Communist Party and the Auto Workers Unions.* Bloomington: Indiana University Press.

Kennedy, D. 2005. *The Dark Sides of Virtue: Reassessing International Humanitarianism.* Princeton: Princeton University Press.

Kennedy, R.F. 1994. *The Enemy Within: The McClellan Committee's Crusade Against Jimmy Hoffa and Corrupt Labor Unions.* New York: Perseus Books.

Kenrick, D.T., and J.A. Simpson. 1997. Why social psychology and evolutionary psychology need one another. In *Evolutionary Social Psychology,* ed. J.A. Simpson and D.T. Kenrick, 1–20. Mahwah, NJ: Lawrence Erlbaum.

Kernberg, O. 1995. Narcissistic personality disorders. *Journal of European Psychoanalysis,* 1, 7–18.

Kick, R., and R. Metzger. 2002. *Everything You Know Is Wrong: The Disinformation Guide to Secrets and Lies.* New York: Disinformation Company.

Kiehl, K.A., A.M. Smith, A. Mendrek, B.B. Forster, R.D. Hare, and P.F. Liddle. 2004. Temporal lobe abnormalities in semantic processing by criminal psychopaths as revealed by functional magnetic resonance imaging. *Psychiatry Research: Neuroimaging,* 130, 1, 27–42.

Kim, Y.R., and P. Tyrer. 2010. Controversies surrounding classification of personality disorder. *Psychiatry Investigation,* 7, 1, 1–8.

Kiyosaki, R. 1995. *If You Want to Be Rich & Happy Don't Go to School: Ensuring Lifetime Security for Yourself and Your Children,* rev. ed. Fairfield, CT: Aslan.

Klose, D.A. 1995. M. Scott Peck's analysis of human evil: A critical review. *Journal of Humanistic Psychology,* 35, 3, 37–66.

Kramer, L.S. 2000. *The Religion That Kills.* Lafayette, LA: Huntington House.

Kreisman, J.J., & Straus, H. 2004. *Sometimes I Act Crazy.* New York: John Wiley & Sons.

Lafer, G. 2007. Neither Free Nor Fair: The Subversion of Democracy Under National Labor Relations Board Elections. An American Rights at Work Report. www.americanrightsatwork.org/dmdocuments/ARAWReports/NeitherFreeNorFair.pdf.

Langer, L.L. 1999. Satan's biographers. *Atlantic Monthly*, 283, 1, 99–104.

Langer, W. 1972. *The Mind of Adolf Hitler: The Secret Wartime Report*. New York: Basic Books.

Lash, J.P. 1964. *Eleanor Roosevelt: A Friend's Memoir*. Garden City, NY: Doubleday.

LeBor, A. 2006. *"Complicity with Evil": The United Nations in the Age of Modern Genocide*. New Haven: Yale University Press.

Leichsenring, F., H. Kunst, and J. Hoyer. 2003. Borderline personality organization in violent offenders. *Bulletin of the Menninger Clinic*, 67, 4, 314–327.

Li, Z. 1994. *The Private Life of Chairman Mao*. New York: Random House.

Lieberman, M. 1997. *The Teachers' Unions: How the NEA and AFT Sabotage Reform and Hold Students, Parents, Teachers, and Taxpayers Hostage to Bureaucracy*. New York: Free Press.

Livesley, W.J., and K.L. Jang. 2008. The behavioral genetics of personality disorder. *Clinical Psychology*, 4, 1, 247–274.

Lykken, D.R. 1996. *The Antisocial Personalities*. Hillsdale, NJ: Erlbaum.

MacMullen, R. 1988. *Corruption and the Decline of Rome*. New Haven: Yale University Press.

Manes, C. 1990. *Green Rage: Radical Environmentalism and the Unmaking of Civilization*. New York: Little, Brown.

Martindale, C., N. Hasenfus, and D. Hines. 1976. Hitler: A neurohistorical formulation. *Confinia Psychiatrica*, 19, 2, 106–116.

Mason, P.T., and R. Kreger. 1998. *Stop Walking on Eggshells: Taking Your Life Back When Someone You Care About Has Borderline Personality Disorder*. Oakland, CA: New Harbinger.

Matthews, G., R.D. Roberts, and M. Zeidner. 2004. Seven myths about emotional intelligence. *Psychological Inquiry*, 15, 3, 179–196.

Mauchnik, J., and C. Schmahl. 2010. The latest neuroimaging findings in borderline personality disorder. *Current Psychiatry Reports*, 12, 1, 46–55.

McGrath, M., and Oakley, B. 2011. Codependency and pathological altruism. In *Pathological Altruism*, ed. B. Oakley, A. Knafo, G. Madhavan and D.S. Wilson, 49-74. New York: Oxford University Press.

McHoskey, J.W. 1995. Narcissism and Machiavellianism. *Psychological Reports*, 77, 3, 755–759.

———. 2001. Machiavellianism and personality dysfunction. *Personality and Individual Differences*, 31, 791–798.

McHoskey, J.W., W. Worzel, and C. Szyarto. 1998. Machiavellianism and psychopathy. *Journal of Personality and Social Psychology*, 74, 1, 192–210.

McLean, B., and P. Elkind. 2003. *The Smartest Guys in the Room: The Amazing Rise and Scandalous Fall of Enron*. New York: Penguin.

McPherson, M., L. Smith-Lovin, and J.M. Cook. 2001. Birds of a feather: Homophily in social networks. *Annual Review of Sociology*, 27, 415–444.

Mealey, L. 1995. The sociobiology of sociopathy: An integrated evolutionary model. *Behavioral and Brain Sciences*, 18, 523–599.

Meekings, C., and L. O'Brien. 2004. Borderline pathology in children and adolescents. *International Journal of Mental Health Nursing*, 13, 3, 152–163.

Methvin, E.H. 1998. A corrupt union and the mob. *Weekly Standard*, August 31. www.thelaborers.net/COIA/magazines/a_corrupt_union_and_the_mob.htm.

Miliora, M. 2004. The psychology and ideology of an Islamic terrorist leader: Usama bin Laden. *International Journal of Applied Psychoanalytic Studies*, 1, 2, 121–139.

Miller, F.T., T. Abrams, R. Dulit, and M. Fyer. 1993. Substance abuse in borderline personality disorder. *American Journal of Drug and Alcohol Abuse*, 19, 4, 491–497.

Miller, S.G. 1996. Borderline personality disorder in cultural context: Commentary on Paris. *Psychiatry: Interpersonal & Biological Processes*, 59, 2, 193–195.

Millon, T. 2004. *Masters of the Mind: Exploring the Story of Mental Illness from Ancient Times to the New Millennium*. New York: Wiley.

Moldea, D.E. 1992. *The Hoffa Wars: The Rise and Fall of Jimmy Hoffa*. New York: SPI Books.

Molina, J.D., F. López-Muñoz, D.J. Stein, M.J. Martín-Vázquez, C. Alamo, I. Lerma-Carrillo, C. Andrade-Rosa, M.V. Sánchez-López, and M. Calle-Real. 2009. Borderline personality disorder: A review and reformulation from evolutionary theory. *Medical Hypotheses*, 73, 3, 382–386.

Montefiore, S.S. 2004. *Stalin: The Court of the Red Tsar*. New York: Alfred A. Knopf.

Moo, G.G. 1999. *Power Grab: How the National Education Association Is Betraying Our Children*. Washington, DC: Regnery.

Morgan, P.W., and G.H. Reynolds. 1997. *The Appearance of Impropriety: How the Ethics Wars Have Undermined American Government, Business, and Society*. New York: Free Press.

Moriya, N., Y. Miyake, K. Minakawa, N. Ikuta, and A. Nishizono-Maher. 1993. Diagnosis and clinical features of borderline personality disorder in the East and West: a preliminary report. *Comprehensive Psychiatry*, 34, 6, 418–423.

Moyo, D. 2009. *Dead Aid: Why Aid Is Not Working and How There Is Another Way for Africa*. New York: Farrar, Straus & Giroux.

Mullins, B., T. McGinty, and J. Zweig. 2010. Congressional staffers gain from trading in stocks. *Wall Street Journal*, October 11. http://online.wsj.com/article/SB10001424052748703431604575522434188603198.html.

Muslin, H. 1992. Adolf Hitler: The evil self. *Psychohistory Review*, 20, 3, 251–270.

Nathan, A.J. 1994. Foreword. In *The Private Life of Chairman Mao*, Zhisui Li, vii–xiv. New York: Random House.

National Institute for Labor Relations Research. 2004. The economic consequences of "Card-Check" forced unionism. *Study,* August. www.nilrr.org/node/31/.

Nesse, R.M. 1990. Evolutionary explanations of emotions. *Human Nature,* 1, 3, 261–289.

———. 1999. The evolution of hope and despair. *Social Research*, 66, 2, 429–469.

———. 2000. Motivation and melancholy: A Darwinian perspective. Paper presented at Nebraska Symposium on Motivation, Lincoln, Nebraska.

———. 2001. *Evolution and the Capacity for Commitment*. New York: Russell Sage Foundation.

Nesse, R.M., and G.C. Williams. 1996. *Why We Get Sick: The New Science of Darwinian Medicine*. New York: Vintage Books.

Norwood, R. 1990. *Women Who Love Too Much*. New York: Simon & Schuster.

Oakley, B. 2007. *Evil Genes: Why Rome Fell, Hitler Rose, Enron Failed and My Sister Stole My Mother's Boyfriend*. Amherst, NY: Prometheus Books.

Oakley, B., A. Knafo, and M. McGrath. 2011. Pathological altruism—An introduction. In *Pathological Altruism*, ed. B. Oakley, A. Knafo, G. Madhavan and D.S. Wilson, 3–9. New York: Oxford University Press.

Oakley, B., A. Knafo, G. Madhavan, and D.S. Wilson, ed. 2011. *Pathological Altruism*. New York: Oxford University Press.

Oberauer, K., R. Schulze, O. Wilhelm, and H.-M. Süß. 2005. Working memory and intelligence—their correlation and their relation: Comment on Ackerman, Beier, and Boyle (2005). *Psychological Bulletin*, 131, 1, 61–65.

Paige, R. 2007. *The War Against Hope: How Teachers' Unions Hurt Children, Hinder Teachers, and Endanger Public Education*. Nashville, TN: Nelson.

Paris, J. 1996. Cultural factors in the emergence of borderline pathology. *Psychiatry: Interpersonal & Biological Processes,* 59, 2, 185–192.

———. 1997. Antisocial and borderline personality disorders: Two separate diagnoses or two aspects of the same psychopathology? *Comprehensive Psychiatry*, 38, 4, 237–242.

———. 2009. The treatment of borderline personality disorder: implications of research on diagnosis, etiology, and outcome. *Annual Review of Clinical Psychology*, 5, 277–290.

Peck, M.S. 1983. *People of the Lie: The Hope for Healing Human Evil*. New York: Simon & Schuster.

Pert, C.B. 1997. *Molecules of Emotion: Why You Feel the Way You Feel*. New York: Scribner.

Peter, L.J., and R. Hull. 1994. *The Peter Principle: Why Things Always Go Wrong.* New York: HarperCollins.

Pitrone, J.M. 1989. *Tangled Web: Legacy of Auto Pioneer John F. Dodge.* Hamtramck, MI: Avenue.

Popper, M. 2000. The development of charismatic leaders. *Political Psychology*, 21, 4, 729–744.

Posner, G.L., and J. Ware. 2000. *Mengele: The Complete Story.* New York: Cooper Square Press.

Posner, M.I., M.K. Rothbart, N. Vizueta, K.N. Levy, D.E. Evans, K.M. Thomas, and J.F. Clarkin. 2002. Attentional mechanisms of borderline personality disorder. *Proceedings of the National Academy of Sciences,* 99, 25, 16366–16370.

Posner, M.I., M.K. Rothbart, N. Vizueta, K.M. Thomas, K.N. Levy, J. Fossella, D. Silbersweig, E. Stern, J. Clarkin, and O. Kernberg. 2003. An approach to the psychobiology of personality disorders. *Development and Psychopathology*, 15, 4, 1093–1106.

Post, J.M. 1993a. Current concepts of the narcissistic personality: Implications for political psychology. *Political Psychology*, 14, 1, 99–121.

———. 1993b. *When Illness Strikes the Leader: The Dilemma of the Captive King.* New Haven: Yale University Press.

———. 2003. *The Psychological Assessment of Political Leaders: With Profiles of Saddam Hussein and Bill Clinton.* Ann Arbor: University of Michigan Press.

———. 2004. *Leaders and Their Followers in a Dangerous World: The Psychology of Political Behavior.* Ithaca: Cornell University Press.

Redlich, F. 1998. *Diagnosis of a Destructive Prophet.* New York: Oxford University Press.

Ressler, J. MARKETING > Big Fat Inc. http://hellocoolworld.com/files/TheCorporation/Ressler.pdf.

Riby, D., V. Bruce, and A. Jawaid. 2011. Everyone's friend? The case of Williams syndrome. In *Pathological Altruism*, ed. B. Oakley, A. Knafo, G. Madhavan and D.S. Wilson, 116–127. New York: Oxford University Press.

Robb, P. 1996. *Midnight in Sicily.* New York: Vintage Books.

Robins, L.N., J. Tipp, and T. Przybeck. 1991. Antisocial personality. In *Psychiatric Disorders in America,* ed. L.N. Robins and D.A. Reiger, 258–290. New York: Free Press.

Robins, R.S., and J.M. Post. 1997. *Political Paranoia: The Psychopolitics of Hatred.* New Haven: Yale University Press.

Ronningstam, E. 1996. Pathological narcissism and narcissistic personality disorder in Axis I disorders. *Harvard Review of Psychiatry*, 3, 6, 326–340.

Rosenbaum, R. 1999. *Explaining Hitler: The Search for the Origins of His Evil.* New York: Random House.

Rosenthal, M.Z., K.L. Gratz, D.S. Kosson, J.S. Cheavens, C.W. Lejuez, and T.R. Lynch. 2008. Borderline personality disorder and emotional responding: A review of the research literature. *Clinical Psychology Review*, 28, 1, 75–91.

Rosett, C. 2005. Oil for Food: The list goes on—Congress gets deeper inside the U.N.-sponsored "Saddam Bribery System." *National Review*, May 12. http://old.nationalreview.com/rosett/rosett200505121840.asp.

Rummel, R.J. 1994. *Death by Government.* New Brunswick, NJ: Transaction.

———. 1999. *Statistics of Democide: Genocide and Mass Murder Since 1900.* Berlin: Lit Verlag.

Simon, H.A. 1990. A mechanism for social selection and successful altruism. *Science*, 250, 1665–1668.

———. 1991. Altruism: Docility or group identification [Response to L. R. Caporael R. M. Dawes]. *Science*, 252, 192.

Simpson, O.J. 1995. *I Want to Tell You: My Response to Your Letters, Your Messages, Your Questions.* New York: Little, Brown.

Skeem, J.L., and D.J. Cooke. 2010. Is criminal behavior a central component of psychopathy? Conceptual directions for resolving the debate. *Psychological Assessment*, 22, 2, 433–445.

Sleigh, A. 1966. Hitler: A study in megalomania. *Canadian Psychiatric Association Journal*, 11, 3, 218–219.

Sokal, A. 1996. Transgressing the boundaries: Toward a transformative hermeneutics of quantum gravity. *Social Text*, 46/47, 217–252.

Sprock, J., T.J. Rader, J.P. Kendall, and C.Y. Yoder. 2000. Neuropsychological functioning in patients with borderline personality disorder. *Journal of Clinical Psychology*, 56, 12, 1587–1600.

Steele, H., and L. Siever. 2010. An attachment perspective on borderline personality disorder: Advances in gene-environment considerations. *Current Psychiatry Reports*, 12, 1, 61–67.

Stills, S. 1970. *Love the One You're With*. New York: Atlantic Records.

Stone, M.H. 1983. Special problems in borderline adolescents from wealthy families. *Adolescent Psychiatry*, 11, 163–176.

———. 2003. Borderline patients at the border of treatability: At the intersection of borderline, narcissistic, and antisocial personalities. *Journal of Psychiatric Practice*, 9, 4, 279–290.

Sutton, R.I. 1994. *The No Asshole Rule: Building a Civilized Workplace and Surviving One That Isn't*. New York: Warner Business Books.

Swenson, C.R. 2000. How can we account for DBT's widespread popularity? *Clinical Psychology: Science & Practice*, 7, 1, 87–91.

Taylor, S.E., and J.D. Brown. 1988. Illusion and well-being: A social psychological perspective on mental health. *Psychological Bulletin*, 103, 2, 193–210.

———. 1994. Positive illusions: Creative self-deception and the healthy mind. *Psychological Bulletin*, 116, 1, 21–27.

Terrill, R. 1998. Mao in history. *National Interest*, 52, 54–63.

Thieblot, A.J. 2006. Perspectives on union corruption: Lessons from the databases. *Journal of Labor Research*, 27, 4, 513–536.

Tierney, John. 2011. Social scientist sees bias within. *New York Times*, February 7. www.nytimes.com/2011/02/08/science/08tier.html.

Time Magazine. 1987. Religion: Enterprising Evangelism. *Time*, August 3. www.time.com/time/magazine/article/0,9171,965155-1,00.html.

Timmerman, K.R. 2001. *Shakedown: Exposing the Real Jesse Jackson*. Washington, DC: Regnery.

Tooby, J., and L. Cosmides. 1990a. On the universality of human nature and the uniqueness of the individual: The role of genetics and adaptation. *Journal of Personality*, 58, 17–68.

———. 1990b. The past explains the present: Emotional adaptations and the structure of ancestral environments. *Ethology and Sociobiology*, 11, 375–424.

———. 1992. The psychological foundations of culture. In *The Adapted Mind: Evolutionary Psychology and the Generation of Culture*, ed. J.H. Barkow, L. Cosmides, and J. Tooby, 19–136. New York: Oxford University Press.

Torgersen, S., E. Kringlen, and V. Cramer. 2001. The prevalence of personality disorders in a community sample. *Archives of General Psychiatry*, 58, 590–596.

Turner, M.L. 2003. *Kmart's Ten Deadly Sins: How Incompetence Tainted an American Icon*. New York: John Wiley & Sons.

Turvey, B.E. 2011. Pathological altruism: Victims and motivational types. In *Pathological Altruism*, ed. B. Oakley, A. Knafo, G. Madhavan and D.S. Wilson, 177–192. New York: Oxford University Press.

U.S. Department of Justice. 1993. A comprehensive strategy for serious, violent, and chronic juvenile offenders: Program summary. Report No. NCJ-1434530, December. Washington, DC.

Volkogonov, D. 1994. *Lenin: A New Biography*. New York: Free Press.

Wachs, T.D. 1992. *The Nature of Nurture*. Newbury Park, CA: Sage.

Waite, R.G.L. 1977. *The Psychopathic God: Adolf Hitler*. New York: Basic Books.

Walker, K., and M. Schone. 2001. *Son of a Grifter: The Twisted Tale of Sante and Kenny Kimes, the Most Notorious Con Artists in America: A Memoir by the Other Son*. New York: William Morrow.

Weiner, J. 1995. *The Beak of the Finch: A Story of Evolution in Our Time*. New York: Vintage Books.

Weiss, M., P. Zelkowitz, R.B. Feldman, J. Vogel, M. Heyman, and J. Paris. 1996. Psychopathology in offspring of mothers with borderline personality disorder: a pilot study. *Canadian Journal of Psychiatry/Revue Canadienne de Psychiatrie*, 41, 5, 285–290.

Westhues, K. 1998. *Eliminating Professors: A Guide to the Dismissal Process*. Lewiston, NY: Edwin Mellen Press.

Widiger, T.A., and A.J. Francis. 1989. Epidemiology, diagnosis, and comorbidity of borderline personality disorder. In *American Psychiatric Press Review of Psychiatry*, ed. A. Tasman, R.E. Hales and A.J. Francis, 8–24. Washington, DC: American Psychiatric Press.

Willner, A.R. 1984. *The Spellbinders: Charismatic Political Leadership*. New Haven: Yale University Press.

Wilson, D.S., D. Near, and R. Miller. 1996. Machiavellianism: A synthesis of the evolutionary and psychological literatures. *Psychological Bulletin*, 119, 2, 285–299.

Wilson, J.Q., and R.J. Herrnstein. 1985. *Crime and Human Nature*. New York: Simon & Schuster.

Wright, R. 1994. *The Moral Animal: The New Science of Evolutionary Psychology*. New York: Pantheon Books.

Wright, R., and N. Cummings, ed. 2005. *Destructive Trends in Mental Health: The Well-Intentioned Path to Harm*. New York: Brunner-Routledge.

Zahn-Waxler, C., and C. Van Hulle. 2011. Empathy, guilt, and depression: When caring for others becomes costly to children. In *Pathological Altruism*, ed. B. Oakley, A. Knafo, G. Madhavan, and D.S. Wilson, 321–344. New York: Oxford University Press.

Zanarini, M.C., F. Frankenburg, R.E.D. Dubo, A.E. Sickel, A. Trkha, A. Levin, and V. Reynolds. 1998. Axis II comorbidity of borderline personality disorder. *Comprehensive Psychiatry,* 39, 5, 296–302.

Zheng, W., W. Wang, Z. Huang, C. Sun, J. Zhu, and W.J. Livesley. 2002. The structure of traits delineating personality disorder in a Chinese sample. *Journal of Personality Disorders,* 16, 5, 477–486.

4

Evil in Public Administration

A Contrary Perspective

H. George Frederickson

Since the publication of Guy B. Adams and Danny L. Balfour's *Unmasking Administrative Evil* (2009), the subject of evil has been fashionable in some public administration circles. Indeed, the publication of this collection of essays attests to a continuing interest in evil in public administration. This interest happens to coincide with a resurgence of the use of the word "evil" among elected officials, particularly since the attack on the World Trade Center and other sites on September 11, 2001. Rather than take up a consideration of the claims and examples found in *Unmasking Administrative Evil,* or the use of the word "evil" in contemporary politics, in this chapter I contemplate and recommend a much broader and more general conception of evil, the conception of evil developed by Mohandas K. Gandhi. Then, I turn to the classic public administration ethics canon and argue for its salience.

"Evil" is certainly among the most powerful and evocative words and concepts in contemporary public discourse. The Union of Soviet Socialist Republics was described by President Ronald Reagan in the last stages of the cold war as an "evil empire." President George W. Bush, in his second State of the Union Address, used the phrase "axis of evil" to characterize Iraq, Iran, and North Korea. The phrase "axis of evil" was developed by David Frum (2003), a presidential speechwriter, to help justify efforts to dislodge the government of Saddam Hussein in Iraq and, in time, the Iraq War.

If, among Americans, the Saddam Hussein regime in Iraq was understood to be evil, and the Iraqi public administrators in that regime were engaged in evil, were the actions of the government of the United States, based on false information, to engage in a so-called preemptive war on Iraq evil? Most Americans would probably agree with the first claim but disagree strongly with the second. And, to put a finer point on it, were the U.S. military and civilian public administrators engaged in the Iraq War evil? To Americans such a claim is repellent and jarring. This being so, "evil" may be powerful political word and a useful label to describe persons and organizations doing horrible things, but "evil" is not an especially useful academic concept or theory.

Evil regimes and leaders are abroad in the world—dangerous, threatening, dark, and mysterious. There is evil among us, and some of it, we are told, is administrative evil that needs to be unmasked. Evil, and its opposite, good, are, it is said, categories into which individuals and their actions, groups and their actions, ideologies, and even cultures can be reliably divided. Are such claims and categories, however provocative and alarming, useful as part of the building blocks of theories of public policy, public administration, or administrative ethics? Are they useful as guides for the practice of public administration and public policy?

As is said of the Ten Commandments, the *Unmasking Administrative Evil* approach is considerably stronger on what should not be done than on what should be done. To more completely understand administrative evil is to understand what not to do. In the case of *Unmasking Administrative Evil,* the understanding of evil reduces to pinning the blame on modernity and technical rationality. Even if administrators influenced by modernity and technical rationality can be held accountable for evil, particularly for the Holocaust, we are still dealing with things that should not have been done and actions that should not have been taken. Can a useful public administration ethic be built either in whole or in part on not being evil? I do not think so. Would it not be preferable to attempt to build a public administration ethic on doing good? Even something as evil as the Holocaust and the actions of public administrators during the Holocaust can be usefully viewed from the perspective of good (Frederickson and Hart, 1985).

Instead of approaching evil in public administration from the perspective suggested in *Unmasking Administrative Evil*, a much broader and significantly more elevating and useful approach to evil in public administration is found in the description of it by Gandhi. He used dichotomous categories to describe good and evil but, rather than characterizing particular leaders, their regimes, or their policies as evil, he found evil to be well within each individual's capacity to understand and to act. He had good reason for characterizing the particular leaders, regimes, or actions of his time, the late stages of colonialism, as evil but chose, instead, to set out an understanding of evil that is abstract and therefore particularly useful and enduring. In his description, Gandhi did not include those evils so obvious and fundamental to human understanding that they require little elaboration, such as involuntary servitude or the taking of innocent life. An abstract and even philosophical approach to evil by a political leader was unusual in Gandhi's time and would be even more unusual today, when the word "evil" is so frequently and casually used. What follows in summary form and with a few minor changes to put them into our present context and in the context of public policy and administration scholarship are Gandhi's descriptions of six forms of evil.

POVERTY AMID PLENTY

To Gandhi, poverty amid plenty is evil, and those policies and actions that consciously favor the interests of those with plenty at the expense of those in poverty are likewise evil. Such a view of evil is hardly novel. It is, after all, "easier for a camel to go through the eye of a needle than for a rich man to enter the kingdom of Heaven." Virtually all forms of theology teach that those with resources have responsibilities toward those without resources. Persons and groups of persons who have plenty have responsibilities toward those who do not. Better-off countries have responsibilities toward less-well-off countries. Nothing—not race, not gender, not ideology, not geography—can mitigate the evil of those with plenty who are ignoring the needs of those with little.

The evil of poverty amid plenty may seem an enduring aphorism or a good Sunday school lesson, but is it relevant to policy and policy implementation? Yes, and the reason is as much empirical as it is philosophical. Richard Wilkinson and Kate Pickett, in their brilliant book *The Spirit Level: Why Greater Equality Makes Society Stronger* (2009), conclusively demonstrate that in rich societies the poor have shorter lives and suffer more from almost every social problem. One common factor linked the healthiest and happiest societies is the degree of equality among their members—not wealth, not resources, not culture, not climate, not diet, and not form of government. Further, more unequal societies are bad for everyone within them—the rich and middle class as well as the poor. A wide survey of policy issues or social problems—poor health, violence, lack of community life, teen pregnancy, mental illness—are more likely to occur in less-equal societies. Using data comparing countries and comparing the fifty states in the United States, Wilkinson and Pickett conclusively demonstrate that the United States, by most measures the richest country, has shorter life spans, more mental illness, more obesity, and more of its people in prison per capita than any other developed country. And the same pattern is found in the fifty states—the states with the highest inequality also have the most severe social problems.

This is powerful evidence that poverty amid wealth not only is evil as Gandhi claimed but is terrible public policy. And, of course, that public policy is implemented by public administrators. If the policy is evil, are those who carry it out, ipso facto, evil? Such a question broadens the subject of evil, but does it help? Yes, because it points to the policy (the message) and not the implementing agents (the messengers) as evil. If the policy is evil, what can be done to change policy? What can public administrators do to point out the evil of policy and be forces for policy change? Or, one might consider Rosemary O'Leary's guerrilla government argument (O'Leary, 2006) or Albert Hirschman's "exit, voice, and loyalty" choices (Hirschman, 1970).

That subject has been part of public administration for nearly a generation and is called social equity (Frederickson, 2010a). The reason the concept of social equity has such resonance as a core ethic in American public administration is that we instinctively recognize the evil of poverty amid plenty.

WEALTH WITHOUT WORK

Wealth without work is evil. Because the poor in our uneven world usually work tirelessly just to survive, it is evil for those with plenty to be idle. Recall the little 1915 rhyme by Sarah Cleghorn that so profoundly captured the evil of wealth without work that it influenced the development of much stronger British and American child labor laws:

> The golf links lie so near the mill
> That almost any day
> The laboring children can look out
> And see the men at play. (Cleghorn, 1936)

Although there has been progress in many parts of the world, the challenges of child labor and human exploitation are no less now than they were in Gandhi's time. Our wealth can easily be seen by others, but it is not easy for us to see their privation.

Gandhi's aphorisms on evil were developed during the latter stages of colonialism. At the time and, to some extent, even today, wealth in both India and Great Britain was associated with large land holdings, an owner class with leisure, and a working class taking care of land and property. In our day, great wealth tends to be associated with commerce rather than large land holdings. The modern captains of industry and the great Western families of commerce—Rockefeller, Vanderbilt, Carnegie, Walton, Gates, and so on—would not ordinarily be associated with leisure (golf, perhaps). The ethical issue of our time most nearly resembling Gandhi's "wealth without work" is the issue of government policy, particularly tax policy. Which—wealth or work—shall bear the primary burden of taxation and government support?

Taxation in the United States reflects our federated model of government. Units of local government tend to tax real property with some reliance on consumption taxes. States rely on consumption taxes and, increasingly, on income taxes. The national government relies on the taxation of income, both wages and capital gains. Of these forms of taxation, only local property taxes are based on the taxation of wealth, at least in the form of real property. In our time, most large accumulations of wealth are not in real property. And so it is that, with the exception of inheritance taxes (the so-called death taxes), personal wealth is left untaxed, following Justice Oliver Holmes's metaphor of taxing the fruit but not the tree from which it has fallen. One result of these arrangements is the huge concentration of wealth in the hands of a relatively few Americans (Knoll, 2000).

While this may not be evil in the way that Gandhi saw wealth without work, it is certainly the perpetuation of the advantages of a few over the welfare of many. As Warren Buffett put it in defense of raising taxes on the wealthy, "It's class warfare, my class is winning, but they shouldn't be" (2005).

David Shakow and Reed Shuldiner make an interesting case for a comprehensive flat wealth tax (2000; see also Knoll, 2000). In the context of considerations of simplification of the Federal Income Tax Code and in the context of debates over the fairness of the income tax, the inheritance tax, and the feasibility of a flat tax, the feasibility of a general federal consumption tax, the idea of a federal tax on wealth could inform policy deliberations.

We are left with this question: Is the present pattern of taxation of wealth, compared with the taxation of work, good or evil? I suspect Gandhi would say: evil!

COMMERCE WITHOUT MORALITY

Commerce without morality can be evil. In most respects, modern corporations and their operations in the marketplace are a positive force for good in the world, forming the base of gainful work for millions while improving products and providing services. The development of modern commerce in Asia and the Indian subcontinent greatly benefit millions of people in much the same way as market economies serve as the basis of highly developed economies in Europe and the Americas. Nevertheless, there are many contemporary examples of Gandhi's description of the evil of commerce without morality. Environmental degradation and the depletion of natural resources are associated primarily with commerce. Predatory lending and unregulated trading in so-called derivatives, among other things, appear to account for the present (since 2008) "Great Recession" in most Western economies. Suffering from the Great Recession has not been limited to the poor and marginally employed. Many traditionally middle-class families and individuals have lost homes and jobs. Because of the thicket of banks, bond-rating firms, accounting firms, insurance firms, financial management firms, and so forth involved in causing the Great Recession, assigning responsibility for the recession is difficult and the subject of debate and disagreement. There can be no disagreement, however, that the Great Recession of the early twenty-first century is an example of the evil of commerce without morality.

SCIENCE AND TECHNOLOGY WITHOUT HUMANITY

Science and technology without humanity can be evil. The fruits of science give us better food, better health, and longer lives. Technology can reduce human toil and greatly enhance human communication and knowledge. Science and technology can be instruments for a more humane world. But when science and technology are used for inhumane purposes, they are evil. The moral implications of nuclear war, on one hand, and suicide bombers, on the other, are clear. Modern science and technology both bless us and cause us to face potential evils never before faced by humankind.

Many, if not most, developments in science and technology involve calculable trade-offs. The use of fossil fuels provides cheap and fast transportation but at steep environmental and health costs. Often the benefits of science and technology are enjoyed by present generations, the "hidden" trade-offs to be borne by future generations in the form of ruined soil, climate change, and the like. The potential future costs of such trade-offs can be ameliorated by permitting systems that include environmental impact calculations and statements, rigorous drug-testing protocols, and similar temporal requirements designed to protect future generations. Sophisticated risk assessments are now commonplace and can be informative in designing licenses, permits, and other forms of policy control over science and technology. Such forms of control tend to be "country specific," while the processes of science and technology tend to be regional or global. Because of globalization, those who implement country-specific systems of control over science and technology must increasingly cooperate with their counterparts in other countries to ensure against the specter of rent-seeking countries with weak controls over the negative side-effects of science and technology (Koppell, 2010).

The contemporary "intergenerational social equity" argument in public administration might hold some promise (Frederickson, 2010a). Intergenerational social equity is the application of the logic of sustainability to public policy and administration.

POLITICS AND ADMINISTRATION WITHOUT PRINCIPLES

The practices of politics and administration without principles can be evil. In his time, Gandhi was probably most concerned with the evils associated with European policies of empire and their implementation in India. In our time, we face the challenges of political and administrative evil in Iraq, for example, the evil of Saddam Hussein, on one hand, and the evil of prisoner abuse, on the other. We should never tire of asking these questions: What exactly are our political and administrative principles, and do we believe them to be good? For whom are our principles good? How do current policies or proposed policies achieve those purposes? How can those policies be implemented without doing evil?

KNOWLEDGE WITHOUT CHARACTER

Knowledge without character can be evil. Although we live, it is said, in a knowledge society, knowledge never was the same thing as either wisdom or character. One way to ensure greater character in the application of knowledge to human affairs is to do all that can be done to make knowledge widely available and to demand transparency. Knowledge comes in many forms, and in the hierarchies of knowledge, local knowledge tends to be discounted. This is nonsense because all knowledge, when it is applied, must be applied locally. It is at the local level, where policy is carried out, that character is most likely to meet knowledge and ideas passing for knowledge. Consider, for example, local school districts. It would seem that local school officials do not know as much about education as do politicians and expert policymakers at the state and national level. It requires little character to support knowledge-based arguments that one is not asked to carry out. The denial of local knowledge reduces the prospects of bringing real character to policy implementation at the level where it matters most.

All six forms of the Gandhian perspective on evil are modal, common everyday ethical challenges. In confronting these challenges, there are, I would argue, far more acts of administrative goodness than of administrative evil. There were and still are evil individuals—Adolf Hitler, Joseph Stalin, Osama bin Laden, Saddam Hussein, Kim Jong Il. There were and are collective acts of evil—slavery, the Holocaust, the killing fields, Rwandan genocide, the Sudanese genocide. There were and are still, evil regimes—the mullahs in Iran, and until recently Muammar Gaddafi in Libya and Kim Jong Il in North Korea, but somehow not the House of Saud in Saudi Arabia (could it be oil?). And evil exists in the world as an independent disembodied force—such as greed and avarice, which appeal to our worst instincts—that seeks to lead people from doing good to doing bad.

THE INSTITUTIONAL? PUBLIC ADMINISTRATION ETHICS CANON

Rather than dwelling on evil, particularly on large-scale past evil acts, I suggest that public administration ethics specialists do what we do best. What we do best can almost always be found in what I describe here as the "traditional public administration ethics canon."

Public administration ethics during the early government-reform era is associated with a well-known list of accepted standards, agreed-upon assumptions, and preferred practices. Let us call the list below the "traditional public administration ethics canon" or, simply, "the canon." The canon includes claims regarding:

- prohibitions against conflicts of interest
- merit-based appointments and promotions as an alternative to political spoils
- public office as a public trust
- formal adoption of ethics rules
- objective and transparent procurement and contracting procedures
- standardized internal accounting and auditing protocols and annual external auditing
- both institutional and professional codes of ethics
- clear lines between day-to-day professional administration and political office holding, particularly electoral or campaign politics
- prohibitions against nepotism
- prohibitions against bribery
- fair and equal treatment of citizens
- ethics training
- NASPAA Commission on Peer Review and Accreditation requirement that master of public administration degrees include ethics education
- prohibition against the use of public property or time for personal or political purposes
- encouragement of and support for whistleblowers
- transparency

In the past forty years, the government-reform basis of public administration was challenged on multiple fronts. Rational choice or market model economists found bureaucracy to be inefficient and regulation to reduce business efficiency. The reinventing government movement likewise found bureaucracy wanting, favoring contracting out most public services to businesses. Customer-based government would, it was claimed, work better and cost less. The "new public management" emerged, combining market economics with reinventing government. What began as program evaluation evolved into an influential performance measurement movement. And the word "accountability" increasingly came to be used to describe a new approach to ethics. Many in the practice of public administration embraced these movements. A few professors, including me, argued that downsizing, contracting out, and deregulation would, in the long run, be a recipe for both ineffective government and corruption. Issuing such warnings is, after all, what professors do—that is why we have tenure. But our warning made little difference.

Public administration is now part of a considerably different public life, a new life of highly influential public but nongovernmental institutions; many autonomous and semiautonomous quasi-governmental institutions; many single-purpose governments, often financed by fees for service rather than general revenues; increasing percentages of government-financed work performed by nonprofit and corporate agents; elaborate patterns of both formal and informal interjurisdictional collaboration and cooperation in the so-called new geogovernance.

The canon of traditional public administration ethics, rooted in general-purpose governments and in early government reform, is no longer adequate to the task of bringing ethical virtue to this *new governance*. That being so, and if necessity is the mother of invention, the necessities of contemporary public life call for the invention or creation of a public administration ethics better suited to our times, in other words: a new ethics canon.

PUBLIC ADMINISTRATION ETHICS IN THE ERA OF GOVERNANCE

What might be the elements or components of public administration ethics in the era of new governance?

First, while perceptions of government, particularly of big government, are not particularly positive, perceptions of "publicness," particularly "grassroots publicness," are rather positive. For example, the cluster of fashionable concepts and ideas—such as civil society, social capital, community, civic engagement, and citizen participation—associated with David Mathews (1999), Theda Skocpol and Morris Fiorina (1999), and Robert Putnam (2000) are promising. Closely associated with the civic engagement advocates are those working on both individual and institutional cooperation and collaboration, including Robert Axelrod (1984) and Robert Agranoff and Michael McGuire (2003). And, perhaps most interesting, Elinor Ostrom (1990) in 2009 received the Nobel Memorial Prize in economic sciences for her work on the commons, in particular her demonstration of the several ways that the "tragedy of the commons" can be avoided. All these versions of grassroots publicness seem to arrive at the same conclusions: that effective "publics" have *trust*, make and enforce rules, build structures, practice reciprocity, and have cultures of ethical leadership. Governments, especially local governments, are only part of this grassroots publicness.

Public dependence on our high-reliability systems—such as commercial air travel and the provision of electricity and gas, electronic and particularly digital electronic communication, such as television, radio, and the Internet—is so ingrained that any lapses in service are met with citizen outrage (Frederickson and La Porte, 2002). Again, governments are part of these public high-reliability systems, but only a part.

In between the grassroots and high-reliability systems are a wide variety of public services and functions. Some are distinctly governmental, such as the criminal justice system, the education system, and the Social Security system. Others, such as national defense, are highly mixed partnerships with commercial firms and nonprofit organizations. And others, such as the health-care system, are based primarily on contractors and grantees.

From the standpoint of ethics, the issue, then, is not the degree to which a particular system is governmental but, rather, the degree to which a particular system is understood to be public. The more a system is thought to be public, the more the public will expect that system to be ethical.

The public administration task, therefore, is to take the lead in identifying the various organizations and professions in each public system and bring those organizations and professions together around the subject of ethics.

By now, it will have been noticed that I have given little attention to public administration ethics scholarship. While I have been part of that scholarship over the years, I have come more recently to identify with the vulgar ethics perspective (Frederickson, 2010b; Mainzer, 1991). I have no quarrel with the study of ontology, for that matter, deontology (the study of moral idealism or of utilitarianism), claims made about either dirty hands or many hands, the ethics of regime values, or even the further study of my own beloved arguments about the patriotism of benevolence. All of them add to the body of ethics knowledge.

I suggest the use of ordinary cases, examples, or models, rather than extraordinary cases. The excellent work of Steven Maynard-Moody and Michael Mushno (2003) comes to mind. In their *Cops, Teachers, and Councilors*, they describe how and why street-level bureaucrats make moral choices in the face of scarce resources and high variation in the legitimacy of client claims. Using standard, ordinary cases, they describe how ethics actually works. An understanding of the ethics of ordinary cases demonstrates why a too great focus on aberrant cases, such as those that are evil, results in aberrant ethics standards.

Finally, those who study ethics will find here a decided emphasis on institutional and organizational forms, on rules and regulations, on organizational behavior. This draws from my conviction that most public administrators, almost all the time, make good moral choices and adhere to public sector ethics. The big question before us is whether those engaged in the public's work as contractors and grantees will also, almost all the time, make good moral choices and adhere to public sector ethics. For those tempted to be unethical, there must be policies, rules, regulations, oversight, audits, and other forms of institutional arrangements to help them be virtuous.

These are the primary challenges and tasks facing the field of ethics in public administration. A preoccupation with evil diverts public administration from these challenges and does little to elevate public service. Public administrators do have ethics challenges, but they should not be subjected to the assumption that, if unmasked, they are evil.

REFERENCES

Adams, G.B., and D.L. Balfour. 2009. *Unmasking Administrative Evil*, 3d ed. Armonk, NY: M.E. Sharpe.

Agranoff, R. and M. McGuire. 2003. *Collaborative Public Management: New Strategies for Local Governments.* Washington, DC: Georgetown University Press.

Axelrod, R. 1984. *The Evolution of Cooperation.* New York: Basic Books.

Buffett, W. 2005. CNN interview, May 25.

Cleghorn, S. 1936. Through the needle's eye. In *Threescore: The Autobiography of Sarah Cleghorn.* Manchester, NH: Ayer.

Frederickson, H. George. 2004. Contemplating evil. *PA Times*, September.

———. 2010a. *Social Equity and Public Administration: Origins, Developments, and Applications.* Armonk, NY: M.E. Sharpe.

———. 2010b. Searching for virtue in the public life. *Public Integrity*, 12, 3, 239–246.

Frederickson, H.G., and D.K. Hart. 1985. The public service and the patriotism of benevolence. *Public Administration Review*, 45, 5 (September/October), 547–553.

Frederickson, H.G., and T. LaPorte. 2002. Airport security, high reliability, and the problem of rationality. *Public Administration Review*, 62, September (special issue), 33–43.

Frum, D. 2003. *The Right Man: The Surprise Presidency of George W. Bush.* New York: Random House.

Hirschman, A. 1970. *Exit, Voice, and Loyalty: Responses to Decline in Firms, Organizations and States.* Cambridge: Harvard University Press.

Knoll, M.S. 2000. Commentary of fruit and trees: The relationship between income and wealth taxes. *Tax Law Review*, 53, 587.

Koppell, J.G.S. 2003. *The Politics of Quasi-Government: Hybrid Organizations and the Dynamics of Bureaucratic Control.* New York: Cambridge University Press.

———. 2010. *World Rule: Accountability, Legitimacy, and the Design of Global Governance.* Chicago: University of Chicago Press.

Mainzer, L.C. 1991. Vulgar ethics for public administration. *Administration & Society*, 23, 1, 3–28.

Mathews, D. 1999. *Politics for People*, 2d ed. Urbana: University of Illinois Press.

Maynard-Moody, S., and M. Musheno. 2003. *Cops, Teachers, Counselors: Stories from the Front Lines of Public Service.* Ann Arbor: University of Michigan Press.

O'Leary, R. 2006. *The Ethics of Dissent: Managing Guerilla Government.* Washington, DC: CQ Press.

Ostrom, E. 1990. *Governing the Commons: The Evolution of Institutions for Collective Action.* Cambridge: Cambridge University Press.

Putnam, R.D. 2000. *Bowling Alone: The Collapse and Revival of American Community.* New York: Simon & Schuster.

Shakow, D., and R. Shuldiner. 2000. A comprehensive wealth tax. *Tax Law Review*, 53, 3, 107–140.

Skocpol, T., and M.P. Fiorina, ed. 1999. *Civic Engagement in American Democracy.* Washington, DC: Brookings Institution Press.

Wilkinson, R., and K. Pickett. 2009. *The Spirit Level: Why Greater Equality Makes Societies Stronger.* New York: Bloomsbury Press.

5

On the Psychology of Evil in Interpersonal and Corporate Contexts

David R. Mandel

Evil is a difficult topic to explore from an analytic, let alone scientific, perspective because the concept of evil is primarily emotive and moralistic. Like the perception of risk (Sandman, 1989; Slovic, 1987), the perception of evil is often accompanied by feelings of outrage and dread, even terror. Alford (1997) found that people tend to describe evil mainly in terms of a sense of impending doom, suggesting that the phenomenology of evil is closely tied to emotional responses to perceived actors and events—namely, to people's "gut feelings." Evil, though, is also clearly related to attributions of extreme moral wrongdoing (Darley, 1992), suggesting that its phenomenology (again like risk perception) may be one that we would characterize as "hot cognition," linking to the layperson's prosecutorial and perhaps even theologian mindsets (Tetlock, 2002).

"Organizational evil" poses even greater challenges for discussion because one must decide whether the term refers to the organizational side of evil, as it were—that is, how organizational or social processes support the production of evil (e.g., Darley, 1992)—or whether it refers to evil wrought by organizations; and, if the latter, are we to take a broad or a narrow view of the organization? Are we talking broadly about evil states (e.g., Nazi Germany) and other organizational structures (e.g., al Qaeda) or narrowly about only evil for-profit corporations (e.g., Enron)? In either case, it is clear that we will need to cultivate our sense of what evil represents before we can say anything meaningful about organizational evil. In the latter half of this chapter, I will reflect on the latter sense of organizational evil—namely, *corporate evil*.

I suppose a good place to start, however, is with a warning. And, here, Whitehead's Fallacy of Misplaced Concreteness seems quite apropos to the task that lies ahead. As Whitehead (1925/1997) made clear, it is all too easy to mistake an abstract notion for an aspect of concrete reality. Theoreticians, who, of course, specialize in abstractions, are particularly good at this; and, in some sense, the measure of their success is marked by the degree to which they can convince others that their favored abstractions are, in fact, aspects of an objective, external reality. It is only a small cadre of thinkers who have reflected carefully on how effortlessly the human mind reifies the concepts that it conjures up. I do not wish

The author carried out his research on behalf of Defence Research and Development Canada.

to delve here into philosophical arguments that I admit I am, in any event, ill prepared to discuss. May it suffice to say that the study of evil would seem to lure the misperception of concreteness and that I prefer to treat evil as a concept to be analyzed from different intellectual vantage points, rather than as a thing in the world to be "dissected."

A LEXICAL ENTRY POINT

From among those various perspectives, let me start with an authoritative lexical definition of the term. The 2005 revised edition of *The Oxford English Dictionary* (OED) defines evil, in its primary adjectival sense, as "the antithesis of good in all its principal senses." The principal noun entry unfortunately offers no greater insight—quite simply, "that which is evil." The specific interpretations of the term provided by OED are numerous but cover so much "antithesis-of-good" ground as to make precising definitions for our purposes here seem arbitrary. Nor does an examination of the date chart seem to help much either. Even if archaic and obscure entries are ruled out, we are still left with a wide range of descriptors, including "morally depraved," "wicked," "mischievous," "hurtful," "unpleasant," "disagreeable," "unlucky," and "disastrous."

There is one rather striking feature of the date chart, however; namely, that the term "evil" seems to hardly have been used in the twentieth century but for a resurgence following President Ronald Reagan's deprecatory use of the expression "Evil Empire" to refer to the Soviet Union, which resulted in a 2005 draft addition to the *Oxford English Dictionary*. I strongly suspect that future additions will include President George W. Bush's expression "axis of evil." One wonders whether, but for Reagan and Bush, there would even be scholarly discussion of evil in the social and behavioral sciences.

The etymology of the term is somewhat more revealing. According to OED, the Medieval English term "uvel" usually referred to the roots "up" or "over," suggesting that the primary sense of the term would have been either "exceeding due measure" or "overstepping proper limits." Hence, evil is not merely the antithesis of good but a subset that in some sense exceeds due measure or oversteps proper limits. The sense or senses in which this excess is wrought is still unclear, but it appears that we have zeroed in here on an important attribute of the term—in a word, excess.

THE NOTION OF EXCESS IN CONTEMPORARY PSYCHOLOGICAL PERSPECTIVES ON EVIL

Contemporary perspectives on evil have picked up on the theme of excess in a number of ways. For instance, Darley writes,

> To be labeled as evil, the wrongdoing act often has to have a quality of egregious excess, such as a murder gratuitously committed in the course of a crime. . . . At other times, the evil actor shows an equal disregard for humanity, but the evil act is not so much described as egregious excess as depraved excess. Those individuals who derive pleasure from the torture of children display this aspect of evil. (1992, 201)

As Darley points out, evil represents a subset of moral wrongdoing in which the harm caused to the victim seems disproportionately greater than the resulting benefit to the perpetrator. Excess, in this sense, is a relative notion: a ratio of victim loss to perpetrator gain in the attributor's moral calculus.

However, the examples that Darley (1992) offers suggest something more akin to an absolute notion of excess underlying the attribution process. Senseless murders and child torture are deemed evil not only because the losses to the victims are immeasurably greater than the gains to the perpetrators—that is, out of proportion in a relative sense— but also in an absolute, albeit qualified, sense—namely, the harm inflicted on the victim is perceived as both severe *and* exceptionally unwarranted.

Take murder, for instance. Murder is always severe, but, as Darley notes, not all examples of murder seem to qualify as evil. A murder committed in self-defense or in defense of a helpless individual may not even be considered a wrongful act. Indeed, the "responsibility to protect" principle—or R2P, as it is commonly referred to in the international relations arena—embodies the latter example as a moral imperative of bystander states in the international community to use armed force when it is deemed necessary to protect victims of mass atrocity crimes when the state or states in which they are occurring fail to do so (International Commission on Intervention and State Sovereignty, 2001). R2P was prompted by the failure of the international community to effectively intervene during the Rwandan genocide, and it is, in some sense, an organizational response among states in the international community to what they agree (through a United Nations resolution) is an evil inter- or intrastate act of aggression. A recent study of more than a hundred International Studies Association members found that R2P was ranked as the third-strongest justification for going to war, after self-defense and prevention of imminent attack but ahead of justifications based on supporting allies, preemption, avenging a prior attack, and territorial conquest (Dorn, Mandel, and Cross, 2011).

Baumeister (1997) offers another psychological perspective on evil that draws on the notion of excess in a comparative manner by contrasting the perspectives of victims, bystanders, and perpetrators. In his view, attributions of evil are far more likely to be made by victims and bystanders than by perpetrators because the latter simply do not regard their behavior or the consequences of their behavior in such terms. That is, they do not, as a general rule, put themselves in their victims' shoes, experiencing even vicariously the excessive costs that they bestow upon their victims. Indeed, perpetrators tend to give much less consideration to their evildoing than victims.

Hence, what may be a life-transforming or even life-terminating event for the victim could be no more than a fleeting, thoughtless act of fancy for the perpetrator. For Baumeister, then, the question of how perpetrators can bring themselves to perform evil acts is often an inappropriate one to pose because perpetrators often fail to see those acts as excessive or evil. Rather, he proposes, such questions reflect the fact that those concerned with questions of evil are usually more sensitized to the perspective of the victims than of the perpetrators that they seek to understand.

Baumeister's (1997) intersubjectivist stance can, in some sense, be read as an indictment of the enterprise: How can one understand why someone perpetrates evil when the perpetrator and victim cannot even agree on the evilness of the acts in question, and when the theorists are biased in favor of the victim's perspective? The concept of evil, therefore, seems to share much with the concept of radicalization that is currently *en vogue* in the terrorism domain (Mandel, 2010)—both are inextricably subjective: My evil may be your good, much like what strikes me as radicalism may strike you as the defense of honor or tradition.

The notion of excess in psychological perspectives on evil takes on yet another facet in the evolutionary account of evil proposed by Duntley and Buss. According to those authors:

> At a first approximation, those [products of the evolutionary process of selection] we label as "evil" are behaviors or behavioral dispositions that result in a *massive* imposition of fitness costs on another individual or group. (2004, 104; emphasis added)

Evil, in this sense, is the result of an evolutionary strategy that favors imposing genetic fitness costs on competitors rather than directly acquiring benefits that aid one's own genetic fitness. All else being equal, the more excessive the fitness costs imposed, the more likely they are to be regarded as evil. Killing is an extreme example of imposing fitness costs on others because it not only removes the ability of the victim to further reproduce, which means that any children the victim might otherwise have had are also denied not only their turn at life but also the ability to reproduce, and so forth through the counterfactual generations that might have been. Moreover, killing a parent significantly reduces the evolutionary fitness of the victim's existing children for several reasons that Duntley and Buss describe.

From an evolutionary perspective, humans' ability to think in terms of evil and to attribute it to others coevolved with the "evil" cost-inflicting strategies as a counter-cost-inflicting strategy. That is, in order to defend against individuals or groups that used cost-inflicting strategies, opponents who evolved the ability to communicate with one another in ways that described the severity of the opponent's fitness-impeding acts or plans would have an advantage over those who might not have developed such an ability. These "evil understanding" individuals could better organize deterrent or punitive counterresponses to plans or acts that threatened their genetic fitness.

The "language of evil" could also be used in offensive maneuvers designed to impose fitness costs on opponents through a variety of "influence operations." In everyday terms, think of examples such as framing someone for a heinous crime that the person did not commit or making a particular group a scapegoat for a negative personal or societal consequence or set of consequences that, in turn, results in violence directed toward that group. As I have discussed elsewhere (Mandel, 2002a), attributions of evil have been used by instigators of collective violence and political leaders to drum up support for confrontational measures. Both Osama bin Laden and George W. Bush frequently invoked the term "evil" to refer to the adversary.

Of course, the evolutionary view does not presuppose that people explicitly think about evil in terms of genetic fitness costs. As Duntley and Buss point out:

We do not think to ourselves: "Gee, the damage done to Sally inflicts a large cost on her fitness, which impairs her relative gene replication . . . hence, it's evil." Rather, we propose that humans have evolved evaluative psychological mechanisms that function to gauge the magnitude of fitness costs inflicted on themselves, their allies, their children, and their extended families—roughly, the degree of evil. (2004, 104)

A distinct advantage of the evolutionary account seems to be that it is well equipped to bypass the morally prescriptive issues associated with the topic, while advancing a descriptive theory replete with testable predictions. By defining evil, roughly speaking, in terms of the degree of genetic fitness cost imposed, several predictions can be tested. For instance, all else being equal, murder should be seen as more evil when the victims are very young and, thus, would not have had a chance to reproduce. Behaviors that are intended and well planned out to inflict fitness costs on others should be more likely to be seen as evil than heat-of-the-moment acts that result in similar costs, because only the former seem to reflect the strategic nature of the act. The theory also predicts that, holding the act constant—say, murder—attributions of evil will be more likely and more severe as the genetic relatedness of the victim to the attributor increases. Indeed, the same act perpetrated against a hated enemy might very well be seen as a virtuous act.

The evolutionary account of evil developed by Duntley and Buss (2004) differs from other accounts of evil proposed thus far in the psychological literature in at least one important respect—namely, it does not assume that evil is the result of improbable, abnormal, or deficient conditions in either the evildoer or his or her environment. Rather, evil is seen as the result of a series of genetic adaptations, making both its expression and the expression of countervailing adaptations aimed at deterring or punishing evil normal within the species. The variance between this view and that of competing theories, including common folk psychological theories of evil, is so striking that it deserves some comment, to which I now turn.

DISPOSITIONIST AND SITUATIONIST PERSPECTIVES ON EVIL

Owing to intellectual tradition of social psychology, which strongly favors situationist explanations of human behavior and its motives (Ross and Nisbett, 1991), it is hardly surprising that most psychological attempts to provide a conceptual framework for understanding evil have either tacitly or explicitly rejected the sort of dispositional attributions that seem prevalent in the everyday folk psychology of the layperson. Psychologists are thus apt to reject the notion that there is something intrinsic in the moral fiber of the evildoer that makes him or her behave in evil ways. Their accounts for the most part offer a rebuttal to the view that there is a quantum or kernel of evil, to use Darley's (1992) expression, in the perpetrator of evil acts. Rather, their accounts focus on situational factors that make expressions of evil more likely to occur.

There is certainly some merit in the situationist message insofar as it makes us think critically about simplistic dispositionist perspectives on evil. Earlier, I warned against reifying the concept of evil, and yet folk psychological notions of evil seem to do just that. That is, people seem disposed, if not predisposed, to regard evil as a thing—as that dispositional "quantum of evil" in the psychological makeup of the purported evildoer that compels him to undertake evil acts. In this intuitive "dispositional" view, evil is seen as part of the "moral fiber" of the evildoer, and those who see it that way seem to be unclear about whether the fiber in question is real or metaphorical.

As noted earlier, because evil is an intuitive moral notion, it is difficult for most people to examine the topic from a dispassionate perspective that is free of wishful thinking or, worse, self-deception. This difficulty owes much, I believe, to our desire to avoid Moore's (1903) *naturalistic fallacy* or Hume's (1739) *is-ought* problem—that is, our tendency to succumb to the conclusion that "what is" is also "what ought to be." The worry here is that, if the behaviors that we call evil can be explained in normal biological, psychological, or social terms, then it seems to follow that we must accept evil as inevitable, if not, in some sense, right.

Ironically, however, dispositionists and situationists alike often fall prey to overreaction to the "is-slips-into-ought" concern. For the dispositionists, a view of the world as fundamentally benevolent is achieved by placing the quantum of evil not in man as species but in only those who have warranted the title of evildoer (Darley, 1992). The quantum might be natural, but it is also, thankfully, rare. For example, in Baumeister and Vohs's (2004) account, the proximal cause of evildoing is impulsivity or lack of self-control. Those individuals who exhibit a high level of this dispositional characteristic are more prone to committing evil acts. For the situationists, by contrast, that quantum is traded for a confluence of factors, mainly situational, that transform benevolent individuals into evildoers. And, though the psychological processes that are proposed to bring about the transformation are emphasized to be "ordinary," the confluences that produce evil are themselves thought to be, in a fundamental sense, aberrant or abnormal.

We see this same feature recur in a number of psychological perspectives on evil. It is perhaps best captured by Zimbardo's (2004) claim that evil acts are mainly the result of putting good people in bad situations. Different theorists have focused on different situational conditions. For example, whereas Milgram (1974) focused on obedience to malevolent authority figures, Staub (1989) focused on the frustration or deprivation of "basic human needs." The net result is the same: Evil may be more like a wave—a situational ripple—than a quantum, but such waves, much like their quantal equivalents, are generally seen as aberrations, as deviations from a more positive norm.

A serious problem with this view is that it reflects a belief that what ought not to be a certain way is, in fact, not that way—what Davis (1978) called the "moralistic fallacy." In the present context, the moralistic fallacy implies that because people ought not to be evil, they must, in fact, not be evil, at least not intrinsically. Following the situationist's train of reasoning, if people are not intrinsically evil, then the situations in which they find themselves somehow must "conspire" to make them act in evil ways.

Of course, I do not want to suggest that situational forces do not exert psychological and social pressures on individuals that can influence their chances of committing evil deeds. I believe that they do. My point is simply that the moralistic fallacy, perhaps inadvertently, leads theorists and laypeople alike to favor a type of "wishful thinking" account of evil in which the putative determinants of evildoing allow the belief holder to preserve a vision of humanity as basically good, much like many seem to hold onto a belief that the world is fundamentally a just place in which to live (Lerner, 1980). Aside from biasing descriptive accounts of evil, such motivational tendencies favor a kind of simplistic situationism that is all too willing to accept the default goodness of man—one that has also inadvertently provided an alibi to past and would-be evildoers (for an extended discussion of this issue, see Mandel, 1998; see also Berkowitz, 1999).

Obviously, the evolutionary perspective offered by Duntley and Buss (2004) is an exception to the social psychological rule. According to that view, what humans call evil is the result of genetic adaptations in our evolutionary history that favored such behavioral expressions. Situational and dispositional factors can affect the likelihood of such expressions, but the capacity for evildoing, much like the capacity for altruistic behavior, is an evolved characteristic within our species. Hence, there is no reason to view evildoing as the result of either abnormal conditions in the environment or deficiencies in the evildoer. Evil exists as part of the human behavioral repertoire because, in our evolutionary past, it had a net benefit on the reproductive fitness of those who carried out such acts.

The evolutionary perspective also strikingly differs from other accounts by proposing that evil-promoting and evil-mitigating strategies have coevolved. The view that emerges from this co-evolutionary pattern is highly dynamic. The benefits of engaging in acts that improve one's own reproductive fitness by harming others' reproductive fitness are counteracted by the harms that the perpetrator may, in turn, receive as a result of the victims' counteractions, which themselves reflect adaptations designed to protect against various forms of harm. For instance, killing competitors can bring severe repercussions to the perpetrator: Victims or their allies could injure or kill perpetrators in the process or at a later time; members of society could constrain the perpetrator's free movement (e.g., through imprisonment).

Adaptations to counter evil, as noted earlier, also involved developing the ability to categorize human actions in terms of good and evil. Such categorizations may have originally served an informational function, allowing humans to warn their kin and allies of others who may be likely to harm them. This would be an important precursor in many instances to invoking behavioral responses aimed at thwarting the would-be perpetrator's actions or taking retaliatory actions after the fact.

Over time, however, such communicative functions probably evolved into persuasion tactics that could be used to harm adversaries. By casting adversaries in a negative light, some individuals could motivate others to inflict harm on those labeled as evildoers. Language aimed at depersonalizing, dehumanizing, and or attempting to scapegoat others falls into this category of influence tactics. Indeed, prescriptive accounts of evildoing could be seen as attempts to outline a system of conduct that is aimed, broadly speaking, at reducing the likelihood of evildoing or setting the foundation for a system of punishment for those who commit evil transgressions.

The evolutionary perspective is also, in a broad sense, a social and organizational perspective. Evil reflects the basic fact that humans have, over their evolutionary history, been in competition for scarce resources. Their chances of procuring resources that would increase their evolutionary fitness—access to mates, natural resources, and so forth—could be increased by self-improvement or by damaging their competitors. The co-evolution of adaptive strategies for countering evil is, of course, "organizational" at the broadest level, as is the eventual mutation of some of those strategies for evil purposes (here, I am thinking of the influence tactics noted earlier). That is, these adaptations reflect the evolution of a coordinated response to intentional harm-inflictors.

THE LOCUS OF CORPORATE EVIL: CORPORATIONS VERSUS PERSONS

The foregoing discussion examined a variety of psychological perspectives on evil, most of which have yet to be applied to what might be called corporate evil—namely, evil acts that are committed by modern-day corporations. It would be tempting to move straight from that discussion to an extrapolation to the corporate case, but that would be premature. I do not think that we can take as a given what I suppose is the premise of this book—that there is such a thing as organizational evil—at least not if we are referring to corporations. Corporations are, after all, human constructions designed to serve human wants and desires. Whatever harm they may bring about seems, ultimately, to be the responsibility of people who play a role in the organization or in relation to it, such as its executives or stockholders.

One wonders, however, whether the corporation itself can be an evildoer. The corporation is most often, if not always, an intermediary in cases of harm. Of course, from a legal perspective, it may be that corporations have social obligations as entities or "legal persons" in their own right, but those legal conventions are themselves examples of human social organization. If humans created a shared reality in which corporations are "beings" with social or moral obligations, then that fact reflects something about the behavior of humans. However, it does not somehow turn the corporation into a moral being. I say this because, today, it appears that many people believe quite the opposite: that corporations, laws, proclamations about rights (especially those deemed to be of the "inalienable human" variety), and other abstractions are the stuff of which reality is made and that we humans are the undefined, malleable, almost hypothetical constructs, which are given shape by those structures.

Certainly, it is true that the organizations and conventions we create shape our thinking and behavior. Because each person living today was born into a world replete with complex organizations and legal frameworks at every level, from the municipal to the international, it is not difficult to see how one could forget that those structures have themselves developed over time, fully as a consequence of human social interaction. The long view backward that accompanies the evolutionary perspective could be a useful tool for disabusing oneself of the erroneous view that human social products are temporally and causally prior to humans themselves. Obviously, if we trace back far enough in human history, none of those products—those structures that both enable and constrain modern-day human expression—existed.

Thus, at a minimum, we ought to distinguish between the notion of evil perpetrated by corporations per se and evil perpetrated by individuals who do so in an organizational role or capacity—as a president, chief executive officer (CEO), or stockholder. The distinction is not merely academic because it is likely to affect our understanding of who (or dare I say *what*) should be responsible in cases of moral wrongdoing. If a corporation commits an act of evil as a consequence of its CEO's decision making, should the corporation as a whole be held accountable or only the executive?

The CEO, after all, is an employee of the corporation—the agent in a principal-agent relationship, in which the stockholders represent the principals. As Milton Friedman put it:

> In a free-enterprise, private-property system, a corporate executive is an employee of the owners of the business. He has direct responsibility to his employers. That responsibility is to conduct the business in accordance with their desires, which generally will be to make as much money as possible while conforming to the basic rules of the society, both those embodied in law and those embodied in ethical custom. (1970, 1)

Thus, the proper locus of responsibility seems to depend on the degree to which the executive was acting in accordance with the stakeholders' wishes. If the stakeholders expressed a desire to employ proper risk-mitigating procedures that might prevent certain types of foreseeable harm caused by the corporation's activities, and the CEO failed to implement those procedures because he wanted to increase profits even more substantially (perhaps since his own earnings were pegged to corporate profits), then the CEO should be responsible for any evil that ensued as a result of his decision making.

If, however, the stockholders instructed an executive to cut corners in order to maximize profits, then their share of the responsibility would appreciably increase and the CEO's responsibility would conversely decrease. Whether it ought to be eliminated completely depends on one's personal theory of social obligations. Does an executive have social responsibilities in addition to his responsibility to the principals? Certainly, even a laissez-fair capitalist such as Friedman notes that an executive is expected to conform to the "basic rules of the society, both those embodied in law and those embodied in ethical custom." Corporate executives cannot simply avoid responsibility because they were "just following orders." Some orders are illegal; others are legal but of dubious moral stature.

If a corporation's stakeholders are found to be at fault for a case of corporate evil, are all stakeholders equally responsible? Stakeholders who vote against an evil measure implemented by the majority of stakeholders seem to fit the category of righteous objectors more than evildoers. Are two stakeholders who support the same evil measure evil to the same extent if one holds 1 percent of the company's stocks and the other holds 10 percent? And how might the answer to that question change if the latter held 51 percent instead, thus having majority power?

The foregoing questions should highlight some of the difficulties that arise when we move from a notion of corporate evil in which the corporation as a single entity is considered as a potential evildoer to a notion of corporate evil in which specific individuals with roles in relation to the corporation are assigned responsibility. Attributing evil to corporations rather than apportioning it to persons acting in relation to corporations may be a suboptimal solution, but it certainly helps to simplify discussion of evil in the corporate context. This is most often the case for attributions levied by the general public, who may have little or no knowledge of the individuals acting on behalf of the corporations under scrutiny.

EVIL IN THE CORPORATE CONTEXT: EVIL WITHOUT MALICE

Even if one maintains that corporate evil is the moral responsibility of certain individuals, it strikes me that the drivers of evil, and indeed the expression of evil, may be quite different in the corporate context. Examples of evil considered in psychological literature on the topic often focus on violent crimes, such as murder, rape, and torture. In these cases, the perception of evil will be a function of both consequence and intent. In terms of consequence, as noted earlier, the more excessive the harm inflicted, the more likely the act will be labeled evil. In terms of intent, most theorists (e.g., Darley, 1992; Duntley and Buss, 2004) agree that, all else being equal, intentional acts are regarded as more evil than unintentional acts. Intentional acts that cause great harm to the victim and yet seem to yield little or fleeting benefit to the perpetrator are what most observers would regard as prototypically evil. This combination of factors tends to create a feeling that the acts committed were senseless, monstrous, or both. Instigators of collective violence such as Hitler and Stalin fall into this category, as would serial killers such as Ted Bundy in the United States and Robert "Willie" Pickton in Canada (the former pig farmer from Port Coquitlam, British Columbia, who was convicted of second-degree murders of six women, charged in the deaths of an additional twenty women, and believed to be implicated in the deaths of yet others).

In the corporate context, examples of evildoing are different. They, too, involve harm, but the harm produced often seems to be an incidental rather than an intended consequence. Greed rather than malice appears to be the driving motive for corporate evil. Perhaps, more precisely, one could say that evil in the corporate world is usually the result of an unbridled desire for profit maximization. When the corporate activities leading to profit making involve serious risks of harm to others, a singular focus on maximizing profit increases the likelihood that proper risk-mitigating measures will not be implemented. Greed increases the likelihood that the foreseeability of harm to others—even in extreme forms—will be insufficient to lead corporate decision makers to avoid it, especially when the harm is perceived to be improbable.

Of course, foreseeable harm is not the same as intentional harm. In the latter case, the victimization that arises is often part of the perpetrator's goal, which is why evil by individuals as principals often reflects an act of malice. In contrast, in the corporate context, evil is a by-product of other goals, such as profit maximization. In these cases, the perpetrator would usually prefer that the evil act had not occurred, much as a reckless driver would prefer not to cause a fatality. Nevertheless, negligence implies moral responsibility since it involves reasonably foreseeable risk brought about by a lack of due care in behavior (D'Arcy, 1963; Hart, 1968; Mackie, 1977). Not surprisingly, actors who commit intentional harm tend to be seen as more morally responsible for their behaviors than those who commit unintentional negligent harm, but the latter, in turn, tend to be seen as more responsible than those who commit accidental harm (Karlovac and Darley, 1989; Shultz and Wright, 1985).

Extrapolating from these findings, one might hypothesize that attributions of evil would follow the same pattern, in which case one might also expect there to be fewer attributions of evildoing in the corporate context than in situations where harm is brought about intentionally. In cases where attributions of evil are assigned in the corporate world, the magnitude of harm caused will probably be severe, because negligence culminating in moderate harm seems inconsistent with the sense of excessiveness that is central to the notion of evil.

One might further predict that companies that cause multiple acts of harm through negligence or misconduct are also more likely to be labeled evil than ones that cause one-time harm, except perhaps when the single case constituted a sustained event that itself appeared to be unnecessarily prolonged or consisting of a series of minicases. Multiple or sustained acts of negligence or misconduct indicate a pattern that reflects a conscious (and callous) disregard for human safety or the environment in which we live. A willingness by a corporate perpetrator to tolerate the conditions that led to past evils lends itself to the perception of the corporation and its representatives as contemptuous and remorseless, perceptions that seem fitting to the label "evildoer."

Safety warnings by frontline employees at risk of harm that go uncorrected because of their costs or slowdown effects on production seem to fit the profile of corporate evil. The BP-Transocean Deepwater Horizon oil rig explosion in 2010, which killed eleven workers and led to the largest oil spill in U.S. territory, provides a modern case in point. A confidential survey of rig employees conducted only weeks before the explosion revealed widespread concern over safety, with about half of respondents indicating that they did not feel as if they could voice concerns over risks without repercussions (Urbina, 2010). In a similar vein, the Exxon *Valdez* oil spill in Alaska in 1989 has been blamed in part on a failure to repair the ship's sonar, which was known to be broken for over a year before the disaster but which Exxon's management deemed too expensive to fix (Palast, 1999).

As we move from cases in which corporations tolerate probable harm to ones in which they contribute knowingly—or even worse, enthusiastically—to certain harm, we concurrently move up the staircase of evil. Companies that willfully exploit the vulnerable (e.g., by using child laborers) or destroy that which is irreplaceable (e.g., by contributing to species extinction or rainforest destruction) serve as good examples. It would appear that Darley's (1992) notion of egregious excess plays a role here too. For example, it has been easier for animal rights activists to change public opinion to a perception of the fur industry as evil than it has to do the same to the animal farming industry. Because the latter produces food products that most people regard as necessary for survival, and on which they accordingly depend, it is not surprising that the food industry elicits little moral outrage, except by committed activists. Killing animals, such as seals, for their fur seems excessive and utterly cruel to a much larger segment of the population.

Companies that directly enable other evildoers to do intentional harm are also well up the staircase of evil. IBM's critical role in providing Nazi Germany with the technology to stratify the German population and, later, the populations of occupied countries is, without a doubt, one of the worst cases of corporate evil ever committed. As Edwin Black describes in his book *IBM and the Holocaust: The Strategic Alliance Between Nazi Germany and America's Most Powerful Corporation*, Thomas John Watson Sr., IBM's first president, licensed to the Nazis, through its German subsidiary, Dehomag, the punch card and sorter technology that was used to "identify, sort, and quantify the population to separate Jews from Aryans" (2001, 47).

The evil in this case has many contributing factors. First, of course, is the scale of the harm perpetrated. IBM's technology was a direct enabler of the Holocaust, which led to the murder of approximately six million Jews. Second, the technology would not have been available in IBM's absence, as it did not have any competitors on the market at the time that could have done so instead. Thus like instigators of collective violence themselves (Mandel, 2002b), IBM played a noninterchangeable role in bring about this human catastrophe. Though a refusal by IBM to support the Nazi regime would not have prevented the Holocaust altogether, it would almost certainly would have greatly slowed down the ability of the Nazis to perpetrate genocide. Without that technology, the Nazis simply would not have been able to efficiently and effectively identify and refine the classification of Jews and other undesirables that they targeted for extermination. Third, Watson knew what the technology was being used for and spoke openly in defense of Germany's right to govern in a manner of its own choosing. Indeed, Hitler created the second-most-prestigious medal in Nazi Germany, the Merit Cross of the German Eagle with Star, for Watson to, as Black quotes from a July 2, 1937, *New York Times* article, "honor foreign nationals who made themselves deserving of the German Reich" (2001, 131). Finally, not only did Watson aid the Nazis knowingly and for a staggering profit, but he did so in violation of U.S. law, which at the time prohibited doing business with Germany.

THE ROLE OF VALUE TRADEOFFS IN UNDERSTANDING EVIL: THE CASE OF GOOGLE

Both the psychological literature on evil, which has mainly focused on evil that takes the form of interpersonal or collective violence (e.g., Baumeister, 1997; Miller, 2004; Newman and Erber, 2002; Staub, 1989), and the foregoing discussion of corporate evil suggest that the evildoer is usually faced with a value tradeoff in which the satisfaction of some form of selfish interest is exchanged for harm to one or more others. For instance, in Duntley and Buss's (2004) evolutionary account, the evildoer seeks to increase his or her genetic fitness by impeding the fitness of competitors. In Baumeister and Vohs's (2004) account, the evildoer seeks to satisfy impulsive desires that involve harming others. And, likewise, in the foregoing discussion of corporate evil, I suggest that the evildoer often seeks to maximize profit at the cost of harm to others.

In all these descriptions, the evildoer is portrayed as one who experiences little conflict over the value tradeoff. Moreover, the evildoer resolves the tradeoff in what, from a communal perspective, is surely "the wrong way." It is not merely that the evildoer has caused harm but that his indifferent and remorseless attitude toward the harm caused is itself felt by others as a violation of sacred, communal values—or, more simply, as inhuman. Not only does the evildoer experience little conflict but he experiences what others regard as *insufficient* conflict, both before and after having made the immoral choice.

The attribution of evil, therefore, is influenced not only by the manner in which observers perceive an actor's deeds and their objective consequences but also by how observers perceive and evaluate the propriety of the actor's feelings and attitude regarding those deeds and their consequences. Perhaps because feelings seem to be less controllable than behavior, they seem to provide better indicators of the essential qualities of the actor and thus a better test of whether the actor possesses the quantum of evil.

In concluding this chapter, I reflect briefly on another characterization of evil that has gained some attention in the corporate realm in recent years, largely as a result of Google's use of the term "evil" in outlining its corporate code of conduct, which I discuss below. In contrast to the view just described, that characterization suggests that there may also be such a thing as a "conflicted evildoer"—one who knowingly commits evil but does so because he believes it to be the lesser of evils among a set of evil options. The individual who, facing considerable moral conflict (see Mandel and Vartanian, 2008), lets one person die so that five others can be saved represents this type of "evildoer." Indeed, most of us would not consider the individual in this moral dilemma an evildoer at all and might even feel sorry for that person because of having to make the choice. The political ethics of value tradeoffs between civil liberties and national security in the post–9/11 world have also been described in terms of choosing the lesser evil (Ignatieff, 2004).

Google originally adopted the motto "Don't be evil" to describe its overarching corporate philosophy. In an initial public offering letter, Google cofounders Larry Page and Sergey Brin (2004) stated:

> *Don't be evil. We believe strongly that in the long term, we will be better served—as shareholders and in all other ways—by a company that does good things for the world even if we forgo some short term gains.*

The "don't be evil" creed strikes one as an absolutist injunction: be good, not evil. However, Google's confrontation with China over censorship issues led to a moral conflict, which prompted a more moderated "lesser evil" perspective. When Google decided to enter the Chinese market in spite of China's censorship of "unauthorized sites," it realized it was about to commit a form of evil by complying with the government's authoritarian demands. Google justified its subsequent actions, arguing that it had committed the lesser evil because, for the Chinese population, restricted access to information was better than no access at all. As Google CEO Eric Schmidt explained at the 2006 Davos conference,

> We concluded that although we weren't wild about the restrictions, it was even worse to not try to serve those users at all. We actually did an evil scale *[sic]* and decided not to serve at all was worse evil. (quoted in Paczkowski, 2010)

Google's moral wrangling is interesting for a couple of reasons. First, it illustrates that considerations of evil do play a role in the corporate context. Second, the Google example illustrates that such considerations are not "only" moral but also strategic. As cofounders Page and Brin made clear in their earlier quotation, they believe that a philosophy that emphasizes communal values will benefit stockholders in the long run. In other words, corporate greed, according to them, is a flawed model for long-term success. Shermer (2008) contrasts Google and Enron, arguing that Google's success and Enron's failure reflect their choice of different evolutionary strategies. Although both companies ultimately exist in a competitive environment, Enron favored fierce competition, even internally among its employees. Google favors communal principles such as reciprocity, fairness, and cooperation.

FINAL REMARKS

The view of the evildoer as a morally conflicted character is itself an interesting one to consider, given our entry point. That is, if the essence of evil is excessive harm, then how can we reconcile this notion with one of the evildoer who tries to minimize harm? How can the same term be applied to individuals who seem devoid of moral consideration and, as well, to those who seem to honestly wrestle with moral dilemmas in an attempt to do as good as humanly possible? Perhaps it speaks to the ambiguity of the concept of evil. Perhaps, though, an analysis of that ambiguity will itself reveal important aspects of how we think about the morality of others and ourselves.

A program of research on our understanding of evil is long overdue. In psychology, there are a handful of scholars whose work on the social psychological determinants of collective violence sometimes falls under the "psychology of evil" banner (for an overview, see Miller, 2004). That body of literature, however, does not address in any empirical manner how people understand the term "evil" in different cultures and contexts. The fact that the meaning of the term is itself hard to pin down suggests that it is a multidimensional construct. Future research could, for instance, investigate the "factor structure" of the construct by having people rate both the extent to which various attributes of evil are present or absent in different cases and the extent to which the focal acts in the cases are judged to be evil.

The present chapter suggests some possible attributes to investigate: egregious harm, depraved harm, fitness costs to the victim, fitness costs to the victim's genes, accepting foreseeable risks to others or the environment, greed, the degree of accompanying moral conflict, and so forth. A study such as that would also shed light on redundancies in these attributes by allowing researchers to examine the intercorrelations of the various attribute ratings. If the cases were structured in a systematic way—for instance, by keeping a number of factors constant but changing the context from, say, individual harm to corporate harm—then studies along these lines could also shed valuable light on how perceived attributes of evil change across contexts.

The definitional problems associated with the concept of evil make it a poor scientific construct. I suspect that will not change. However, the enduring legacy of the construct also indicates that it occupies a fairly stable position in our collective consciousness. That fact alone makes it worthy of study as a social psychological and organizational phenomenon.

REFERENCES

Alford, C.F. 1997. The political psychology of evil. *Political Psychology*, 18, 1–17.

Baumeister, R.F. 1997. *Evil: Inside Human Violence and Cruelty*. New York: Freeman.

Baumeister, R.F., and K.D. Vohs. 2004. The four roots of evil. In *The Social Psychology of Good and Evil*, ed. A.G. Miller, 85–101. New York: Guilford Press.

Berkowitz, L. 1999. Evil is more than banal: Situationism and the concept of evil. *Personality and Social Psychology Review*, 3, 246–253.

Black, E. 2001. *IBM and the Holocaust: The Strategic Alliance Between Nazi Germany and America's Most Powerful Corporation*. New York: Crown.

D'Arcy, E. 1963. *Human Acts: An Essay in Their Moral Evaluation*. Oxford: Clarendon.

Darley, J.M. 1992. Social organization for the production of evil. *Psychological Inquiry*, 3, 199–218.

Davis, B.D. 1978. The moralistic fallacy. *Nature*, 272, 5652, 390.

Dorn, A.W., D.R. Mandel, and R. Cross. 2012. Expert Survey of Justifications for Armed Conflict and War. Manuscript in preparation. Defence R&D Canada-Toronto.

Duntley, J.D., and D.M. Buss. 2004. The evolution of evil. In *The Social Psychology of Good and Evil*, ed. A.G. Miller, 102–123. New York: Guilford Press.

Friedman, M. 1970. The social responsibility of business is to increase its profits. *New York Times Magazine*, September 13. www.colorado.edu/studentgroups/libertarians/issues/friedman-soc-resp-business.html.

Hart, H.L.A. 1968. *Punishment and Responsibility*. Oxford: Clarendon.

Hume, D. 1739. *A Treatise of Human Nature*. London: John Noon.

Ignatieff, M. 2004. *The Lesser Evil: Political Ethics in an Age of Terror*. Toronto: Penguin.

International Commission on Intervention and State Sovereignty. 2001. The Responsibility to Protect. Report, December. Ottawa. www.iciss.ca/report2-en.asp.

Karlovac, M., and J.M. Darley. 1989. Attribution of responsibility for accidents: A negligence law analogy. *Social Cognition*, 4, 287–318.

Lerner, M.J. 1980. *The Belief in a Just World: A Fundamental Delusion*. New York: Plenum Press.

Mackie, J.J. 1977. *Ethics: Inventing Right and Wrong*. New York: Penguin.

Mandel, D.R. 1998. The obedience alibi: Milgram's account of the Holocaust reconsidered. *Analyse & Kritik: Zeitschrift fur Sozialwissenschaften*, 20, 74–94.

———. 2002a. Evil and the instigation of collective violence. *Analyses of Social Issues and Public Policy*, 2, 101–108.

———. 2002b. Instigators of genocide: Examining Hitler from a social psychological perspective. In *Understanding Genocide: The Social Psychology of the Holocaust*, ed. L.S. Newman and R. Erber, 259–284. New York: Oxford University Press.

———. 2010. Radicalization: What does it mean? In *Home-Grown Terrorism: Understanding and Addressing the Root Causes of Radicalisation Among Groups with an Immigrant Heritage in Europe*, ed. T.M. Pick, A. Speckhard, and B. Jacuch, 101–113. Amsterdam: IOS Press.

Mandel, D.R., and O. Vartanian. 2008. Taboo or tragic: Effect of tradeoff type on moral choice, conflict, and confidence. *Mind and Society*, 7, 215–226.

Milgram, S. 1974. *Obedience to Authority: An Experimental View*. New York: Harper and Row.

Miller, A.G. 2004. *The Social Psychology of Good and Evil*. New York: Guilford Press.

Moore, G.E. 1903. *Principia Ethica*. Cambridge: Cambridge University Press.

Newman, L.S., and R. Erber. 2002. *Understanding Genocide: The Social Psychology of the Holocaust*. New York: Oxford University Press.

Paczkowski, J. 2010. Chinese scientists recalibrate Google's evil scale. CNET News, February 26. http://news.cnet.com/8301-1023_3-10460345-93.html.

Page, L., and S. Brin. 2004. "An owner's manual" for Google shareholders. Google.com. http://investor.google.com/corporate/2004/ipo-founders-letter.html.

Palast, G. 1999. Ten years after but who was to blame? *Guardian/The Observer,* March 21. www.gregpalast.com/ten-years-after-but-who-was-to-blame/.

Ross, L., and R.E. Nisbett. 1991. *The Person and the Situation: Perspectives of Social Psychology.* New York: McGraw-Hill.

Sandman, P. 1989. Hazard versus outrage in the public perception of risk. In *Effective Risk Communication: The Role and Responsibility of Government and Nongovernment Organizations,* ed. V.T. Covello, D.B. McCallum, and M.T. Pavlova, 45–49. New York: Plenum Press.

Shermer, M. 2008. Don't be evil. *Scientific American Mind,* 19, 58–65.

Shultz, T.R., and K. Wright. 1985. Concepts of negligence and intention in the assignment of moral responsibility. *Canadian Journal of Behavioural Science,* 17, 97–108.

Slovic, P. 1987. Perception of risk. *Science,* 236, 280–285.

Staub, E. 1989. *The Roots of Evil: The Origins of Genocide and Other Group Violence.* New York: Cambridge University Press.

Tetlock, P.E. 2002. Social-functionalist frameworks for judgment and choice: The intuitive politician, theologian, and prosecutor. *Psychological Review,* 109, 451–472.

Urbina, I. 2010. Workers on doomed rig voiced concern about safety. *New York Times,* July 21. www.nytimes.com/2010/07/22/us/22transocean.html?pagewanted=all.

Whitehead, A.N. 1925/1997. *Science and the Modern World.* New York: Free Press.

Zimbardo, P.G. 2004. A situationist perspective on the psychology of evil: Understanding how good people are transformed into perpetrators. In *The Social Psychology of Good and Evil,* ed. A.G. Miller, 102–123. New York: Guilford Press.

Part II

Understanding Organizational Evil

6

Power in Organizations

Good vs. Evil

Arthur D. Martinez, Gerald R. Ferris,
Miriam Moeller, and Michael Harvey

Organizations need to develop a priority for addressing the evil use of power.

—Claudia Card (2002)

Organizational scholars seem to have a fascination with studying "bad" behavior by managers. Of course, in their defense, they would argue that there is so much bad, evil, dysfunctional behavior in organizations that we would be remiss as scientists if we failed to address such behavior. Whether it is a concern with the "dark side" or political behavior in organizations (e.g., Griffin and O'Leary-Kelly, 2004; Perryman, Sikora, and Ferris, 2010), unethical or just plain mean or evil bosses (Byrne, 2003; Dunlap, 1996), leaders as bullies (e.g., Ferris, Zinko, Brouer, Buckley, and Harvey, 2007; Harvey, Buckley, Heames, Zinko, Brouer, and Ferris, 2007), or the transformation of otherwise good people into mean and sadistic creatures (Milgram, 1969; Zimbardo, 2007), we perhaps have never witnessed greater interest in the "dark side" issues in organizations.

If there is an increase in "dark side" behavior, it may be a function of organizations' tendency to attract, select, and retain seemingly "impaired" managers, in whom impairment speaks to their dysfunctional nature as manifested in their psychological, cognitive, and behavioral characteristics. These dysfunctional characteristics can derive from several personality disorders or learning disabilities: (1) general personality disorders or learning disabilities; (2) borderline personality disorder; (3) bipolar disorder; (4) diminished learning capacity and dementia; (5) obsessive-compulsive behavior; and (6) destructive/dysfunctional employees. The argument we make is that a continuous state of dysfunctionality (i.e., a continued exposure to and accumulation of personality disorders or learning disabilities) will eventually lead to a pool of managers in supervisory positions who manage with malicious/evil as opposed to good intentions.

The notion of evil (i.e., malevolence, misuse of power, and abuse) is triggered by the accumulation and persistence of personality disorders or learning disabilities. An evil or destructive manager might follow a scheme of repeated and malicious behaviors that are in direct opposition to the organization's goals (Einarsen, Aasland, and Skogstad,

105

2007). The relationship between personality disorders or learning disabilities and evil is not unimportant as the dynamics present an issue that is not atypical in today's organizational context. The fact that these disabilities are commonly portrayed as basic concerns to modern society provides further evidence that these personality disorders or learning disabilities are part of the root cause of the evil power exercised in organizations today.

The ongoing impact of these disabilities represents challenging issues, which must be addressed with caution to the extent they may affect other employees, whether peers, superiors, or subordinates. Therefore, we are suggesting that a continuous state of dysfunctionality may spill over to other levels in the organization, such as teams, departments, and the organization itself, and ultimately result in what could potentially be a plethora of counterproductive work behaviors. In an attempt to address these dynamics, the chapter proceeds as follows. First, we briefly address the various personality disorders or learning abilities and their impact on the formation of evil managers. Second, by means of an empirical study, we attempt to describe and clarify a set of antecedents of evilness and its antithesis, goodness. Third, we provide ideas for identifying and testing for dysfunctional managers in the hiring of managers. Finally, implications and future research directions are offered.

PERSONALITY DISORDERS OR LEARNING DISABILITIES AND THEIR IMPACT ON EVIL

General Learning Disabilities

Learning disabilities may be categorized as follows: (1) arithmetic disability (AD); (2) reading disability (RD); and (3) reading and arithmetic disability (RAD). Lyon (1994) indicates that individuals categorized into these groups significantly differ when using standardized testing assessments such as reading, spelling, memory, and other cognitive measures. The variation in these types of learning disabilities is great, and thus it requires focused attention to identify the type of disability the individual has. If this is not identified and addressed, it can complicate the continued development of managerial competencies.

Ultimately, the repercussions of learning disabilities may be visible in the organization, as managers, with their falsely advertised level of competency (i.e., in reading, writing, or arithmetic), are destined to become characterized by a strong need for the justification of their position caused by a continuous striving to overcome low self-esteem. The managers' façade might put the organization at a disadvantage, as the managers' actions could be destructive or deleterious (i.e., evil), rather than positive (i.e., good).

Borderline Personality Disorder

Common characteristics of individuals diagnosed with borderline personality disorder include: (1) showing excessive anxiety/emotional instability; (2) irritability; (3) being erratic; (4) being hypocritical; (5) indifference; (6) being overprotective of their personal power; and (7) overindulgence of the same. The characteristics of borderline personality disorder can manifest under circumstances in which managers sense a personal attack on their character or status. For example, the culmination of excessive amounts of information or uncertainty about one's future in the organization, or the future of the organization itself, can activate psychological/cognitive/behavioral processes that inhibit a "healthy" adaptation to new surroundings (see Andrews, Stewart, Morris-Yates, Holt, and Henderson, 1990).

Given the state of hypercompetitiveness in today's work environments, it appears to be more likely that the fast pace of business and ambiguities encountered may lead to feelings of anxiety, contributing to enhanced irritability and erratic behaviors. This argument sets the foundation for the notion that a perceived inability to perform as initially hoped may lead to frustrations that are then acted out in terms of "evil" behaviors toward other employees.

Bipolar Disorder

Bipolarity is a manic–depressive state (Johnson, 2005) that may interfere with a person's ability to fulfill self-imposed or externally determined responsibilities. The disorder is grounded in the idea that episodes of disturbances in mood not only are recurrent but may be diagnosed to the degree to which they occur. Clinically speaking, bipolar disorder is composed of two groups (i.e., Bipolar I and II), which allows for the distinction between different rates of mood swings. Bipolarity and borderline personality disorder are related in that the more frequent the emotional episodes become, the more likely it is for individuals to be classified as possessing borderline personality disorder due to the stable psychological nature of personality (Kernberg and Michels, 2009). The frequency with which these neurotic emotional behaviors occur influences the destructive state of managers.

Diminished Learning Capacity and Dementia

Experiencing a diminished learning capacity appears to be a common denominator among many societies. The deterioration of the learning/intellectual capacity is a process that worsens over time and is difficult to address in a society to halt. For example, the loss of memory and concentration can damage managers' level of self-confidence in their ability to fulfill the responsibilities required by the organization—indicating that there is a relationship between learning/intellectual capacity and self-efficacy/self-esteem.

Similarly, dementia refers to situations in which managers experience a serious loss of cognitive ability beyond what is expected of an aging person. One of the many causes of dementia may be that managers may not be exposed to a very stimulating environment or one fosters creative and continuous learning which in turn may help to bring on the occurrence of dementia, especially in older workers. Managers who show signs of diminished intellectual capabilities or dementia are likely to entrench themselves in the organization, using most of their efforts to justify their presence and participation. As a result, they inhibit the organization from being productive by their unwillingness/inability to admit their deteriorating cognitive state.

Obsessive-Compulsive Behavior

Obsessive-compulsive disorder (OCD) refers to behaviors that are continuous, repetitive, inflexible, and unchanging and that are likely to increase with the level of stress in one's environment. For example, a constant concern over the cleanliness of one's surroundings can indicate a case of OCD that might lead to lower levels of performance over time and lead managers' of such employees to feel frustration because they are not able to achieve their planned objectives and consequently take out their frustration on other employees.

ANTECEDENTS TO GOOD AND EVIL

Scholarly interest in bad behavior in organizations, either implicitly or explicitly, focuses on the root cause or inferences about intentionality of such behavior. Interest in good versus evil as causes of human behavior has long been evident in the literature (e.g., Miller, 2004). Furthermore, it is clear that imputed motives or intentions strongly affect not only the perception and interpretation of behavior in organizations but also others' reactions to it (e.g., Fedor, Eder, and Buckley, 1989; Ferris, Bhawuk, Fedor, and Judge, 1995). The question is: Why do managers engage in behaviors considered evil when managing others in an organization—is dysfunctional, destructive, evil behavior a learned behavior or is it caused by personality/learning disabilities?

Evil has two foundations. The first foundation of evil involves the shadow archetype, first theorized by Carl G. Jung. With regard to the notion of evil, the American poet Robert Bly said, "the shadow energies remain a part of or belong to the human community," but "there may be powers in the universe outside the human community and hostile to the human community" (1988, 59). Hence, the first foundation of evil involves the shadow energies (or the shadow archetype), and the second foundation involves hostile powers outside of the human community.

Organizational power is appropriate to investigate in the context of good and evil because power has the potential to be both constructive and destructive, for the person who wields it and others. Most of us have heard that "power corrupts, and absolute power corrupts absolutely," which implies that power itself might be evil. Yet others have drawn on arguments such as "the finger pulls the trigger" in order to maintain that evil is something that emanates from people, not from power per se. We draw on Carl G. Jung's theory of archetypes to view evil as a kind of instinctual intolerance to potential human tendencies (i.e., the shadow archetype). So, perhaps both of the previous arguments are valid because both actors and their social structures are affected by the shadow archetype.

In this chapter, we were compelled to consider negative managerial behavior that might be associated with the evil use of power. Thus, we relied on the fact that evil is the necessary opposite of good (i.e., a result of the structure of the human psyche). We reasoned that antithesis factors of the well-known supervisory dimensions "Initiating Structure" and "Consideration" would probably suffice. Our intuition paid off as the results of a vignette study supported our claims. In short, one primary contribution of this study is to attempt to provide a more concrete conceptualization of evil managerial behavior. We discuss important implications of our research for organizations and offer suggestions for future research on the topic.

THEORY AND HYPOTHESES

The Collective Unconscious and Archetypes

Carl G. Jung (1959, 3–4) theorized that a collective unconscious is inborn in all of us. The collective unconscious is universal, such that it exists in everyone and its contents are the same. The contents of the collective unconscious consist of archetypes. Archetypes are "patterns of instinctual behavior" (44). Continuous repetitions of "typical situations in life" eventually engraved these experiences onto the psyche, primarily in the form of possible types of perception and action. Now, when a typical situation in life occurs, the corresponding archetype is activated, and something like an instinctual drive can override all reason and will.

The Shadow Archetype and Evil

According to Jung, "The shadow personifies everything that the subject refuses to acknowledge about himself and yet is always thrusting itself upon him directly or indirectly—for instance, inferior traits of character and other incompatible tendencies" (1959, 284–285). Content that individuals refuse to acknowledge can be based on personal experience (i.e., things that they have learned are intolerable) or collective experience (i.e., things that are instinctively intolerable). Indeed, the parts of the shadow that go far beyond anything personal can be compared to the principle of evil (322).

The human psyche is structured in a polar structure, an energetic system dependent on the tension of opposites—namely, between the conscious and unconscious. According to Jung (1959), evil is the necessary opposite of good, which means that good could not exist without evil and vice versa. Therefore, an understanding of good facilitates an understanding of evil. We use this principle later to develop the types of supervisory behavior most likely associated with evil. Another useful aspect of the shadow is that it is commonly projected onto the environment (e.g., onto a suitable person).

Good and Evil Use of Power

Of course, there are numerous "typical situations in life" and hence just as many archetypes. "Supervising" or leading others is unquestionably a typical situation in life, so it must have an archetype. Indeed, popular media has elaborated on the subject. For example, Robert Moore and Douglas Gillette (1990) described a "king" archetype as possessing two general functions: "ordering" (e.g., organizing reality from chaos) and "providing fertility and blessing" (e.g., creating and affirming those who are deserving). Coincidentally, these functions are comparable to the two supervisory behavioral dimensions identified in the Ohio State Leadership Studies.

The Ohio State Leadership Studies (Stogdill and Coons, 1957) took a behavioral approach to studying leadership, finding that Initiating Structure and Consideration were important behavioral dimensions. Initiating Structure is associated with the establishment of things like work roles, goals, and communication. Consideration includes behavior associated with things such as respecting others, looking out for others' welfare, showing appreciation, and providing support. The validity of these factors has been relatively robust over diverse samples. For example, the meta-analyses carried out by Judge and colleagues (2004) confirmed that Consideration and Initiating Structure were significantly related to important and positive leadership outcomes (e.g., job satisfaction and performance). In sum, Initiating Structure and Consideration are classes of behavior that are typically associated with "good" supervision.

Power

Power can be defined in various ways. For example, Tjosvold and Wisse (2009) listed several alternative viewpoints: It can be defined as the "potential" to influence, overcome resistance, affect outcomes, or bring about a desired change or as the "actual" influence or overcoming of resistance. The use of power is a crucial aspect of supervision as it reveals the state of the dual nature of power: Power is potentially creative and destructive. Winter (2009) described several ways to tame power, including the use of love, reason, religion, and responsibility. Naturally, most organizations wish to manage the use of power, but the first step is the measurement of the use of power. We propose one way to measure the use of power: via the semantic differential poles of good and evil. Antecedents of a "good" use of power likely involve positive supervisory behavior. As explained above, the dimensions Initiating Structure and Consideration are typically associated with positive supervision. Therefore, we formulate the following hypotheses:

Hypothesis 1: Initiating Structure is positively related to the "good" use of power.
Hypothesis 2: Consideration is positively related to the "good" use of power.

Note that we do not imply that the mere lack of Initiating Structure and Consideration necessarily indicates the "evil" use of power. Other, more negative, behavior is necessary before the use of power is deemed "evil." Which supervisory behavioral dimensions might be associated with evil use of power? Given that evil is the necessary opposite of good, and assuming that Initiating Structure and Consideration are associated with good use of power, we propose dimensions that are directly opposed to Initiating Structure and Consideration. One opposite dimension to Initiating Structure could be labeled Destroying Structure. One opposite dimension to Consideration could be labeled Aggression. Therefore, we hypothesize that:

Hypothesis 3: Destroying Structure is positively related to the "evil" use of power.
Hypothesis 4: Aggression is positively related to the "evil" use of power.

Again, we are not implying that the lack of these dimensions necessarily indicates good use of power. Furthermore, we suggest that subordinates provide the data concerning their supervisors (i.e., supervisors should not provide data about themselves) because the shadow archetype is normally projected onto suitable others. In other words, people are not likely to identify with evil consciously but are likely to project evil onto someone else. Also, attentive observers can more objectively detect another's actual behavior—the unconscious has a way of influencing the actor's behavior without his awareness (Jung, 1959).

METHOD

Sample

A convenient sample ($n = 44$) was used that consisted of undergraduate students (majoring in business administration) at a large public university in the southeastern United States. The average age of the respondents was twenty-two. About 40 percent were female. We asked respondents to use their imagination to place themselves in the hypothetical situation portrayed in the scenario. Therefore, although we did not require the respondents to necessarily possess and draw from their own personal experiences with particular supervisors with whom they might currently be working, it could collectively draw from their prior work experiences.

Specifically, our instructions were: "Please carefully read the short scenario concerning a hypothetical supervisor, then answer the question about how you think the supervisor is using his/her power." Our two research designs relied upon responses to short vignettes. The first design (good use of power) incorporated four vignettes representing the most essential scenarios: low and high Initiating Structure × low and high Consideration. Similarly, the second design (evil use of power) also incorporated four vignettes: low and high Destroying Structure × low and high Aggression. For each of the two designs, only one of the four scenarios was randomly selected and presented to respondents.

Variables

Use of Power

A one-item measure was used to capture the good or evil use of power. The item was "The supervisor uses his/her power for:" with the endpoints 1 = "good" to 9 = "evil," and the midpoint 5 = "neither or neutral." The statements used to construct the scenarios for Initiating Structure and Consideration were inspired by some of the items from the questionnaire designed by Stogdill and Coons (1957).

Initiating Structure

The statement developed to represent a scenario of high Initiating Structure was "The supervisor frequently assigns employees to particular tasks. The supervisor frequently lets employees know what is expected of them. And the supervisor frequently schedules the work to be done." Alternatively, the statement representing low Initiating Structure was "The supervisor rarely assigns employees to particular tasks. The supervisor rarely lets employees know what is expected of them. And the supervisor rarely schedules the work to be done."

Consideration

The statement corresponding to high Consideration was "The supervisor frequently appears to look out for the personal welfare of employees. The supervisor frequently finds time to listen to employees. And the supervisor frequently appears friendly and approachable." The statement corresponding to low Consideration was "The supervisor rarely appears to look out for the personal welfare of employees. The supervisor rarely finds time to listen to employees. And the supervisor rarely appears friendly and approachable."

Destroying Structure

The statement constructed to represent a scenario of high Destroying Structure was "The supervisor frequently assigns employees to vague or unreasonable tasks. The supervisor frequently conceals what is expected of employees. And the supervisor frequently complicates or disarranges the work to be done." Alternatively, the statement representing low Initiating Structure was "The supervisor rarely assigns employees to vague or unreasonable tasks. The supervisor rarely conceals what is expected of employees. And the supervisor rarely complicates or disarranges the work to be done."

Aggression

High level of Aggression was represented with "The supervisor frequently appears to threaten the personal welfare of employees. The supervisor frequently appears to ignore employees. And the supervisor frequently appears unfriendly and unapproachable." The low level of Aggression was represented by "The supervisor rarely appears to threaten the personal welfare of employees. The supervisor rarely appears to ignore employees. And the supervisor rarely appears unfriendly and unapproachable."

Data Analysis Technique

Results were analyzed using two discrete two-way analysis of variance (ANOVA) procedures, which is preferable when testing differences between more than two groups. ANOVA requires independent observations, so we randomly assigned one vignette from each design

Table 6.1

Means, Standard Deviations, and Sample Sizes for "Good" Use of Power Model

Level of Initiating Structure	Level of Consideration	N	Mean	Standard Deviation
Level of Initiating Structure				
Low		21	4.67	2.03
High		23	5.43	2.25
Level of Consideration				
Low		21	3.43	1.54
High		23	6.57	1.44
Level of Initiating Structure	Level of Consideration	N	Mean	Standard Deviation
Low	Low	9	3.00	1.58
Low	High	12	5.92	1.31
High	Low	12	3.75	1.48
High	High	11	7.27	1.27

Table 6.2

Means, Standard Deviations, and Sample Sizes for "Evil" Use of Power Model

Level of Destroying Structure	Level of Aggression	N	Mean	Standard Deviation
Level of Destroying Structure				
Low		13	4.38	2.10
High		31	3.19	1.78
Level of Aggression				
Low		23	4.78	1.76
High		21	2.19	0.98
Level of Destroying Structure	Level of Aggression	N	Mean	Standard Deviation
Low	Low	7	5.57	2.15
Low	High	6	3.00	0.89
High	Low	16	4.44	1.50
High	High	15	1.87	0.83

to each respondent. Tukey's HSD ("honestly significant difference") tests were used for multiple comparisons, as this procedure is useful for groups with unequal sizes.

RESULTS

Descriptive Statistics

Means, standard deviations, and group/cell sizes are listed in Tables 6.1 and 6.2 for the good and evil use of power models, respectively.

Two-Way ANOVA Results for "Good" Use of Power Model

Table 6.3 is an ANOVA summary table for the good use of power model. Results indicated that Initiating Structure demonstrated a significant main effect on the use of power

Table 6.3

ANOVA Table for "Good" Use of Power Model ($N = 44$)

Source	df	SS	MS	F	Sig.	Partial Eta²
Initiating Structure (A)	1	12.03	12.03	6.07	.02	.13
Consideration (B)	1	112.47	112.47	56.70	.00	.59
A×B Interaction	1	1.00	1.00	0.50	.48	.01
Within Groups	40	79.35	1.98			
Total	43	200.80				

Table 6.4

ANOVA Table for "Evil" Use of Power Model ($N = 44$)

Source	df	SS	MS	F	Sig.	Partial Eta²
Destroying Structure (A)	1	11.72	11.72	6.22	.02	.14
Aggression (B)	1	60.28	60.28	31.98	.00	.44
A×B Interaction	1	0.00	0.00	0.00	1.00	.00
Within Groups	40	75.39	1.89			
Total	43	160.91				

$[F(1, 40) = 6.07, p = .02]$. The effect size was relatively small (partial $\varepsilon^2 = .13$). Tukey's HSD test revealed that the difference in means between the high and low conditions was in the hypothesized direction and statistically significant ($.76, p < .01$). Hence, H1 is supported.

Results also indicated that Consideration exhibited a significant main effect on the use of power $[F(1, 40) = 56.70, p < .01]$. The effect size (partial $\varepsilon^2 = .59$) was relatively large. Tukey's HSD test revealed that the difference in means between the high and low conditions was in the hypothesized direction and statistically significant ($3.14, p < .01$). Hence, H2 is strongly supported.

Two-Way ANOVA Results for "Evil" Use of Power Model

Table 6.4 is an ANOVA summary table for the evil use of power model. Results indicated that Destroying Structure had a significant main effect on the use of power $[F(1, 40) = 6.22, p = .02]$. The effect size was relatively small (partial $\varepsilon^2 = .14$). Tukey's HSD test revealed that the difference in means between the high and low conditions was in the hypothesized direction and statistically significant ($1.19, p < .01$). Hence, H3 is supported.

Results also indicated that Aggression demonstrated a significant main effect on the use of power $[F(1, 40) = 31.98, p < .01]$. The effect size (partial $\varepsilon^2 = .44$) was relatively large. Tukey's HSD test revealed that the difference in means between the high and low conditions was in the hypothesized direction and statistically significant ($2.59, p < .01$). Hence, H4 is strongly supported.

Exploratory Analyses

As noted above, we reasoned that the mere lack of Initiating Structure and Consideration would not necessarily imply the evil use of power. We performed a post-hoc test to investigate this notion more formally: If the mean use of power was less than 5.0 (i.e., Neither or Neutral) for the low Initiating Structure and low Consideration scenario, then we would have to conclude that evil may be viewed as the mere absence of these factors. We found that the value for this scenario ($M = 3.0$, $SD = 1.58$) was indeed significantly less than 5.0. Therefore, the mere absence of Initiating Structure and Consideration was associated with the evil use of power.

A similar analysis was conducted to see whether the mere absence of Destroying Structure and Aggression is associated with the good use of power. If the mean use of power was greater than 5.0 (i.e., Neither or Neutral) for the low Destroying Structure and low Aggression scenario, then we would have to conclude that good can be viewed as the mere absence of these factors. However, we found that the value for this scenario ($M = 5.6$, $SD = 2.15$) was not significantly greater than 5.0. Also, while not formally hypothesized, we wondered whether there were significant interaction terms in the models. The interaction between Initiating Structure and Consideration was nonsignificant [$F(1, 40) = .50$, ns]. Also, the interaction between Destroying Structure and Aggression was nonsignificant [$F(1, 40) < .01$, ns].

DISCUSSION

The use of power can be deemed evil when the associated supervisory behavior is perceived as intolerably destructive (e.g., destroying Structure and Aggression). Can this behavior be tamed? We think it can, but there may be unintended consequences, depending upon the manner in which it is managed. In fact, we learned that "taming" behavior is actually the root of evil! This kind of behavior existed before we arrived and will surely continue after we depart. It is an expression of the shadow archetype described by Jung (1959), which is something we all inherit. But doing nothing about it is certainly unacceptable.

So, how do we deal with this behavior? Perhaps a more preliminary question is: What's the purpose of this kind of behavior? Maybe there is some sort of value in destructive behavior, for instance, the destruction of dysfunctional systems (e.g., when the unconscious knows that a higher order social structure is inherently more evil than the individual behavior aimed at destroying it). Or, maybe there is no point to it at all, except that the shadow simply demands to be part of the personality and is exerting itself. In any case, it is probably wise to acknowledge and address this type of behavior when it occurs in organizations.

Controlling Evil Through Establishing Barriers to Organization Entry

Three general categories of learning disability can play a role in the misuse of power and the apparent increase in evil in organization today, which are: (1) arithmetic disability

(AD), (2) reading disability (RD), and (3) reading and arithmetic disabilities (RAD) (Brown and Campione, 1986; Kavale and Forness, 1996; Mazzocco, 2001). It is difficult to believe, but these apparently fundamental disabilities might account for a significant extent of the misuse of power and dysfunctional behavior in organizations. Therefore, examining the existence of these disabilities in relationship with evil could be an important step in reducing the level of the misuse of power.

It has been hypothesized that each of these personality/learning disability categories differ significantly from the others on standardized tests of reading, spelling, memory, and other cognitive measures. Both the RD and RAD categories of learning disabilities indicate a deficit in phonological processing, vocabulary, and spelling standardized tests (Lyon, 1994). The RAD category of learning disabled performs worse when compared to the other two categories, in particular on visual-spatial tasks. One of the problems associated with clarifying the impact of learning disabilities on employees is overidentification, variation, and nuisances in particular learning disabilities.

This can be reduced or even eliminated by increasing adherence to identification criteria when assessing/hiring various groups of employees (Scruggs and Mastropireri, 2002). It is debated whether there is a 6–8 percent prevalence rate of learning disabilities, but most researchers would agree that identification and recognition rates have increased due to better research, a broader definition of learning disabilities, and more recently a greater identification of girls/women with learning disabilities (Geary and Hoard, 2001; Lyon, 1996).

There are also issues associated with understanding the genesis of personality/learning disabilities associated with dyscalculia (e.g., number, counting, and arithmetic inabilities associated with learning). The procedural deficits and some forms of retrieval deficit appear to be associated with functions in the prefrontal cortex of the brain. Retrieval deficit also appears to be tied into the left parieto-occipito-temporal areas of the brain (Geary and Hoard, 2001). The learning disability is difficult to address due to the multiple sources of the dysfunction but, nonetheless, these disabilities can be more harmful to the employee with the learning disability (e.g., reading can be faked more easily given the subjective nature of learning through reading rather than calculating precise numeric answers).

Researchers believe that this dysfunction results from either overt brain injury or neuro-developmental abnormalities. A great deal of research has been conducted to probe the psychological impact on brain functions, specific learning disabilities, and resulting dysfunctional behaviors of managers (Dehaene and Cohen, 1997; McCloskey and Macaruso, 1995; Pesenti, Seron, and Van der Linden, 1994; Semenza, Miceli, and Girelli, 1997).

The use or misuse of power is a classic example of enacted behavior that may evolve out of personality/learning disabilities. In view of the connection between learning disabilities and the use/abuse of power, testing for learning disabilities might be a fruitful way to reduce evil power in organizations. To that end, six learning disabilities are identified that could contribute to the exercising of evil power in organizations. These disabilities are: (1) general personality disorders or learning disabilities; (2) borderline personality disorder; (3) bipolar disorder; (4) diminished learning capacity and dementia; (5) obsessive/compulsive behavior; and (6) destructive/dysfunctional/evil managers. If there is a connection between learning disability and the excising of evil power in organizations, then it would seem reasonable to measure these disabilities when hiring or promoting managers in organizations. To that end, methods for measuring learning disabilities can be the first line of defense against the increase in evil power in organizations.

Means to Measure General Learning Disabilities

Given the breadth of personality/learning disabilities under consideration, there are a number of tests that can be administered to determine whether an employee has a one of these disorders or disabilities and, at the same time, to determine its severity. The following measures can be used to assess personality disorders or learning disabilities: (1) ARC's Self-Determination Scale (Wehmeyer and Kelchner, 1995); (2) Nowicki-Strickland Internal-External Scale (Nowicki and Duke, 1974); (3) Lyon, 1994, 1996; (4) Kubiszyn and Borich, 2007; (5) Woodcock-Johnson Psycho-Educational Test Battery (Lyon et al., 2001).

Means to Measure Borderline Personality Disorder

It is estimated that 10 percent of outpatients in mental-health clinics and almost 20 percent of psychiatric inpatients have a diagnosis of borderline personality disorder (BPD) (American Psychiatric Association, 2001). The disorder is five times more common in first-degree relatives of persons with the disorder than in the general population, and it is diagnosed three times more often among women than among men. There is no standard test given to determine the prevalence of BPD. Given the complexity of BPD, ongoing contact with a professional psychiatrist is most frequently recommended on an outpatient basis. Personality disorders are most frequently based on extensive psychological evaluation and on the history of severity of the symptoms. The severity of the disorder is most frequently diagnosed by conducting a mental-health assessment, which is frequently supplemented with lab tests and other assessment of the general physical health of the employee.

Measurement of Bipolar Disorder

There are no biological tests to confirm the presence of bipolar disorder (MacQueen and Young, 2001). One of the best indicators of problems with bipolar disorders is usually reports from the employee his/herself, as well as abnormalities observed by friends, co-workers, or family members (husband/wife). These early indicators include depression/manic episodes (George et al., 2003). The next stage of diagnosis is frequently a battery of physical exams to measure thyroid-stimulating hormone (TSH) levels to determine hypo- or hyperthyroidism, assessment of basic electrolyte levels, an electroencephalogram (EEG) to exclude epilepsy, computed tomography (CT) scan to exclude brain lesions, and an assessment of the erythrocyte sedimentation rate (ESR) to rule out inflammation and serology to exclude syphilis or HIV infection. Several psychiatric illnesses are examined, such as schizophrenia and BPD. The key is that no one test will pinpoint bipolar disease, and, therefore, diagnosis is difficult and will depend on longitudinal observation by individuals who are familiar with the employee.

Measurement of Diminished Learning Capacity and Dementia

Currently, there is no validated screening device through which dementia can be identified in older adults (Janicki et al., 1995). The most frequently used method to determine the advance of diminished learning capacity is based upon observation by trained caregivers relative to a person's normal cognitive functioning. This type of skilled professional observational measurement is next to impossible in nonclinical environments such as in the workplace. Therefore, employees can slip into advanced stages of diminished capacity without the knowledge of the management. Sometimes employees are aware of the early stages of diminished capacity and learn to mask or cover up their loss of capabilities. Therefore, by the time the diminished capacity is recognized, the employee might be beyond assistance and the management is left with the very difficult decision of how to effectively remove the employee from the work environment.

In an effort to provide means to measure the progression of diminished intellectual capacity, the following tools/measures are recommended: (1) Facts on Aging (FOA) quiz—a twenty-five-item questionnaire administered on a longitudinal basis (e.g., biannually for employees over sixty years old); (2) Dementia and Intellectual Disability (DID) quiz—a seventeen-item questionnaire administered biannually opposite the FOA; and (3) Attributional Style Questionnaire (ASQ)—a three-dimensional questionnaire that measures stability, globality, and controllability of attributions (i.e., causes of behavior) that relate to the process and rate of employees' diminished intellectual capacity (Whitehouse and Chamberlain, 2000). These tests should be administered on an ongoing basis, which could create an adversarial relationship with older employees. In addition, the firm should have a clear idea of the legal consequences of testing one category of employee and not others, to avoid future liability or litigation.

Means to Measure Obsessive-Compulsive Behavior

An effective measure of obsessive-compulsive behavior in the workplace needs to account for the following facts.

1. The actions of the employee are repetitive and formalized;
2. The employee feels driven to perform these actions;
3. The acts are performed to reduce distress and are not ends in themselves;
4. The employee might recognize that the behavior is unreasonable and unrealistic; and
5. The employee finds the behavior disturbing and attempts to resist or avoid situations where ritualizing will become necessary.

There have been a number of methods to measure obsessive-compulsive behavior: (1) the Yale-Brown obsessive compulsive scale; (2) Leyton Obsessional Inventory Adult Version; (3) assessment of frontal lobes and the hippocampus-amygdala complex though the use of magnetic resonance imaging (MRI); (4) Obsessive-Compulsive Inventory, and (5) Rey-Osterrieth Complex Figure Test (RCFT) (Flament et al., 1988; Foa et al., 1998; Goodman et al., 1989; Szeszko et al., 1999).

Measuring Destructive/Dysfunctional Employees

Given the nature of these maladies and the breadth of the disorders, it is nearly impossible to devise one test that can be used to determine the level of an employee's disorder. Researchers have studied dysfunctional, destructive, abusive, bullying, and even evil employees, but the scales to measure these disorders are not well developed and do not capture a composite assessment of bad behavior. Therefore, it is recommended that management audits are used to identify individual as well as groups of disgruntled employees so that individual clinical treatments and counseling sessions can be implemented that is appropriate to the perceived extent of the disorder.

Many dysfunctional or destructive individuals exhibit narcissism or self-interest that can be tied closely to their overvaluation of their ideas and justification of power motives and outcomes. The individual gains from his/her own decisions, which may be in juxtaposition to what is best for the organization or others in the organization. Although narcissism can have positive aspects (e.g., a high level of self-confidence, infectious enthusiasm, unrelenting drive to gain power, political skill, relationships [frequently superficial], and "street smarts"), the same positive attributes can become negative (e.g., exaggeration, belief in being special, devalues the contributions of others, demanding constant attention, expecting favorable treatment and automatic compliance with what the individual wants) (Boyett, 2006). This type of attitude promotes the substitution of organizational goals or goodwill for that of the employee.

Figure 6.1 illustrates the potential impact of destructive managers' use of evil power throughout the organization. It is important to note that the destructive manager can have an impact on individuals, groups, and the organization as a whole. Therefore, corrective measures have to focus not only on the level that is directly affected but also the interaction of various levels. The use of evil power, therefore, can demonstrate an impact not only directly on the individual but also indirectly on groups and ultimately the entire organization, thus setting a pattern of evil/destructive behavior throughout the organization.

Implications

We recommend that organizational leaders proactively monitor for Destroying Structure and Aggression in their organizations. Just as important, we recommend that they maintain open minds in order to consider deeper issues that might be related to the behavior. For example, does the behavior occur in part because aspects of the

Figure 6.1 **Model of Diversity, Personal Maladjustment, and Power in Organizations**

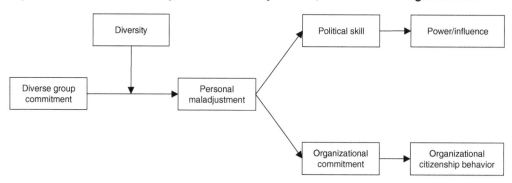

organization drive its supervisors to engage in it? Or, are employees projecting these behaviors onto their supervisors because the organizational climate somehow stirs up their shadow archetypes (e.g., they work in rigid job environments intolerant to healthy conflict)? Or, are there any apparent external societal factors having an affect on organizational behavior (e.g., international disputes, a troubled economy, terrorist attacks)? Organizations have good reason to check their uses of power. The "iron law of responsibility" is the notion that entities that do not use their power responsibly will eventually lose it (Davis and Blomstrom, 1966). Organizations not only need to know how power is being used within them (via its organizational members); they also need to know how their external stakeholders perceive them. Are they viewed as aggressive or destructive organizations?

Future Research Directions

Future research could address more basic matters, such as the frequency, intensity, duration, antecedents, and consequences of Destroying Structure and Aggression in various organizations. In addition, more valid measures could be developed. Potentially important moderators (i.e., boundary conditions) could also be investigated, especially those that attenuate destructive behavior and its undesirable consequences. Evil in organizations is certainly a multilevel phenomenon. Hence, future research could take a more macro-level approach to studying the shadow. How does the shadow manifest itself at the organizational level of analysis? Are there organizational tendencies that resonate with what's considered evil? Moreover, a mesolevel approach could be used to investigate how particular organizational factors affect individual behavior.

Of course, future research could also focus on actor-target dyads other than the supervisor-employee dyad. For example, employee-employee, employee-supervisor, or employee-customer dyads could be investigated. Future research could also consider networks of actors (i.e., go beyond the dyadic level). More advanced ideas could be examined: Can organizations be "too" good? In other words, "Where did the evil go?" Perhaps "holy-like" organizations are actually jack-in-the-box structures ready to "spring" unexpectedly.

REFERENCES

American Psychiatric Association. 2001. What is Borderline Personality Disorder? *Psychiatric Services*, 52, 12, 1569–1570.

Andrews, G., Stewart, G. Morris-Yates, A., Holt, P., and Henderson, S. 1990. Evidence for a General Neurotic Syndrome. *British Journal of Psychiatry*, 157, 6–12.

Bly, R. 1988. *A Little Book on the Human Shadow*, ed. William Booth. San Francisco: Harper & Row.

Boyett, J. 2006. Surviving the destructive narcissistic leader. Report, April. Boyett and Associates, Alpharetta, GA. www.jboyett.com/files/Surviving_the_Destructive_Narcissistic_Leader.pdf.

Brown, A., and J. Campione. 1986. Psychological theory and the study of learning disabilities. *American Psychologist*, 14, 10, 1059–1068.

Byrne, J.A. 2003. *Chainsaw: The Notorious Career of Al Dunlap in an Era of Profit-at-Any-Price*. New York: HarperCollins.

Card, C. 2002. *The Atrocity Paradigm: A Theory of Evil*. New York: Oxford University Press.

Davis, K., and R. Blomstrom. 1966. *Business and Its Environment*. New York: McGraw-Hill.

Dehaene, S., and L. Cohen. 1997. Cerebral pathways for calculation: Double dissociation between rote verbal and quantitative knowledge of arithmetic. *Cortex*, 33, 219–250.

Dunlap, A.J. 1996. *Mean Business: How I Save Bad Companies and Make Good Companies Great*. New York: Fireside.

Einarsen, S., M.S. Aasland, and A. Skogstad. 2007. Destructive leadership behavior: A definition and conceptual model. *Leadership Quarterly*, 18, 3, 207–216.

Fedor, D.B., R.W. Eder, and M.R. Buckley. 1989. The contributory effects of supervisor intentions on subordinate feedback responses. *Organizational Behavior and Human Decision Processes,* 44, 396–414.

Ferris, G.R., D.P.S. Bhawuk, D.B. Fedor, and T.A. Judge. 1995. Organizational politics and citizenship: Attributions of intentionality and construct definition. In *Advances in Attribution Theory: An Organizational Perspective*, ed. M.J. Martinko, 231–252. Delray Beach, FL: St. Lucie Press.

Ferris, G.R., R. Zinko, R.L. Brouer, M.R. Buckley, and M.G. Harvey. 2007. Strategic bullying as a supplementary, balanced perspective on destructive leadership. *Leadership Quarterly,* 18, 195–206.

Flament, M., A. Whitaker, J. Rapoport, M. Davies, C. Berg, K. Kalikow, W. Sceery, and D. Shaffer. 1988. Obsessive compulsive disorder in adolescence: An epidemiological study. *Journal of American Academy of Child & Adolescent Psychiatry,* 27, 6, 1120–1131.

Foa, E., M. Kozak, P. Salkovskis, M. Coles, and N. Anir. 1998. The validation of a new obsessive-compulsive disorder scale: The Obsessive Compulsive Inventory. *Psychological Assessment,* 10, 3, 206–214.

Geary, D., and M. Hoard. 2001. Numerical and arithmetical deficits in learning-disabled children: Relation to dyscalculia and dyslexia. *Aphasiology*, 15, 7, 635–647.

George, E., D. Miklowitz, J. Richards, T. Simoneau, and D. Taylor. 2003. The comorbidity of bipolar disorder and axis II personality disorders: Prevalence and clinical correlates. *Bipolar Disorders*, 5, 2, 115–122.

Goodman, W., L. Price, S. Rasmussen, C. Manure, R. Fleischmann, C. Hill, G. Eninger, and D. Charney. 1989. The Yale-Brown obsessive compulsive scale: Development, use, and reliability. *Archives of General Psychiatry*, 48, 1006–1011.

Griffin, R.W., and A. O'Leary-Kelly, ed. 2004. *The Dark Side of Organizational Behavior.* San Francisco: Jossey-Bass.

Harvey, M.G., M.R. Buckley, J.T. Heames, R. Zinko, R.L. Brouer, and G.R. Ferris. 2007. A bully as an archetypal destructive leader. *Journal of Leadership and Organizational Studies,* 14, 117–129.

Janicki, M., T. Heller, G. Sletzer, and J. Hogg. 1995. *Practice Guidelines for the Clinical Assessment and Care of Management of Alzheimer and Other Dementia's Among Adults with Mental Retardation.* Washington, DC: American Association on Mental Retardation.

Johnson, S. 2005. Mania and dysregulation in a goal pursuit: A review. *Clinical Psychology Review*, 25, 2, 241–262.

Judge, T.A., R.F. Piccolo, and R. Ilies. 2004. The forgotten ones? The validity of consideration and initiating structure in leadership research. *Journal of Applied Psychology*, 89, 36–51.

Jung, C.G. 1959. *The Archetypes and the Collective Unconscious*, trans. R.F.C. Hull. Princeton: Princeton University Press.

Kavale, K., and S. Forness. 1996. Social skill deficits and learning disabilities: A meta-analysis. *Journal of Learning Disabilities,* 29, 3, 226–237.

Kernberg, O.F., and F. Michels. 2009. Borderline personality disorder. *American Psychiatry,* 166, 5, 505–508.

Kubiszyn, T., and G. Borich. 2007. *Educational Testing and Measurement: Classroom Application and Practice.* New York: John Wiley & Sons, Inc.

Lyon, R. 1994. *Frames of Reference of Learning Disabilities: New View on Measurement Issues.* Baltimore: Paul H. Brookes.

———. 1996. Learning disabilities. *Special Education for Students with Disabilities*, 6, 1, 54–62.

Lyon, R., J. Fletcher, S. Shaywitz, B. Shaywitz, J. Torgesen, F. Wood, A. Schulte, and R. Olson. 2001. Rethinking learning disabilities. In *Rethinking Special Education for a New Century*, ed. C.E. Finn, A.J. Andrew, and C.R. Hokanson, 259–287. Washington, DC: Progressive Policy Institute and Thomas B. Fordham Foundation.

MacQueen, G., and T. Young. 2001. Bipolar II disorder: Symptoms, course, and responses. *Psychiatric Services*, 52, 3, 358–361.

Mazzocco, M. 2001. Math learning disability and math LD subtypes: Evidence form studies of Turner syndrome, Fragile "X" syndrome, and neurofibromatosis Type 1. *Journal of Learning Disabilities*, 34, 6, 520–533.

McCloskey, M., and P. Macaruso. 1995. Representing and using numerical information. *American Psychologist*, 50, 351–363.

Milgram, S. 1969. *Obedience to Authority.* New York: Harper and Row.

Miller, A.G. 2004. *The Social Psychology of Good and Evil.* New York: Guilford Press.

Moore, R., and D. Gillette. 1990. *King, Warrior, Magician, Lover: Rediscovering the Archetypes of the Mature Masculine.* New York: HarperCollins.

Nowicki, S., and M. Duke. 1974. A locus of control scale for noncollege as well as college adults. *Journal of Personality Assessment*, 38, 2, 136–137.

Perryman, A.A., D. Sikora, and G.R. Ferris. 2010. One bad apple: The role of destructive executives in organizations. In *The "Dark" Side of Management*, ed. C. Schriesheim and L. Neider, 27–48. Charlotte, NC: Information Age.

Pesenti, M., X. Seron, and M. Van der Linden. 1994. Selective impairment as evidence for mental organization of arithmetical Facts: BB, a case of preserved subtraction? *Cortex*, 30, 661–671.

Scruggs, T., and M. Mastropieri. 2002. On babies and bathwater: Addressing the problems of identification of learning disabilities. *Learning Disability Quarterly*, 25, 3, 155–168.

Semenza, C., L. Miceli, and L. Girelli. 1997. A deficit for arithmetical procedures: Lack of knowledge or lack of monitoring? *Cortex*, 33, 483–498.

Stogdill, R.M., and A. Coons. 1957. Leader behavior: Its description and measurement. Bureau of Business Research, Ohio State University.

Szeszko, P., D. Robinson, J. Alvir, R. Bilder, T. Lencz, M. Ashtari, H. Wu, and B. Bogerts. 1999. Orbital frontal and amygdala volume reductions in obsessive-compulsive disorder. *Archives of General Psychiatry*, 56, 913–919.

Tjosvold, D., and B. Wisse. 2009. *Power and Interdependence in Organizations*. New York: Cambridge University Press.

Wehmeyer, M., and K. Kelchner. 1995. Whose future is it anyway? Student-directed transition planning process, *Arc National Organization on Mental Retardation*.

Whitehouse R., and P. Chamberlain. 2000. Dementia in people with learning disability: A preliminary study into care staff knowledge and attributions. *British Journal of Learning Disabilities*, 28, 148–153.

Winter, D. 2009. How can power be tamed? In *Power and Interdependence in Organizations,* ed. D. Tjosvold and B. Wisse, 33–51. New York: Cambridge University Press.

Zimbardo, P. 2007. *The Lucifer Effect: Understanding How Good People Turn Evil*. New York: Random House.

7

Holy Evil

J. Patrick Dobel

For many people, religious belief lies at the core of the human experience. The influences of spiritual belief ripple across society, engulfing believers and nonbelievers alike. Individuals discover meaning and direction through an experience that they believe links them to a truth or presence that lies beyond the boundaries of nature. The religious experience grounds meaning in a chaotic natural world. It produces an anchor for purpose and morality because it arises from a supernatural domain beyond the reach of ordinary perceptions and the cognitions that humans employ to make sense of the world. This supernatural status gives this experience a unique position and privilege to guide human beings. This chapter discusses how people's religious experiences can shape their understanding of good and evil. This religiously formed meaning profoundly influences the capacity of people and organizations to engage in evil. The chapter maps out the internal moral and religious logic of organizations that are anchored in the experience of holiness for their legitimacy. The inner moral logic illuminates how holy organizations evade external categorization as evil by annulling such external claims in their internal moral world.

The power of the religious domain grows from the experience of the Holy or Sacred as domains that remain inaccessible in mundane life. When a person experiences what Rudolph Otto (1923/1958) calls this "numinous" domain, the contact transforms the person. Living through the experience of the Holy directly or through contact with the bearers of supernatural truth (re)forms people's identity and affiliation. These sacred intermediaries take on immense importance in the question of organizational evil. Most people have neither the time nor the gifts to encounter the Holy. This chapter, however, identifies a wide range of relationships that demarcate those who serve as contacts or intermediaries with the sacred. I use the word "cleric" to describe this diverse group, which can comprise shamans, oracles, soothsayers, prophets, monks, nuns, anchorites, priests, deacons, elders, scribes, preachers, holy men, and imams. The concept of a cleric covers the religiously and morally privileged individuals who speak on behalf of or bring to people the experience or truths of the Holy.

People's experience of holiness can be central to organizational evil. To the extent that people believe that the experience of the Holy, Sacred, or Divine reveals truths that exist beyond nature and reason, the purity and power of the experience of the Holy morph into an extraordinarily potent source of authority. The experience of the

Holy makes sense of the world by dividing it into what Mercia Eliade (1957/1987) called the "Sacred" and the "Profane." This division comprehends the nature of evil and produces institutions and people who define good and evil and guide people in engaging them.

The ineffable experience of the Holy can evolve into religion and generate organizations. The development of religion grounded in sacred truth and experience of mystery provides an unfathomable and warranted source of meaning and authority. A sacred experience can lead people to establish holy institutions anchored in supernatural knowledge to define evil and good grounded in the experience of holiness. They provide justification or forgiveness for people who embark upon actions that people outside the religion might call morally evil. This chapter refers to evil in the secular and traditional moral sense of intended harm or destruction imposed by humans upon other beings or the world who are innocent in a moral sense (Adams and Balfour, 2009). Traditional moral theory argues that evil actions depend upon intentionality and awareness of the impact. Adams and Balfour in their path-breaking study, along with thinkers like Václav Havel and East European critics of totalitarianism, argue that the deepest danger with modern organizations lies in their ability to mask organizational evil through instrumental rationality that narrows or hides the moral nature of decisions (Adams and Balfour, 2009; Havel, 1987). Sheldon Wolin (2004) pointed in a similar direction when he argued that politics and self-aware discussions over the nature of the political order and good became sublimated in the theory and practice of modern organizations. Organizations anchored in holy purpose pose a different challenge because they actively define evil and justify actions for members to confront and eradicate evil in the world. Holiness can inspire crusades and inquisitions to build a good world and eradicate evil.

In this chapter, the words "holy," "sacred," and "divine" elide into each other. Their meanings suggest nuanced variations but grow from the same Indo-European roots and the experience of human beings with a supernatural domain (Mallory and Adams, 1997; Watkins, 2000). This experience of a supernatural domain forms the core encounter that floods human feeling and changes the human being. The chapter builds on the experience of the Holy as described in Rudolph Otto's (1923/1958) classic study of the origin of religion. The word and domain of the Sacred extends this idea but also expresses the active principle that humans use to extend holiness when they consecrate, bless, or sanctify. Divine highlights the experiences that lead humans to vest the holy and sacred in supernatural beings. At many points, the three dwell together and are used interchangeably.

This chapter explores the nature of the Holy by examining the etymological roots that reveal insights about the primordial human experience of it. Building upon these insights and Otto's study, the chapter analyzes the different relationships that people can develop with this primeval religious experience. These relationships generate different patterns of authority and organization that shape organizational morality when its members possess a privileged relation to holiness. This matters because holiness divides the world and defines evil. The chapter concludes by discussing the organizational implications for power and action that flow from drawing upon a sacred relation to the Holy.

THE IDEA OF THE HOLY

The concept of the Holy derives from the old English "hali" and old German *Heilig*; both suggest a sense of wholeness or completeness. Another variation, *Halig*, emphasizes separateness and points to a domain that cannot be transgressed and is inviolate as a separate or complete domain. The deep Indo-European root *kailo* emphasizes wholeness, health, and good omens that bind together into a hallowed separate domain (Barnhart, 1999; Onions, 1966; Watkins, 2000). The origins of Holy begin with otherworldly associations. The word points to an existence beyond the everyday natural world and beyond normal perceptions and apprehension. The Holy intimates a domain of reality that possesses stability and existence beyond the bustle and change of daily life. Human reason and concepts cannot capture the essence of this realm.

The idea of the Holy carries immense importance for humans because of what Otto called its "numinous" quality; the experience exits beyond reason and floods human consciousness and changes a person's sense of self. Otto (1923/1958) coined the term *mysterium tremendum* to describe the sense that humans took away from their awareness of the Holy. The Holy offered human beings access to a different realm. The holy presence induced a sense of being a creature before a higher world and provoked a sense of humility, submission, and trembling before the numinous world. Touching the holy realm was experienced as not only a higher encounter, but the unpredictable luminosity inspired awe and fear. The ancient Vedas, the *Upanishads*, the Bible, and the Koran all express this awe, adoration, and subordination before the holy presence.

The Holy possesses a "Truth" beyond the comprehension of language. This numinous experience eludes apprehension in conceptual or ethical terms, and all attempts to articulate the truth remain incomplete. The transcendent nature of the Holy means that the domain of holiness remains obscure, unpredictable and ultimately nonverifiable except as fragmentary insights from humans who touch it. Awe, fear, and trembling before the immensity of the Holy ground this new identity for a human facing the luminous power and demands humble surrender before it. This experience offers immunity to the vicissitudes of life and offers human beings meaning and a different way of being in the world. The self can be anchored in truth and purpose guaranteed by insight from beyond the natural and rational.

The Holy conjoins with the Sacred as another aspect of this domain. The Indo-European root *sak* or *sak-ro* emphasizes separateness but one set aside for the gods. *Sak* and its derivations point to how aspects of life can be consecrated or sacrificed or express how the holy presence shines through. It can identify the holy or sacred presence at a place or time (Mallory and Adams, 1997; Watkins, 2000). The concepts of the holy and the sacred unify the awareness of a domain of life that is separate, whole, and bound together (Barnhart 2003; Mallory and Adams, 1997). The roots of language and pervasive cultural data suggest that this experience lies at the core of the religious experience of life.

The ethical importance of the Holy and Sacred lies in their ability to complete and make sense of life. Because the Holy defies explanation but remains above and beyond the mundane, it provides the possibility of knowledge and truth that endure amid change and give meaning and direction to life. The luminous nature of the *mysterium tremendum* offers stability and clarity if it can be discovered and known in a world of infinite flux and death.

The autonomy of the Holy makes it unpredictable but also divides the world. The world of the Sacred and Holy defines a domain of higher existence and enduring truth and purity that the natural world cannot attain or even aspire to. The existence of the Holy and Sacred changes the status of nature. In Eliade's words, it becomes "profane" compared to the sacred. Its root, *sak,* means "separate and set aside for the gods." One does not learn to be holy; rather, people live a process by which they are transformed by contact with the Holy or Sacred. The natural world resembles one seen darkly through a mirror, as Saint Paul suggests after he was struck dumb on the road to Damascus. Plato argues that life resembles a world of shadows in a cave reflected by fire. This shadow world fades to insignificance when a person escapes the cave into the blinding light of the truth. Moses discovers a blinding, burning bush that transforms his knowledge. The stories, analogies, and myths provide a consistent view of how the world of daily life pales in comparison to the exalted realm of the Holy and Sacred (Eliade, 1957/1987; Plato, VII, 507–520 1968; Exodus 3 1966; Acts of the Apostle 9 1966; 1 Corinthians 13 1966).

This division into sacred and profane or holy and unholy has profound implications for living and ruling. It hints that life on earth possesses less meaning or importance than life in the domain of the Holy and Sacred. The two realms can lie side by side, barely touching, or entangle in such a way that sacredness shines through constantly. The gods may venture down or influence existence, but the life on earth proceeds largely independent of the Holy. This distinction cleaves the world and living can become a vale of tears, a fallen state, or a sojourn for pilgrims seeking a higher state. This insight lies deep in the human condition. Almost four thousand years ago, the first great written work of human literature, *The Epic of Gilgamesh*, recounts the quest of the great King Gilgamesh to escape the world and sorrows and attain immortality (Mitchell, 2004). The world does not become evil or horrible, just less than perfect and incomplete. Often, however, holiness or sacredness seeps through into the mundane world. Holy places, signs, and divine openings saturate the world. The Sacred can erupt into the world in unpredictable and disruptive ways as well as pervade it in a quiet or tranquil way (Eliade, 1957/1987; Otto, 1923/1958). The possibility of touching or discovering holiness permeates the world; one has to know how to look and how to discover and then face what to do with the knowledge imparted by being (trans)formed by sacredness.

RELATIONSHIPS WITH THE HOLY

The organizational and governing implications of the Holy or Sacred grow from the point of contact and what happens to individuals who touch it. Because the Holy remains supernatural, it is not usually accessible to everyone. At the same time, mundane and profane reality is shot through with Holy and Sacred openings. The key lies in how to discover or come into contact with them and the implications for living of this contact.

A person does not learn to be holy; a person is transformed in a deep emotional, cognitive and spiritual way by contact with the Holy (Eliade, 1957/1987; Otto, 1923/1958). This experiential foundation of religion and awareness poses the unique point of challenge as to how holiness and sacredness influence organizations and governing. If the domain of holiness possesses a higher truth and a guide to a higher purer path, then connecting to the Holy or Sacred can engender legitimacy for people yearning for meaning or seeking an anchor for their place and way of life. Holiness can evolve into a strong source of ethical guidance and political legitimacy. The *mysterium tremendum* or the Holy, however, does not necessarily possess a strong ethical or political import. The religious impulse flowing from experience of the holy can just as easily lead to quietism or withdrawal to exalt or contemplate, or worship. It might lead to prayer or adoration but not necessarily to organization (Otto, 1923/1958).

The relation between human beings and the august realm of holiness flows in two directions. First, Holiness might descend to the person. Second, the human might seek out contact with the Holy. In the first case, the Holy or Sacred often erupts into the world. Holiness often visits people or pursues them. In some cases, it takes possession of them. The realm of holiness remains mysterious and can be wild and unpredictable, and this in itself can make it an unreliable foundation for organizational or governing consistency (Machinist, 2003). In the second, humans seek to tame holiness by devising ways to discover and formalize relations to it. In this section I divide how Holiness contacts a person into three approaches: visitation, possession, signs, and symbols.

Visitation

Divine visitation occurs in many ways. The Holy descends in dreams with coded messages. Holiness can descend when we are least aware, as Buddha experienced beneath a tree. The Holy can speak to someone, such as dictating to Mohammed or speaking to Abraham or talking to Moses. The Holy can stalk someone, as Yahweh did Jeremiah through the streets of Jerusalem or the Furies sought the Greeks or the Holy Spirit converges on a person. Visitations saturate life in the world, and a creature's presence, a place, or a tree can open to the essence of the Holy with a message. Natural signs abound, so a person must be aware of them or trained to see them. The underlying reality here emphasizes the wildness and unpredictability of the Holy, so prophets or people privileged with divine visitation and insight can arise at any time and place (Brown, 1997; Machinist, 2003).

Possession

The Holy can take possession of a person. The sacred presence can fill a person or creature, and the person represents the incarnate divine or serves as a vessel for the word and insights of the sacred realm like a living god or oracle illustrated by the Pythian priestess at Delphi. If a person manifests as the avatar or surrogate for the sacred on earth, this generates immense power and legitimacy for them in ruling or organizing. Such a ruler or holy person embodies the living divine presence on earth. The actions of the Emperor God or divine right king or of the incarnated one inscribe the divine will onto the world (Figgis, 1965; Potter, 1997).

Sign and Symbol

The Holy remains ineffable—this is critical. Signs can provide a wide range of emanations or openings into the domain of holiness. People who are aware, and sometimes those caught unawares, can discover the holy domain in many places. The impulse to build altars to honor a visitation from an animal or nature spirit or to acknowledge the presence in a sacred tree, grove, or stream occurs constantly (Eliade, 1957/1987). These signs can evolve into a sacred place and can pervade a land or place with sacred import. This sacredness marks the land and settlement as divinely inspired and reinforces a people's view of their place or as justified by the sacred grant. Sacred places can be co-opted by other religions over time (Brown, 1997; Casey, 1997).

The decision to build shrines or to acknowledge sacred presence nurtures the development of symbols to express the emotional, cognitive and spiritual importance of the truth emerging from the experience of the Holy. Most important for the exercise of ruling or organizational power becomes the development of written symbols or the need to set aside and protect holy places. The word, the *logos*, is recorded by the privileged ones who are touched by the Holy. These insights come down as stories as in the ancient Vedas or collected oral traditions that become the basis of sacred scriptures. But once the words of God, the truth of the Holy, produced divinely inspired scripture, the organizational importance of the Holy changed fundamentally.

Visitation, possession, signs all fuse in the divine word, the *logos*. Reciting or reading the scriptures became a moment of possible visitation. More important, the ability to read was not widely distributed, so access to the truth of the Holy now narrowed. In the wild and unpredictable world of visitations, prophets and possession the Holy or Sacred could erupt anywhere any time without regard to status or literacy, but scriptures potentially changed the entire balance of connection and access and created an entirely different approach to the divine world (Machinist, 2003; Rousseau, 2010).

The other direction of the relation with the divine involves the active search of humans to connect to the Holy in a more predictable way. In this discussion I examine five approaches: the quest, study and discipline, lineal descent, ritual or sacrifice, and text. These approaches intensely influence organizing and ruling because they generate ritualized patterns or institutions to regularize relations to holy truth. This approach builds religion and fuses sacredness to organizations and authority.

Quest

In this path, humans do not wait for a visitation but initiate a quest to find the Holy. Many cultures hand down prescribed methods of seeking the divine, such as sojourns in places known to be full of sacred presence. Cultures develop rituals to cleanse and prepare for journeys or for entering the divine presence. Other cultures create rituals of dance or ecstatic substances to embark on the quest. Humans change the direction and discover reliable paths or rituals to make a person receptive to the presence of the divine and holy. More important, this sets the stage for organizing and training people to seek holiness (Brown, 1997; Rousseau, 2010).

Study and Discipline

The quest to find divine presence leads easily to creating paths of study, training, and discipline to ensure continuing access. This pattern can be as simple as becoming an apprentice with a master who has achieved communion with the Holy or can entail elaborate rituals and disciplined living. The relations become more formalized when a community forms around a master or saint and organizes a rule for monastic or communal life. The rules try to replicate the experience of the master or saint and sanctify the path of study and practice that helps others achieve the experience that makes them holy (Adolphson, 2007; Benedict, Saint, Abbot of Monte Cassino, 1981; Nigg, 1959). The rules pervade communal life to maximize the chances of encountering the Holy presence. The community may produce initiation rites and stages of growth that require discipline, study, and practice. Monastic or seminary rules harmonize and adapt to create knowledge but also create specialization to provide resources, security, and handing down of the path and knowledge. The imperative to maintain and hand down the sacred truths leads to systematic organizing with rules, rituals, and authority. The organization guarantees the quality and precision of the path followed by novices, students, and initiates (Kerr, 2009; McMillan and Fladenmuller, 1997; Singh, 1997).

The community rules establish a pattern of authority. The individuals who found the divine or had been transformed by the holy presence assume privileges as teachers and leaders. The community grows as others seek the way to holy truth but also as disciples leave the community, seminary, or monastery to spread the word and practice. Schools of thought and practice develop organized around the insights and learning of different masters, priests, sages, or saints (Kerr, 2009; McMillan and Fladenmuller, 1997; Singh, 1997).

This clerical authority structure usurps options once widely distributed. Divine signs of nature and life may once have been open to the entire community. Now the interpretation of auguries and signs becomes the province of priests or holy members of the community. This specialization such as interpreting signs or dreams or sacrificing gives greater significance to the holy clerics who now become mediators between people and the divine (Cole, 2005; Rousseau, 2010).

This formalization is enhanced with the creation of sacred texts. A text-based spirituality summons forth far more organizational complexity. Two forces drive this. First, the existence of scriptures beyond oral tradition can drive the creation of a canon. The development of a canon narrows the wild and unpredictable prospect of visitation, signs, and prophecy. The canon presses toward regularity and prescribed versions. Sacred texts highlight the importance of literacy that creates a barrier—literacy that means that only the educated may discover the truth and then hand it on to the illiterate. The institutions of writing, reading, and record keeping become critical for communities driven to find and sustain a relationship with the Holy. Second, the scripture-driven spirituality opens up the world of interpretation and schools of thought. The essence of the Holy remains its ineffable and incomplete presence in the world. Any word or concept will be incomplete in its apprehension of the divine. The ultimate elusiveness of words will lead to battles and clashes between schools of interpretation especially as texts prove elusive or reflect compound histories and traditions as the Vedas or Hebrew Talmud. The battle over which books count as canon and differences between those who accept some and not other texts can set off endless conflict and inspire the formation of different sects.

Lineal Descent

The political and religious world can depend upon blood descent and familial affiliation. The assumption that privileged access to the divine flows from blood affiliation easily influences the establishment of a clerical estate. The development of a Vedic caste system, the Hebrew priesthood descending from the tribe of Levi or the early Christian insistence that Jesus must be a lineal descendent of David illustrates the strength of lineage and holiness. Some schools of Islamic interpretation depend heavily upon inherited privilege and access to scriptures; likewise, the spirit may flow from one preacher to his children in evangelical Christianity. This familial claim allies with blood loyalty becomes a source of power and privilege as the family becomes a gatekeeper to the truth of text or revelation (Cole, 2005).

Ritual and Sacrifice

The formalization of access to the divine presence and truth grows into discipline and practice. These often take on ritualized and sacrificial aspects. The rituals provide recurring patterns of action that have proven efficacy in achieving spiritual connection. The rituals often etch the pattern of sacred life into the everyday world. A sacred festival or ceremony will recreate and make present sacred actions or moments. The rituals memorialize and evoke the divine presence. The rituals, however, require training and practice to ensure that they are done well and that there are acolytes to prepare them. Ritual and ceremony require organizing to collect the resources, train people, and ensure quality in their performance to evoke and sustain the divine relationship with the Holy. Often rituals and rites require the construction of holy spaces such as temples, churches, mosques, or synagogues to provide the physical infrastructure for the divine connection (Jones, 1966; Rousseau, 2010).

The Holy and Sacred remain inextricably bound with the practice of sacrifice in human history. The sacrifice unites humans with the divine presence. Providing sacrifice solidifies the relationship between the community and the Holy presence. The provision of sacrifice makes the sacrificed object holy and reinforces this relationship. Sacrifices affirm both the surrender and the relation to the divine presence. Sacrifices can supplicate or restore moral and relational equilibrium with the domain of holiness. The sacrifices accrete rituals to ensure that the sacrifice is worthy and acceptable because the sacrifice transforms the mundane into the sacred. Rituals govern the place, timing, and nature of the victim and the type of person who offers the sacrifice. The ritual sacrifice requires organization to train, gather resources, and maintain the place for the sacrifice.

Text

I have already mentioned the central importance of text to all these relations with the sacred. The existence of text, literacy, and routinized access to the *logos* initiates the true organizational revolution around holiness. The canonical text sanctioned as the emanation of divine knowledge in the world provides immense power and legitimacy to those who possess access to it and claim interpretative primacy over it. It breeds a class of people and interpretations that generate more rules that the text reveals in its stories of how to live in accordance with the demand of holiness. The divine word proclaims the way of life and rules required to live up to the demands of the supernatural domain. Control and battles over control of the text and its meaning become primarily important for the organizational impact of the Holy.

THE DIVIDED WORLD AND SACRED POWER

The emergence of organizations sanctioned and sanctified by a privileged relation to the sacred truth profoundly shapes the contour of administrative evil. This privileged access can occur in many ways such as visitation, possession, quest, sacrifice, study and discipline and text. The Holy presence divides the world into the aspects that support the quest for holiness and aspects that undermine it. This division creates an experiential and moral chasm between the holy and the profane. Some spiritual traditions so enmesh the sacred and mundane that this division matters less, but organizational patterns arise from the claims of individuals and groups to speak on behalf of the sacred truth, and they demarcate the world.

While some religious traditions retreat from the world or remain quietist, most holiness traditions spill into the mundane world with moral claims that affect ruling and daily life. This impact lurks in the division of the universe into two domains: Holy and Profane. This division influences the moral status of creatures and nature because their position and worth can hinge upon their relation to the Holy. If they contribute or manifest holiness, they gain worthiness for those who see the sacred as the axis of value and worth in the world. To the extent that people, creatures, or nature are indifferent, their moral worth shrinks but does not necessarily become a problem. If they are perceived as standing in the way of, rejecting, or undermining holiness, they fall into a damning moral category of unholy and profane; they can be categorized as evil.

This divided world affects all assessments and delineates the boundaries of good and bad, right and wrong, holy and profane. This division lies behind the modern English concept of evil. Evil is relatively recent in the Indo-European tradition. Its precursor Indo-European root, *upelo,* strongly suggests the idea of exceeding or transgressing proper limits. This fits well with the original sense of holiness and sacred as a realm apart that should not be violated. Middle and Old German applied the more recent cognate *yvil* indiscriminately to cover a wide array of bads, wrongs, and harms. Only recently has evil emerged as a darker, more morally commanding concept. The deeper Indo-European root *uergh* saved what we call evil for actions associated with a criminal or vile being or malign presence. The idea points to the violation or transgression dimension of an evil act. Profoundly wrong or evil actions exceed bounds, violate codes, and destroy the integrity or wholeness of a situation. Modern English usage sets evil against the sacred. The stories of the origin of evil speak of individuals or gods intentionally violating the norms of sacred order that held together peace and community. In another vein, Augustine and others argued that evil really represented an absence of the good, and this imposes an obligation upon religious people to bring good into the void (Augustine, 1958; Barnhart 2003; Mallory and Adams, 1997; Watkins, 2000).

UNITING HOLY WITH ORGANIZATIONS

This divided world and the boundary between holy and evil heightens the importance of the claim to speak on behalf of the Holy. If a person or institution gains the authority to articulate the truth of the divine presence, then that person or institution can define what is evil and what is not. Holy and evil arise against each other as defining axes of not only spiritual but also moral meaning. Evil as a concept unites worldly wrong with spiritual transgression, and the privilege of defining it carries immense organizational and political import for the idea of organizational evil. If an organization derives its legitimacy and culture from this approach, it not only monopolizes definitions of evil but claims immunity from secular or other judgments about the evil of its own actions.

Evil takes on more importance when it becomes an active, intentional force. Demonic beings turn the world into a battlefield of forces of good against forces of evil. These demonic forces pose an incessant threat to efforts to be holy or create good. They can possess humans, take over spaces, and tempt or seduce humans into following an unholy path. An active evil force reinforces the perception of the world as a battleground where protectors of holiness must be always on guard against the pull and glamour of evil. This approach militarizes holiness movements to gird for war against evil and puts even greater pressure on them to attend to their own holiness and purity (Adolphson, 2007; Nigg, 1959; Tesfai, 2010; Walzer, 1965/1982).

The holy domain usually is articulated as supernatural beings that possess a unique autonomy. While this domain can evolve into a formal religion with mature institutions, rituals, teachings, texts, and doctrines, no dynamic forces it into the realm of political life. Governing institutions can remain autonomous even parallel to religious institutions. This relationship between the state and sacred institution influences the ends of the state and the means of state power. The regime and the holy need not unite, but more often than not they collide, merge, and conflict.

When the domains unite, the Holy can hallow the governing and the person of the ruler. More important, when the holy domain bonds with organizational governing, this bond transforms law and authority. When holiness permeates state rule, the entire moral rubric of justification changes. The ends of the state, however pursued, combine the holy with the interests of the ruler. A sacred veneer covers ruling and organizations. Violating a law not only becomes disobedience but a sin. Disrespecting the state not only becomes disrespect but a sacrilege. Disagreeing not only becomes dissent but blasphemy. Fighting a war transforms into a holy sacrifice. The procedures of court and governance turn into sacraments and incarnations of the divine on earth. Punishing a lawbreaker becomes administering God's wrath on the unholy. Legal processes turn into liturgical interpretations of divine decrees (Adolphson, 2007; Jones, 1966; Tesfai, 2010).

Holy organizations raise the stakes very high for the notion of evil. The key lies in the ability of the clerics speaking on behalf of the Holy to define the evil. If the ruler merges with the divine, as with a god/king or divine/emperor, no cognitive or spiritual space exists for dissent or questioning. When governing is hallowed by religion, then organizational actors do not have to worry about doing evil. The organization does not need to mask evil being done because the culture of justification builds upon a sacred purpose that saturates daily actions and identities. By definition, administrators engage in evil by divine mandate. Their obedience to orders and their discretion are sanctified by prayer and religion. They become moral and spiritual duties. This unity of holy and organizational leaves no room for questioning or opposing the decisions of the ruler because the ruler's decisions manifest the divine will. Appointments to posts accrue by adherence to orthodoxy, and merit is construed by spiritual worthiness rather than technical expertise. The organizational culture creates a strong push to display orthodoxy in thought and action. This manifestation of one's holiness means that the organizational goals cannot be questioned. Organizational actions and procedures are consecrated, and the devout administrator must carry them out in their quest for holiness. The organizational logic of a holy organization tends toward closure and insulation of its moral judgments.

The paradox remains that the domain of the Holy remains fundamentally unknowable and unpredictable. Spiritual insight has launched revolutions and remains continuously available in many forms such as visitation, descent, or textual interpretation. Seemingly monolithic religious cultures generate immense disagreement and battles over heresy and bring about persecutions and wars among their own kind. But sustaining religion and relations with the Holy requires consistent ritual performance, resources, training, and teaching as well as consistent control. The unpredictable world of the spirit needs a mundane bureaucracy and administrators to maintain its practices, hand them down to the next generation, and maintain relations with the divine source of legitimacy (Davis, 2006). This uneasy relationship between the demand for consistency and predictability needed by all organizations and the untamed potential of the divine informs the dynamics of holy governing within both the holy and the governing estate.

The sanctification of organizational action informs internal moral attitudes and expands the ends of governing. Consecrated or devout governors increase their range of concern to guide and enforce the means of becoming holy in daily life (Davis, 2006; Potter, 1997). The holy state can intrude itself into daily actions to ensure the moral formation required for ordinary people to live and achieve the discipline of being holy. Just as holiness can become an object of discipline and practice, the holy state can now enforce that discipline on its people to increase holiness in the world. The internal moral logic of holy organizations faces three critical challenges, in which the organization must confront the possibility of evil and generate solutions: dissent, unbelievers, and exoneration or forgiveness.

Dissent

The infusion of sacred purpose into governing organizations deeply alters the state organization's relation to "others." Once state purpose encompasses a sacred mandate to form the character of the ruled, then anyone who does not fit the religious norms becomes suspect. For instance, opposition and dissent within the governing and religious establishment takes on a different tone. What might be considered normal policy debate transmutes to heresy or unorthodoxy that evokes greater moral wrath and warrants harsher punishment. Internal inquisitions against heretics and the unorthodox can be unleashed, resulting in ritualized castigation. Opposition equates with evil and warrants harsh actions or purges against dissenters. At the same time, the ineffable and unpredictable nature of the Holy opens up the constant potential for heterodoxy to come forward. Just as holiness can augment organizational power and narrow dissent, so can it release new genii of opposition and debate (Anderson, 2002).

Unbelievers

From inside the organization the dividing line of holy and evil extends to anyone not under the umbrella of the blessed or faithful. Anyone not committed to the path of holiness ordained by the uniting of governing and holiness becomes, by definition, potentially evil. Infidels or unbelievers are categorized as unholy and lie outside the norms of required treatment for the devout. This characterization enormously increases the potential for organizations to unleash immense suffering upon infidels, but the infliction of pain is not masked or hidden; rather, it is experienced as conquering evil in the world. People may be infidels through ignorance or, worse, obduracy, but both fall outside the scope of normal morality and could represent evil or threaten the holiness of the organization and its people. A world inhabited by active evil forces compounds the problem of unbelievers who may be controlled by or allies with the demonic. Holy administrators or soldiers do not need to worry about doing evil against the unbelievers because the unbelievers pose dangerous threats (Nigg, 1959; Tesfai, 2010).

The holy state, whether a theocracy, divine ruler, or consecrated by holy clerics, must deal with the nonbelievers in its midst. Because nonbelievers fall outside moral norms and can be evil, one clean solution is to exterminate them. A secular or traditional morality might call this genocide because it destroys humans who have done no harm to the ruler or others. The extermination, however, can be justified by the holy organization because unbelievers put themselves outside the realm of holiness and may be either threats or unredeemable. Here is where so much secular or traditional evil can be done, but because the people destroyed are by holy edict evil, then genocide or extermination becomes a positive good within the organization's moral logic. Extermination removes ungodliness or evil from the earth and makes the world more holy.

Another approach forces conversion. The conversation, forced or voluntary, has several advantages. It eliminates the unholy but also saves individuals from their infidelity and increases the holiness in the world. More than a few holy crusades across all religious traditions extend the range of the divine mandate by not only conquering the unholy but also forcibly converting them to a new way of life. The secular or moral evil would lie in violating people's conscience-bound beliefs by forcing them to live a way of life they abhor or find evil, but within the institutional intent, these unbelievers, by virtue of either ignorance or evil intent, lie outside normal moral categories and their conversion transmogrifies into a good.

Finally, holy governing can impose differential rights or treatment on the infidels. Differential taxes or property rights or restrictions on participation in society can all be regulated and limited by religious status. This differential treatment avoids the costs of extermination or forced conversion but over time limits the lives of those who keep their religious identity but suffer the daily erosion of position and freedom. In secular or traditional moral terms, this differential treatment violates conditions of fair and equal treatment before the law. Over time, these punitive costs either lead to emigration or conversation or mark the unbelievers as possible targets of pogroms or inquisitions. The union of ruling and holy narrows internal dissent and discussion and creates immense moral costs and differential treatment for anyone not linked to the tradition of holiness that pervades the ruling estate.

Exoneration and Forgiveness

Many religions generate sacred laws and rules that possess divine sanction and certainty. In a holy organization with absolute rules, administrators and soldiers may be called on to violate these laws. The rules often emerge from sacred texts or revelations and have great sacred moral weight. Administrators or warriors may be asked to violate the rules to achieve sacred goals, and they know that their actions violate their own sacred laws. They know that they are committing evil and do not hide from this. The sacred estate, however, whether ruler or clerics, addresses this dilemma. It is important to remember that in this case the individuals accept responsibility for their decisions and evil actions, so they do not hide from, mask, or pretend that what they are doing constitutes pure right. Holy organizations create rituals to provide forgiveness or exoneration for the warriors or administrators who perform the heinous acts. The forgiveness may require penance or atonement to restore moral balance. This sacred forgiveness or pardon permits religious orthodoxy to acknowledge objectively evil actions that violate sacred laws but enables organizations to exonerate the organizational actors who commit them.

This dynamic of merging holiness, organizations, and rule has many permutations, but this analysis focuses on two patterns. The first unites the ruler or ruling estate with the divine. The second mandates that clerics dominate the state in a theocracy. In the first, many rulers or families claim descent from their god and create blood-based sacred legitimacy for their lines. Divine emperors or divine-right kings also make claims based on other grounds such as divinely sanctioned conquest, but all reflect a strategy to insulate the rulers from external religious claims or secular-reasoned claims. This approach imbues rulers' actions with liturgical and sacred legitimacy. The force of divine writ supports the ruler's commands. The unity of rule and sacred sanctifies state and human actions.

Ascension to rule involves becoming divine as well as a ruler and requires worship as well as obedience. The ruler may be incarnate, visited, or possessed—it hardly matters, given the apparatus and consequences. Elaborate theologies can be developed to explain the divine and human nature of the ruler (Kantorowicz, 1957). The ruler does not need everyone to convert, just to worship or accede to the divine ruler. This solution simply abolishes the problem of organizational evil by making it impossible.

In the second relationship, theocracy unites state and holy but places the rule of clerics at the center, and the state becomes an instrument of the clerisy. The key lies in the autonomous religious clerical estate. The clerics claim a monopoly on the rituals and teaching that allow access to the divine presence. They control the sacrifices, the holy places, the training, and the discipline needed to acquire intimate familiarity with the insights and truth of the Holy. This monopoly over truth and moral rectitude anchor their claims to control the direction of government. Their monopoly over interpreting the sacred texts augments this. Both approaches deny the applicability of human reason and concepts to critique their logic and pronouncements. They develop a legal system to apply the sacred mandates to daily life. The clerics also maintain control over who is permitted to govern as gatekeepers. This widespread strategy is illustrated by Cromwell's revolution of the saints or Calvinist regimes in Europe (Walzer, 1965/1982). Medieval Europe witnessed endless disputes over legitimate succession after the Roman Catholic Church claimed the right to sanction the ruler and crown the ruler (Keen, 1987). While the medieval clerics never gained the level of control over the entire apparatus of governing that a theocracy requires, the medieval Church could depose rulers or incite rebellion among restless nobles by excommunicating rulers. The pope could place an entire realm under interdiction, which meant that the population could not receive sacraments, and it broke the bonds of fealty upon which feudal kings depended. The great Islamic caliphates experienced the same tensions.

One hallmark of a theocracy or strong holy organizations is the ability of the clerics to govern and judge themselves. This judicial independence grants the sacred estate autonomy that enables them to rule states through indirection. The modern Iranian state exhibits a very sophisticated modern form that unites theocratic power with the apparatus of the modern rational state. The clerical estate monopolizes interpretation of the text, controls seminary training, and the public education curriculum. It possesses a Guardian Council and Assembly of Experts to decide legal interpretations of the sacred text and Islamic law. Islamic law and its adjudicators trump secular law. The clerical institutions screen the people allowed to run for election, so the government is constrained by the clerical interpretation of orthodoxy. Advancement in the bureaucracy and military is monitored by the clerics, and senior appointments are made by the supreme leader, who is the supreme cleric appointed for life. Cleric-dominated foundations control the majority of the economy. The regime has evolved to the stage where the supreme leader is no longer regarded as merely the final interpreter of the text but as God's surrogate or God's voice on earth (Cole, 2005; Shapera, 2010). The Iranian and other recent experiments demonstrate the extent to which it is possible to meld the rational bureaucratic and technological state with orthodoxy grounded in the Holy (Cole, 2005; Tesfai, 2010).

Two dynamics influence these relationships between the holy and ruling estates. First, the clerical estate fights to control the definition of evil. All the issues associated with organizational evil are resolved if either the ruler or the clerics define evil and can exonerate violators of sacred laws. The clerics use their ability to delegitimize leaders to keep a tight rein on the aspiration of the rulers to establish an autonomous political domain (Machiavelli, 1977; Wolin, 2004). Second, the self-enclosed and self-enforcing monopoly on religious reality insulates the clerical estate from any effective accountability outside itself. The monopoly on holiness expands to immunity from state or popular control. Quite predictably, this clerical impunity results in the erosion of the integrity of the clerics. The capacity of people to delude themselves and rationalize their interests as moral endeavors can be a powerful draw in self-insulated elites (Festinger et al., 1987; Zimbardo, 2007). It engenders hubris not only to be the interpreter of the divine will but also to dismiss all questioning as heresy or blasphemy. Power, wealth, unquestioned will, deference, and the ability to dismiss opposition to one's will erode internal piety and undermine people's belief. The monopoly motivates careerists to enter the organization to acquire power, and these mixed motives as well as arrogance and immunity combine to create organizations that develop strong self-interest and goal displacement while becoming blinded to their own limitations by the sacred mission (Downs, 1967). The ability of clerics to define evil as opposition to their will permits unquestioned organizational evil to occur under the guise of holy good.

CONCLUSION

Organizational evil matters because organizations possess the power, the durability, and the ability to act on enormous scales. The achievements can involve evil—the intentional harm or destruction of human beings, creatures, and nature that are morally innocent. The magnitude and scale of harm rise as the quality and size of the organization grow, and the past century's slaughters demonstrate the sustained capacity of organizations to unleash hellish consequences. The question of how organizations and the people within them develop so that they can do evil and live with themselves becomes extremely important. I suggest that it goes beyond Václav Havel's concern that people subordinate their identity as rational tools of organizations; rather, humans can willingly destroy secularly innocent people, creatures, and nature when sustained by the power of the Holy (Havel, 1987).

I believe that the internal moral and cultural logic of organizations that are sustained by a relation to holiness exemplifies one way that this can occur. The human experience of a domain of existence that Rudolph Otto identified as the Holy or *numinous* inspires humans from awe and ecstasy to subordinate themselves to pursue the supernatural domain and truth. A person conceives of him or herself as a holy warrior devoted to a sacred cause sanctioned by clerics who articulate the mandates of the divine domain. The actions of these administrators, soldiers, and clerics express their quest to become holy as they eradicate evil and build a more perfect and holy world.

The paradox of holy organizations and their capacity for evil actions lies in the need for organizations to build strong organizational cultures to flourish (Collins, 2001; Schein, 2010;

Wilson, 1989). An organizational culture exists when cultural norms frame individual's relations, judgments, and actions (Bolman and Deal, 1997). A strong culture provides meaning and purpose for people in organizations and transforms organizations into communities of belief and practice (Weick, 2005). The culture helps people make sense of their world, frames their judgments, and builds strong norms of authority and role (Schein, 2010; Weick, 2005). Good leaders and strong organizations create robust cultures (Collins, 2001; Schein, 2010). The culture enables individuals to move from a relatively indifferent or compliance orientation to a commitment to the mission. This commitment increases morale, performance, and adaptability (Bolman and Deal, 1997; Senge, 1990).

The sanctification of an organization achieves all the goals of a strong organizational culture. The sacred purpose strengthens the norms, rituals, and commitments of people by making them liturgical actions with a holy purpose. Holiness consecrates the dictates of organizational rationality and enables organizations to exploit the power of specialization, consistency, routine, and resource allocation with a powerful parallel motivation to be holy, eradicate evil, and perform one's role in achieving divine purpose. This merges with the needs of a holy enterprise to enforce orthodoxy through consistency, goals, control, expertise, and confirmation for members.

The ends and the means of an organization are now consecrated to a high spiritual and moral end. This motivates individuals and anchors their identity in a sacred purpose and place. Holy actors can expand the range of organizational attention into any aspect of life that the clerics deem necessary to achieve holiness or exterminate heresy or blasphemy. Holy organizations seek to address and control the frailties of life that profane the world and block the path to holiness. It keeps the organization on high alert against the wiles and depredations of active evil forces in the world. The normal daily routines are hallowed and blessed, and mundane actions in organizations even of obscure specialists take on a moral luster of contributing to sacred ends. The internal moral logic of a holy organization, religious, state, or economic, pulsates with a deep moral purpose and certainty (Davis 2006).

Anchoring an organization in the experience and authority of holiness buttresses its culture and moral purpose. It narrows internal dissent to terms of orthodoxy and requires vigilance by clerics to ensure purity and holiness among themselves but also among the people in organizations. This leads to incessant internal inquisitions and creates an unstable and uncertain dynamic. This incessant self-scrutiny breeds different independent power bases within holy organizations. At the same time, the organizational rhetoric and moral appraisal escalate and any differences or disagreements spiral to more intense moral and religious conflicts. This intensifies the stakes of any disputes because arguments involve holy and sacred stakes, not just differences of opinion about policy, professional judgment, or ways of living. It becomes very hard to negotiate with holy organizations when other groups are seen as unbelievers or evil. Contracts, treaties, or agreements are reduced to mere resting points in an endless conflict. Often only exhaustion will generate peace with such organizations.

The key lesson for the study of organizational evil is in how holy organizations annul the issue of evil. This is not about evil being masked or misunderstood but, rather, about an organization that possesses the legitimacy to define evil and escalate any conflict into rhetoric about good versus evil. The entire realm of nonbelievers poses an unending challenge as unholy threats but also possible converts. The nonbelievers, however, exist in a moral category outside the range of holy rules and can be treated as such. Holy organizations return to the early origins of the concept of evil, which encompassed a wide array of wrong and bad action. Now daily organizational life and mundane actions take on moral urgency because they have sacred significance while orthodoxy permeates the rituals of daily, not just organizational, life.

People in consecrated organizations rest assured in the belief that the mediators of the holy domain bless their actions. Even when institutional actors must violate sacred rules, clerics offer forgiveness, exoneration, or even heavenly rewards for this sacrifice, and they laud the moral risk for a greater holy aim. Holy evil makes moral evil irrelevant to organizational life.

REFERENCES

Adams, G., and D. Balfour. 2009. *Unmasking Administrative Evil*, 3d ed. Armonk, NY: M.E. Sharpe.
Adolphson, M.S. 2007. *The Teeth and Claws of Buddha: Monastic Warriors and Sohei in Japanese History.* Honolulu: University of Hawaii's Press.
Anderson, J.M. 2002. *Daily Life During the Spanish Inquisition.* Westport, CT: Greenwood.
Augustine, Saint, Bishop of Hippo. 1958. *The City of God: An Abridged Version*, trans. Gerald Walsh and ed. V.J. Bourke. Garden City, NY: Image Books.
Barnhart, R.K., ed. 1999. *Chambers Dictionary of Etymology.* New York: Chambers.
Benedict, Saint, Abbot of Monte Cassino. 1981. *The Rule of Saint Benedict in Latin and English*, ed. Timothy Fry. Collegeville, MN: Liturgical Press.
Bolman, L., and T. Deal. 1997. *Reframing Organizations: Artistry, Choice and Leadership.* San Francisco: Jossey Bass.
Brown, P. 1997. *The Rise of Western Christendom.* Oxford: Blackwell.
Casey, E.S. 1997. *The Fate of Place: A Philosophical History.* Berkeley: University of California Press.
Cole, J. 2005. *Sacred Space and Holy War: The Politics, Culture and History of Shi'ite Islam.* New York: I.B. Tauris.
Collins, James C. 2001. *Good to Great.* New York: Harper Books.
Davis, A.J. 2006. *The Holy Bureaucrat: Eudes Rigaud and Religious Reform in Thirteenth Century Normandy.* Ithaca: Cornell University Press.
Downs, A. 1967. *Inside Bureaucracy.* Boston: Little, Brown.
Eliade, M. 1957/1987. *The Sacred and Profane: The Nature of Religion*, trans. Willard R. Trask. New York: Harcourt.
Festinger, L., H.W. Riecken, and S. Schachter. 1987. *When Prophecy Fails: A Social and Psychological Study of a Group That Predicted the Destruction of the World.* New York: Harper & Row.
Figgis, J.N. 1965. *The Divine Right of Kings.* New York: Harper & Row.
Havel, V. 1987. *Living in Truth*, ed. Jan Vladislav. London: Faber.
Jones, Alexander, ed. 1966. *The Jerusalem Bible.* Garden City, NY: Doubleday.
Jones, A.H.M. 1967. *Constantine and the Conversion of Europe.* New York: Macmillan.
Kantorowicz, E. 1957. *The King's Two Bodies: A Study in Medieval Political Theory.* Princeton: Princeton University Press.
Keen, M. 1987. *The Pelican History of Medieval Europe.* Harmondsworth, UK: Penguin.
Kerr, J. 2009. *Life in the Medieval Cloister.* London: Continuum.

Machiavelli, N. 1977. *The Prince*, trans. Robert M. Adams. New York: Norton.

Machinist, P., ed. 2003. *Prophets and Prophecy in the Ancient Near East*. Boston: Brill.

Mallory, J., and D.Q. Adams. 1997. *Encyclopedia of Indo-European Culture*. London: Adams Taylor.

McMillan, D.J., and K.S. Fladenmuller. 1997. *Regular Life: Monastic, Canonical and Mendicant Rules*. Kalamazoo, MI: Medieval Institute.

Mitchell, S. 2004. *Gilgamesh: A New English Translation*. New York: Free Press.

Nigg, W. 1959. *Warriors of God: The Great Religious Orders and Their Founders*, ed. and trans. by Mary Ilford. New York: Knopf.

Onions, C.T., ed. 1966. *Oxford Dictionary of English Etymology*. Oxford: Oxford University Press.

Otto, R. 1923/1958. *The Idea of the Holy*, trans. John W. Harvey. Oxford: Oxford University Press.

Plato. 1968. *The Republic*, trans. Allan Bloom. New York: Basic Books.

Pocock, J.G.A. 1975. *The Machiavellian Moment: Florentine Political Though and the Atlantic Republican Tradition*. Princeton: Princeton University Press.

Potter, D. 1997. *Prophets and Emperors: Human and Divine Authority from Augustus to Theodosius*. Cambridge: Harvard University Press.

Rousseau, P. 2010. *Ascetics, Authority and the Church in the Age of Jerome and Cassian*. Notre Dame: Notre Dame University Press.

Schein, E.H. 2010. *Organizational Culture and Leadership*. San Francisco: Jossey-Bass.

Senge, P.M. 1990. *The Fifth Discipline: The Art and Practice of the Learning Organization*. New York: Currency.

Shapera, P. 2010. *Understanding Iran: Iran's Religious Leaders*. New York: Rosen.

Singh, N. 1997. *The Origin and Development of Buddhist Monastic Education in India*. Delhi: Indo-Asian Publishing.

Tesfai, Y. 2010. *Holy Warriors, Infidels, and Peacemakers in Africa*. New York: Palgrave Macmillan.

Walzer, M. 1965/1982. *The Revolution of the Saints: A Study in the Origins of Radical Politics*. Cambridge: Harvard University Press.

———. 1992. *Just and Unjust Wars: A Moral Argument with Historical Illustrations*. New York: Basic Books.

Watkins, C. 2000. *The American Heritage Dictionary of Indo-European Roots*, 2d ed. Boston: Houghton Mifflin Harcourt.

Weick, K.E. 2005. *Making Sense of the Organization*. Oxford: Blackwell.

Wilson, J.Q. 1989. *Bureaucracy: What Government Agencies Do and Why They Do It*. New York: Basic Books.

Wolin, S.S. 2004. *Politics and Vision: Continuity and Innovation in Western Political Thought*. Princeton: Princeton University Press.

Zimbardo, P. 2007. *The Lucifer Effect: How Good People Turn Evil*. New York: Random House.

8

Imagining and Managing Organizational Evil

Melvin J. Dubnick, Jonathan B. Justice, and Domonic A. Bearfield

In this chapter, we argue—less paradoxically than it might at first appear—that organizational evil (OE) is, at the same time, a fundamentally nonsensical idea and a concern of real importance for those studying or leading organizations. Nonsensical, we believe, because the senses in which the expression "organizational evil" is typically used—to describe a property or characteristic of organizations generally or a form of conduct perpetrated by particular organizations—do not correspond in any meaningful way to actual social or natural phenomena. Genuinely important, however, because the use of the language is subjectively meaningful, and therefore consequential and actionable for a wide range of actors in (and concerned with) organizations. The uniquely strong reactive attitudes (Strawson, 1962; Wallace, 1994) that give rise to the use of the language of organizational evil (or simply "evil" in any context), and the often equally strong behavioral responses by a variety of stakeholders to such attitudes, are undeniably real and may have consequences ranging from scholarly confusion (see Dubnick, 2000) to destructive social and organizational convulsions, including moral panics, witch hunts, and the like (cf. Alford, 1997b).

Thus, the often nonsensical language of organizational evil motivates organizational stakeholders in ways that may have very significant consequences, for good (such as preventing or correcting wrong and destructive behavior) or ill (such as substituting a new wrong for the original one). By understanding how the meaning of organizational evil is constructed and acted upon, organizational scholars and leaders may be able to manage (or, at the least, anticipate and cope with) that construction and respond in more consistently beneficial ways. Accordingly, we attempt here to explain our reasoning and its significance and to identify its implications for organizational researchers and leaders.

The chapter is organized into three major sections. First, we make the case that, because organizations and evil are both quintessentially *social facts* (see Searle, 1995) with no existence independent of their social context, the common ways of speaking about organizational evil as a thing in-and-of-itself (i.e., existing independently of the volition and actions of individuals) are largely nonsensical. Yet organizational evil understood as a contextually contingent, functional social construct is, in fact, a socially meaningful concept. Next, we explore how that understanding helps us to make sense of the very real ways in which scholars, managers, and laypeople respond to acts and actors that seem so egregiously bad as to be morally incomprehensible. Developing a typology of expressive as well as instrumental reactions to perceived evil acts and actors associated with organizations allows us to categorize some familiar historical cases and to see how certain types of reactions can have either destructive or constructive consequences.

Finally, we conclude by noting paradoxically that so-called organizational evil, if properly understood, may (if also properly managed or accommodated) be functionally beneficial, serving to promote constructive moral vigilance and correction among an organization's members and other stakeholders. We offer as both tentative prescription and research hypothesis the central claim that the ordinary practical ethical reasoning employed by nonsociopaths in their daily life provides a firm underlying basis for the prevention, detection, and correction of actions that would be regarded as organizational evil. This can fruitfully be nurtured by organizations' leaders, with any tradeoffs of individual ethical empowerment against efficiency and obedience adapted to the circumstances of specific organizations and tasks. Moreover, because ethical reasoning is a learned skill, it can also be further developed in specific organizational environments and task contexts and for specific members of organizations, in appropriate degrees.

IMPORTANT NONSENSE

For students of philosophy, the problem of evil has long been regarded as theological: if God is a beneficent, omnipresent, and omniscient force in the universe, how does one explain the presence and power of evil in the world (Kremer and Latzer, 2001)? In contrast, the central problem faced by students of organizational evil is ontological, focused directly on the issue of whether organizational evil is metaphysically real (that is, exists outside our mental construction of it) or whether it is a product of our individual and collective cognition of our world.

In this chapter, we assume the latter position, viewing organizational evil as an important social construct that serves a functionally significant role in the way that organizations deal with extreme threats or forms of deviance from their norms and practices. But before offering our limited insights into the functionality of OE as a social construct, we need to address the basic ontological issue. Our goal in this section is to provide a preemptive defense to anticipated charges that our analysis avoids the central issues related to OE by defining out of existence the "evil-is-real" views held by many of our colleagues. Our response is "guilty as charged," but with the qualifier that our position is not merely defensible but necessary if we are to advance the work of the organizational sciences. Just as modern philosophy flourished when Enlightenment thinkers abandoned the obsessive preoccupation with theodicy (the study of the classic "problem of evil"),[1] so the administrative sciences have made (and will continue to make) substantial progress by "naturalizing" the supernatural concept of OE and bringing it into the arena of empirically grounded social theory.

Putting our perspective in context ontologically requires revisiting one of the most fundamental questions in philosophy: What is reality? More specifically, is reality mind-independent, or is its existence contingent on the workings of the human mind and experience? This seemingly esoteric concern (after all, few of us ever stop in the middle of our busy days to consider whether our interactions with the world are truly real or merely figments of our imagination) does have a significant impact on how we approach questions related to OE. They are questions that predate the foundational philosophies of Plato and Aristotle, but their respective responses have effectively established the alternatives that define the debate. For Plato and Platonists (typically noted as the "idealists" in this debate), reality is metaphysical, and although we are capable of capturing the particular manifestation of that reality in our thoughts and actions, its essence is beyond our mental or physical reach. In contrast, Aristotle's realism is "naturalist" and grounded in the belief that people and things are of this world and can indeed be captured intellectually as well as materially. Transformed, extended, and reconstructed in many ways over the centuries, the distinction endures. And although no particular labels can capture the complexity of the resulting debate generated by that philosophical division, for present purposes we settle on two: metaphysical realism and pragmatic realism.

"Metaphysical realism" is the label we apply to the perspective that assumes the existence of a mind-independent world with an objective existence. Although we can develop various strategies for conceptualizing and dealing with that objective reality, its existence does not rely on our mental gymnastics or imagination. "Pragmatic realism,"[2] in contrast, assumes an agnostic stance when addressing the issue of an objective reality. Rather, it is through our practical experience and intellectual engagement with the world that reality becomes manifest, therefore rendering reality contingent on situations and surroundings.

How does this distinction relate to the study of OE? For students of modern organizations, the nature of "truth" remains an open and divisive question. This is especially true for those engaged in the examination of organizational evil, in which the phrase itself begs for clarification at the outset. Are we dealing with a compound noun, or is "organizational" indicative of a particular form of evil? Assuming the latter (as we do in this chapter), are we to focus on the evil *of* organizations? The evil done *by* organizations? Or the evil that takes place *within* organizations? All can be posited as legitimate focal points for analysis.

But responses to those conceptual and analytic choices pale in importance before how we approach the ontological standing of organizational evil. Are we dealing with a metaphysical reality that is not mind-dependent, or is it a pragmatic mental or social construct created in response to some condition or change in our surroundings? Or is it a variation of the two extremes—a phenomenon that takes on the characteristics of a meaningful condition that must be addressed as an objective reality in order to deal with it?

The significance of these somewhat abstract options is plotted in Figure 8.1, where we have transposed the alternative perspectives for the two keywords in our subject: organizations and evil. At the two extremes (A/D) are studies that approach the subject in completely opposite ways. Cell "A" posits the existence of organizations as distinct (albeit typically collective)[3] social actors that can be treated as if they possess a malevolent will (mission) and operate under an explicitly destructive logic. Finding credible organizational studies scholarship of this sort is difficult, for it requires an initial effort to establish a warrantable connection between organizational evil and its empirical referent in the world of

Figure 8.1 **Alternative "Realities" of Organizational Evil**

The "reality" of evil:	The "reality" of organizations:	
	Metaphysical	Pragmatic
Metaphysical	A. Pure organizational evil	C. Organizations as instruments used by evil persons
Pragmatic	B. Organizations create evil acts/ actors	D. Perceived (constructed) organizational evil

organizations. There are perhaps no more obvious candidates for such a study than those organized efforts identified with the structure and operations of the Holocaust, especially the network that made the *Shoah*—a term applied to the explicit and systematic policy to exterminate Jews conducted by the Nazi regime—possible. Even more likely candidates are studies that zero in on the structure and operations of the five Nazi extermination camps (Arad, 1987; see also Sofsky, 1996; Todorov, 1996)[4]—Auschwitz-Birkenau, Chelmno, Belzec, Sobibor, and Treblinka. All five[5] were part of "Operation Reinhard," established in 1941 with the express purpose of carrying out the Final Solution to the Jewish "problem" in Poland, although they also served as destinations for others from throughout Nazi-ruled Europe. As horrific as these studies are, any claim to be the study of organizational evil per se effectively begs the core question as to the metaphysical existence of OE and thus undermines the value of such analytic efforts.[6]

At the same time, the more coldly analytic studies that fall under the pure pragmatic reality category (organizational evil as a social construct) may be regarded as detracting from the very special nature of the functions and productions—the horrific destructiveness—of such organized efforts as the extermination camps. In its most extreme form, the social constructionist perspective seems best suited for "deniers" who believe that the evidence of the horror is merely a faulty interpretation of the historical facts imposed by those with a political agenda (see Hacking, 1999, 3–5). Moreover, such a perspective can be regarded as nurturing a nonjudgmental, amoral position that can create an ethical indifference among students of organizations: In place of "never again," social constructivism promoted the view that "stuff happens."

Our schema points to two alternative perspectives to the "pure" types, and each has had major impacts on the study of so-called organizational evil. The metaphysical view of organizations gives "life" to such entities as unique collectivities that must be treated as if they had a distinct form of agency in our social milieu. Whatever our view about the fantastical nature of this assumption about organizations, it is one ensconced in laws (and legal systems as a whole) that treat corporations as "persons" with the rights and privileges of all other persons under law. Under type B of Figure 8.1 are studies that take such a view of organizations seriously in teleological terms. Most often associated with the Weberian view of modern bureaucracies, organizations are potentially all-encompassing (totalizing) contexts that pursue the rationalization of collective behavior by subtly (but intentionally) imposing a logic of technical rationality on those who are either engaged in or affected by it. This technical rationality is central to the *evil created by* modern organizations (Adams and Balfour, 2004; Hummel, 2008). While not denying the objective reality of evil, studies of "administrative evil" stress that it is the product of a dehumanization process that creates thoughtless and inhumane actors out of otherwise "ordinary people" (e.g., Bauman, 1989; Browning, 1992; Hilberg, 1985, 1992).[7] Here, in short, it is the evil *of* (perpetrated by) organizations that is most crucial, and individuals within the organizations are portrayed as nearly helpless dupes or pawns of some flatly inhuman entity—the organization itself.

This approach to organizational proves problematic in a number of respects, not the least being the credibility of its foundational premise regarding the inherent evilness of organizations (Dubnick, 2000) and its all too simple (and dangerously careless) attribution of evildoing to those who may lack evil intentions (cf. Singer, 2004).[8]

In contrast to type B, C-type studies emphasize the objective reality of evil and regard organizations as mere venues or vehicles for carrying out evil agendas. Here we find the historical and fictional narratives of evil persons creating of assuming control of the organizational apparatus required to fulfill malevolent goals. Finding exemplars of evil persons in the sense offered by Marcus Singer is, sadly, not difficult.

> The term "evil" is the worst term of opprobrium that can be applied to a human being. . . . Evil deeds must flow from evil motives, the volition to do something evil, by which I mean something horrendously bad. One cannot do something evil by accident or through thoughtlessness. Through accident or misadventure one can do something wrong or bad, even terrible, but not something evil. So when we say that someone did something evil, we are saying something about that person, that person's motives and consequently about that person's character. (Singer, 2004, 190)

But finding examples of evil persons who make use of organizations with the explicit intention of carrying out their evil schemes proves more difficult. The one obvious example that comes to mind is Adolf Hitler, but, as Ron Rosenbaum has argued, he may in fact be a unique and unprecedented case (Rosenbaum, 1998)—a point that Hannah Arendt stresses about the more general existence of evil in her writings on what took place in Europe during the 1930s and 1940s (see Baehr, 2002). Ian Kershaw, in making the case against treating Hitler and Stalin as similar, argued that it is more fruitful to view Hitler as a charismatic force that overwhelmed and subjected the German state to his will. "What occurred in the Third Reich was not the supplanting of bureaucratic domination by 'charismatic authority,' but rather the superimposition of the latter on the former" (Kershaw, 1993, 112).

The choice we make from among these four OE perspectives as students of organizations can prove significant not merely in terms of how we carry out our analyses but also how the results are to be perceived and evaluated. Explicating the rationale behind that choice is therefore important in at least two respects: First, it offers the reader/consumer of such studies (including other researchers) an explicit standard by which to judge the work, and, second, it offers the researcher an opportunity to reflect upon what intentions and biases are influencing the effort (cf. Bunge, 2006; Tsoukas, 2000).

As already noted, our choice among the four viewpoints is to consider both dimensions of OE as social constructs (Type D). Moreover, we take the position that this perspective is the only credible option if the intention is (as it is in our case) to advance the study of organizations as an empirically grounded phenomenon that pervades our lives at all levels. The central question for us at the outset was whether this particular aspect of modern organizations—that is, the widespread presence of a belief in the existence of OE—can be explained and, if so, whether the belief in OE can be framed in a way that further enhances our knowledge about social life within and among organizations.

MAKING SENSE OF ORGANIZATIONAL EVIL

To reiterate our focus in this chapter, we are considering how and why so-called evil emerges within organizations as well as various scenarios for dealing with it when it does emerge. We begin with the (Type D) assumption that both organizations and the concept of evil are functional social constructs, constituted in specific situations and cultural milieus. They are, for all intents and purposes, historically and culturally contingent *social facts* (Searle, 1995).

Regarding organizations, we assume the constructivist position that they are ongoing social enactments, the dynamic product of the intersubjective institutionalization of social norms and practices (see Gergen and Thatchenkery, 1996; Weick, 1979; cf. Fleetwood, 2005). Thus, even to talk about an organization as a distinct entity that behaves or takes meaningful action is, at best, a convenient form of reification that, while pragmatically and rhetorically useful, can prove dysfunctional in both practical and analytical terms.

Relying on this dereified perspective, organizations can be viewed analytically in a number of ways, ranging from a relatively neutral setting for individual or social interaction (e.g., a stage upon which the human drama of "organizing" is played out) to a cognitive factor that helps constitute and mediate purposeful social activity. In that sense, the organization cannot be regarded as either agent or actor, yet in so-called organizational evil it is treated as a contingency or (at best) causal factor.

Similarly, evil is also treated as a social construct with specific functionality and characteristics. Functionally, evil is used in social situations as an attribution of either an act or actor under a variety of circumstances. A distinction can be made between attributions that are made with intention and purpose (instrumental) and those that reflect a strong subjective response to act or action that is perceived as threatening, deviant in the extreme—that is, outside the attributor's moral frame of reference—unconscionable or otherwise socially unfathomable (expressive).

Sociologists would regard the act of attribution—whether instrumental or expressive— as a form of "labeling" that, whatever its intent, stigmatizes the targeted act/actor while giving some degree of affective satisfaction to those who apply or accept it.[9] Figure 8.2 provides some perspective on the types of responses reflected in attributions. An expressive attribution that focuses on the deviant actor will be judgmental, asserting that the individual

Figure 8.2 **Types of Attribution Responses**

Focus on:	Attribution is:	
	Expressive	Instrumental
Actor	Judgmental	Stigmatizing
Act	Indignation	Condemnation

acted in an unacceptable way (bad, wrong, inappropriately) (see Kaplan, 1942). When applied with intent, the attribution can be extended to characterizing—stigmatizing—the actor (Goffman, 1963; Link and Phelan, 2001). When applied expressively to a particular act, the response usually rises to the level of indignation and resentment (reflecting what P.F. Strawson called a "reactive attitude" in the attributor) (Russell, 1992; Strawson, 1962). In more strategic hands, the attribution of the act amounts to condemnation and calls for sanctions and other forms of punishment (see Piven, 1981).

When it comes to the label "evil," these characteristics of attributions are more extreme. All attributions of acts and actors are likely to generate responses in the form of changes and adjustments in the perceptions and actions at all levels of the organization (e.g., individual, group), but those that tend to warrant the designation as evil seem to create an imperative for a response, especially if motivated by intent (instrumental).

Those responses can take various forms in society, ultimately leading to the "neutralization" or "destigmatization" of the labeled actor or act (Sykes and Matza, 1957; Warren, 1980). In some instances, the evil attribution can result in the demonization of labeled populations and result in "moral panics" (see below; Cohen, 2002; Goode and Ben-Yehuda, 1994). This, in turn, can lead to the expansion of moral regulations designed to preclude and preempt future evils (Critcher, 2009; Hier, 2002). At other times, an attribution can be modified, using processes that sociologists call "delabeling" or "relabeling." Many of these studies focus on the changing of labels from implying deviance (e.g., alcoholic) to designating some form of malady (e.g., alcoholism) (Preston et al., 1998; Trice and Roman, 1970). In the same way, they imply a process in which acts and actors initially attributed as evil might be regarded as merely deviant or suffering from an illness that caused the depraved behavior.

We believe these same dynamics apply when dealing with so-called organizational evil. When, through either expressive or instrumental attribution, organizational acts/actors are stained with the label of evil, a number of processes take place that can either aggravate or ameliorate the situation established by the attribution. In the following analysis we consider three such processes: (1) demonization, (2) relabeling, and (3) recasting.

The basis for our analysis is the framework in Figure 8.3, which distinguishes between how acts and actors are perceived in the context of a problematic situation in which they are the focus of attention. In the most extreme situation (Cell D), both the act and actor are regarded as evil, creating a state that is most appropriately termed "wickedness." This is the focus of our examination of demonization and moral panics. Cells B and C are central to our analysis of relabeling, because both involve reconsideration of the motivations and circumstances under which terrible acts occur. In Cell B, the evil sup-

Figure 8.3   **Forms of Socially Constructed Organizational Evil**

Act perceived as:	Actor is perceived as:	
	Transgressor	Evil
Transgression	(A) Accountability	(B) Agentic state
Evil	(C) Grey Zone	(D) Wickedness

Source: Based on Dubnick and Justice, 2006.

posedly resides in the actor who is thoughtlessly "just following orders" or doing what is expected without reflecting on the contribution of his or her minor transgressions to the unspeakable outcomes. This situation was famously described by Hannah Arendt as the banality of evil, and it was Stanley Milgram who described such individuals as being in an "agentic state" of mind. In Cell C, by contrast, are actors who operate in what Primo Levi (1989) called the moral "gray zone," in which their awareness of the horrible acts they are committing is offset by the need to survive (or succeed) within their social milieu. Finally, in Cell A we find examples of both delabeling and the neutralization of evil attributions through accountability and other means.

Demonization: Wickedness and Moral Panics

As a social construction, perceived wickedness in organizations can take a variety of forms. The act-actor tie is almost an identity. In the evident cases found in the literature, the connection was strong and perhaps inseparable: bullying-bully (Rhodes et al., 2010; Vickers, 2001, 2010), racism-racist (Brief et al., 2000; Cortina, 2008; Griffith et al., 2007; Mistry and Latoo, 2009), and child abuse-child abuser (deYoung, 1996, 2008; Hier, 2008; Murray, 2001; Richardson, Reichert, and Lykes, 2009). In such extreme cases, the reaction both inside and outside an organization is to extend the process of labeling through "demonization," a basis for the development of moral panics.

Here we focus on the case of racism as a "moral evil." Given the long and troubled history in the United States concerning issues of race, the racism-racist tie has become (rightfully so) a rich target for demonization. In recent years, overt discrimination on the basis of color has often resulted in strong and severe rebukes for those accused. This is especially true of those who can be described as possessing a "racist heart," an individual committed to and completely unrepentant about racist acts (Garcia, 1996, 1997; cf. Shelby, 2002).

> In its central and most vicious form, it is a hatred, ill-will, directed against a person or persons on account of their assigned race. In a derivative form, one is a racist when one either does not care at all or does not care enough (i.e., as much as morality requires) or does not care in the right ways about people assigned to a certain racial group, where this disregard is based on racial classification. Racism, then, is something that essentially involves not our beliefs and their rationality or irrational-

ity, but our wants, intentions, likes, and dislikes and their distance from the moral virtues. . . . Such a view helps explain racism's conceptual ties to various forms of *hatred* and contempt. (Garcia, 1996, 6–7)

Garcia's view (he terms it "volitional racism"), ironically, frees the moral evil of racism from its racial moorings. White on nonwhite racism might have been the initial focus of antidiscrimination efforts and policies, but minorities in positions of power have increasingly been called to account for their actions concerning discrimination toward people outside their own racial/ethnic group.

For instance, shortly after the election of Barack Obama in 2008, several conservative media personalities suggested that the country's first black president would exact revenge on the white population as a means of payback for years of historical discrimination. Media outlets argued that the Justice Department's refusal to charge the fringe activist group the New Black Panther Party with voter intimidation, and an incident in which a young white student was beat up on a school bus by a group of blacks provided evidence of what the future would look like in "Obama's America."

In July 2010, Big Government, a Web site owned by new media entrepreneur Andrew Breitbart, posted a video of a speech given by Shirley Sherrod, an official with U.S. Department of Agriculture, at an awards dinner for the National Association for the Advancement of Colored People (NAACP). In the video, Sherrod, an African-American woman, was telling a story about how, earlier in her career, she had discriminated against a white farmer who went to her for help. Soon afterward, other media outlets began showing the video, claiming it as evidence that an Obama administration official had engaged in racial discrimination. Within days, the fury surrounding Sherrod's speech had become so intense that she was forced to resign, with Agriculture Secretary Tom Vilsack pointing to the administration's "zero tolerance" on discrimination as the reason for her separation.

Sociologists would describe this incident as a "moral panic," a term first used by Stanley Cohen in his classic study of English youth gangs (Cohen, 2002). There he describes an exaggerated reaction to phenomena or events that are perceived as threatening or upsetting traditional norms. At the center of a moral panic is the folk devil: a group, entity, or object that emerges as the target of disdain. Described as "the personification of evil" (Hier, 2002), folk devils serve as "visible reminders of what we should not be" (Cohen, 2002, 2). In this respect, folk devils are, in Goffman's terms, stigmatized: discredited individuals or groups that bear the markers of their stigmatism as a part of their social identity (Goffman, 1963). What makes the folk devil different is that it has been demonized and, as a consequence, it has been marked as evil—a burden much greater than that carried by most discredited groups. While "normals" may shun those they have stigmatized, they are still allowed to coexist. But how does one coexist with evil? One cannot, thus the demonized folk devil must be defeated or purged.

As soon as the video went viral on the Internet, Sherrod was transformed into the face of wickedness. Here was a relatively high-placed black public official who seemed to relish telling the story of how she had once discriminated against the white farmer, and for many the image presented of "Obama's America" became strikingly real. In an agency that had recently been accused of perpetuating discriminatory policies with regard to African-American farmers, the emergence of Sherrod as a folk devil in the media was too much to bear. A moral panic gripped the Department of Agriculture's decision makers and only seemed to subside after evil was exorcised by the organization's zero-tolerance policy.

Yet the rush to judgment that frequently surrounds moral panics has an inherent danger. Because these events can erupt and subside quite rapidly, one could be demonized and purged before all the facts have come to light. In case of Sherrod, days after her firing, another video version of her speech emerged, revealing that Sherrod's comments had been edited and were clearly presented out of context. In a full, unedited version, Sherrod tells a story of racial reconciliation, about how she fought to overcome her initial prejudice toward the white farmer. Instead of a tale of a public official who abused her position by engaging in racial discrimination, the video captured the story of how she went above and beyond to help this particular farmer save his family's farm.

The feeding frenzy surrounding the Sherrod case and its very quick unfolding in the media offers a public example of what likely occurs on a less-visible level in organizations in which the social construction of wickedness is perhaps more common than many would admit. Despite the existence of potential pathways out of the demonization trap, however, the attribution of moral evil is a powerful force that is just as likely to degenerate into dysfunctional and destructive moral panics.

Relabeling I: Constructing the Evil Agent

Demonization and moral panics are not the only options after the perception of evil takes hold in an organizational setting. When socially constructed evil becomes dysfunctional—that is, when its emergence in response to an unspeakable act or actor itself becomes a threat to the very existence of the organized effort—a variety of psychological and strategic mechanisms can come into play that can make the perception itself more "manageable" in the sense of allowing both organization members and external observers to "make sense" of what was initially unfathomable. Many of these sense-making mechanisms (see Weick, 1979, 1995) involve altering the meaning of the attribution—a process termed "relabeling" by those who study the sociology of deviance (e.g., Preston et al., 1998; Trice and Roman, 1970).

The relabeling path out of the wickedness zone takes two forms, each an attempt to provide a meaningful explanation or excuse for the perceived evil act or actor without necessarily rendering it forgivable or legally actionable. One path involves viewing the so-called evil-doers as submissive agents who are oblivious or indifferent to the horrific implications of the organized endeavor in which they are engaged. This is the view reflected in Arendt's "banality of evil" (1976), and it represents the evil-doers as thoughtless and unreflective, yet willing, participants operating as cogs in a destructive machine. From this perspective, the core evilness lies primarily in the thoughtless actor who, rather than being regarded as some hapless dolt, bears moral responsibility for assuming an "agentic state" and not asserting the inherent human capacity to "choose to do otherwise." The alternative path, discussed below, builds on Primo Levi's observations regarding the moral "gray zone" that formed the setting of consciously complicit evil-doers.

To understand the agentic state form of evil, we turn to Stanley Milgram's famous (and infamous) study of obedience (Milgram, 1963, 1974), an explicit test of this model of evil. In those well-known experiments, he placed his subjects in a setting that required and fostered the legitimate expectation for obedient behavior. On a strictly objective level, the organizational setting for the experiments could hardly have been more benign: a lab on a university campus overseen by an authoritative-looking figure (the "scientist" in a white lab jacket) and an explanation that gave the impression that this was a justifiable experiment related to the improvement of learning. In the waiting area, each subject met and chatted informally with the other "participant" in the experiment, and both were evidently being compensated for their time. In short, everything was done to drive the primary subject of the real experiment into what Milgram terms an agentic state in which there are clear expectations of carrying the operations to a successful completion.

Putting aside the ethical issues raised by the design and conduct of the Milgram experiment, its results provide support for a view that ordinary people, placed in objectively benign settings, can carry out significant acts of torture without a "second thought" about the moral consequences of their behavior. For Arendt and others who adhere to a Kantian notion of "radical evil," the agentic state assumed by individuals is an inherent aspect (and danger) of modern organizational life that can be overcome by making moral choices not to participate (as did some subjects in Milgram's study). Those who do not do so—those who render themselves "superfluous"—are condemnable as thoughtless evil-doers.

Shifting the socially constructed perception of OE from the demonization of wickedness to the thoughtlessness of agentic evil does not, at first, seem like an "improvement" in the situation. But the Arendtian formulation carries the implied sense that those operating under the pressures of an inherent "radical evil" could choose not to do so, if only they exercised the moral will to reflect on what they are doing or being asked to do. As social constructs, demons are hopeless; agents are salvageable.

Relabeling II: Entering the Gray Zone

The alternative relabeling path to dealing with the perceived OE is to render the act or actor's behavior as understandable (but not excusable) "under the circumstances." To comprehend this perspective, we turn to the concept of "gray zone" morality associated with the work of Primo Levi. A Holocaust survivor, he used the phrase to situate those individuals—the kapos, Sonderkommandos (the "Special Squads" of inmates who ran the crematoriums), and others who directly implemented the evil of the Holocaust—whose transgressions pose a true dilemma for those trying to make sense of them. The acts that they commit in the process of operating the deadly machinery of their Nazi Lagers are wicked by definition, and yet those who commit the acts can be regarded as no less victims than the other inmates of the camps. "Conceiving and organizing the[se special] squads was National Socialism's most demonic crime," declares Levi—not only for the obvious reason that hundreds of thousands perished as a result but also for the moral depravity forced upon those who literally implemented those plans (1989, 37). The organizational setting did not merely "induce" horrendous actions; it often demanded open complicity in the effort (cf. Berger, 1995).

Unlike those who enter the psychological agentic state fostered by Milgram's experimental setting, occupants of the gray zone were not oblivious or indifferent to the reprehensible nature of their acts. If anything, they surrendered to their circumstances and (in too many instances) developed a sense of enthusiasm and accomplishment in a job well done. In contrast to Arendtian expectations, a reflective and thoughtful actor does not necessarily become less evil but may, in fact, become even more deserving of the attribution. But there is an added factor at play: empathy for the perceived evil-doer and a palpable inability to pass judgment (*impotentia judicandi*) (Levi, 1989, 60). In Levi's gray zone, traditional categories of morality collapse, and the problem emerges of having to deal with evil acts undertaken by actors who cannot be judged under any of the extant ethical categories or standards (see Agamben, 2000).

For support of this view, we turn to another set of experiments associated with the study of the human capacity for so-called evil. The Stanford Prison Experiment (Zimbardo, 1972) is often viewed as a confirmation of the Milgram study, but it points to something quite different: the power of organizational roles in the fostering of malevolent behavior. The setting and the orientations of participants to their "jobs" in the short-lived experiment are well documented in film footage and postevent interviews as well as writing, and what the evidence indicates is that ordinary individuals can transform themselves into enthusiastic accomplices in shocking behavior. In recent years, Zimbardo and his colleagues have extended the lessons drawn from his experiment to a more extended analysis that addressed events such as Abu Ghraib, making the case for what he terms the "Lucifer effect" in organizational settings (Zimbardo, 2007).

What the gray zone perspective shares with the agentic state construction of evil is the implication that something can be done to alter the Lucifer effect of organizational settings. In reflecting on the Stanford experiments twenty-five years later, Craig Haney and Zimbardo made a plea for actions to deal with (alter or eliminate) those settings (Haney and Zimbardo, 1998) in the real world of prisons. But they also note that while malformed prison settings can transform ordinary ("normal") individuals into abusive role takers, those settings can also magnify pathological tendencies to escalate the evil-doing (Haney and Zimbardo, 1998, 719–720). Still, moving so-called evil into the gray zone provides a greater opening to actionable changes than that offered by the demonizing alternative.

Recasting: Transformation of Evil Construct

Thus far we have considered three ways of dealing with constructed OE, involving demonization and two forms of "relabeling." What these approaches share is a commitment to retaining the concept of evil as a way to make sense of the unconscionable act and the unfathomable actor. There is, however, a wide range of options for dealing the evil label itself, which we bring together under the idea of "recasting."

Some of these involve "delabeling" tactics by which it is demonstrated that the attribution itself was inappropriate from the outset or is not relevant under present conditions. The case of Shirley Sherrod, discussed above, is exemplary, although rarely is the process so visible as was this widely covered incident. Delabeling of that sort is extremely difficult if the process of demonization has already created a moral panic that seems to permanently stigmatize the individuals involved even when the accusations eventually prove to have been completely without merit.[10] Other forms of delabeling noted in the deviance literature involve efforts to have attributions expunged from the "record." In the case of OE in which personnel files or similar institutional (e.g., school) records might be a consideration, there might be methods for eliminating or modifying one's past involvement in flagrant bullying or horrendous acts committed as a juvenile (Mahoney, 1974).

Another type of recasting involves efforts to neutralize the impact of the evil attribution. In a classic article addressing tactics used by juvenile delinquents to offset accusations and their stigma, Sykes and Matza highlight five approaches that can be related to the neutralization of OE attributions: (1) denying responsibility for the act, (2) denying that an injury occurred, (3) denying the existence of a real victim, (4) challenging the motives or veracity of the accusers, or (5) appealing to some other ("higher") loyalty (Sykes and Matza, 1957). Haines (1979) associates neutralization with steps taken to "depoliticize" a deviant behavior by a process he calls "enclosure," which effectively removes the act or actor from the political arena in which demonization and moral panic are likely to hold sway. In an approach similar to relabeling, groups such as Alcoholics Anonymous and Gamblers Anonymous have long been known for their efforts to have their focal behaviors and actors treated as illnesses (i.e., "medicalization") (Preston et al., 1998; Trice and Roman, 1970) or otherwise regarded as genetically predisposition (i.e., "scientization") (see Wasserman, 2004). In their initial efforts to neutralize the impact of child abuse committed by clergy, some leaders of the Catholic Church relied on claims of demonic possession and effectively formed an enclosure by implying that this was an internal matter that could best be handled by other members of the Church hierarchy (Benyei, 1998; Scheper-Hughes and Devine, 2003). Impression and reputation management techniques can also be relied on as a means of neutralizing OE attributions (Bromley, 1993; Frink and Ferris, 1998; Leary and Kowalski, 1990).[11]

In contrast to recasting aimed at neutralizing the OE attribution, criminalization (or its organization equivalent) is an effective way of rendering OE acts or actors legally actionable. By criminalization, we mean the formal designation of some act (or actor committing the act) as sanctionable, through either the criminal justice system outside the organization and/or the disciplinary system within an organization.

That "and/or" phrase is an important one to keep in mind. Although some behaviors within an organization might not rise to the level of criminality as defined by the external legal system, they can be regarded as sanctionable within the organization. Bullying, for example, may be perceived as an evil act within an organization and made subject to personnel sanctions (Vickers, 2001), but it is not necessarily subject to actual criminal prosecution until it rises to the level of physical threats and violence (Rhodes et al., 2010). Pernicious behavior such as sexual harassment might be prohibited as part of agency policy and employment contracts, but the standards for making a juridical claim outside the organization are typically much more elaborate and involved. Nevertheless, the sense of "sanctionability" can be reproduced to some extent within organizations.

Although many acts that may come to be regarded as evil are already subject to legal action because they fall under traditional definitions of criminal activity (e.g., physical attacks can be prosecuted as assaults), their status as a form of evil often generates the creation of laws or regulations that deal directly with the perceived "evil nature" of the behavior. The most obvious contemporary examples involve the prosecution of some assaults as "hate crimes," a recasting that serves the demand that such misbehavior be prosecuted and judged for what motivated the act, not just the physical harm caused (Iganski, 2001; Jenness and Grattet, 1996). Iganski's study found support for such recasting-through-criminalization as a reflection of the sense that hate-motivated crimes "hurt more," but one cannot overestimate the value of transforming evil behavior into a criminal act that can be prosecuted. The criminalization process has also been applied to many other acts, such as drug use (Nadelmann, 1989), driving while intoxicated (Gusfield, 1981; Reinarman, 1988), and actors deemed so behaviorally deviant (i.e., evil) as to warrant severe formal sanctioning in law or its equivalent within organizations (e.g., the mentally ill; see Quanbeck, Frye, and Altshuler, 2003; Teplin, 1983).

One significant characteristic of this form of recasting is that the focal act or actor is rendered subject to account, and here we see the connection between accountability and its role in preventing and dealing with perceived OE. Many of the organizational mechanisms put in place to monitor or prevent misfeasance or malfeasance (e.g., reporting, auditing) can be rationalized on grounds that there needs to be some way of blunting the potential for OE (Lubit, 2004; Whicker, 1996). Similarly, making explicit the organization's commitment and willingness to take action against (i.e., hold accountable) those who might engage in bullying, racism, sexual harassment, and other widely condemned behaviors can be regarded as part of the general effort to preclude and preempt behavior that might take on OE qualities.

These various recasting processes, and the tactics associated with them,[12] have a paradoxical relationship with attributions of OE that go to the core of our view that OE is a social construct and, therefore, is subject to reconstruction in order for the organization and its members to make sense of and deal with perceived evil. The paradox of evil is that efforts to deal with it must effectively transform it into something other than evil. Delabeling, neutralization, and criminalization accomplish this by undermining the unfathomableness of OE by different means. Delabeling seeks to eliminate the attribution, while naturalization attempts to reduce or offset the impact of demonization. Criminalization transforms evil into an actionable phenomenon by rendering it illegal and sanctionable—undermining its power as a supernatural factor in our lives. Using accountability mechanisms and policies to preclude or preempt the emergence of behaviors that might spark concerns about OE should also be part of the response in organizations that are sensitive to the threats posed by the attribution.

THE IMPLICATIONS OF ORGANIZATIONAL EVIL

Organizational evil is not real in the sense of existing as a coherent thing-in-itself independent of the contextually contingent and moral community-specific beliefs of specific stakeholders. To view it as such, we contend, is of little practical or empirical value. Rather, OE is a highly useful concept if we acknowledge it as a functional social construct that identifies morally incomprehensible behavior. Because responses to (inter)subjectively observed or experienced organizational evil can vary along a continuum ranging from horrifically bad to enormously beneficial, it is important to understand how those responses are generated and, in particular, how the more potentially beneficial types of response can be reliably produced instead of the more harmful or unproductive ones. Our exploratory, case-based analysis recounted in the preceding section leads us to a tentative prescription for organizational practice, which also serves as a hypothesis that we believe merits systematic testing in organizational research.[13]

In a nutshell, we believe that in order to increase the likelihood of successfully preventing or remediating horrifically bad (evil) acts in organizational settings, all members of organizations, but especially those with more than trivial amounts of discretion, can be encouraged to develop and use their skills in practical ethical reasoning. This, admittedly, may come at the cost of diminished employee obedience (and, perhaps, losses in bureaucratic efficiency) to the extent that organizational members are encouraged or take it upon themselves to question the moral authority and instructions of their hierarchical superiors. However, as in other matters of organizational routines and cultures, the precise balance of the tradeoff can be adjusted by adept leadership to suit the requirements of specific organizations, missions, contexts, and contingencies. This requires that a form of ethical risk analysis be performed, involving assessment of the probability that inept reactions to perceived evil (or unthinking obedience to instructions or impulses that might yield actions that would qualify as evil in the first place) pose a threat to individuals or to the organization's mission.

Although another sometimes recommended prophylactic is to determine and promulgate a central set of values for public servants generally or members of specific public service organizations, we have argued elsewhere that such an approach can create more problems than it solves (see Dubnick and Justice, 2006). The examples of appalling, systematized brutality by organizations and grossly inappropriate behavior by individuals that have provided the impetus for prescribing thoroughgoing ethical stipulation and surveillance appeared to us in fact to be illustrations precisely of the dangers of that prescription. While we certainly hope that public servants will obey ethically and instrumentally correct instructions from the leaders of public organizations, we also believe that they must be willing and able to recognize when basic obedience to instructions is insufficient or even contrary to the fulfillment of their public and ethical duties. This requires that ordinary stakeholders as well as leaders possess both ethical competence and a willingness to act accordingly.

Developing such ethical competence throughout an organization is unquestionably a nontrivial task, and it is likely that the balance struck in practice between obedience and independent judgment may not always be exactly right for every organization at every point in its life cycle. Nonetheless, it seems more constructive to work toward developing ethical competence at all levels of an organization than to presume the inevitability of incompetence and attempt to compensate for that by indoctrinating an organization's members in lieu of developing their skills. In fact, ethical development as opposed to stipulation seems likely to be a requisite for the kind of distributed leadership advocated by some contemporary experts in organizational leadership as a way to enhance organizational efficiency. We would expect effective independent practical ethical reasoning to lead individual stakeholders to work to advance what they believe to be the legitimate (in both the instrumental and ethical senses) work of the organization. To the extent an organization's leaders can convince ethically competent stakeholders that their instructions are reasonably designed to advance ethically and instrumentally legitimate purposes, the conclusions drawn from independent reasoning should reinforce those instructions and actually promote obedience.

When independent reasoning and obedience are at odds, it is possible that there has been a failure of leadership, stakeholder ethical reasoning, or both. Where leaders' instructions are not well suited to advancing the organization's legitimate mission, ethical independence provides a check against large-scale error. Where appropriate instructions are resisted, due to poor communications by leaders or errors in judgment by other members of the organization, inefficiency and error may well result. But it seems reasonable to hypothesize that organizations whose members have been adequately prepared and empowered to practice ethical judgment will find this risk (as measured by the combination of likelihood and severity of undesirable behavior) to be smaller over time than the risks associated with 'organizational evil' or other consequences of thoughtless obedience.

Finally, we note that this is not a pie-in-the-sky impossibility and might be barely more difficult that simply indoctrinating employees simply to obey instructions or a single overriding set of organizational or societal norms. Practical wisdom, to use Aristotle's term, is a skill that can be developed through practice aided by deft instruction and encouragement. Examples of potentially appropriate instructional approaches for various settings include those embodied in books targeting public administration trainees (e.g., Lewis and Gilman, 2005; Svara, 2007) and the general public (see Schwartz and Sharpe, 2010).[14] Any of these approaches could conceivably be adapted for use within organizations as well as in standard academic settings. In sum, while the bad news is that treating organizational evil as a thing-in-itself is a counterproductive approach, the good news is that a more pragmatic understanding of "organizational evil" implies some possible directions for the development of a practical and practicable approach to organizational ethics that can decrease the likelihood of so-called organizational evil without unacceptably degrading organizations' ability to perform their legitimate missions effectively and efficiently. Just as organizations have proven capable of contending with the limits of human attention and cognitive abilities (e.g., bounded rationality) and the imperfections of markets and other institutions, so it can develop that means for dealing with those unfathomable events and behaviors that all too often fall under the label of organizational evil.

NOTES

1. The problem of evil debate remains active, but more as an argument in logic than in philosophy (see Cooper, 1983).

2. The concept of "pragmatic realism" is attributable to Charles Peirce but is today most often associated with the writings of Hilary Putnam in the 1990s (he has since modified his views on realism). See Putnam, 1981, 1982.

3. We will not tackle here the issues raised by the inclination of those who espouse Type A perspectives to focus on the collective (as opposed to the individualistic) nature of society, other than to acknowledge that bias and to highlight the fact that there are alternative, more individualist perspectives that can be applied. For classic expositions on this issue as it relates to methodological individualism, see Arrow, 1994; Elster, 1982. Even more relevant to the examination of OE is the ongoing debate over collective and shared responsibility, e.g., Feinberg, 1968; May, 1992.

4. On the decision making behind Operation Reinhard, including the fact that the organizational technology for carrying out the extermination process was already in place before the policy was formalized, see Musial, 2000.

5. Auschwitz-Birkenau was also classified as a "concentration camp" that engaged in extended imprisonment. Arad's study highlights Belzec, Sobibor, and Treblinka as the three major death camps.

6. See Putnam, 1981, 1982; cf. Bunge, 2006; Devitt, 1991.

7. It is tempting to put Goldhagen (1996) among this list of relevant Type B studies, but a close reading indicates that Goldhagen might be more relevant for A or C types; see Alford, 1997a.

8. The position assumed by advocates of Type B views is almost ideological in nature given its commitment to the Weberian view of modern organizations. Such a commitment is in part based on a misreading (mistranslation) of that Weberian view (e.g., Baehr, 2001; Kent, 1983) or a myopic indifference to perspectives drawn from alternative (e.g., Hegelian) traditions (see Sebastiaan and Patrick, 2008; Shaw, 1992).

9. For a classic overview and reflection on labeling, see Becker, 1973.

10. See deYoung, 2007. DeYoung, a sociologist who closely followed the infamous McMartin Preschool case involving charges of ritual child abuse (e.g., deYoung, 1994) conducted a follow-up assessment of what happened to those charged or convicted twenty-five years after the associated moral panic began.

11. Berbrier takes note of a particular form of impression management—intellectualization—used by white supremacist groups to offset the taint of racism that places them squarely among the demonized in American society (Berbrier, 1999).

12. For an excellent overview of relabeling and recasting from the perspective of tactics, see Rogers and Buffalo, 1974. They offer a framework that generates "nine modes" of adaptive responses to deviance, and most are relevant to the present analysis.

13. This is not an unusual situation for scholars of organizations. Some other examples of theories of motivation that were adopted as managerial prescriptions on the basis of hypothetical formulations in advance of rigorous empirical testing include Maslow's hierarchy of human needs, Herzberg's identification of "hygiene factors" and "motivators," and arguments in favor of Douglas McGregror's managerial "Theory Y" over "Theory X."

14. The Schwartz and Sharpe (2010) book is based on an elaborate and ingenious course designed by the authors for advanced undergraduates at Swarthmore College.

REFERENCES

Adams, G.B., and D.L. Balfour. 2004. *Unmasking Administrative Evil*, rev. ed. Armonk, NY: M.E. Sharpe.

Agamben, G. 2000. *Remnants of Auschwitz: The Witness and the Archive*. New York: Zone Books.

Alford, C. Fred. 1997a. Hitler's willing executioners: What does "willing" mean? *Theory and Society,* 26, 719–738.

———. 1997b. *What Evil Means to Us.* Ithaca: Cornell University Press.

Arad, Y. 1987. *Belzec, Sobibor, Treblinka: The Operation Reinhard Death Camps.* Bloomington: Indiana University Press.

Arendt, H. 1976. *Eichmann in Jerusalem: A Report on the Banality of Evil.* New York: Penguin Books.

Arrow, K.J. 1994. Methodological individualism and social knowledge. *American Economic Review,* 84, 1–9.

Baehr, P. 2001. The "iron cage" and the "shell as hard as steel": Parsons, Weber, and the Stahlhartes Gehäuse metaphor in the Protestant ethic and the spirit of capitalism. *History and Theory,* 40, 153–169.

———. 2002. Identifying the unprecedented: Hannah Arendt, totalitarianism, and the critique of sociology. *American Sociological Review,* 67, 804–831.

Bauman, Z. 1989. *Modernity and the Holocaust.* Ithaca: Cornell University Press.

Becker, H.S. 1973. Labelling theory reconsidered. In *Outsiders: Studies in the Sociology of Deviance,* 177–212. New York: Free Press.

Benyei, C.R. 1998. *Understanding Clergy Misconduct in Religious Systems: Scapegoating, Family Secrets, and the Abuse of Power.* New York: Haworth Pastoral Press.

Berbrier, M. 1999. Impression management for the thinking racist: A case study of intellectualization as stigma transformation in contemporary white supremacist discourse. *Sociological Quarterly,* 40, 411–433.

Berger, R.J. 1995. Agency, structure, and Jewish survival of the Holocaust: A life history study. *Sociological Quarterly,* 36, 15–36.

Brief, A.P., J. Dietz, R. Reizenstein Cohen, S.D. Pugh, and J.B. Vaslow. 2000. Just doing business: Modern racism and obedience to authority as explanations for employment discrimination. *Organizational Behavior and Human Decision Processes,* 81, 72–97.

Bromley, D.B. 1993. *Reputation, Image and Impression Management.* New York: John Wiley & Sons.

Browning, C.R. 1992. *Ordinary Men: Reserve Police Battalion 101 and the Final Solution in Poland.* New York: HarperCollins.

Bunge, M. 2006. *Chasing Reality: Strife Over Realism.* Toronto: University of Toronto Press.

Cohen, S. 2002. *Folk Devils and Moral Panics.* New York: Routledge.

Cooper, K.J. 1983. Here we go again: Pike vs. Plantinga on the problem of evil. *International Journal for Philosophy of Religion,* 14, 107–116.

Cortina, L.M. 2008. Unseen injustice: Incivility as modern discrimination in organizations. *Academy of Management Review,* 33, 55–75.

Critcher, C. 2009. Widening the focus. *British Journal of Criminology,* 49, 17–34.

Devitt, M. 1991. *Realism and Truth.* Cambridge, MA: Basil Blackwell.

deYoung, Mary. 1994. One face of the devil: The satanic ritual abuse moral crusade and the law. *Behavioral Sciences and the Law,* 12, 389–407.

———. 1996. A painted devil: Constructing the satanic ritual abuse of children problem. *Aggression and Violent Behavior,* 1, 235–248.

———. 2007. Two decades after McMartin: A follow-up of 22 convicted day care employees. *Journal of Sociology and Social Welfare,* 34, 9–33.

———. 2008. The day care ritual abuse moral panic: A sociological analysis. *Sociology Compass,* 2, 1719–1733.

Dubnick, M.J. 2000. The case for administrative evil: A critique. *Public Administration Review,* 60, 464–474.

Dubnick, M.J., and J.B. Justice. 2006. Accountability and the evil of administrative ethics. *Administration & Society,* 38, 236–267.

Elster, J. 1982. The case for methodological individualism. *Theory and Society*, 11, 453–482.

Feinberg, J. 1968. Collective responsibility. *Journal of Philosophy*, 65, 674–688.

Fleetwood, S. 2005. Ontology in organization and management studies: A critical realist perspective. *Organization*, 12, 197–222.

Frink, D.D., and G.R. Ferris. 1998. Accountability, impression management, and goal setting in the performance evaluation process. *Human Relations*, 51, 1259–1283.

Garcia, J.L.A. 1996. The heart of racism. *Journal of Social Philosophy*, 27, 5–46.

———. 1997. Current conceptions of racism: A critical examination of some recent social philosophy. *Journal of Social Philosophy*, 28, 5–42.

Gergen, K.J., and T.J. Thatchenkery. 1996. Organization science as social construction: Postmodern potentials. *Journal of Applied Behavioral Science*, 32, 356–377.

Goffman, E. 1963. *Stigma: Notes on the Management of Spoiled Identity*. New York: Touchstone/ Simon and Schuster.

Goldhagen, D.J. 1996. *Hitler's Willing Executioners: Ordinary Germans and the Holocaust*. New York: Alfred A. Knopf.

Goode, E., and N. Ben-Yehuda. 1994. Moral panics: Culture, politics, and social construction. *Annual Review of Sociology*, 20, 149–171.

Griffith, D.M., E.L. Childs, E. Eng, and V. Jeffries. 2007. Racism in organizations: The case of a county public health department. *Journal of Community Psychology*, 35, 287–302.

Gusfield, J.R. 1981. *The Culture of Public Problems: Drinking-Driving and the Symbolic Order*. Chicago: University of Chicago Press.

Hacking, I. 1999. *The Social Construction of What?* Cambridge: Harvard University Press.

Haines, H.H. 1979. Cognitive claims-making, enclosure, and the depoliticization of social problems. *Sociological Quarterly*, 20, 119–130.

Haney, C., and P. Zimbardo. 1998. The past and future of U.S. prison policy: Twenty-five years after the Stanford prison experiment. *American Psychologist*, 53, 709–727.

Hier, S.P. 2002. Conceptualizing moral panic through a moral economy of harm. *Critical Sociology*, 28, 311–334.

———. 2008. Thinking beyond moral panic. *Theoretical Criminology*, 12, 173–190.

Hilberg, R. 1985. *The Destruction of the European Jews*, student ed. New York: Holmes & Meier.

———. 1992. *Perpetrators, Victims, Bystanders: The Jewish Catastrophe, 1933–1945*. New York: Harper.

Hummel, R.P. 2008. *The Bureaucratic Experience: The Postmodern Challenge*, 5th ed. Armonk, NY: M.E. Sharpe.

Iganski, P. 2001. Hate crimes hurt more. *American Behavioral Scientist*, 45, 626–638.

Jenness, V., and R. Grattet. 1996. The criminalization of hate: A comparison of structural and polity influences on the passage of "bias-crime" legislation in the United States. *Sociological Perspectives*, 39, 129–154.

Kaplan, A. 1942. Are moral judgments assertions? *Philosophical Review*, 51, 280–303.

Kent, S.A. 1983. Weber, Goethe, and the Nietzschean allusion: Capturing the source of the "iron cage" metaphor. *Sociological Analysis*, 44, 297–319.

Kershaw, I. 1993. "Working towards the Führer": Reflections on the nature of the Hitler dictatorship. *Contemporary European History*, 2, 103–118.

Kremer, E.J., and M.J. Latzer, ed. 2001. *The Problem of Evil in Early Modern Philosophy*. Toronto: University of Toronto Press.

Leary, M.R., and R.M. Kowalski. 1990. Impression management: A literature review and two-component model. *Psychological Bulletin*, 107, 34–47.

Levi, P. 1989. *The Drowned and the Saved*. New York: Vintage International.

Lewis, C.W., and S. Gilman. 2005. *The Ethics Challenge in Public Service: A Problem-Solving Guide*. San Francisco: Jossey-Bass.

Link, B.G., and J.C. Phelan. 2001. Conceptualizing stigma. *Annual Review of Sociology*, 27, 363–336.

Lubit, R.H. 2004. *Coping with Toxic Managers, Subordinates—and Other Difficult People.* Upper Saddle River, NJ: FT Prentice Hall.

Mahoney, A.R. 1974. The effect of labeling upon youths in the juvenile justice system: A review of the evidence. *Law and Society Review*, 8, 583–614.

May, L. 1992. *Sharing Responsibility.* Chicago: University of Chicago Press.

Milgram, S. 1963. Behavioral study of obedience. *Journal of Abnormal and Social Psychology*, 67, 371–378.

———. 1974. *Obedience to Authority: An Experimental View.* New York: Harper.

Mistry, M., and J. Latoo. 2009. Uncovering the face of racism in the workplace. *British Journal of Medical Practitioners*, 2, 2, 20–24.

Murray, S.B. 2001. When a scratch becomes "scary story": The social construction of micro panics in center-based child care. *Sociological Review*, 49, 512–529.

Musial, B. 2000. The origins of "Operation Reinhard": The decision-making process for the mass murder of the Jews in the "Generalgouvernement." *Yad Vashem Studies*, 28, 113–153.

Nadelmann, E.A. 1989. Drug prohibition in the United States: Costs, consequences, and alternatives. *Science*, 245, 939–947.

Piven, F.F. 1981. Deviant behavior and the remaking of the world. *Social Problems*, 28, 489–508.

Preston, F.W., B.J. Bernhard, R.E. Hunter, and L.B. Shannon. 1998. Gambling as stigmatized behavior: Regional relabeling and the law. *Annals of the American Academy of Political and Social Science*, 556, 186–196.

Putnam, H. 1981. *Reason, Truth and History.* New York: Cambridge University Press.

———. 1982. Three kinds of scientific realism. *Philosophical Quarterly*, 32, 195–200.

Quanbeck, C., M. Frye, and L. Altshuler. 2003. Mania and the law in California: Understanding the criminalization of the mentally ill. *American Journal of Psychiatry*, 160, 1245–1250.

Reinarman, C. 1988. The social construction of an alcohol problem: The case of Mothers Against Drunk Drivers and social control in the 1980s. *Theory and Society*, 17, 91–120.

Rhodes, C., A. Pullen, M.H. Vickers, S.R. Clegg, and A. Pitsis. 2010. Violence and workplace bullying. *Administrative Theory & Praxis*, 32, 96–115.

Richardson, J.T., J. Reichert, and V. Lykes. 2009. Satanism in America: An update. *Social Compass Social Compass*, 56, 552–563.

Rogers, J.W., and M.D. Buffalo. 1974. Fighting back: Nine modes of adaptation to a deviant label. *Social Problems*, 22, 101–118.

Rosenbaum, R. 1998. *Explaining Hitler: The Search for the Origins of His Evil.* New York: Random House.

Russell, P. 1992. Strawson's way of naturalizing responsibility. *Ethics*, 102, 287–302.

Scheper-Hughes, N., and J. Devine. 2003. Priestly celibacy and child sexual abuse. *Sexualities*, 6, 15–40.

Schwartz, B., and K. Sharpe. 2010. *Practical Wisdom.* New York: Riverhead Books.

Searle, J.R. 1995. *The Construction of Social Reality.* New York: Free Press.

Sebastiaan, P.T., and O. Patrick. 2008. Escaping the iron cage: Weber and Hegel on bureaucracy and freedom. *Administrative Theory & Praxis*, 30, 71–91.

Shaw, C.K.Y. 1992. Hegel's theory of modern bureaucracy. *American Political Science Review*, 86, 381–389.

Shelby, T. 2002. Is racism in the "heart"? *Journal of Social Philosophy*, 33, 411–420.

Singer, M.G. 2004. The concept of evil. *Philosophy*, 79, 185–214.

Sofsky, W. 1996. *The Order of Terror: The Concentration Camp.* Princeton: Princeton University Press.

Strawson, P.F. 1962. Freedom and resentment. *Proceedings of the British Academy*, 48, 1–25.

Svara, J.H. 2007. *The Ethics Primer for Public Administrators in Government and Nonprofit Organizations.* Sudbury, MA: Jones and Bartlett.

Sykes, G.M., and D. Matza. 1957. Techniques of neutralization: A theory of delinquency. *American Sociological Review*, 22, 664–670.

Teplin, L.A. 1983. The criminalization of the mentally ill: Speculation in search of data. *Psychological Bulletin*, 94, 54–67.

Todorov, T. 1996. *Facing the Extreme: Moral Life in the Concentration Camps*. New York: Henry Holt.

Trice, H.M., and P.M. Roman. 1970. Delabeling, relabeling, and Alcoholics Anonymous. *Social Problems*, 17, 538–546.

Tsoukas, H. 2000. False dilemmas in organization theory: realism or social constructivism? *Organization*, 7, 531–535.

Vickers, M.H. 2001. Bullying as unacknowledged organizational evil: A researcher's story. *Employee Responsibilities and Rights Journal*, 13, 4, 205–216.

———. 2010. Introduction—Bullying, mobbing, and violence in public service workplaces. *Administrative Theory & Praxis* 32, 7–24.

Wallace, R.J. 1994. *Responsibility and the Moral Sentiments*. Cambridge: Harvard University Press.

Warren, C.A.B. 1980. Destigmatization of identity: From deviant to charismatic. *Qualitative Sociology*, 3, 59–72.

Wasserman, D. 2004. Is there value in identifying individual genetic predispositions to violence? *Journal of Law, Medicine & Ethics*, 32, 24–33.

Weick, K.E. 1979. *The Social Psychology of Organizing*. Reading, MA: Addison-Wesley.

———. 1995. *Sensemaking in Organizations*. Thousand Oaks, CA: Sage.

Whicker, M.L. 1996. *Toxic Leaders: When Organizations Go Bad*. Westport, CT: Quorum Books.

Zimbardo, P.G. 1972. Pathology of imprisonment. *Transaction/Society*, 9, 6, 4–8.

———. 2007. *The Lucifer Effect: Understanding How Good People Turn Evil*. New York: Random House.

9

For "the Greater Good"

Exposing the Parody of Necessary Evil—
Exemplars from Organizational Life

Margaret H. Vickers

NEEDING TO THINK ABOUT EVIL AT WORK

> It is most appropriate to talk of evil when all the defining elements are present: intensely harmful actions, which are not commensurate with instigating conditions, and the persistence or repetition of such actions. A series of actions also can be evil when any one act causes limited harm, but with repetition, these acts cause great harm. (Staub, 1999)

It is once again time to think carefully about our workplaces as potential perpetrators of evil. I am not suggesting that workers will necessarily witness genocide, torture, or others acts of physical violence on a grand scale as they go about their working day (although history suggests that they might). If one thinks carefully about evil, what it is and what it might be, we find that there is much in our modern workplaces that can reasonably be considered evil and that can result in evil outcomes for organizational members. Workplace violations of any kind in our workplaces—physical, psychological, or emotional—are a serious occupational health concern and merit the attention of employers, researchers, and government (Schat and Kelloway, 2003). However, if the organizational response to genuine workplace violations and subsequent requests for support in response to those violations is to enact evil, even assuming it to be a form of necessary evil, then a parody is produced: the organizational response purported to help workers facing adversity is likely to do them more harm, while the response is still being framed as being for the greater good.

Many forms of workplace adversity exist: bullying, mobbing, violence, harassment, incivility, wrongdoing, misbehavior, and other forms of organizational misconduct and mistreatment (Delbecq, 2001; Frost, 1999, 2003; Hamilton and Sanders, 1999; Hutchinson et al., 2005, 2006a, 2006b; Leather et al., 1998; Vickers, 2010). Toxic leaders, followers, and organizational environments have all been identified (Frost, 1999, 2003; Padilla, Hogan, and Kaiser, 2007), and, unfortunately, such violations in organizational life are frequent. For example, in 1999, 1 in 20 American workers was physically assaulted, 1 in 6 was sexually harassed, and 1 in 3 was verbally abused. The most serious form of workplace violence—homicide—has been found to be the second-leading cause of workplace death (Schat and Kelloway, 2003). All forms of violence and aggression in the workplace, whether physical or psychological, are capable of causing harm to both the individual and the organization (Leather et al., 1998). Indeed, some have already characterized these kinds of violations in organizations as evil in themselves, and those doing them as perpetrators of evil (see, e.g., Boddy, 2006; Boddy, Ladyshewsky, and Galvin, 2010a, 2010b; Delbecq, 2001; Hamilton and Sanders, 1999; Tracy, Lutgen-Sandvik, and Alberts, 2006; Vickers, 2001). Still others have described the associated problem of passive evil in organizational life, describing the muteness of those who witness unethical behavior, harm, or suffering inflicted in organizations and who choose to do nothing (Samier, 2008). However, it is not my intention to offer another examination of these kinds of organizational outcomes as acts of evil, even though I agree that, in many instances, they are.

I intend to draw attention to another recognized form of evil in organizations: "necessary evil." I intend to demonstrate the parody that is created when organizations say one thing and do another, especially when the harm they actually do is purported to be "for the greater good." It is acknowledged that organizations can normalize negative behaviors, such as bullying, violence, and corruption, so, over time, these negative behaviors and outcomes become embedded in that organization or community, taken for granted, and perpetuated (Ashforth and Anand, 2003; Staub, 1999; Vickers, 2010). As a result of being normalized, such negative behaviors are likely to increase and the need for support for workers being violated is likely to increase. When a genuine need for support exists and is neglected, workers experience alienation, burnout, and withdrawal; employers are seen to be engaging in management rhetoric rather than genuine dialogue and action in response to employees' often-valid concerns (Arthur, 2004; Herriot, 2001). This is especially painful when the organization claims to support workers in need, via advertised policy and process, and yet many of these same organizational responses become harmful to those seeking help (Hoque and Noon, 2004; Jewson et al., 1990, 1992, 1995; Vickers, 2006a, 2010; Vickers and Kouzmin, 2001).

Using the construct of "necessary evil" (Molinsky and Margolis, 2005, 245), I argue that many of the purported support mechanisms in organizational life—those designed and constructed to support organizational members faced with adversity—are deemed necessary evils by those who are responsible for enacting and upholding them. Evil in organizations is generally associated with an imbalance between the magnitude of the gain received by the wrongdoer and the injury done to the target (Berkowitz, 1999). What makes these organizational outcomes forms of necessary evil—and a parody—is not just that additional harm is produced. It is that the additional harm done to that worker is not in response to any negative provocation by that worker. Instead, the harm is directed at workers who are seeking help as a result of harm already done to them in that organization. When organizational support processes are then performed as if they are necessary evils, something that must be done, the negative organizational response is framed as being undertaken for the greater good, at once making a mockery of the espoused support process and enhancing the sense of betrayal for those seeking help—and all the while treating organizational support processes as necessary evils, whereas enacting them in this way is not *necessary* at all.

In the next section, I outline some ideas and definitions regarding what is currently understood about the notion of evil. I then explore three espoused sources of support in organizations in terms of their enactment as potential exemplars of necessary evil in organizations. I show how treating organizational support processes as necessary evils creates a parody of the support process, enhancing the sense of betrayal for recipients and framing the negative outcomes as being enacted for the greater good.

SOME THOUGHTS ABOUT EVIL IN ORGANIZATIONS

> Both in groups and individuals, the evolution of evil starts with the frustration of basic human needs and the development of destructive modes of need fulfillment. (Staub, 1999, 181)

In recent years in particular, there has been increasing recognition of the problem of evil in and around organizations. The slaughter of millions of people in the twentieth century has prompted considerable discussion of the cause and nature of evil (Berkowitz, 1999). Evil is generally believed to include extreme human destructiveness, as in genocide and mass killing (Staub, 1999), and is usually seen as intentional, planned, and morally unjustified injury of others (Berkowitz, 1999). Evil has been defined by a number of elements: first, extreme harm, which can include pain, suffering, loss of life, or loss of human potential; second, the extremely harmful acts committed are not commensurate with any instigation or provocation by those targeted; and, third, evil is determined by the repetition or persistence of these harmful acts. Even if one act causes limited harm, with repetition, these repeated acts can become evil if they cause great harm (Staub, 1999).

At its most general sense, evil is understood as something very bad that causes extreme harm to others (Anderson, 2006). The term "evil" originates in religious or metaphysical discourse; evil is regarded as the opposite of good and is often anthropomorphized (Anderson, 2006). Evil generally has religious connotations and includes ideas of Satan, the devil, and demons (Anderson, 2006). Evil has also been conceived of that which deprives innocent people of their humanity, and some believed that it is inherent in the human condition (Dillard and Ruchala, 2005). Evil, for some, is defined by its special quality of badness: It involves pleasure in causing pain. Evil has been described as "hurting fun" (Alford, 1997, 15; Furman, 1993, 263; Vickers, 2001). The evil individual at work has been described as someone who sucks the life juices from the organizational group with his/her unusually destructive behavior, crippling the group and ensuring that all positive spirit is lost (Delbecq, 2001).

Hamilton and Sanders (1999, 222; citing Simpson and Weiner's *Oxford English Dictionary,* 1989, 471) select two useful definitions of evil. The first definition they cite involves actions that are "morally depraved, bad, wicked, vicious," which they claim highlights the intentional nature of engaging in morally blameworthy and reprehensible acts toward others. Many agree that the term "evil" generally goes beyond "bad," "aggressive," and "destructive" (Alford, 1997; Berkowitz, 1999) and that the use of terms like these tend not to convey the sense of moral repugnance that we usually associate with acts and outcomes of evil (Berkowitz, 1999). Alford (1997) wrote of the organization of evil, arguing that evil was not just about individuals going along with malevolent authority but that evil derives from identifying with that authority and deriving pleasure and satisfaction from its destructiveness. Although the problem of evil is frequently defined in moral terms, as something causing harm to others through human agency (Samier, 2008), others have observed that evil is defined, not by any moral category but as something experienced in terms of one's own terror and a sense of impending doom (Alford, 1997). Still others ask whether it is actions or people that are evil and whether it is intention or outcome that matters most (Anderson, 2006).

There has been recognition of the need to acknowledge degrees of evil, from the truly egregious injustices, such as the Nazis' Final Solution (the campaign to exterminate the Jews) to what some might consider lesser wrongdoings such as domestic violence (Berkowitz, 1999). Some determinations of evil are considered dependent on the intentions of the perpetrator as the factor deciding whether the actions are evil (Anderson, 2006; Staub, 1999). Others suggest that evil is relational: It occurs between people when one or more persons do evil to another. Evil, in this sense, is always about making someone else suffer (Geddes, 2003; cited by Adams and Balfour, 2008, 883). Evil has also been noted as repetitive or persistent, as developing or evolving over time, and of not being commensurate with provocation (Staub, 1999). It has been suggested that evil must involve not only intentional and deliberate acts, not only killing and other excessive acts of horrendous cruelty, but that the outcomes of these acts materially or psychologically diminish people's dignity, happiness, and capacity to fulfill basic material needs and therefore can also include petty cruelties and minor transgressions (Baumeister, 1999; Dillard and Ruchala, 2005; Staub, 1999).

Hamilton and Sanders (1999, 222) also highlighted a second way of thinking about evil, what they termed the second "face" of evil: one that is less purposeful and less clearly accompanied by what the law calls the "guilty mind." This second definition includes the "doing or tending to do harm; hurtful, mischievous, prejudicial" (Hamilton and Sanders, 1999, 222; citing Simpson and Weiner, 1991, 471) and is without connotations of deliberateness and intention to harm. As Hamilton and Sanders (1999) have suggested, not all evildoers are vicious individuals hatching diabolical and cruel schemes of torture on others; rather, many social and organizational processes may have a large part to play in the encouragement, development, and enactment of evil. Ordinary individuals have been recognized for some time as performing acts of evil when they are caught up in complex social forces (Berkowitz, 1999, 247; Darley, 1992, 204). Analyses of evil in recent years have pointed to Milgram's graphic and groundbreaking work on obedience, in which experiments showed obedient followers inflicting great pain and suffering on others because someone in authority told them to; they were just following orders (for examples, see Anderson, 2006; Berkowitz, 1999; Cunha, Rego, and Clegg, 2010; Darley, 1992; Hamilton and Sanders, 1999). The suggestion from Milgram's work is that people could be obedient to authority in an extreme and unquestioning way (Cunha, Rego, and Clegg, 2010), and one of Milgram's clearest messages was that those who gave the electric shocks did not want to but simply could not extricate themselves from the situation or challenge the authority that they faced (Hamilton and Sanders, 1999).

Similarly, Arendt's (1964) thesis on the banality of evil has also been considered by many (see, for example, Alford, 1997; Anderson, 2006; Berkowitz, 1999; Darley, 1992; Samier, 2008). Arendt's analysis portrays Eichmann as an uninspired bureaucrat carrying out instructions and, concurrently, as an individual who would not normally be considered evil. As Arendt explains, Eichmann did not appear to be a sociopath; he talked normally and even spoke of compassion. Arendt categorized such dispassionate, impersonal disconnection from human suffering as banal evil (Anderson, 2006; Arendt, 1964). Arendt's analysis of Eichmann is relevant, not only in exposing the great evils perpetrated under totalitarianism but for recognition of the minor evils committed by administrators in democratic countries in peacetime (Samier, 2008). Both Milgram's and Arendt's work point to the reality of individuals doing evil things out of a sense of obligation or obedience, rather than being particularly psychopathic or having especially aggressive tendencies.

Adams and Balfour (1998) revealed the problem of administrative evil in organizations. They argued that the modern organization, especially with its emphasis on technical rationality, offers a way of thinking and doing that applauds the scientific-analytical and a belief in the inherent goodness of technological progress (Adams, Balfour, and Reed, 2006; Moreno-Riaño, 2001). Acknowledging this way of thinking enabled the recognition of the bewildering form of evil known as administrative evil to emerge (Adams and Balfour, 1998). Administrative evil is masked; people engage in acts of administrative evil when they are, in fact, thinking that they are doing nothing wrong. Administrative evil can be undertaken by ordinary people who are acting appropriately in their organizational role—what most of those around them would agree that they should be doing—and, at the same time, they are participating in what a critical and reasonable observer, usually well after the fact, would call evil (Adams and Balfour, 1998). Worse, under conditions of moral inversion, acts of evil can be convincingly redefined as good; ordinary people can all too easily engage in acts of administrative evil while believing that what they are doing is not only correct within that organization but good (Adams and Balfour, 1998; Adams, Balfour, and Reed, 2006). Evil, then, becomes masked in technique and technology, transforming the moral administration of others into a "muted" organizational reality that includes instances in which humans knowingly and deliberately inflict pain and suffering on others. Through language manipulation and moral inversion, administrators can practice evil unintentionally, even unconsciously, making their behavior potentially more dangerous than those who do evil knowingly (Adams and Balfour, 1998; Samier, 2008).

Beyond the notion of administrative evil is Molinsky and Margolis's (2005) work on necessary evil. Necessary evil refers "to those work related tasks in which an individual must, as part of his or her job, perform an act that causes emotional or physical harm to another human being in the service of achieving some perceived greater good or purpose" (Molinsky and Margolis, 2005, 245). Layoffs are recognized as the most prevalent and widely researched example of necessary evils, but there are others. Cited examples include a nurse injecting a child with a drug necessary to cure disease or a police officer delivering the news of a child's death to a parent (Molinsky and Margolis, 2005). Although the debate as to whether each of these last two examples of necessary evil are actually evil at all is beyond the scope of this paper, what is important to note is that necessary evils are considered necessary by the performer in that they believe some greater good is produced as a result of the performer knowingly inflicting harm on another. This benefit—the greater good—can accrue to an individual, an organization, or society.

Necessary evils have three distinguishing characteristics: (1) a valued objective that makes them necessary; (2) the infliction of ineradicable harm on another that makes them evil; and (3) they are integral to the role the performer occupies, making them mandatory (Molinsky and Margolis, 2005, 247). The organization exemplars cited below become necessary evils if the valued objective motivating their use is protecting the organization, rather than the worker in need. I ask readers to keep in mind the defining characteristics of necessary evils when considering the exemplars that follow. I also suggest that what performers of these necessary evils are doing is creating a parody of what is supposed to be supportive practice; rather than giving support to those in need, further harm is being inflicted on those seeking help. Identified exemplars of potential areas of necessary evil include policy and process, management response, and the language of organization.

EXEMPLARS OF NECESSARY EVIL IN ORGANIZATIONAL LIFE

> Evil can be defined as the knowing infliction of pain and suffering—physical and/or psychological—on another human being. It can be perpetrated by individuals, by organizations, and by nation states, among others. It can take the form of administrative evil, in which people participate in acts of evil while thinking they are just doing what they should be doing in their organizational role. Under conditions of moral inversion, evil can be engaged in under the guise of doing good. (Adams and Balfour, 2008, 881)

Policy and Process as Necessary Evil

Services, policies, and processes that are set up to support people but that actually serve to harm them may be far more widespread than might routinely be imagined. Many of the organizational responses routinely and publicly proffered by workplaces that claim to assist those who have been violated in the organizational context—such as protective legislation, internal workplace policies, training, counseling, employee assistance programs, and alternative dispute resolution—have also been claimed to harm those seeking support in organizational life (Hoque and Noon, 2004; Jewson et al., 1990, 1992, 1995; Vickers, 2006a, 2010; Vickers and Kouzmin, 2001). Support and equity policies can also be used in response to internal complaints, problems identified by the community, or the media (Hoque and Noon, 2004; Jewson et al., 1990, 1992, 1995; Vickers, 2006a).

A study in the UK confirmed that the existence, for example, of equal opportunity policies does not actually ensure enactment of that policy in the form of action plans or enhanced opportunities for minority groups. They found that while nearly three-quarters of the 208 companies that they surveyed had a disability policy, implementation of the policies was poor: Only 40 percent monitored job applications for disability, only 25 percent had arrangements in place to consult people with disabilities, and only 53 percent allowed time off for rehabilitation and treatment (Hoque and Noon, 2004). Problems identified as a result included organizational members paid lip service to policies; few clear procedures developed from the policy; and managers were able to subvert the procedures that were developed if they wished to (Hoque and Noon, 2004; Liff and Dale, 1994). Adopting a policy can become an end in itself for the organization rather than an intended first step toward equality (Dickens, 2000; Hoque and Noon, 2004). In these circumstances, the adoption of equity policies has been found to constitute little more than an empty shell and, thus, good for business by offering perceived benefits such as a competitive advantage in the labor market, better employee relations, and a positive company image (Hoque and Noon, 2004). While an appropriate policy and a documented complaint-handling process may be a necessary condition for resolving complaints (Hubert, 2003; Vega and Comer, 2005), as we have seen, any written document or policy is only as effective as the employees and managers who know about them, support their use, and enact them (Vega and Comer, 2005). Equity and support policies and processes considered necessary evils by organizations can go beyond cynical organizational attempts at self-preservation and public relations, to offer paradoxical outcomes that are potentially damaging and harmful to those seeking help under their guise (Vickers, 2006a, 2010). They also make a mockery of the organization's espoused claims to support staff in need.

Employee assistance programs (EAPs) are another putative workplace support service that emerged from an embryonic focus on problems of staff alcohol abuse. EAPs purport to offer a range of services for employees whose performance might be suffering as a result of what the organization deems personal problems such as individual health and wellness, financial problems, child-care responsibilities, elder-care responsibilities, and stress (Weiss, 2010). They are frequently recommended to staff who complain of violence or bullying (Ferris, 2004). However, based on the absence of scientific evidence to confirm their efficacy (Arthur, 2000; Weiss, 2010), EAPs have been widely criticized and have been targets of accusations that EAP research has been conducted by internal providers with a clear self-interest and insufficient scientific rigor (Arthur, 2000).

In addition, EAPs have also been criticized for their failure to provide the support that they supposed to offer, and it has been suggested that they can be used as instruments of coercion (Vickers and Kouzmin, 2001; Weiss, 2010). EAPs in organizations are *claimed* to identify poorly performing or troubled workers (Prince, 1998; Vickers and Kouzmin, 2001; Weiss, 2010), yet their *actual* use has been found to facilitate dismissals. Such an outcome appears to be common knowledge in some quarters (Weiss, 2010), as are the coercive practices proffered under a paternalistic and humanitarian guise (Vickers and Kouzmin, 2001). Employees receiving EAP counseling, perhaps advice on how to deal with bullying and other adversity, might also find their situation worsening if the counselor directs them to return to the organization, perhaps to human resources (HR) or line management for assistance, without considering the harm that following such advice might cause (Ferris, 2004). However, despite these numerous and widely held concerns, EAPs remain in use by employers as a low-cost management "tool" purported to improve workplace performance and respond to critical incidents (Weiss, 2010).

Similarly, rather than being designed to change the organization to eliminate the stressors encountered by workers, organizational stress management programs are designed, instead, to respond to stress as a problem experienced by individual employees or by enhancing employees' resistance to stress (Arthur, 2004; Weiss, 2010). Emphasis is still placed on the "problem" of the individual worker, allowing stressful practices to remain unchallenged (Arthur, 2004; Dewe and O'Driscoll, 2002) with programs that are focused on the individual rather than developed in response to organizations' accepting responsibility, in whole or in part, for occupational stress that arises in that environment (Arthur, 2004; Dewe and O'Driscoll, 2002). The negative health-related consequences for targets of workplace violations *should* be mitigated by interventions that enhance support for employees under stress, instead of further contributing to the difficulties that they may be experiencing (Schat and Kelloway, 2003; emphasis added). However, it remains the case that retaining an individual-based organizational response to stress allows the organization to continue to deflect responsibility from the organization and its role in creating stressors for workers, allowing stressful and potentially harmful organizational practices to remain unchallenged (Dewe, 1989; Dewe and O'Driscoll, 2002). Little attempt is made by the organization to find the source of the stress or the extent to which the organization is responsible for it (Arthur, 2000; Dewe and O'Driscoll, 2002).

When organizations proffer equity and support policies, EAPs, and stress management programs, without a genuine intention to help workers in need, they are doing evil. The outcomes are evil because the use of these procedures, as described above, can result in the infliction of further pain and suffering on those in need. This potentially harmful response is in no way justifiable, especially when made in response to those seeking support. It becomes a necessary evil when those in charge of the process believe that the approach they are taking is necessary and that any further harm to workers in need is undertaken under the guise of being required and the belief in doing good.

Management Response as Necessary Evil

When an employee experiences adversity or violations at work, a routine organizational response is to suggest that person seek help from their supervisor, manager, or HR representative. However, it has been suggested that few employees will approach their organization for assistance in dealing with bullying or other similar violations (Ferris, 2004). Rayner (1998) suggested that asking for help could result in threats of dismissal or of exacerbation of the bullying behaviors. Others have claimed that HR personnel are ineffective when dealing with bullying, and some found that management and HR personnel were the principal supports for the bully (Namie and Namie, 2000). Still others have reported that HR practitioners initially appeared to be supportive but, over time, became more and more unresponsive and unhelpful and demonstrated no real intention to resolve the issue or respond in a meaningful way (D'Cruz and Noronha, 2010). The response of managers approached for help by a person being bullied might also be to side with the bully or perpetrator of violence, dismiss the concern, or threaten the employee who has complained—all of which serve to further harm the person targeted (Ferris, 2004). In some organizations, an employee who makes an allegation of bullying has been demonstrably at risk of greater harm (Ferris, 2004).

Organizational responses of "seeing no evil" have also been reported. Here, negative behaviors are identified but not responded to by the organization and subsequently became normalized by that organization (Ferris, 2004; Vickers, 2010). Targets might be treated as if they are participants in a conflict in which both parties (rather than just the bully) are considered responsible. A "blame the victim" approach is then taken with respect to targets for not communicating properly or for somehow provoking the bullying behaviors (Ferris, 2004; Vickers, 2006a). Parties in the "conflict" are then advised to sort it out themselves, attend mediation, or told that the negative behavior being reported is not covered under relevant protective legislation anyway, which further confirms a fundamental misunderstanding of the bullying construct (Ferris, 2004) and enhances the sense of betrayal experienced by those targeted. Any negative behaviors acknowledged by the organization might then be accompanied with an identification of the target's "weakness" or "problem," with suggestions that the target should "toughen up" or "not be so sensitive" and with suggestions given about training courses to enhance that person's "problematic" communication skills or referrals made to EAP counseling to enhance that person's resilience and ability to cope (Ferris, 2004; Vickers, 2006a; Vickers and Kouzmin, 2001). Mediation outcomes are also often unsuccessful, as mediation often does not take into account power differentials and the mediation process implicitly apportions blame to whichever parties come to the table (Ferris, 2004; Vickers, 2006a). When workplace policies are not enacted, supported, and implemented appropriately, employees who need support are likely to be left feeling even more betrayed (Ferris, 2004).

It has been claimed that the role of management is critical in determining the outcome of targets' coping responses to violations such as bullying and discrimination (D'Cruz and Noronha, 2010), positive or otherwise. HR professionals have a critical role in influencing—negatively or positively—the experience of those experiencing bullying or other adversity at work (D'Cruz and Noronha, 2010). For example, staff who complained of being bullied while working at a call center in India described their confusion, anger, and stress when the HR staff in their employing organization did not support them as they had anticipated the HR staff would. Those who complained of bullying, instead, reported their view that the HR professionals at their workplace had reneged on their professional mandate to protect employees. The targets of bullying reported feeling doubly victimized: First, they were bullied; then, they received an unhelpful and unsupportive HR response. Complainants subsequently reported feeling cornered and experiencing severe emotional distress, anxiety, depression, a sense of meaninglessness, and associated adverse outcomes to their physical health. Complainants also reported that their task motivation at work was waning, that their job performance was declining, and that they felt a growing distrust toward their employer, replacing what had previously been a very positive and professional relationship—prior to the involvement of HR (D'Cruz and Noronha, 2010).

Researchers have questioned whether managers should reflect upon their motives in the use of stress management interventions, beyond recognizing that such initiatives often fit the generally accepted rhetoric surrounding the management of work stress (Arthur, 2004; Dewe and O'Driscoll, 2002; Reynolds and Briner, 1994). The question has been raised as to whether managers really consider the stress of their employees a priority deserving immediate attention, not because managers are "uncaring" but because they may simply consider occupational stress a risk with which the individuals affected should cope, rather than something that the organization is responsible for managing (Arthur, 2004; Dewe and O'Driscoll, 2002). The stress outcome in individual workers continues to be considered by some line managers as an abnormal reaction by that staff member to a problem, rather than an organizational problem itself (Arthur, 2004). The broader problem of stressors in the organization continues to be disguised by managers treating occupational stress and its outcomes as an individual, rather than an organizational, problem (Arthur, 2000, 2004). Managers frame these programs as necessary evils when adopting such an approach.

Managers are often recognized as the ones to inflict psychological abuse on subordinates, representing one of the most frequent and serious problems confronting employees in today's workforce (Frost, 2003; Lutgen-Sandvik, 2003). Organizational change processes have also been recognized as sources of bullying, incivility, and stress, offering potential vehicles for making the situation worse for those targeted (Hutchinson et al., 2005). Other managers can induce harm by being disinclined to support staff through permitting job-sharing, working at home, or allowing staff to take personal leave for child care or elder care that may be reasonably required (Hoque and Noon, 2004) and is purported to be available. The discretion of managers regarding the implementation of policy initiatives ostensibly designed to support employees is influenced heavily by the level of knowledge that individual managers might have regarding the problem; managers might not, for instance, understand the magnitude of difficulty involved in caring for a chronically ill child by a worker requesting parental leave (Vickers, 2006b). Further, when a staff member who is considered especially valuable to an organization behaves inappropriately toward another, via bullying, harassment, or incivility, formal policies and protocols put in place to support those targeted might fall by the wayside (Vega and Comer, 2005).

Similarly, the outcome of HR professionals' breaching the psychological contract has also been called one of the most distressing experiences for individuals, including the need to contain emotions of betrayal and hurt (Arthur, 2004; Conway and Briner, 2002). In this case, managers might consider that they are just "doing their job," "acting in the interests of the organization," and "protecting the reputation of their employer" by not acting in good faith with employees. Within the organizational context, the necessary evil becomes obscured behind layers of processes and structures (Dillard and Ruchala, 2005) while the perpetrators of necessary evil often see their own actions and attitudes, as being in the service of higher ideals and contributing to beneficial outcomes, even as being beneficial, in some instances, to targets themselves (Staub, 1999).

Managers who respond in ways like those described above may well consider themselves to be doing their job and acting for the good of their employer. When managers respond to claims of stress, bullying, violence, or requests of support via flexible working arrangements, they often react as if they are doing a necessary evil. Managers might not enjoy *not* helping those around them, especially those they understand to be in need, but might feel that they are operating from the perspective of the greater good of their employing organization and doing what is necessary. But such a response, or nonresponse, can be characterized as evil in that their actions can result in a frustration of basic human needs and then evolve into more destructive modes and responses (see Staub, 1999). Management responses become enactments of necessary evil because they result in harm to employees—by not taking complaints of stress seriously, by blaming the victim, or by not recognizing genuine requests for assistance—while being done by those who believe that they are just doing their jobs (see Adams and Balfour, 2008; Molinsky and Margolis, 2005), doing what they think is necessary, and doing it because believe it to be for the greater good (Molinsky and Margolis, 2005).

The Language of Organizations as Necessary Evil

Finally, I point to the use of language in organizations is another potential source of necessary evil. Rhetoric can be the insincere or exaggerated use of language in a way that is calculated to produce some effect (Vickers, 2002; Wilkes, 1979). Through the use of rhetoric, management can use a mild, delicate, or indirect word in place of a plainer or more accurate one (Stein, 1998; Vickers, 2002). Using rhetoric enables organizations not only to deemphasize the bad and shift attention away from a negative reality but to create a new (and inaccurate) reality (Eccles and Nohria, 1992; Vickers, 2002). Managers use rhetoric to persuade employees of the "rightness" of their actions, putting their case simply, forcefully, and in a manner that makes the organization look good. The clarity of such a message is designed to lull the listener into uncritical acceptance of what they are told (Hilmer and Donaldson, 1996; Vickers, 2002).

Organizations can also use euphemisms to replace, override, and reinvent reality. A euphemism is a mild, indirect, or vague expression used to substitute for an offensive or unpleasant one (Vickers, 2002; Wilkes, 1979). Using euphemisms is about devising deliberately slippery language to justify aspects of the organization and its processes—if not to impose them—that also contribute to the degradation and harm of people in organizations (Stein, 1998). Euphemism cloaks the bad as good; euphemisms make things not seem what they actually are but what the organization needs them to seem to be, making their use a potentially obscenely fine art (Vickers, 2002). Organizations frequently use language to minimize negative feedback to workers, for example, to mask the seriousness of an adverse situation. Discharged workers are informed that they have been "downsized," "separated," "severed," "unassigned," or "proactively outplaced" (Micklethwait and Wooldridge, 1996, 11). However, words can be destructive and, because of the associated negative feelings and gestures that may accompany them, are capable of great harm (Stein, 1998). In the case of bullying, for example, euphemisms such as "personalities" that are in "conflict" might be used to minimize emotionally abusive events. Physical violence might be trivialized by management as a "slap" or not be believed to have happened at all in the absence of witnesses. Through the use of rhetorical language, organizational members can justify, normalize, and even glorify the infliction of pain and suffering—what would normally be considered unacceptable—on another (Anderson, 2006). And normalizing pain and suffering not only trivializes it but encourages the continuation of those behaviors (Vickers, 2010).

Organizations have been accused of enacting evil via the infliction of pain and suffering through the use of euphemisms and spin (Anderson, 2006). Rhetoric and spin enable organizational members, including managers and HR practitioners, to discount the significance and magnitude of pain for those who complain, using language that separates those managers from the reality of what has taken place (Anderson, 2006). Euphemisms also enable managers to disassociate themselves from the reality of the outcomes of that pain and suffering and the systems that facilitate such disconnections and disassociations are called administrative evil (Adams and Balfour, 1998; Anderson, 2006). The goals of classic bureaucracy, such as rationality, impersonality, rules, and hierarchy have been recognized as leading to that person's disconnection from the organization and from themselves (LaBier, 1986). Facilitating such disassociation or disconnection from responsibility is seen by some as facilitating evil (Anderson, 2006).

The language of organization can be used to inflict pain and suffering. Using language in organizations to inflict harm, especially if it is done repeatedly and under the guise of doing good, is also evil. Using slippery language, such as euphemisms and spin, to protect the organization at the expense of further harm to employees, is another potential form of necessary evil: Organizational members are doing something that they believe is necessary and that they should be doing, for the greater good of that organization, even it results in harm to their colleagues.

FROM NECESSARY EVIL TO A SUPPORTIVE ORGANIZATIONAL RESPONSE

Organizations have been metaphorically described as instruments of social control and domination (Darley, 1992; Morgan, 1986). In these kinds of organizations, coercive pressures are high and the actors within them do as they are told (Darley, 1992). Clegg (2006; citing Goffman, 1961) recently reminded us of the dangers of ignoring Goffman's notion of the total institution. The total institution is total in that it surrounds the person at every turn. The total institution cannot be escaped by inmates; the institution produces and reproduces the normalcy of that institution—however abnormal it might be. The total institution also demonstrates, in heightened and condensed form, the role and capacity of many underlying organizational processes that are found in many normal organizations (Clegg, 2006).

Beyond total institutions, there are many organizations in which employees are also expected to obey orders as a matter of course (Cunha, Rego, and Clegg, 2010; Jacques, 1996). Corporate hierarchy encourages subordinates to act, not solely in terms of individual self-interest but in terms of the authority's orders (Hamilton and Sanders, 1999). The hierarchy transforms the way in which the individual actor frames the situation and his or her choices within it. Hierarchical frames help explain the behavior of subordinates acting as agents (Hamilton and Sanders, 1999). In crimes of obedience, individuals operate in relation to the social and organizational systems in which they belong. People choose a course of action in response to what they are told to do by superiors and by picking frames within which to view and describe their situations (Hamilton and Sanders, 1999). It appears that within the technical-rational environment of professional practice, good people can learn to do evil, and when individuals and groups harm others in organizations, they tend to develop characteristics that make further and more intense infliction of harm probable (Staub, 1999). As we have seen in the exemplars above, even processes intended to support can shift inexorably into necessary evils, with harmful outcomes, a belief in their necessity, and the organizational hierarchy's protection regarded as the primary goal.

Many organizations, even those considered "normal" organizations, can exert social control through their modernist processes and assumptions and, therefore, have a great propensity for harm. Many (e.g., Adams and Balfour, 1998; Bauman, 1989; Clegg, 2006) have concluded that what is most frightening about the so-called organizations of evil, such as the Nazi concentration camps, is that, organizationally, they were not at all unique; the logic of their systems was as routine as so many of the organizational systems with which we are all so familiar (Clegg, 2006). Many organizations exist that would not conventionally be regarded as organizations of social control or organizations capable of evil, yet they still offer the potential to incubate harm (Darley, 1992). Sometimes though, bluntly put, "normal" organizations also *intend* harm; their corporate ideology makes it appropriate for those within them to harm others, especially if this is done putatively for the good of the organization (Darley, 1992). Organizations can corrupt their members by getting their members to do things that they would not otherwise wish to do—a very human response to a very flawed social situation (Darley, 1992). According to Darley (1992), evildoing is not confined to individuals who are evil at the time of committing the act. Each of us has the capacity to do evil actions if our surroundings—the forces of the situation—press us to do so (Darley, 1992). Within them, perpetrators see their actions as necessary, in the service of higher ideals, and resulting in beneficial outcomes for the organization, and possibly even for the victims themselves (Staub, 1999).

Card suggested that the special nature of modern organizations, even "normal" organizations, can lead to a genuine loss of moral responsibility by the individuals within them (2005; also Cunha, Rego, and Clegg, 2010). This loss of moral responsibility is part of the rational and modernist process (Card, 2005): Machines, professionals, and administrative hierarchies represent the intellectual, physical, and organizational manifestations of instrumental rationality that can, over time, overwhelm and suppress individual morality. Administrative evil is inherent in many of the administrative hierarchies that currently govern work organizations. There is little doubt that instrumentally rational processes are quite capable of morphing into administrative evil (Adams and Balfour, 1998; Dillard and Ruchala, 2005). Morality is expunged when the situation is presented in technical terms and legitimized by organizational authority (Adams and Balfour, 1998; Clegg, 2006; Dillard and Ruchala, 2005), and, under these circumstances, the moral choice becomes redefined through a moral inversion, and the otherwise undesirable action becomes seen as the "right" thing to do (Adams and Balfour, 1998, 2008; Adams, Balfour, and Reed, 2006). The authority of the hierarchy can sanction the belief in the need for necessary evil organizational actions.

Inflicting pain and suffering on another as part of pursuing the greater good is within the realm of human understanding (Anderson, 2006). When those decisions are made within the organizational context and the decision rationale is determined by the prevailing organizational norms, values, and rationalizing hierarchy, decisions become legitimated by, and synonymous with, instrumentally rational decision making. Moral responsibility becomes defined by instrumentally rational logic and supports the implementation of the proposed course of action (Dillard and Ruchala, 2005)—the necessary evil course of action. Progressively, the norms of the group change and institutions and their processes can shift to serve violence and harm (Staub, 1999). Violence and violations become authorized by virtue of their necessity to further the goals of the organization; the pervasive and devastating consequences of modernity run their logical and harmful course (Dubnick and Justice, 2006). Organizations can perpetrate evil even though no single individual harbors evil intentions or foresees the extent of harmful consequences of his or her actions (Darley, 1992). Still others might see the harm and feel the discomfort associated with inflicting the harm, but do it anyway because it is their job (Adams and Balfour, 1998) and because they believe it is a necessary evil that serves the greater good (Molinsky and Margolis, 2005). Good people can do harm to others when they believe that they are doing what they are required to do and, if it is unpleasant, then it must be a necessary evil that is required of them for that organization's greater good.

The literature increasingly confirms that our workplaces have a role to play in making the outcomes of organizational violations worse, by enabling a culture in which bullying continues unabated and HR and management show a lack of support when complaints are made (Arthur, 2004; Dewe and O'Driscoll, 2002; Hutchinson et al., 2005; Schat and Kelloway, 2003; Vega and Comer, 2005; Vickers, 2010). Our workplaces, then, expose employees to further harm when they invoke support policies and processes. The double harm that can accrue from both the initial violation and the subsequent unsupportive response can jeopardize health, impinge on family and community life, and stifle (even destroy) careers (Vickers, 2004). Organizations need to recognize the parody created when support responses are enacted as forms of necessary evil. Rather than creating policy and process that merely purport to support staff, organizations need to actually support staff, when they need it, by standing behind the policies developed. It is not enough to pay "lip service" to policies and programs developed to assist staff in need; what is required is a forthright and honest approach to support staff in need that does not make a mockery of what has been espoused. But recognizing and accepting that necessary evils take place in organizational life is not sufficient, especially when what is believed to be a necessary evil is not necessary at all. Organizations must respond compassionately and honestly to workers in need. For an organization to do what it says it is going to do—that is truly in service of the greater good: for the organization, for its employees in need, and for a society that hopes to retain a proper moral compass.

REFERENCES

Adams, G.B., and D.L. Balfour. 1998. *Unmasking Administrative Evil*. Thousand Oaks, CA: Sage.
———. 2008. Expiating evil: Reflections on the difficulties of cultural, organizational and individual reparation. *Public Administration*, 86, 4, 881–893.
Adams, G.B., D.L. Balfour, and G.E. Reed. 2006. Abu Ghraib, administrative evil, and moral inversion: The value of "putting cruelty first." *Public Administration*, 66, 680–693.
Alford, C.F. 1997. The political psychology of evil. *Political Psychology*, 18, 1, 1–17.
Anderson, J.F. 2006. The rhetorical impact of evil on public policy. *Administration & Society*, 37, 6, 719–730.
Arendt, H. 1964. *Eichmann in Jerusalem: A Report on the Banality of Evil*. New York: Viking.
Arthur, A.R. 2000. Employee assistance programmes: The emperor's new clothes of stress management? *British Journal of Guidance and Counselling*, 28, 4, 549–559.
———. 2004. Work-related stress, the blind men and the elephant. *British Journal of Guidance and Counselling*, 32, 2, 157–169.
Ashforth, B.E., and V. Anand. 2003. The normalization of corruption in organizations. In *Research in organizational behavior*, vol. 25, ed. R.M. Kramer and B.M. Staw, 1–52. Amsterdam: Elsevier.
Bauman, Z. 1989. *Modernity and the Holocaust*. Cambridge, UK: Polity.
Baumeister, R.F. 1999. *Evil: Inside Human Violence and Cruelty*, 2d ed. New York: W.H. Freeman.
Berkowitz, L. 1999. Evil is more than banal: Situationism and the concept of evil. *Personality and Social Psychology Review*, 3, 3, 246–253.
Boddy, C.R. 2006. The dark side of management decisions: Organizational psychopaths. *Management Decisions*, 44, 10, 1461–1475.
Boddy, C., R. Ladyshewsky, and P. Galvin. 2010a. The influence of corporate psychopaths on corporate social responsibility and organizational commitment to employees. *Journal of Business Ethics*, 97, 1, 1–19.
———. 2010b. Leaders without ethics in global business: Corporate psychopaths. *Journal of Public Affairs*, 10, 3, 121–138.
Card, R.F. 2005. Individual responsibility within organizational contexts. *Journal of Business Ethics*, 62, 297–405.
Clegg, S.R. 2006. Why is organization theory so ignorant? The neglect of total institutions. *Journal of Management Inquiry*, 15, 4, 426–430.
Conway, N., and R.B. Briner. 2002. A daily diary study of affective responses to psychological contract breach and exceeded promises. *Journal of Organizational Behavior*, 23, 287–302.
Cunha, P.E., A. Rego, and S. Clegg. 2010. Obedience and evil: From Milgram and Kampuchea to normal organizations. *Journal of Business Ethics*, 97, 2, 291–309.
Darley, J.M. 1992. Social organization for the production of evil. *Psychological Inquiry*, 3, 2, 199–218.
D'Cruz, P., and E. Noronha. 2010. Protecting my interests: HRM and targets' coping with workplace bullying. *Qualitative Report*, 15, 3, 507–534.
Delbecq, A.L. 2001. "Evil" manifested in destructive individual behavior. *Journal of Management Inquiry*, 10, 3, 221–226.
Dewe, P.J. 1989. Developing stress management programmes: What can we learn from the literature? *Journal of Occupational Safety and Health—Australia, New Zealand*, 5, 493–499.
Dewe, P., and M. O'Driscoll. 2002. Stress management interventions: What do managers actually do? *Personnel Review*, 31, 2, 143–165.
Dickens, L. 2000. Still wasting resources? Equality in employment. In *Personnel Management*, 3d ed., ed. S. Bach and K. Sisson, 137–169. Oxford: Blackwell.

Dillard, J.F., and L. Ruchala. 2005. The rules are no game: From instrumental rationality to administrative evil. *Accounting, Auditing and Accountability Journal*, 18, 5, 608–630.

Dubnick, M.J., and J.B. Justice. 2006. Accountability and the evil of administrative ethics. *Administration & Society*, 38, 2, 236–267.

Eccles, R.G., and N. Nohria. 1992. *Beyond the Hype: Rediscovering the Essence of Management.* Boston: Harvard Business School Press.

Ferris, P. 2004. A preliminary typology of organizational response to allegation of workplace bullying: See no evil, hear no evil, speak no evil. *British Journal of Guidance and Counseling*, 32, 3, 389–395.

Frost, P.J. 1999. Why compassion counts! *Journal of Management Inquiry*, 8, 2, 127–133.

———. 2003. *Toxic Emotions at Work: How Compassionate Managers Handle Pain and Conflict.* Boston: Harvard Business School Press.

Furman, E. 1993. *Toddlers and Their Mothers.* Madison, CT: International Universities Press.

Goffman, E. 1961. *Asylums: Essays on the Social Situation of Mental Patients and Other Inmates.* Ringwood, VIC: Penguin Books Australia.

Hamilton, V., and J. Sanders. 1999. The second face of evil: Wrongdoing in and by the corporation. *Personality and Social Psychology Review*, 3, 3, 222–233.

Herriot, P. 2001. *The Employment Relationship: A Psychological Perspective.* Hove, UK: Routledge.

Hilmer, F.G., and L. Donaldson. 1996. *Management Redeemed: Debunking the Fads That Undermine Corporate Performance.* New York: Free Press.

Hoque, K., and M. Noon. 2004. Equal opportunities policy and practice in Britain: Evaluating the "empty shell" hypothesis. *Work, Employment and Society*, 18, 3, 481–506.

Hubert, A.B. 2003. To prevent and overcome undesirable interaction: A systematic approach model. In *Bullying and Emotional Abuse in the Workplace: International Perspectives in Research and Practice*, ed. S. Einarsen, H. Hoel, D. Zapf, and C.L. Cooper, 299–311. London: Taylor and Francis.

Hutchinson, M., M.H. Vickers, D. Jackson, and L. Wilkes. 2005. "I'm gonna do what I wanna do!": Organizational change as a vehicle for bullies. *Health Care Management Review*, 30, 331–338.

———. 2006a. "Like wolves in a pack": Stories of predatory alliances of bullies in nursing. *Journal of Management and Organization*, 12, 235–251.

———. 2006b. "They stand you in a corner and you are not to speak": Nurses tell of abusive indoctrination in work teams dominated by bullies. *Contemporary Nurse*, 21, 228–238.

Jacques, R. 1996. *Manufacturing the Employee: Management Knowledge from the 19th to 21st Century.* London: Sage.

Jewson, N., S. Waters, and J. Harvey. 1990. Ethnic minorities and employment practice: A study of six employers. Research Paper No. 76. Employment Department, Sheffield, UK.

Jewson, N., D. Mason, A. Drewett, and W. Rossiter. 1995. Formal equal opportunities policies and employment best practice. Employment Department Research Series No. 69. Employment Department, Sheffield, UK.

Jewson, N., D. Mason, C. Lambkin, and F. Taylor. 1992. Ethnic monitoring policy and practice: A study of employers' experiences. Research Paper No. 89. Department of Employment, London.

LaBier, D. 1986. *Modern Madness: The Emotional Fallout of Success.* Sydney: Addison-Wesley.

Leather, P., C. Lawrence, D. Beale, T. Cox, and R. Dickson. 1998. Exposure to occupational violence and the buffering effects of intra-organizational support. *Work and Stress*, 12, 2, 161–178.

Liff, S., and K. Dale. 1994. Formal opportunity, informal barriers: Black women managers within a local authority. *Work, Employment and Society*, 8, 2, 177–198.

Lutgen-Sandvik, P. 2003. The communicative cycle of employee emotional abuse: Generation and regeneration of workplace mistreatment. *Management Communication Quarterly*, 16, 4, 471–501.

Micklethwait, J., and A. Wooldridge. 1996. *The Witch Doctors: What the Management Gurus Are Saying, Why It Matters and How to Make Sense of It.* London: Mandarin Paperbacks.

Molinsky, A., and J. Margolis. 2005. Necessary evils and interpersonal sensitivity in organizations. *Academy of Management Review*, 30, 2, 245–268.

Moreno-Riaño, G. 2001. The etiology of administrative evil. *American Review of Public Administration,* 31, 3, 296–312.

Morgan, G. 1986. *Images of Organization.* Beverly Hills, CA: Sage.

Namie, G., and R. Namie. 2000. *The Bully at Work: What You Can Do to Stop the Hurt and Reclaim Your Dignity on the Job.* Naperville, IL: Sourcebooks.

Padilla, A., R. Hogan, and R.B. Kaiser. 2007. The toxic triangle: Destructive leaders, susceptible followers, and conducive environments. *Leadership Quarterly,* 18, 3, 176–194.

Prince, M. 1998. EAPs becoming part of larger programs. *Business Insurance,* 32, 14–16.

Rayner, C. 1998. From research to implementation: Finding leverage for intervention and prevention. 1998 Research Update Conference, Staffordshire University, Staffordshire.

Reynolds, S., and R.B. Briner. 1994. Stress management at work: With whom, for whom and to what ends? *British Journal of Guidance and Counselling,* 22, 75–89.

Samier, E. 2008. The problem of passive evil in educational administration: Moral implications of doing nothing. *International Studies in Educational Administration,* 36, 1, 1–21.

Schat, A.C.H., and E.K. Kelloway. 2003. Reducing the adverse consequences of workplace aggression and violence: The buffering effects of organizational support. *Journal of Occupational Health Psychology,* 8, 2, 110–122.

Simpson, J.A., and E.S.C. Weiner, ed. 1989. *Oxford English Dictionary,* 2d ed. Oxford: Clarendon.

Stein, H.F. 1998. *Euphemism, Spin, and the Crisis in Organizational Life.* Westport, CT: Quorum Books.

Staub, E. 1999. The roots of evil: Social conditions, culture, personality, and basic human needs. *Personality and Social Psychology Review,* 3, 3, 179–192.

Tracy, S.J., P. Lutgen-Sandvik, and J.K. Alberts. 2006. Nightmares, demons, and slaves: Exploring the painful metaphors of workplace bullying. *Management Communication Quarterly,* 20, 2, 148–185.

Vega, G., and D. Comer. 2005. Sticks and stones may break your bones, but words can break your spirit: Bullying in the workplace. *Journal of Business Ethics,* 58, 1, 101–109.

Vickers, M.H. 2001. Bullying as unacknowledged organizational evil: A researcher's story. *Employee Responsibilities and Rights Journal,* 13, 4, 207–217.

———. 2002. "People first-always": Euphemism and rhetoric as troublesome influences on organizational sense-making-a downsizing case study. *Employee Responsibilities and Rights Journal,* 14, 2, 105–118.

———. 2004. The traumatized worker: A concern for employers and employees. *Employee Responsibilities and Rights Journal,* 16, 3, 113–116.

———. 2006a. Towards employee wellness: Rethinking bullying paradoxes and masks. *Employee Responsibilities and Rights Journal,* 18, 267–281.

———. 2006b. *Working and Caring for a Child with Chronic Illness: Disconnected and Doing It All.* London and New York: Palgrave Macmillan.

———. 2010. Bullying, mobbing and violence in public service workplaces: The shifting sands of "acceptable" violence. *Administrative Theory & Praxis,* 33, 1, 7–24.

Vickers, M.H., and A. Kouzmin. 2001. Employee assistance programmes (EAPs): From crisis support to sanctioned coercion and panopticist practices? *Critical Psychology: The International Journal of Critical Psychology,* 2, 61–83.

Weiss, R. 2010. Brinksmanship redux: Employee assistance programs' precursors and prospects. *Employee Responsibilities and Rights Journal,* 22, 4, 325–343. doi: 10.1007/s10672-010-9144-0.

Wilkes, G.A., ed. 1979. *Collins Dictionary of the English Language.* Sydney: Collins.

10

The Truth and Reconciliation Commission in South Africa

Understanding Roots of and Responses to Societal Evil

Edith van't Hof and Dan J. Stein

In the past several decades, many countries have transitioned from nondemocratic to democratic systems and have faced the question of how best to deal with atrocities and human rights violations committed by past regimes (Bouraine and Levy, 1995; Hamber, 2000a). Evil perpetrated by entire social systems can take multiple forms, ranging from neglect of basic human rights to deliberate abuse as exemplified by ethnic cleansing, forced labor, torture, and so on. Although much research exists on such societal evil, many questions remain.

The South African context provides a unique opportunity to address some of these questions. The transition from apartheid to democracy required the development of a response to past societal evils. The specific solution formulated by the new government was the Truth and Reconciliation Commission (TRC), which aimed to move the focus from retributive justice to reparative justice. In this chapter, we provide some of the background to the South African TRC and attempt to address some questions about the responsibility of bystanders, the nature of perpetrators, and optimal responses to survivors of societal evil.

BYSTANDERS VS. PERPETRATORS OF SOCIETAL EVIL

The apartheid system had its roots in earlier colonial role, but was more formally instituted during the rule of the National Party from 1948 to 1994. Apartheid imposed a heavy burden of suffering on black people in South Africa and introduced evil in at least two forms. First, gross violations of human rights occurred, including murder and torture of opponents of the state. More ubiquitous, however, was the day-to-day discrimination against black people, who did not have basic human rights and who were confined to particular geographic areas, where there were fewer employment opportunities, worse education, and poorer health services (Darley, 1992).

Who were the wrongdoers in this system? We argue that, although there is often overlap between categories, it is relevant to distinguish between bystanders, perpetrators, and survivors in situations where evil is committed. While white South Africans participated in implementing the day-to-day system of apartheid, many later claimed that they were unaware of the full extent of the human rights violations taking place. This exemplifies the bystander position, in which many bore significant responsibility for the perpetuation of societal evils by remaining passive.

The credibility of Hannah Arendt's (1994) concept of the "banality of evil," describing the assumption that great evils are conducted not by sociopaths but by ordinary people, is supported by empirical work. After studying Nazi doctors and perceiving them as absolutely normal people, Robert Lifton stated: "ordinary people can commit demonic acts" (1986, 5). Similarly, Ervin Staub concluded from his work, "I believe that, tragically, human beings have the capacity to come to experience killing other people as nothing extraordinary" (1989, 13). Stanley Milgram and Phillip Zimbardo's famous experiments confirm that ordinary people can commit evil acts under particular circumstances (Milgram, 1974; Zimbardo, 1969).

At the same time, our own view is that individuals can have significant variations in their susceptibility to becoming either bystanders who allow evil to occur or perpetrators who actively contribute to the infliction of evil. It is notable, for example, that Milgram and Zimbardo both encountered noncompliance among some participants in their experiments. In Milgram's experiment, about one-third of the participants showed "noncompliant" behavior and refused to administer electric shocks to the "victim" participant. Similarly, only a third of the prison guards in the Stanford prison experiment were regarded as cruel by the prisoners.

A good deal of research has focused on factors contributing to the perpetuation of bystander behavior. Situational factors include the likeliness of potential harm for the victim, the length of perpetrator activity, the visibility of the action, the relationship among victims, perpetrator, and bystanders, and the degree of benefit for bystanders (Bar-On, 2001). Studies have indicated, for example, that the larger the number of bystanders in a certain situation, the smaller the likelihood of one person's helping the victim or opposing the crime (Latane and Nida, 1981). One group has demonstrated that bystanders are more likely to help victims when they are part of their own group as opposed to members of out-groups (Levine, Cassidy, and Braier, 2002).

The construct of an "altruistic personality" has been developed to explain why some individuals seem particularly likely to help others if the opportunity arises. This has been described in terms of a "capacity for extensive relationships—their stronger sense of attachment to others and their feelings of responsibility for the welfare of others" (Oliner and Oliner, 1988). In this theoretical approach, "A bystander is less concerned with the outside world, beyond his own immediate community. A bystander might be less tolerant of differences, thinking 'Why should I get involved? These are not my people. Maybe they deserve it?' They don't see helping as a choice" (Oliner and Oliner, 1988). While some individuals may be able to empathize with a very broad range of people, most people apply their empathy more selectively, perhaps explaining the high prevalence of bystander-related societal evils.

Conversely, in an attempt to explain the Holocaust, Theodor Adorno et al. (1950) argued that an authoritarian personality predisposes people to commit evil acts within organizations. In this theoretical framework, authoritarian personalities have a strong need to show submissiveness for authority, have a blind allegiance to conventional beliefs about right and wrong, have rigid stereotyped thoughts, are superstitious, and display excessive conformity. Our case study of a major perpetrator of apartheid suggests the presence of many similar personality traits among fellow South African perpetrators (Kaminer and Stein, 2001). However, although particular societal organizations might facilitate in the infliction of significant harm on others (e.g., systematic torture), most individuals appear to have a relatively high threshold for such behavior, perhaps explaining the relatively low prevalence of such perpetrator-related societal evils.

Indeed, the question of whether perpetrators suffer from psychopathology has often been raised. Although there are psychiatric symptoms reminiscent of behaviors that are associated with evil, like sexual sadism and aggression, no psychiatric diagnosis exists that overlaps with the commission of evil. The neurobiology of impulsive aggression is, however, a growing area of research. Frontal lobe damage is associated with an increase in superficial emotional responses to stimuli in the immediate environment without considering consequences (pseudopsychopathy) and causing indifferent behavior (Luria, 1980). There is evidence that psychopathology is characterized by specific frontal dysfunctions in the brain and disturbances in serotonergic function and testosterone have also been associated with impulsive aggression (Stein, 2000).

Indeed, the distinction between the more "banal evil" committed by bystanders and the more "sadistic evil" committed by perpetrators may have neurobiological underpinnings. Everyday acts that involve harm to others and that are characterized by decreased empathy may well differ from more aggressive acts that are specifically characterized by an intention to cause injury. Speculatively, banal evil may involve dissociation of corticostriatal processing from limbic input (reason without passion), while sadistic evil may involve a dissociation of limbic processing from frontal controls (passion without reason) (Stein, 2000). Further work is, however, needed in this area, particularly given recent data indicating that social punishments serve important functions and that meting out such punishments can be experienced as rewarding.

Unfortunately, relatively little empirical work was conducted during apartheid on the particular mechanisms that contributed to bystander and perpetrator evil. Nevertheless, we argue that the widespread occurrence of bystander evil points to the relatively normal human capacity for participating in societal evil. At the same time, case studies of perpetrators of more severe gross human rights violations indicate that, although particular forms of society may encourage the emergence of such evils, only a few individuals have the capacity for inflicting these kinds of evil. Finally, while we have suggested a distinction between "banal" and "sadistic" societal evils, we also acknowledge that, in reality, some boundaries may be blurred and under different conditions particular individuals may show different propensities for committing different kinds of evil.

RESPONSES TO PAST SOCIETAL EVILS

Many countries have grappled with determining the best response to gross human right violations committed by past regimes. A number of different responses to these kinds of societal evil are possible. The two most common and simple reactions are either punishment of the perpetrators or choosing to forget. The latter option is exemplified by the infamous words initially spoken by the Cambodian government in 1998 to welcome back highly placed traitors of the Khmer Rouge "with bouquets of flowers, not with prisons and handcuffs" and that "we should dig a hole and bury the past and look ahead to the 21st century with a clean slate" (Chandler, 2000; Crocker, 2009).

More complex responses are also possible. David Crocker, for example, presents a normative framework that incorporates a range of responses. He suggests eight goals that may serve as a framework for deliberating on how to deal with past societal evils: the truth, a public platform for survivors, accountability and punishment of perpetrators, rule of law, compensation to survivors, institutional reform and long-term development, reconciliation, and public deliberation (Crocker, 2009). He argues that the dialectally connected goals of vengeance and disregarding the past in favor of the future are not desirable aims.

Two major and contrasting responses to societal evil are those that fall under the rubrics of "legalistic" and "therapeutic." Legalistic responses emphasize the importance of retributive justice: sanctions imposed for past crimes. Therapeutic responses, by contrast, focus on reparative justice: revealing the truth about the past, in order to allow healing of individuals and of communities. When new democracies are faced with the problem of dealing with past injustice, it may be difficult to accomplish this without the risk of weakening the democracy itself and may therefore prefer a reparative approach. However, the needs of the individual and society may be divergent, with some survivors of societal evil arguing for the importance of retributive justice.

In South Africa, after the election of the first democratic government in 1994, a Promotion of National Unity and Reconciliation Act was passed as a response to the societal evils perpetrated under the apartheid system (Asmal, Asmal, and Roberts, 1996). South Africa decided to work with a commission instead of Nuremberg-style trials for various reasons. Because large numbers of people committed crimes as members of a political organization, it would be hard to ascertain legal responsibility. Furthermore, it was believed that it would be difficult to gather evidence of the crimes committed. Thus, an approach focused solely on retributive justice might not succeed, either in successful prosecutions or in promoting national reconciliation.

Thus, the task of the TRC was to investigate and expose the gross violations of human rights that took place in South Africa from March 1960 to May 10, 1994, to include the Sharpeville Massacre as the first gross human rights violation to the inauguration of president Nelson Mandela. This approach made the granting of amnesty to perpetrators and the granting of reparations to survivors central parts of the process. Perpetrators of gross human rights violations who provided a full account and who could demonstrate a political reason for their behaviors would be given amnesty from future prosecution. At the same time, the focus on gross human rights violations meant that less attention was paid to bystander-related societal evils.

Arguably, the TRC embodied both a "therapeutic approach," based on the concept that revealing the truth about the past would allow healing of individuals and of communities, and a "legal approach," based on the concept that some actions in the past deserved sanction, including imprisonment. The commission focused on restorative justice rather than retributive justice, in order to promote the welfare of South African society as a whole, rather than that of individuals. The idea was that individuals could benefit from the chance to make statements to apply for amnesty and reparation, but the restoration of the harmony of the community was the main aim (Allan, 2000). It therefore had both a sociopolitical (reconciling South Africa's oppressors and oppressed) and individual aim (healing of survivors).

Given that TRCs are often established by people with conflicting interests, it is not surprising that they are targets of a certain amount of criticism. The South African TRC received a good deal of criticism for its approach. Many were skeptical about its rhetoric of forgiveness and reconciliation, arguing that it had sacrificed justice for reconciliation. At the same time, some claimed that, because of its approach of eliding the principles of natural justice, it led to unfair treatment of perpetrators, with unproved allegations made in public hearings. Arguably, the fact that such critique came from a broad political spectrum suggests, however, that the commission succeeded in maintaining a balanced stance in its consideration of both perpetrators and survivors of societal evils.

One important criticism of the TRC was its focus on particular types of evil. Thus the commission made a distinction between gross human rights violations and the "ordinary" legalized administrative violence of apartheid, including pass laws, forced removal, racial discrimination, and inequalities in health care, education, and housing. Thus much of the suffering of black South Africans due to the banal societal evils of apartheid was not addressed fully by the TRC. In particular, neither the moral and political responsibility of white South Africans nor the matter of compensation to survivors of these evils was a major focus. This failure is consistent with that seen in several other transitional justice mechanisms (Fletcher, 2007).

Pumla Goboda-Madikazela (2004), in her volume on interviews with "Prime Evil" Eugene de Kock (a colonel of the counterinsurgency team of the police force), illustrates this point, writing:

> White society had a good life. They were quite happy with what they got, and now they are not so happy with who made it happen. I mean, how many whites really voted against the National Party? Whites say they didn't know, but did they want to know? As long as they were now safe and they had their nice houses and their second cars and their third cars and their swimming pools and kids at good government schools and university, they had no problem with cross-border raids and other counterinsurgency operations of the security. (111)

Brandon Hamber (2000b) notes that, in South Africa, this problem may be compounded by survivors' having to watch some of the perpetrators confess and then walk free while they have to continue to live in poverty, making the struggle even greater.

One important question is whether the therapeutic approach of the TRC led to psychological healing in those who testified before it. Some data tentatively suggests that

testimonial therapy can reduce psychiatric symptoms in survivors of human rights violations (Agger and Jensen, 1990; Cienfugos and Monelli, 1983; Weine et al., 1998), and
it is notable that increased levels of forgiveness are associated with improved mental
health (Freedman and Enright, 1996; Hebl and Enright, 1993). However, in South Africa
giving either public or closed testimony to the TRC did not have a significant effect on
psychiatric health and forgiveness. No association was found between TRC participation and current psychiatric status (Kaminer et al., 2001). In contrast, the predictors of
posttraumatic stress disorder in TRC survivors included exposure to everyday stressors
(Stein et al., 2009).

Thus, while it may be argued that the TRC was beneficial to society as a whole, by
providing knowledge about and acknowledgment of the past, it is unlikely to have addressed completely all the claims of individuals who testified before it. The fact that everyday stressors are a predictor of ongoing illness in those exposed to gross human rights
violations further emphasizes that even if the perpetration of more sadistic societal evils
were fully addressed, the perpetration of more banal societal evils had and continues to
have significant negative impacts. It is not entirely surprising, therefore, that the TRC did
not always meet the expectations of survivors and sometimes led to significant distress
(Byrne, 2004). A national survey found a significant association between attending TRC
hearings, increased distress, and decreased forgiveness (Stein et al., 2008).

Despite these important concerns, it may be argued that the TRC was beneficial to
society as a whole, by providing knowledge about and acknowledgment of the past.
The national survey also found that attitudes of the public toward the commission were
moderately positive (Stein et al., 2008). South Africa continues to serve as an exemplar
of a society that attempted, in a self-conscious and thoughtful process, to address past
societal evils in order to strengthen the possibility of reconciliation. Although many societal evils, including high rates of HIV/AIDS transmission and high rates of domestic
and criminal violence, remain deeply problematic, it can also be argued that had South
Africa not taken the path of the TRC and national reconciliation, its current situation
would be far worse.

CONCLUSION

In this chapter we aimed to address questions around the responsibility of bystanders, the
nature of perpetrators, and the optimal responses to survivors of societal evil. We began
by arguing that there are important differences between bystander and perpetrator evil.
Bystanders bear responsibility for everyday acts of societal evil insofar as these entail
a failure of empathy and of moral courage. At the same time, there may be differences
between these kinds of more banal evil and those that are specifically undertaken in order
to inflict and observe harm in others. Although the vast majority of members of society
may be susceptible to committing ordinary bystander societal evils, fewer may be capable
of actually committing more sadistic societal evils.

Emerging democracies are often faced with the challenge of responding to past societal
evils. A conflict may exist between the needs of the individual and society in the aftermath

of such evils, and such a conflict is mediated by the work of the South African Truth and Reconciliation Commission. On the one hand, the TRC was perceived in a relatively positive global light, bringing not only more knowledge but also public acknowledgment (Ash, 1997; Stein, 1998), and the TRC serves as a model to many other countries dealing with similar aftermaths. On the other hand, a good deal of criticism on the approach of the TRC was also expressed from various corners, and data on psychiatric results of the TRC in South Africa suggest that the TRC was not sufficient to meet the psychological needs of survivors; additional therapeutic interventions for such individuals are still needed.

REFERENCES

Adorno, T., E. Frenkel-Brunswik, D. Levinson, and N. Stanford. 1950. *The Authoritarian Personality*. New York: Harper & Row.

Agger, I., and S.B. Jensen. 1990. Testimony as ritual and evidence in psychotherapy for political refugees. *Journal of Traumatic Stress*, 3, 115–130.

Allan, A. 2000. Truth and reconciliation: A psychological perspective. *Ethnic Health,* 5, 3–4, 191–204.

Arendt, H. 1994. *Eichmann in Jerusalem: A Report on the Banality of Evil*. New York: Penguin.

Ash, T. 1997. True confessions. *New York Review of Books*, 17, 33–38.

Asmal, K., L. Asmal, and R. Roberts. 1996. *Reconciliation Through Truth: A Reckoning of Apartheid's Criminal Governance*. Cape Town: David Philip Publishers, in association with Mayibue Books, University of the Western Cape.

Bar-On, D. 2001. The bystander in relation to the victim and the perpetrator: Today and during the Holocaust. *Social Justice Research*, 14, 2, 125–148.

Bouraine, A., and J. Levy, ed. 1995. *The Healing of a Nation?* Cape Town, Johannesburg: Thorold's Africana Books.

Byrne, C.C. 2004. Benefit or burden: Victims' reflections on TRC participation. *Peace and Conflict: Journal of Peace Psychology,* 10, 3, 237–256.

Chandler, D. 2000. Will there be a trial for the Khmer Rouge? *Ethics and International Affairs,* 14, 67–82.

Cienfugos, A.J., and C. Monelli. 1983. The testimony of political repression as a therapeutic instrument. *American Journal of Orthopsychiatry*, 53, 43–51.

Crocker, D.A. 2009. Reckoning with past wrongs: A normative framework. In *Ethics and International Affairs: A Reader,* 3d ed., ed. J.H. Rosenthal, and C. Barry, 45–64. Washington, DC: Georgetown University Press.

Darley, J. 1992. Social organization for the production of evil. *Psychological Inquiry,* 3, 2, 199–218.

Fletcher, L. 2007. Facing up to the past: Bystanders and transitional justice. *Harvard Human Rights Journal,* 20, 47–52.

Freedman, S.R., and R.D. Enright. 1996. Forgiveness as an intervention with incest survivors. *Journal of Consulting and Clinical Psychology,* 64, 983–992.

Gobodo-Madikizela, P. 2004. *A Human Died That Night: A South African Woman Confronts the Legacy of Apartheid*. Cape Town: Mariner Books.

Hamber, B. 2000a. Repairing the irreparable: Dealing with double-blinds of making reparations for crimes of the past. *Ethnic Health*, 5, 3, 215–226.

———. 2000b. *Righting the Wrongs; Dealing with the Difficulties of Granting Reparations in South Africa. From Rhetoric to Responsibility; Making Reparations to the Survivors of Past Political Violence in South Africa*. Johannesburg: Centre for the Study of Violence and Reconciliation.

Hebl, J.H., and R.D. Enright. 1993. Forgiveness as a psychotherapeutic goal with elderly females. *Psychotherapy*, 30, 658–667.

Kaminer, D., and D. Stein. 2001. Sadistic personality disorders in perpetrators of human rights abuses: A South African case study. *Journal of Personality Disorders*, 15, 6, 475–486.

Kaminer, D., D.J. Stein, I. Mbanga, and N. Zungu-Dirwayi. 2001. The Truth and Reconciliation Commission in South Africa: relation to psychiatric status and forgiveness among survivors of human rights abuses. *British Journal of Psychiatry*, 178 (April), 373–377.

Latane, B., and S. Nida. 1981. Ten years of research on group size and helping. *Psychological Bulletin*, 89, 308–324.

Levine, M., C. Cassidy, and G. Braier. 2002. Self-categorization and bystander non-intervention: Two experimental studies. *Journal of Applied Social Psychology*, 32, 7, 1452–1463.

Lifton, R.J. 1986. *Nazi Doctors: Medical Killing and the Psychology of Genocide*. New York: Basic Books.

Luria, A. 1980. *Higher Cortical Functions in Man*. New York: Basic Books.

Milgram, S. 1974. *Obedience to Authority: An Experimental View*. New York: Harper and Row.

Oliner, S., and P.M. Oliner. 1988. *The Altruistic Personality: Rescuers of Jews in Nazi Europe*. New York: Free Press.

Staub, E. 1989. *The Roots of Evil: The Origins of Genocide and Other Group Violence*. New York: Cambridge University Press.

Stein, D.J. 1998. Psychiatric aspects of the Truth and Reconciliation Commission in South Africa. *British Journal of Psychiatry*, 173 (December), 455–457.

———. 2000. The neurobiology of evil: Psychiatric perspectives on perpetrators. *Ethnic Health*, 5, 3–4, 303–315.

Stein, D.J., S. Seedat, D. Kaminer, H. Moomal, A. Herman, J. Sonnega, and D.R. Williams. 2008. The impact of the Truth and Reconciliation Commission on psychological distress and forgiveness in South Africa. *Social Psychiatry and Psychiatric Epidemiology*, 43, 6, 462–468.

Stein, D.J., S.L. Williams, P.B. Jackson, S. Seedat, L. Myer, A. Herman, et al. 2009. Perpetration of gross human rights violations in South Africa: Association with psychiatric disorders. *South African Medical Journal*, 99, 390–395.

Weine, S.M., A.D. Kulenovic, I. Parkovic, and R. Gibbons. 1998. Testimony psychotherapy in Bosnian refugees: A pilot study. *American Journal of Psychiatry*, 155, 1720–1726.

Zimbardo, P. 1969. The human choice: Individuation, reason and order versus individuated impulse and chaos. In *The 17th Nebraska Symposium on Motivation*, ed. W.T. Arnold and D. Levine, 237–307. Lincoln: University of Nebraska Press.

11

Unconsciousness and Organizational Evil

Gerson Moreno-Riaño

One of the most contentious and difficult aspects of a discussion regarding organizational or administrative evil[1] is the nature of the evil in question. It is contentious given the fact that evil is a contested concept. As Walter Bryce Gallie (1956) argues, a contested concept admits of no final and conclusive definition, given that any attempt to define it is value-laden. It is difficult given that the lack of definitional clarity minimizes the possibility of operationalizing the concept of evil with any degree of validity whatsoever. Ultimately, the contentious and difficult character of evil may directly undermine one's ability to understand evil in its entirety. Billy Graham, the well-known evangelist, echoed this claim when, on September 14, 2001—the National Day of Prayer and Remembrance—he proposed that evil was a kind of "mystery," something amorphous, vague, and beyond one's ability to understand. In spite of the ambiguity surrounding the concept of evil, there has been no shortage of attempts seeking to discuss and understand it. Likewise, evil is a part of everyday, popular vocabulary. Google, for example, at one time employed the term as part of its informal motto: "Don't be evil." Although the term itself may be contested, it appears to be the case that people "know it when they see it."[2]

In spite of the dynamic and complex nature of the term "evil," a growing literature has developed around the concept of organizational or administrative evil. In many respects, it began in 1998 with *Unmasking Administrative Evil*, by Guy B. Adams and Danny L. Balfour. Adams and Balfour argued that evil was "intrinsic to the human condition" and was "deeply woven into the identity of public administration" (1998, 3, 5). More important, administrative evil was a "new and frightening form of evil," given its connection to the modern trinity of science, technology, and rationality (1998, 4). Both Adams and Balfour did admit that the primary manifestations of this new kind of evil were unfortunately commonplace: dehumanization and genocide. What was uncommon, however, was both the root of this evil and its characteristics. As already mentioned, the root was modernity itself. Adams and Balfour further argued that administrative evil was chameleon-like and thus deceptive. It could wear "many masks" and thus facilitate the perpetration of evil actions since it made it "easy for ordinary people to do evil, even when they do not intend to do so" (9). Its deceptive nature was rooted in a process of "moral inversion" in which evil was redefined as good and its perpetrators were unaware of the evil nature of their activities (9).

Adams and Balfour's thesis led to a number of studies that applied the concept of administrative evil to various aspects of organizations and public administration (e.g.,

Adams and Balfour, 1998; Adams, Balfour, and Reed, 2006; Dillard and Ruchala, 2005; Dillard, Ruchala, and Yuthas, 2005; Dubnick and Justice, 2006; Ghere, 2006; Vickers, 2001; Zanetti and Adams, 2000). Others studies explored the etiology and characteristics of administrative evil (e.g., Anderson, 2006a, 2006b; McSwite, 2006; Moreno-Riaño, 2001, 2006). A common thread in the administrative evil literature was the implicit acceptance of administrative evil as a reality that required careful study. Dubnick (2000), however, presented the earliest and most serious critique of administrative evil as a theoretical concept. He did not deny the existence of administrative evil but he did question the logic that Adams and Balfour used to establish its existence. In particular, Dubnick argued that Adams and Balfour had failed to abide by the fundamental tenets of responsible scholarship, which required "warrant—establishing arguments in cases where the claims or their assumptions are novel or controversial" (2000, 465). For Dubnick, administrative evil was such a claim, and its lack of justification was at best irresponsible and at worst suspicious.

This chapter revisits Dubnick's central concerns regarding the concept of administrative or organizational evil. Although Dubnick's central concern is the establishment of a framework of responsible scholarship in this area, Dubnick—both directly and indirectly—facilitates an exploration of other important considerations for any research program that has organizational evil at its subject. In what follows, a brief exposition of Dubnick's critique of the administrative evil concept is presented. This exposition also outlines several key conditions to advance a more rigorous and holistic exploration of administrative evil. The chapter concludes with a brief example of these conditions at work.

CONDITIONS FOR THE STUDY OF ORGANIZATIONAL EVIL

In his critique of Adams and Balfour's *Unmasking Administrative Evil* (1998), Dubnick argues that a serious logical misstep exists in the argument used to establish the reality of administrative evil. He differentiates between warrant-using and warrant-establishing arguments and argues that administrative evil, as presented by Adams and Balfour, requires warrant-establishing, not warrant-using, arguments. In short, the novel concept of administrative evil requires justification, not merely uncritical acceptance and usage. According to Dubnick, Adams and Balfour argue for administrative evil based on the following claims:

A: The existence of evil is a historical reality.
B: Evil is inherent in the human condition.
C: Modernity has given rise to a new kind of evil—administrative evil.
D: Organizations perpetrate administrative evil through unaware organizational members via a process of moral inversion.

As Dubnick sees it, claims C and D are both deeply problematic and require justification. Specifically, Adams and Balfour, as Dubnick argues, have redefined the classic understanding of evil by eliminating human awareness and deliberateness as well as framing administrative evil as a type of supraorganizational, "demonic cultural force" bordering on the "magical" (Dubnick 2000, 467). Further, such redefinition has led to the development of a novel concept of evil that is "hollow . . . [and] useless for purposes of explaining or understanding human behavior" (465).[3]

The questions that Dubnick raises are both philosophical and methodological. The notion of personal responsibility, one of the most central tenets of ethics, is at the core of Dubnick's concerns and critique. How can one discuss human evil in an organizational context—or in any context, for that matter—without a framework of personal responsibility and human agency? Dubnick correctly understands Adams and Balfour's argument. The latter appear to attribute administrative evil to organizations and history, leaving individuals paupers and pawns of metaexistential and social forces. But how can scholars investigate such forces in view of both the almost-mystical character of these forces and the current social and policy sciences methodologies available? It appears that the study of organizational evil needs to be recast both philosophically and methodologically.

In order for administrative or organizational evil to be a rigorous, productive, and relevant area of inquiry in the study of organizations, it should meet at least the following conditions. First, scholarship in this area must guard itself against committing the ecological fallacy: the error of making inferences about collectivities based upon individuals. Adams and Balfour infer that organizations can behave in an evil fashion akin to that of human beings. Both authors admit that evil is an inherent aspect of the human experience and extrapolate from this that evil is an essential characteristic of modern organizations. Consequently, Adams and Balfour generalize from a simpler unit of analysis (human beings) to a more complex unit of analysis (organizations). This is fallacious reasoning because it violates the basic parameter of units of analysis distinctions. Some have advanced this same reasoning in the realm of business ethics under the guise of the "moral projection principle," which holds the following:

> It is appropriate not only to describe organizations and their characteristics by analogy with individuals, it is also appropriate normatively to look for and to foster moral attributes in organizations by analogy with those we look for and foster in individuals. (Goodpaster, 2007, 20)

As Nani Ranken rightly notes, such an approach to moral reasoning concerning organizations and individuals is both unfruitful and "dangerous" (1987, 633).

A rejection of the ecological fallacy as well as respect for basic units of analysis parameters in discussions concerning administrative evil suggests the second important condition for future research in this field. Administrative evil is the result of human agency and, therefore, a broader context of human agency and responsibility must be integrated into future administrative evil scholarship. The ecological fallacy in this area of research leads to the creation of historical impulses that motivate organizations to behave in a certain fashion. The assumption that organizations behave as persons and determine human action makes it impossible to develop a meaningful ethic of human responsibility or organizational ethic. This is what Ranken considers "dangerous," namely, that when an organization "is perceived as a super-person with a life and interest of its own; to that extent some morally important issues will be screened out . . . as irrelevant" (1987, 637). Consequently, in order to address adequately the existence of administrative evil, scholars must begin with the centrality of human agency to organizations. Organizations as moral persons or the "moral projection principle" is deeply problematic and must be dismissed from scholarship in this field.

The third condition for scholarship in the area of organizational evil is related directly to the centrality of human agency in organizations. Scholarship in this field must seriously grapple with the human condition and the nature of evil. Both of these are fundamental questions that, though difficult, must be explored. It is interesting to note that the concept of administrative evil, as Adams and Balfour originally present it, does begin with the human condition yet avoids a substantive discussion concerning the nature of evil itself. Further, although a place in their logic is granted for the human condition, a substantive discussion concerning this theme is not presented. Both authors suggest that the starting place for their understanding of administrative evil is "the premise that evil is inherent in the human condition" (Adams and Balfour, 2008, 3). Somehow this key starting point becomes tertiary to an overwhelming organizational impetus that leads to evil. What do they mean by the "human condition"? What does it mean to suggest that evil is "inherent" in the human condition? What is evil? These are first-principles types of questions that must be answered in an effort to advance knowledge and understanding of organizational evil as well as to develop an appropriate response to its existence.

Inherent in a call to address human nature and the nature of evil is yet another condition for scholarship to advance the academy's understanding of administrative evil. Such scholarship must take seriously the contributions of philosophy and a public theology to the type of first-principles questions raised above. Public administration and organizational theory alone are ill equipped to answer the philosophical anthropology questions that are at the root of administrative evil. A philosophical-theological approach must be systematically embraced and should be deeply interwoven into the theories and methodologies of public administration and organization theory scholarship to make sense of the existential dilemmas that organizational evil raises. Scholarship in this field agrees that administrative or organizational evil is something to be avoided and eliminated. Scholars need to enlarge the space for alternative disciplinary perspectives and influences in advancing both the understanding and elimination of administrative evil. The observation of William Ascher concerning the relationship of policy sciences to other disciplinary approaches is instructive:

> let us not separate ourselves from the other people who agree with us on fundamentals but use different labels. We need all the true allies we can get, and the work of many others fits these criteria even if it is not called "policy sciences." (1986, 366)

Philosophy is perhaps one of the most important disciplines in the study of administrative evil because it is a second-order discipline. As James Moreland and William Craig argue, philosophy functions at a "pre-presuppositional level by clarifying and justifying the presuppositions of a discipline" (2003, 13). Furthermore, philosophy by its very nature seeks to provide a holistic consideration and understanding of a field of inquiry. As such, philosophy is crucial to the study of administrative evil. Unfortunately, scholars in this field have not always thought so. As Charles Fox has noted, in the case of philosophy, "philosophers do not do public administration and public administration is not directly informed by philosophy" (1994, 84). Although this state of affairs has changed since Fox made this observation (e.g., Jun, 2006; Stivers, 2008), there is still much to be done in this area.

If the integration of philosophy in administrative evil scholarship has been slow, then that of theology is at a snail's pace. Daniel Lowery (2005) has decried the virtual silence of public administration scholarship in considering the possible connections between religion and public administration. While Jos Raadschelders (2005) mentions in general the influence of various disciplines on public administration, including theology, he offers no explicit examples, probably because the literature itself demonstrates a sizable gap in this area of scholarship. There are, however, some exceptions. O.P. Dwivedi (1987), for example, made a strong plea for an "administrative theology" to address the moral context of all administrations and organizations. Such a theology, argued Dwivedi, is broadly ecumenical and is focused on service, a doctrine of vocation, and a reinterpretation of secular administrative nomenclature. James Martinez and William Richardson (2008) and Michael Macaulay (2009) briefly consider the importance of various aspects of Christian theology in the history and development of an administrative ethics. Other than these and a few other studies, however, the contribution of theology to administrative and organizational evil scholarship is sporadic.

Just as philosophy is central to the problems organizational evil raises, theology is as well. As the influential theologian Jürgen Moltmann argues concerning theology,

> Its subject alone makes Christian theology a *theologia publica*, a public theology. It gets involved in the public affairs of society. . . . It thinks critically about the religious and moral values of the societies in which it exists, and presents its reflections as a reasoned position. (1999, 1)

Theology can substantively inform questions and provide answers that need to be considered as scholars seek to understand the human condition and the nature of evil in ways that add to the body of knowledge concerning administrative evil. In particular, Campbell and Swift (2004), in their work on theology and medical ethics, suggest that theology can treat and discuss human questions that are too often ignored or deemed irrelevant by narrow disciplinary and methodological parameters. Such parameters, argue Campbell and Swift, actually impoverish a discipline because they keep the latter from being able to address matters central to human existence that lie outside their boundaries. It would appear to be the case that such concerns as the human condition and the nature of evil are the kind of central matters that call for a philosophical–theological exploration.

The fifth and final condition is what Ronald Nash (1994) called the test of human experience. Every concept, theoretical scheme, and worldview must correspond with what human beings know about the world and how they experience it. Logical consistency alone is not enough. There must be a close correspondence between a concept or worldview and the commonalities of basic human experience. Although the reality of organizational evil appears *prima facie* to be true (i.e., it exists), it also appears false in its undergirding logic and structure (e.g., no human responsibility). This appears to be the key disagreement between Adams and Balfour and Dubnick. The latter contends that the conceptualization of organizational evil is fictional (i.e., does not fit human experience), while the former point to genocide and dehumanization as evidence of its reality (i.e., does fit human experience). The missing link is that the reality and existence of a concept must be validated at both a conceptual and an existential stage.

It is certainly possible that other conditions could be added to develop a rigorous organizational evil research program. Yet these five conditions constitute the necessary prerequisites to the development of a robust and rigorous approach to this problem. In what follows, these conditions are individually applied as well as exemplified through an analysis of the contribution of the philosopher Eric Voegelin.

TOWARD A THEORY OF ORGANIZATIONAL EVIL

As was suggested earlier, the following five conditions structure a basic framework for developing a more disciplined study of organizational evil, namely, a theory of organizational or administrative evil:

1. Reject fallacious justifications such as the ecological fallacy or the moral projection principle.
2. Develop and integrate a broader context of human agency and responsibility.
3. Engage first-principles questions surrounding the human condition and the nature of evil.
4. Develop a deliberately interdisciplinary framework for research that integrates philosophy and theology.
5. Assess administrative evil research in terms of both logical consistency and the test of human experience.

How can the study of organizational evil integrate these prerequisites to a more substantive consideration of this very real evil? The following delineates a possible, though by no means perfect, plan of action.

Human Responsibility: The Importance of Character for Organizational Actors

Implementing the first two conditions would mean that administrative evil research programs must focus entirely on the individuals who create, develop, found, maintain, and lead organizations. Ghere (2006) provides a good example of a framework for considering human volition in the context of administrative evil. More specifically, however, a concerted focus must be placed on exploring the character—the second nature of a person—and psychological traits of organizational actors as well as the types of organizational ethos, policies, and protocols that these actors develop and maintain. Research that focuses on the character of the modern organization, though instructive, fails to provide adequate analysis and remedies for the flaws of these organizations because it fails to investigate the key unit of analysis: the organizational actor. Although the "character" of modern administrations and organizations may be more aptly considered in terms of a situational context, it is the cultivated and permanent habits and predispositions of organizational actors that facilitate organizational decisions that are either good or evil. In addition to an investigatory realignment from a focus on organizational character to one on the character of organizational actors, the types of solutions for administrative evil proposed must also reflect this shift. In particular, public administration and organizational theory scholarship needs to focus on the importance of leadership character education and development as antidotes to administrative evil. Gene Klann (2007), for example, illustrates a more agent-centered and character-rooted approach to addressing the moral development of organizational actors and, in turn, that of humane organizations. Such emphasis on the education and development of leadership character is essential if organizational actors, particularly leaders, are to avoid what Bernard Bass concluded were their "pragmatism, their preference for taking risks, and their valuing of short-term maximization or long-term gain" (2008, 197).

The Human Condition, the Nature of Evil, and Moral Unconsciousness

The study of human nature and the human condition is perhaps the most fundamental and important kind of scholarship that can be pursued. David Brooks (2011) argued recently that the knowledge in this area "just keeps on flowing." It is surprising to note, therefore, that administrative evil scholarship does not consistently and substantively address human nature and the human condition. The same can be said for evil and its nature. Adams and Balfour (1998) present perhaps the longest treatment of both of these topics. Yet their treatment lacks theoretical clarity and coherence. Although administrative evil is identified in terms of genocide and dehumanization, one is also left with the impression that evil may be socially constructed. As Jonathan Anderson (2006a, 2006b) and O.C. McSwite (2006) argue in their work on evil and public administration, it may be possible to suggest and demonstrate the social construction of evil, yet human beings all seem to know that, at a foundational level, evil exists and is absolute. Scholarship on organizational and administrative evil must therefore situate its investigations within a philosophical anthropology that considers seriously the existence of a human nature with permanent and situation-bound conditions. Furthermore, such scholarship must carefully delineate the absolute character of evil as well as its situation-bound manifestations while simultaneously articulating the relationship between evil and human nature. These are difficult projects to undertake, but there is some promising work being done in all these areas. Zimbardo, for example, considers dispositional, situational, and systemic accounts of evil and seeks to demonstrate "how people's character may be transformed by their being immersed in situations that unleash powerful situational forces" (2007, 8). Although Zimbardo often uses the moral projection principle in suggesting that institutions are creative and manipulative, his observations concerning the interaction between character, human responsibility, evil, and organizational ethos are important and instructive. Thomas Cushman (2001) considers the action-bound nature of evil. This is important to note, especially given the condition that administrative evil scholarship must be situated within a broader context of human agency. As Cushman argues concerning the evil perpetrated in the war in Bosnia at the end of the twentieth century:

> It was individuals who destroyed Bosnia and they did so not as automatons or dupes of historical or cultural forces, but as willful agents who reflexively responded to the contours of both local and global history, who reflexively adapted themselves to the exigencies and contingencies of the unfolding present, and who reflexively presented an ideal vision of the future that their actions would, ideally, bring about. (2001, 82)

Situational and organizational accounts of evil cannot be denied. It is clear that both of these exist. Yet at the center of these are individuals who willfully choose to act or refrain from acting to bring about or restrain evil through "malice aforethought" (Stone, 2009, 22). In this way, evil is part and parcel of the human condition. The question still remains, however, as to where evil itself originates.

Perhaps a fruitful venue for research discussions concerning evil and its organizational manifestations is to consider the existence of a basic modicum of evil as an inherent human disposition, one that—unless restrained through appropriate moral education and transformation—may affect the creation and use of organizations and administration. This basic modicum of evil could simply be the desire and willingness that all human beings evidence to do the forbidden. Here the importance of philosophy and theology is both evident and instructive. Philosophers and theologians have identified human evil as either supreme lawlessness or the pursuit of the forbidden. In book IX of the *Republic*, for example, Plato argued that the tyrant was completely lawless and had given himself over to the most base and lawless desires within him. Augustine, one of Christianity's greatest philosophers and theologians, recounts in book II of his *Confessions* that human depravity is rooted in the desire and pursuit of the forbidden—as illustrated in children's stealing pears not to eat but to throw at hogs and to rejoice in the mere act of stealing. This observation of a basic modicum of evil in human nature has been articulated in a long and distinguished philosophical and theological scholarly tradition known as natural law. Natural law scholarship validates the prima facie and absolute existence of evil in its notion that good exists within all human agents, which, when violated, may result in the perpetration of human evil.

How the existence of goodness in human beings is violated, thus facilitating the perpetration of evil, is a complex matter. Here, the notion of moral unconsciousness should be introduced. Augustine argued that human evil—the human desire for and pursuit of the forbidden—led to an obfuscation of the mind and extreme self-deception. As Gillian

Evans argues, "Augustine believed that evil has the effect of obscuring the understanding and impeding the working of the mind" (1992, 36). For Augustine, evil illustrated "a deceptive sense of omnipotence from doing something forbidden without immediate punishment" (Augustine, 2006, 32). Aristotle also treats this type of moral unconsciousness or deception in book VII of the *Nicomachean Ethics,* suggesting that it is possible for a human being to have knowledge in one sense and yet not have it in another sense. The full passage is worthy of careful consideration:

> And further the possession of knowledge in another sense than those just named is something that happens to men; for within the case of having knowledge but not using it we see a difference of state, admitting of the possibility of having knowledge in a sense and yet not having it, as in the instance of a man asleep, mad, or drunk. But now this is just the condition of men under the influence of passions; for outbursts of anger and sexual appetites and some other such passions, it is evident, actually alter our bodily condition, and in some men even produce fits of madness. It is plain, then, that incontinent people must be said to be in a similar condition to men asleep, mad, or drunk. The fact that men use the language that flows from knowledge proves nothing; for even men under the influence of these passions utter scientific proofs and verses of Empedocles, and those who have just begun to learn a science can string together its phrases, but do not yet know it; for it has to become part of themselves, and that takes time; so that we must suppose that the use of language by men in an incontinent state means no more than its utterance by actors on the stage. (Aristotle 1812/1984 or Bekker numbers 1147a10–1147a23)

For both Augustine and Aristotle, human beings could know and not know, see and not see. It is as if such a human being could be cognitively conscious of the moral yet volitionally unconscious of the moral. This is paradoxical to say the least, yet substantiated in the literature.

The existence of a moral unconsciousness—variously termed—that renders individuals insensitive to evil is a matter of serious discussion in the scholarly literature. In philosophical discussions, for example, some argue for a type of "moral blindness" or the lack of a "moral conscience" that allows individuals with no cognitive defects to simply engage in evil or fail to remedy evil (e.g., Calhoun, 1996; Foltz, 2001; Kaye, 2001). In the psychoanalysis literature, scholars cite the existence of a "moral blindness" that allows individuals to reject fundamental aspects of moral reality (Strenger, 2009). Other scholars have investigated the psychological roots of moral self-deception, leading to "ethical fading"—the process in which "the moral colors of an ethical decision fade into bleached hues that are void of moral implications" (Tenbrunsel and Messick, 2004, 224). Frederick Bird (1996) argues and provides evidence for the phenomena of moral silence, deafness, and blindness among individuals in complex organizations. In short, moral unconsciousness is a phenomenon attested to from various disciplinary vantage points. A deeper understanding of the logic of moral unconsciousness can be gained from a brief consideration of the work of the German-American philosopher Eric Voegelin.

Moral Unconsciousness and the Philosophy of Eric Voegelin[4]

The importance of Eric Voegelin for scholarship on administrative and organizational evil has already been attested to elsewhere (e.g., Moreno-Riaño, 2001, 2006). In the present context, it is sufficient to note that Voegelin helps clarify that the etiology of administrative evil is rooted in a moral unconsciousness characterized by an intellectual revolt against existential order, truth, freedom, and reason.

To understand the roots of administrative evil, it is important to comprehend Voegelin's theory of consciousness and notion of *nous* (i.e., reason or understanding). As Voegelin writes, "The problems of human order in society and history originate in the order of consciousness. Hence the philosophy of consciousness is the centerpiece of a philosophy of politics" (Ranieri, 1995). Organizations represent the consciousness of the individuals who not only sense these but who continually support them. One way to comprehend Voegelin's understanding of consciousness is to think of consciousness as a process in the acquisition of knowledge and understanding about existence and one's participation therein. Voegelin's concern with modern political actors and the organizations they generated was what he perceived as their lack of consciousness: a lack of knowledge and understanding about reality and their place in it. For Voegelin, such a lack of consciousness led to the devastating human atrocities perpetrated in the twentieth century—the type of administrative evil Adams and Balfour decry.

According to Voegelin, consciousness—the process of acquiring comprehensive knowledge about reality—has three dimensions: intentionality, luminosity, and reflexivity, all of which reflect various degrees of reality.[5] Intentionality is perhaps the most basic attribute of consciousness. It is the object-directedness nature of the human mind. Luminosity is the characteristic of consciousness that awakens humans to the fact that they are participants in a greater reality than the one that they immediately experience through the senses. Reflexivity is the ability of human consciousness to remember and reflect on its experiences of reality—it is the art of contemplation. These dimensions of consciousness illustrate the complexity of reality. On the one hand, intentionality reflects the object-relatedness of reality. Human beings experience reality in terms of objects that they can observe, study, touch, and direct. However, luminosity reflects the "beyondness" of reality—not an object that humans can regulate and control but, rather, the nexus in which humans simply participate, one that has not been created and cannot be controlled. In this sense, reality is simply a given beyond the reach of humans. Reflexivity as the art of contemplation is what allows humans to reflect on their existence and experiences of reality and should lead them to an understanding of the whole of reality, not just a part.

According to Voegelin, Plato and perhaps Aristotle were among the first to recognize these dimensions of consciousness. Insofar as this is correct, a brief digression to explore their thought will help to explicate further Voegelin's theory of consciousness and its bearing on the issue at hand. Both of these thinkers, argues Voegelin, were motivated by a search for order and a resistance to the chaos of their society. In Voegelin's view, Plato's and Aristotle's genius was their discovery of the luminous character of reason.[6] Reason was thus a "force of order" radiating its "stark light . . . on the phenomena of personal and social disorder" (Voegelin, 1978, 91). Reason enlightened human beings to an existential order beyond their immediate reality, an order that not only could imbue life with meaning but could help structure life.

The benefits of this "luminosity" were realized insofar as one seriously and diligently questioned the meaning and grounds of existence (i.e., the capacity of "reflexivity"). The degree of one's "openness" to existence and knowledge about this ground determined not only the level of one's consciousness and rationality but also the type of attitudes and behavior that one would exhibit. Consequently, human beings who were open to questions of existence and who partook of the order to which reason directed them (to the extent that they ordered their lives in accordance with this existential order) were fully rational and moral beings. In contradistinction to these complete human beings were those who "insensitively resisted the advance" of the enlightening power of reason (Voegelin, 1978, 90). These individuals closed themselves off to questions of existence and were thus ignorant of the structure of reality and its implication for their personal lives. According to Voegelin, this raises the specter of two "types" of human being: the conscious and the unconscious. As Voegelin writes:

> For Plato . . . the philosopher is man awake, who communicates to his society the knowledge of its right order, while the tyrant is the sleeper who gratifies his lusts in public and commits crimes belonging to the phantasies of dreams. For Aristotle the *spoudaios* (i.e., mature) is the fully developed man who is in the highest degree permeable for the cosmic-divine movement of being and who, by virtue of this quality, becomes the creator of ethics and the source of knowledge about what is right by nature. (1978, 80)

The conscious human being not only is open to the ground of existence but understands how it is structured and how such order, if followed, can lead both to personal and moral fulfillment. Unconscious human beings, in closing themselves off to the existential order of reality (and to reason), order their lives on the basis of a less-differentiated level of existence—which is real (i.e., the intentional dimension of reality) but is not the essential ground of all existence (i.e., the luminous dimension of reality). For Plato and Aristotle, as well as for Voegelin, this less-differentiated level of existence was characterized not by reason but by human passion or, as Voegelin called it, the *libido dominandi*.[7]

The specter of two types of human beings also led to two different manifestations of reason. As noted, the classical philosophers articulated reason and consciousness in terms of luminosity of and reflexivity toward existential order, conceptualizations that Voegelin accepted and used throughout his works. The other view, which Voegelin decries and criticizes, held reason to be nothing more than an instrument of human passion. Therefore, consciousness was limited to knowledge about experienced objects rather than a luminosity toward a transcendent existential order. This instrumental view of reason resulted from a rejection of the fundamental order of existence (one beyond the immediate experience of humans but illuminated through reason) as the ground for personal and social order. In lieu of this fundamental order of existence, another possible order of existence was posited (one within the immediate experience of humans and at the mercy of their passions) by which humans could ground personal and social life as they saw fit. Human passion became the foundation of social and political life and instrumental rationality (i.e., utilitarian rationality) the means by which to build the edifice. To the extent that this occurred, it blinded human beings to the truth that they were "not . . . self-created, autonomous being[s] carrying the origin and meaning of [their] existence within [themselves]" (1978, 92).

The Test of Human Experience

The above digression into the philosophy of Eric Voegelin as well as the brief discussion regarding Plato, Aristotle, and Augustine and various multidisciplinary observations demonstrates the value and importance of integrating philosophical and theological categories and considerations into an exploration of administrative evil. The development of a robust theory of administrative evil requires no less of scholarship in the field. In concluding this chapter, the final condition for research into the etiology of administrative or organization evil is discussed, namely, the test of human experience.

The notions of human nature, the human condition, and the nature and existence of evil often raise numerous philosophical conundrums and objections. As stated at the outset, such notions are often contested and suspect given their value-laden nature. There is, however, one key assessment matrix that cannot be contested or held suspect: the experience of those who suffer evil, dehumanization, and genocide. As much as scholars may want to decry essentialist and dispositional accounts of evil, those who suffer evil are all too aware of the fact that it has been fellow human beings—not organizations or administrations—who have perpetrated real evil against them. In the face of such suffering, arguments concerning the inappropriateness of philosophical or theological explanations are useless. In the face of the afflicted, arguments concerning the social construction of evil are pointless. These individuals about whom Adams and Balfour and countless others have written know and are conscious of the fact that evil has been done.

To some degree, this intimate understanding concerning the reality of evil is related to the intimate desire for goodness and justice that all human beings share. This is part of the natural law that so many philosophers and theologians have defended. The philosopher Simone Weil argues this point when she writes,

> What is it, exactly, that prevents me from putting that man's eyes out if I am allowed to do so and if it takes my fancy? . . . What would stay it is the knowledge that if someone were to put out his eyes, his soul would be lacerated by the thought that harm was being done him. At the bottom of the heart of every human being, from earliest infancy until the tomb, there is something that goes on indomitably expecting, in the teeth of all experience of crimes committed, suffered, and witnessed, that good and not evil will be done him. It is this above all that is sacred in every human being. (1986, 51)

The expectation that "good and not evil will be done" to oneself is a universal characteristic of human nature and the human condition. Likewise, the knowledge that evil exists and has been perpetrated is a universal characteristic of human nature and the human condition substantiating the earlier "people know it when they see it" claim. Central to both of these claims is the validity of human experience in recognizing the absolute nature of good and evil as well as their situational manifestations.

The logic of human experience must be carefully integrated into any organizational evil research program. This would entail the recognition that evil and good are absolute entities that are real, transcendent, and manifested throughout history. Human experience attests to the reality of a universal good and evil that are manifested by human actors. As already suggested, the logic of human experience should lead to the recontextualization of organizational evil from historical and organizational forces to human agency. Contrary to Adams and Balfour (1998), organizational and administrative evil is not particular to modern organizations. Consider, for example, the evil perpetrated by such massive organizations as the Roman empire and the various inquisitorial offices of the Roman Catholic Church during the Middle Ages. The systematic perpetration of evil has occurred throughout human history with increasing levels of efficiency. While the organizational and efficiency context may have differed, large-scale atrocities have always been committed in human history by human beings. The logic of human experience demonstrates that the real problem is human beings. Organizations and situational contexts are tertiary, not primary causes of administrative evil. Likewise, the logic of human experience testifies to the fact that human beings themselves can offer the best human remedies for organizational evil. Such basic principles as the rule of law, constitutional government, consent of the governed, human rights, transparency and accountability, separation of powers, shared governance, and many other principles have proved immensely valuable in limiting the perpetration of organizational evil in public and private organizations. Some of these antidotes have been generated through conflict. Others have come about through sustained and reasoned reflection. So long as a modicum of evil exists in human nature, administrative evil will continue to hunt human experience. It is only when human beings rise to their better nature that such evil can be suppressed and contained.

NOTES

1. In this essay, "organizational evil" and "administrative evil" are used interchangeably.

2. The actual quotation is "but I know it when I see it" and refers to Justice Potter Stewart's struggle to define obscenity in *Jacobellis v. Ohio*, 378 US 184 (1964).

3. In a response to Dubnick's critique, Adams and Balfour (2000) do not address this criticism. Rather, the authors focus on what they perceive to be the caricature-like nature of Dubnick's critique.

4. This section borrows from Moreno-Riaño (2001, 2006), essays in which a fuller treatment of administrative evil and modernity appears.

5. One of the many places in which Voegelin's account of these is found is his *In Search of Order,* vol. 5 of *Order and History* (1956/1987), pp. 1–45.

6. Here, Voegelin uses "reason" and "understanding" interchangeably with "consciousness."

7. For both Plato and Aristotle, human passion was irrational and "base" because it could not discern between the moral and immoral and between order and disorder. This ability was particular to

"reason" because it was the only element of humanity that enabled humans to discern the existential order of reality and apply it to their soul and society, thereby combating the disorder that arises from a life of passion.

REFERENCES

Adams, G.B., and D.L. Balfour. 1998. *Unmasking Administrative Evil*. Thousand Oaks, CA: Sage.
———. 2000. The authors' response. *Public Administration Review*, 60, 5, 481–482.
Adams, Guy B., Danny L. Balfour and George E. Reed. 2006. Abu Ghraib, administrative evil, and moral inversion: The value of "putting cruelty first." *Public Administration Review*, 66: 680–693.
Anderson, Jonathan. 2006a. The rhetorical impact of evil on public policy. *Administration & Society*, 37, 6, 719–730.
———. 2006b. "Evil" revisited. *Administration & Society*, 37, 6, 737–739.
Aristotle. 1812/1984. Nicomachean ethics. In *The Complete Works of Aristotle*, vol. 2, ed. Jonathan Barnes, 1147a10–1147a23. Princeton: Princeton University Press.
Ascher, W. 1986. The evolution of the policy sciences. *Journal of Policy Analysis and Management*, 5, 2, 365–389.
Augustine, Saint, Bishop of Hippo. 2006. *Confessions*, trans. F.J. Sheed. Indianapolis: Hackett.
Bass, B.M. 2008. *The Bass Handbook of Leadership*. New York: Simon & Schuster.
Bird, F.B. 1996. *The Muted Conscience*. Westport, CT: Greenwood.
Brooks, David. 2011. Hello. *New York Times*, March 6. http://brooks.blogs.nytimes.com/2011/03/06/hello/?scp=1&sq=oped%20human%20nature&st=cse/.
Calhoun, L. 1996. Moral blindness and moral responsibility: What can we learn from Rhoda Penmark? *Journal of Applied Philosophy*, 13, 1, 41–50.
Campbell, Alastair, and Teresa Swift. 2004. In search of the virtuous patient: an essay in empirical theology. *Public Theology for the Twenty-first Century*. ed. Duncan B. Forrester, 267–284. London: Continuum International Publishing Group.
Cushman, T. 2001. The reflexivity of evil. In *Evil After Postmodernism*, ed. J.L. Geddes, 79–100. New York: Routledge.
Dillard, Jesse F., and Linda Ruchala. 2005. The rules are no game: From instrumental rationality to administrative evil. *Accounting, Auditing & Accountability Journal*, 18, 5, 608–630.
Dillard, Jesse F., Linda Ruchala, and Kristi Yuthas. 2005. Enterprise resource planning systems: A physical manifestation of administrative evil. *International Journal of Accounting Information Systems*, 6, 107–127.
Dubnick, Melvin J. 2000. Spirited dialogue: the case for administrative evil: A critique. *Public Administration Review*, 60, 5, 464–482.
Dubnick, Melvin J., and Jonathan B. Justice. 2006. Accountability and the evil of administrative ethics. *Administration and Society* 38, 236–267.
Dwivedi, O.P. 1987. Moral dimensions of statecraft: A plea for an administrative theology. *Canadian Journal of Political Science/Revue Canadienne de Science Politique*, 20, 4, 699–709.
Evans, G.R. 1992. *Augustine on Evil*. Cambridge: Cambridge University Press.
Foltz, B.V. 2001. Hidden patency: On the iconic character of human life. *Christian Bioethics*, 7, 3, 317–331.
Fox, C.J. 1994. The use of philosophy in administrative ethic. In *Handbook of Administrative Ethics*, ed. T.L. Cooper, 83–106. New York: Marcel Dekker.
Gallie, W.B. 1956. Essentially contested concepts. *Proceedings of the Aristotelian Society*, 167, 130–131.
Ghere, Richard K. 2006. Watching the borders of administrative evil: human volition and policy intention. *American Review of Public Administration* 36, 419–436.
Goodpaster, K.E. 2007. *Conscience and Corporate Culture*. Malden, MA: Blackwell.

Jun, J.S. 2006. *The Social Construction of Public Administration.* Albany: SUNY Press.

Kaye, H.L. 2001. On moral blindness. *Society,* 38, 5, 30–32.

Klann, G. 2007. *Building Character.* San Francisco: John Wiley & Sons.

Lowery, D. 2005. Self-reflexivity: A place for religion and spirituality in public administration. *Public Administration Review,* 65, 3, 324–334.

Macaulay, M. 2009. The I that is we: Recognition and administrative ethics. In *Ethics and Integrity in Public Administration,* ed. R. Cox, 26–39. Armonk, NY: M.E. Sharpe.

Martinez, J.M., and W.D. Richardson. 2008. *Administrative Ethics in the Twenty-First Century.* New York: Peter Lang.

McSwite, O.C. 2006. The problem of evil: What a postmodern analysis reveals. *Administration & Society,* 37, 6, 731–736.

Moltmann, J. 1999. *God for a Secular Society.* London: SCM Press.

Moreland, J.P., and W.L. Craig. 2003. *Philosophical Foundations for a Christian Worldview.* Downers Grove, IL: InterVarsity Press.

Moreno-Riaño, Gerson. 2001. The etiology of administrative evil. *American Review of Public Administration,* 31, 3, 296–312.

———. 2006. Modernity, administrative evil, and the contribution of Eric Voegelin. In *Handbook of Organization Theory and Management: The Philosophical Approach,* 2d ed., ed. T.D. Lynch and P.L. Cruise, 449–467. New York: Taylor & Francis.

Nash, R. 1994. *Faith and Reason.* Grand Rapids, MI: Zondervan.

Raadschelders, J.C.N. 2005. Government and public administration: Challenges to and need for connecting knowledge. *Administrative Theory & Praxis,* 27, 4, 602–627.

Ranieri, J.J. 1995. *Eric Voegelin and the Good Society.* Columbia: University of Missouri Press.

Ranken, N.L. 1987. Corporations as persons: Objections to Goodpaster's "principle of moral projection." *Journal of Business Ethics,* 6, 8, 633–637.

Stivers, C. 2008. *Governance in Dark Times.* Washington, DC: Georgetown University Press.

Stone, M.H. 2009. *The Anatomy of Evil.* Amherst, MA: Prometheus Books.

Strenger, C. 2009. The psychodynamics of self-righteousness and its impact on the Middle Eastern conflict. *International Journal of Applied Psychoanalytic Studies,* 6, 3, 178–196.

Tenbrunsel, A.E., and D.M. Messick. 2004. Ethical fading: The role of self-deception in unethical behavior. *Social Justice Research,* 17, 2, 223–236.

Vickers, M.H. 2001. Bullying as unacknowledged organizational evil: A researcher's story. *Employee Responsibilities and Rights Journal,* 13, 4, 205–217.

Voegelin, E. 1956/1987. *Order and History,* vols. 1–5. Baton Rouge: Louisiana State University Press.

———. 1978. *Anamnesis,* trans. and ed. G. Niemeyer. Notre Dame: University of Notre Dame Press.

Weil, S. 1986. Human personality. In *Simone Weil: An Anthology,* ed. S. Miles, 51. New York: Grove Press.

Zanetti, L.A., and G.B. Adams. 2000. In service of the Leviathan: Democracy, ethics and the potential for administrative evil in the new public management. *Administrative Theory & Praxis,* 22, 3, 534–554.

Zimbardo, P. 2007. *The Lucifer Effect.* New York: Random House.

12

The Four Roots of Organizational Evil

Michael R. Ent and Roy F. Baumeister

It was Peter's and Jack's custom to have a beer together every Friday evening after work. Typically, their conversations were based on their mutual love of baseball and blues music. Despite the general levity of these meetings, on one Friday in 2009, Jack sat down at the bar with an uncharacteristically grave look on his face. That day, Jack lost his job, which he had held for 17 years, due to his company's new "streamlining initiative." This company had taken some big financial risks; when the risks did not pay off, the company began to fire lower-level managers. Jack was very upset. He felt as though he was paying for the mistakes of his organization's executives, who continued to hold lavish parties and meetings in exotic locations around the world. This could not have come at a worse time for Jack; he had recently seen the value of his pension fall by half because of the worldwide financial crisis. He was not alone in feeling resentment toward the financial and government leaders who were expected to prevent something like this from happening. As Jack was woefully discussing his predicament, Peter was quietly attentive to Jack's every word. Jack ended his tale with a shrug and began to pick at the label of his beer bottle.

Peter thought that he should say something, so he began to discuss the cost-benefit analysis that the executives in Jack's company likely went through before making their risky investments. Then, Peter explained that Jack's company had to make up for the money lost in unfruitful investments. He reasoned that, because of their expendability, lower-level managers such as Jack were a wise place to make cuts. Peter went on to explain why executive parties and trips are necessary to impress potential investors. Peter also provided a lucid explanation of how the financial collapse that caused Jack's diminished pension was due to systemic problems and was not really anyone's fault. Jack sat in amazement during Peter's pontification, thinking, "What the hell is this guy's problem?" Peter probably thought that he was helping Jack by explaining the reasons behind his misfortune. Nevertheless, Peter's lack of compassion indicates that he most likely missed the point of why Jack wanted to talk about his problems. The trouble was not that Peter was ignoring Jack's problems; the trouble was that Peter was viewing the situation from the vantage point of those by whom Jack felt victimized. There is something inherently distasteful about explaining a problem from the perpetrator's perspective, as opposed to relying solely on the victim's account. Explaining evil may seem dangerously close to making excuses for the perpetrators of evil or to justifying evil actions. Peter and Jack's story illustrates a formidable obstacle in the way of an objective assessment of evil: the primacy of the victim's perspective. Although there may be countless ways to view an occurrence of evil, evil is typically identified by the victim and described from the victim's perspective.

Evil exist primarily in the eye of the beholder, and the beholder tends to adopt the victim's perspective. Most perpetrators of evil do not see themselves as evil. Hence, characterizing something as evil involves taking the victim's perspective. For every evil deed, someone suffers. If no one suffered from an action, it would be difficult to make the case that the action was evil. Some religious doctrines might classify actions as evil based on more abstract criteria, such as divine command. This type of classification is not germane to our discussion and usually turns out to be an extension of the notion of victimization anyhow. In basic terms, evil requires a victim.

There are problems with relying on victims to identify evil. For example, people can be victimized unknowingly. In such cases, the victim is incapable of identifying evil, at least right away. The people who invested their money with Bernard Madoff did not realize that they were being victimized until the truth was revealed about Madoff's massive Ponzi scheme. These investors were the victims of fraud for years. However, for a long time, they were unable to claim victimization and identify evil because of inadequate access to information. Another problem is that people's standards for what constitutes victimization may vary considerably. For example, some people feel victimized by their government when income taxes are increased. Others view the same tax increase as necessary and appropriate. So, should tax increases be regarded as evil?

Although defining organizational evil is an important task, it is probably one best left to philosophers and theologians. This chapter addresses organizational evil from a social-psychological perspective. Our focus is to explain the causes and processes of organizational evil. For this purpose, a sufficient guideline is that evil exists in the eye of the beholder. Therefore, we use the term "organizational evil" to refer broadly to any organizational activity that causes people to feel victimized.

VICTIM AND PERPETRATOR PERSPECTIVES

Victim accounts might seem more vivid, moving, or worthy of attention, but they are insufficient for a full understanding of evil. At the same time, perpetrator accounts are few and far between. This scarcity is due in part to perpetrators' reluctance to see themselves as evildoers. The people who let evil into the world do not usually recognize that their actions are evil. Not surprisingly, victim and perpetrator accounts of the same incident tend to diverge considerably. One reason for this inconsistency is that instances of evil tend to be perceived as much more important by the victim than by the perpetrator. This discrepancy is known as the "magnitude gap" (Baumeister, 1997). The core idea of the magnitude gap is that the victim loses more than the perpetrator gains. This is most obvious with murder, insofar as it is almost inconceivable that the perpetrator could gain as much as the victim loses (life itself). But even in less severe cases, such as sex crimes, assault, and property crimes, the victim's loss typically exceeds the perpetrator's gain.

In 2002, the residents of a Houston neighborhood observed a few individuals pouring buckets of liquid along the streets near their homes. These concerned citizens reported the unusual activity, and subsequent tests revealed dangerous levels of cadmium, cyanide, and chromium in properties adjacent to the clandestine dumping grounds. Exposure to these hazardous materials can lead to serious health problems, such as decreased kidney function and cancer. When improperly disposed of, these chemicals eventually make their way through the soil and into the groundwater. Small businesses in the Houston area were using the chemicals to add a protective coating to metal products, such as pistons and ball bearings. Residents of nearby neighborhoods were put in danger when these businesses began to dump their waste along the side of the road instead of paying the fees associated with proper disposal (Cappiello, 2002). In this case, the perpetrators were metal-plating businesses that financially benefited from illegally dumping waste. The victims, those who lived in the communities where the dumping was taking place, were exposed to hazardous chemicals. To the metal-plating businesses, dumping the chemicals may have seemed to be a relatively insignificant action to save a little bit of money. Members of the local community, however, saw the same action as extremely significant. They likely focused on the potentially devastating health effects associated with exposure to these chemicals. The magnitude gap can lead victims and perpetrators to see the same action in very different ways. If, in the process of dumping the chemicals, the workers were to be asked what they were doing, the description would likely be a mundane statement such as, "We're getting rid of this stuff so that we don't have to pay for the disposal fee." A neighborhood resident, however, may describe the same action by saying, "Those guys out there are poisoning my children." Neither of these accounts tells the whole story. The human tendency to identify with victims as opposed to perpetrators may lead us to view victim accounts as the correct view, and perpetrator accounts as hopelessly skewed. Actually, victims and perpetrators both distort the truth to fit with their differing agendas. Perpetrators who are motivated to reduce their guilt may seem to have more reason to lie or to delude themselves. Nevertheless, victims also distort the truth for their own purposes, such as to reassure themselves of their own goodness and innocence.

In a laboratory study, Baumeister, Stillwell, and Wotman (1990) instructed participants to describe an incident in which they had made someone else angry. Participants in this study also described a time when someone else had made them angry. Thus, each participant provided one "perpetrator" story and one "victim" story. This study uncovered several important differences between victim and perpetrator accounts. Overall, actions seem less evil to the perpetrators than to the victims. Even when perpetrators admit a degree of wrongdoing, they tend to view the victims as blowing things out of proportion. Perpetrators also attempt to mitigate their culpability by pointing to external causes to explain their behavior. Individuals who are accused of wrongdoing commonly use phrases such as "I had no choice" and "I was just following orders." One of the most important disparities between victim and perpetrator accounts involves the perpetrator's motives and intentions. Victims' accounts come in two particularly prevalent versions. In one, the victim emphasizes the senselessness of the perpetrator's actions. The act seems random and unwarranted. This view helps to reinforce the innocence of the victim. If an evil action were totally random, then the victim would have absolutely no responsibility for its occurrence. If questioned, perpetrators typically do give reasons for their actions. Whether or not these reasons are adequate justification is another story. Of course, perpetrators may provide reasons for their actions that are thought to be more socially acceptable than their actual reasons. The other reigning view of victim accounts identifies the perpetrator as deliberately malicious, acting out of a sadistic desire to do harm as an end in itself. Perpetrators rarely view their actions in this way.

It is important to keep in mind that, in their study, Baumeister et al. (1990) had each person write both a victim story and a perpetrator story. Each person's style of thinking seemed to change when shifting from the victim to the perpetrator role. In that study, victims and perpetrators were not different kinds of people (indeed, they were precisely the same people); rather, "victim" and "perpetrator" are roles that all people play from time to time. To truly understand evil, it is necessary to acknowledge that everyone is capable of behaviors that could be categorized as evil and that evildoers are not a separate species.

WHO ARE THE EVILDOERS?

Seeing perpetrators of evil as a distinct type of human being is one of many broad stereotypes about evil. Collectively, these stereotypes may be referred to as the "myth of pure evil" (Baumeister, 1997). The typical movie villain exhibits many, if not all, of the common stereotypes of evildoers. Villains are often sadistic, capricious perpetrators who seek out and harm innocent, well-meaning victims. This portrayal of evil is not unique to movie villains. News stories and even children's cartoons (Hesse and Mack, 1991) reinforce the stereotypical view of evil. There are many inaccuracies in the myth of pure evil. One common misperception is that it is easy to tell the good guys from the bad guys.

Sometimes, actions may seem virtuous or evil depending on one's viewpoint. For example, buying a Toyota Prius is seen by many environmentally conscious people as a virtuous decision. The Prius can travel more than 40 miles on one gallon of gasoline (U.S. Environmental Protection Agency, 2006). Therefore, driving a Prius can result in less carbon emissions, less dependence on oil for fuel, and possibly a feeling of doing one's part to help the earth. Nevertheless, some individuals might see the same action as contributing to evil. According to the National Labor Committee (NLC; Institute for Global Labour and Human Rights, 2008), the parts supply chain used to make the Prius is full of sweatshop abuse. Tens of thousands of guest workers are brought to Japan from neighboring countries to work in the factories that produce Toyota's auto parts. These guest workers are stripped of their passports and forced to work for substantially less than minimum wage, as guest workers are not covered by Japan's labor laws. The virtue of purchasing a Prius is called into question when considering these worker rights violations. What one person sees as an environmentally positive action may be seen by another as contributing to the practice of human trafficking.

DIFFUSION OF RESPONSIBILITY

According to the myth of pure evil, responsibility is generally crystal clear, with one person or one group wholly responsible for the suffering of others. In reality, the delineation of responsibility can be tricky. For example, let us consider the horrendous conditions faced by workers in modern-day sweatshops. A report by the NLC (Institute for Global Labour and Human Rights, 2010) indicates that, starting in 2006, National Football League (NFL) jerseys have been produced by Reebok at the Chi Fung factory in San Salvador. Workers at this factory toil in poorly maintained facilities for approximately 60 hours per week with the constant threat of abuse from supervisors. Twelve to fifteen of these hours are mandatory, unpaid overtime. For each NFL jersey that these workers sew, they are paid roughly one-tenth of one percent of the jersey's retail price. These wages are not sufficient for even the basic subsistence needs of the workers. If the stereotypical conception of evil were accurate, then it would be simple to point to a handful of diabolical masterminds pulling the strings behind these injustices. The reality is much less clear cut. So, who is to blame for the suffering of the workers at Chi Fung? Is it the managers and owner of the sweatshop, the subcontractor who set up Reebok with the sweatshop, Reebok, the NFL for choosing to have Reebok make the jerseys, the governments of El Salvador or the United States for letting these worker rights violations occur, the consumers of the jerseys who are unaware or indifferent to the injustice, or the multimillionaire athletes who wear the prototypes and cause consumers to want to buy these items? Even if one or many of these groups were chosen, responsibility is often difficult to ascertain even within the organization.

The concept of "diffusion of responsibility" was introduced by Darley and Latané (1968) to explain why bystanders often fail to help victims in emergencies. In laboratory studies, the researchers found that lone bystanders are likely to intervene on behalf of a victim, whereas bystanders who are part of a group are likely to remain idle. This work was stimulated by the murder of Kitty Genovese in 1963. This Queens, New York, resident was assaulted for nearly an hour while more than 40 witnesses neglected to intervene or call the police. Darley and Latané proposed that, because there were so many witnesses, no individual felt a personal responsibility to help. Accordingly, there was no need for any one person to feel guilty about the woman's death. When responsibility is shared by members of a large group, individuals within the group feel less personally responsible.

When a large group is acting in a morally reprehensible way, no one person is likely to feel enough pressure to condemn the behavior. In completing tasks that require the concerted effort of many individuals, no one is likely to feel a strong sense of identification with the product or end result. Because of its efficiency, division of labor is an indispensible aspect of modern organizations. However, when one's attention is narrowly focused on one aspect of a larger undertaking, the greater purpose or meaning of one's actions may become obscured. Under the Nazis, Germany had in place a euthanasia program designed to kill individuals who were severely handicapped (Lifton, 1986). A combination of oversight committees and senior physicians was responsible for deciding who would be euthanized, while a separate group of young physicians actually administered the lethal injections. Dividing these tasks diffused responsibility so that each group had the impression that a separate party had the final say. The committees, the senior physicians, and the administering physicians could all complete their tasks while believing that someone else was ultimately responsible for the killings.

Deliberate diffusion of responsibility is also used in corporations in order to control who receives blame for mistakes. When there is no obvious guilty party, the reigning authority can easily assign blame to a scapegoat while maintaining the appearance of innocence (Jackall, 1988). Thus, diffusion of responsibility reduces the incentive for acting ethically. If accused of wrongdoing, the guilty party can claim someone else bears responsibility. Intraorganizational diffusion of responsibility makes it difficult to accurately identify perpetrators of evil and assign blame to the appropriate parties. Perhaps more importantly, this ambiguity can facilitate evil.

FROM THE VICTIM'S PERSPECTIVE

The numerous factors that contributed to the worldwide financial crisis of 2008 are beyond the scope of this chapter, but it may be helpful to discuss the manner in which people have responded to this ordeal. Anger aimed at financial and government leaders has led to protests around the world, some of which have turned violent (e.g., Fuller, 2009; Lyall, 2010; Saltmarsh, 2009). These protests stem from a pervasive feeling of victimization associated with the financial collapse. The economic crisis has likely affected all of us in some way. The effects range from losing one's job, home, or retirement fund to having one's promotion delayed or cancelled to postponing vacation plans or an anticipated new car purchase. Whatever the effect, many people have felt victimized by the crisis in general or by specific groups or individuals thought to be responsible.

It is common for victims to seek a meaningful explanation for their suffering (Baumeister, 1991). The suffering that has resulted from this economic crisis has been blamed on poor regulation, manipulation by lobbyists, failure of credit rating agencies, the mistakes of lawmakers, a culture of greed, and numerous other factors (Borak, 2010; Powell and Zeleny, 2008; Puzzanghera, 2010). As already discussed, the feeling of victimization can hinder one's ability to objectively assess evil. Victims are often tempted to fall back on common stereotypical ideas of evil and to view the actions of perpetrators in a way that reinforces their own innocence and virtue. Because so many people have felt victimized by this financial debacle, it may be difficult to avoid being swept up in the current of biased thinking that so often accompanies the role of "victim."

Outrage may be augmented in this particular case because the perpetrators seem to be organizations and corporations, rather than individuals. There is some evidence that people tend to hold organizations, such as corporations, to a higher standard than they do individuals. In a laboratory study, Hans and Ermann (1989) found that people scrutinized an individual's wrongdoing differently than a corporation's wrongdoing. In this study, half the respondents read a scenario in which workers were hired, and subsequently harmed, by an individual named Mr. Jones. The other half read an identical scenario, except that in their story the "Jones Corporation" hired the workers and was responsible for harming them. In these scenarios, five workers were hired to clear debris. All the workers were exposed to hazardous chemicals and experienced differing degrees of respiratory problems. As a result, Jones faced the workers in civil court, and the local prosecutor in criminal court. The respondents in this study were asked to act as mock-jurors in these hypothetical court cases. Across varying dimensions, the Jones Corporation faced harsher judgments than did Mr. Jones. The respondents awarded greater compensation in civil court when the Jones Corporation was the defendant. In addition, the Jones Corporation was more likely to be found guilty of criminal negligence. Finally, the Jones Corporation was rated as more reckless, more deserving of punishment, and more morally culpable.

The authors of this study offered a few possible reasons for these discrepancies. The "resource superiority" of corporations may lead people to expect them to pay greater penalties. Corporations may be expected to have a greater ability to analyze possible risks and safety issues. This may lead people to view corporations as more liable when things go wrong. Also, the potential power of corporations makes them capable of greater possible harm, which may be related to higher standards of judgment. In addition, corporations may be expected to pay greater penalties simply due to their greater financial resources. The cynicism that respondents displayed toward corporations led the researchers to speculate that negative stereotypes about corporations may have also contributed to the effect (Hans and Ermann, 1989). The cynicism noted by Hans and Ermann could be due simply to the fact that corporations are groups. In general, people tend to be leery of groups. For example, Hoyle, Pinkley, and Insko (1989) found that people expect more abrasive interactions when dealing with a group as opposed to dealing with an individual.

THE ROOT CAUSES

In *The Corporation: The Pathological Pursuit of Profit and Power*, one of the most scathing commentaries on corporate evil, author Joel Bakan (2004) commented that most corporate executives are good, moral people. This incongruity raises the question: How can seemingly good people be the perpetrators of evil deeds?

Every instance of evil has a root cause. The four root causes of evil are: the desire for material gain (instrumental evil), idealism, threatened egotism, and sadism (Baumeister, 1997). Not all of these causes are responsible for the same amount of evil. For example instrumental evil is responsible for the lion's share. Although sadism is popular in mythical accounts of evil, it is rarely the cause of evil.

INSTRUMENTAL EVIL

One of the most widely discussed occurrences of instrumental evil involved a subcompact car called the Ford Pinto. In the early 1970s, the Pinto was a relatively popular car, however, major engineering flaws caused this small car to pose large safety risks for its occupants. Mark Dowie (1977) explained the Pinto controversy in detail. According to Dowie, precarious placement of the Pinto's fuel tank made it likely that a relatively low-speed, rear-end collision would result in an explosion. The Ford Motor Company had conducted crash tests revealing the potential dangers associated with the Pinto, but put the car on the market anyway. Its justification was based on cost-benefit analysis. Ford analysts estimated that it would cost $11 per Pinto to save approximately 180 lives per year. Ford executives reasoned that it would cost more to fix the problems with the Pinto than to deal with the consequences of continuing to sell the faulty cars. On one side of the analysis were the financial benefits of ignoring the problem and selling the defective autos; on the other side were the potential losses resulting from civil suits and bad publicity associated with people being killed or injured in defective Pintos. Their calculations concluded that a human life was worth approximately $200,000 (Dowie, 1977). This type of cold calculation is a common feature of instrumental evil. If it had been cost-effective, Ford would have issued a recall.

The defining criterion of instrumental evil is that the perpetrator would be willing to abandon the harmful behavior if he or she could achieve the same goal without it. In cases of instrumental evil, a change in the situation is often sufficient to change the actions of potential perpetrators. Let us turn to the situation faced by the Mexican drug cartel in Los Angeles. Violence may be employed in the illegal drug trade to ensure that the agreed-upon terms of a transaction are met or to prevent competitors from stealing customers (Luhnow and Casey, 2010). The violence involved in the illegal drugs trade fits the primary criterion for instrumental evil; drug cartels seem to be willing to abandon violence if it negatively affects profits. In Los Angeles, the Mexican cartel has discouraged shootings on the grounds that they could scare away potential customers (Sounder, 1995). This led to a long-standing truce among rival gangs. The pursuit of profit led the Mexican cartel to work cooperatively with white supremacist groups such as the Aryan Brotherhood (Johnson, 2010). The Mexican cartel was not issuing an edict to refrain from violence on the grounds of morality. Quite simply, the violence of rival gangs in Los Angeles was interfering with the group's pursuit of profit, so it had to be reduced. The call for a ceasefire in Los Angeles is an exception to the violence that is the modus operandi of the Mexican drug cartel, but is it significant in that it demonstrates the instrumental nature of the group's violence.

The principal consideration of both the Mexican drug cartel and the Ford executives was money. There is nothing inherently evil about this viewpoint. One might desire money for a variety of morally acceptable reasons. Many people probably seek money simply to provide comfort and security for themselves and for their families. So, why do some people resort to evil means to reach acceptable ends? One reason is that legitimate means may not seem feasible to the perpetrator. In the case of criminal organizations, such as the Mexican drug cartel, members are often drawn to the group because of the perception that they lack any suitable alternatives (Pawel, 2010). Despite its lack of effectiveness, people turn to criminal activity in the hope of reaching legitimate goals, such as money, security, and social status. A lack of education or employment opportunity can lead individuals to turn to illegitimate means, such as gang-related activity, to reach legitimate goals. In the white-collar world, people sometimes regard illegitimate means as the only way to get ahead. A global survey carried out by the American Management Association (2006) found that pressure on managers and executives to meet unrealistic goals was the number one factor that led people to disregard their organizations' ethical codes.

People also resort to evil means because they often appear to be easier to carry out or more lucrative than legitimate means. Ford was aware of multiple methods for fixing the Pinto's safety problem. A few of these methods were even cheaper than the $11-per-Pinto estimate (Dowie, 1977). Nevertheless, the easiest and most lucrative solution, from the perspective of the Ford executives, was to sell the Pintos and ignore the safety hazards. That is what the executives chose to do.

BENEFITING FROM ORGANIZATIONAL EVIL

Regardless of whether an organization benefits from unscrupulous behavior, breaking the rules can be beneficial for individuals within the organization. In his analysis of corporate ethics, Robert Jackall (1988) described the pervasive practice of "milking" facilities. Because corporate managers change jobs so frequently, they can forestall spending money on maintenance and safety issues, inventory, waste disposal, and staff replacement. Managers leave these problems for whoever takes over the facility after they leave. Frequent promotions are common, so up-and-comers are not likely to stay at one particular job for very long. According to Jackall, milking a facility can pay off for a manager if he or she "gets out in time" (1988, 98). In many large organizations, attribution for failure is concentrated at the bottom of the ladder, while accolades for success are concentrated at the very top. Therefore, as long as a manager kept getting promotions, he or she could avoid being held responsible for whatever trail of destruction was left behind. This is an example of how misdeeds can actually reward individuals within an organization. Because milking is easy to get away with, it is typically continued and expanded. Managers who successfully milk facilities are able to rise up the corporate ladder quickly; the exploitive management style that aided their ascent accompanies them to the top. As a result, milking is tolerated, if not encouraged, by upper-level managers. Thus, getting away with unethical behavior leads to a continuation and proliferation of that behavior. This pattern is common in all types of evil.

At first glance, the drastic cost-reducing strategies involved in milking a facility may seem to be a standard business practice, not deserving of the term "evil." The victims of cost-cutting strategies may tell a different story. For example, as seen with the Pinto case, cost-cutting strategies that ignore safety issues can result in the loss of human life. The U.S. Chemical Safety Board (2007) found that irresponsible cost-cutting by British Petroleum (BP) had played a causal role in the 2005 Texas City refinery explosion that killed 15 workers and injured 180 others. More recently, the oil spill that devastated the Gulf coast has been blamed on BP officials' favoring cost-effectiveness over safety (Urbina, 2010).

IDEALISM

We have discussed how evil is used by organizations to reach utilitarian goals, but when an organization's goals are of the highest order, where the ends are believed to justify the means in an absolute sense, evil can take on an entirely different face. Idealists and zealots may pursue various types of political, ideological, or religious goals. Evil ensues when idealists resort to extreme means to achieve these goals. Religion provides a clear example of how the pursuit of high ideals can lead to supreme evil. The directives of spiritual leaders and gods are typically seen by followers as unimpeachably good. If God is regarded as the ultimate good, then God's instructions must be in the service of good. Even if an action harms others, it may be seen as acceptable, and even praiseworthy, if it follows from what followers are told is a divine edict.

Since the September 11, 2001, terrorist attacks on the World Trade Center, the Pentagon, and Shanksville, PA, increased attention has been paid to Islamic extremist organizations. The House Permanent Select Committee on Intelligence (2006) defined Islamic extremism as a philosophy that promotes violence as a means to defend a specific vision of Islam. This specific vision stands in stark contrast to the otherwise peaceful religion. In Islamic extremist groups, such as al Qaeda, members believe that violence is commanded by God. In an attempt to realize a religious vision, these extremist groups have killed thousands of innocent people. Absolutism often leads idealists to the conclusion that anyone who is not for them is against them. From the terrorists' perspective, the victims of their attacks are not really innocent. In fact, terrorists generally view themselves as victims fighting against the forces of evil (Post, 1990). This viewpoint enables them to commit atrocities without suffering guilt.

The goals of Islamic extremist groups are of the highest order: divine commandment. Therefore, these groups are willing to pay virtually any price to achieve them. Thousands of innocent lives have been lost in terrorists' pursuit of these goals, but individuals within these groups are also willing to give their lives for the cause. Many terrorist groups rely on suicide bombers to fight their enemies (Bergen and Tiedemann, 2010). Suicide bombers differ significantly from the perpetrators of strictly utilitarian evil. One may be willing to face substantial risks or costs in order to reach utilitarian goals, such as money or prestige, but these risks and costs are insignificant when compared to that of suicide bombers, who sacrifice themselves in the service of their cause.

In the attempt to combat Islamic terrorist organizations, the U.S. government has faced questions as to which means are acceptable to achieve the lofty goal of protecting civilians. Since 9/11, there has been an ongoing debate over which types of interrogation techniques are legally justifiable in the questioning of suspected terrorists (Lichtblau and Shane, 2010). On one side of the debate, wall-slamming, sleep deprivation, and the simulated drowning known as waterboarding, are regarded as acceptable means of interrogation that should be used if the information gained by their implementation could save innocent lives. On the other side, such practices are condemned as torture and are considered immoral regardless of what they may accomplish in terms of intelligence gained. The topic of this debate is whether the ends justify the means when it comes to "enhanced interrogation." In this debate, it is evident that the U.S. government is not subscribing to the kind of absolutism found among idealists and extremist groups. Nevertheless, the protection of innocent lives is a high-order goal; goals of a high order encourage the consideration of extreme means. In most circumstances, people view torture as evil. Even so, when torture is seen as a means of protecting innocent lives, people may consider its use.

The type of absolutism that is evident in the ideologies of Islamic extremist organizations can also be found in groups of Christian extremists. Small factions of anti-abortion activists, such as the Army of God, encourage violence as a way to stop abortions and promote their message. On their Web site, the Army of God hails violent activists such as Paul Hill as "American heroes." Hill, a former Presbyterian minister, was found guilty of the murders of a doctor who performed abortions and the doctor's bodyguard. In 2003, before being put to death for his crimes, the unrepentant Hill argued that the murders were "justifiable homicide" (Campo-Flores, 2003). When faced with his execution, Hill explained that he considered himself a martyr and that he was expecting to be rewarded in heaven. With reference to his murders, Hill stated, "I honestly feel better now about myself, about life and about everything than I ever have because I know I did the right thing" (Dahlburg, 2003). Beyond a simple lack of guilt, Hill was proud and satisfied with his violent actions. Christian extremists like him are willing to die and willing to commit murder in order to obey what they see as God's commandments. Again, it is evident that idealism can lead to evil when the ends are perceived to justify the means in an absolute sense.

THE ROLE OF THE GROUP

A key feature of idealistic evil is that it is almost always fostered by groups. One person's idealistic convictions are rarely sufficient to result in evil. Before one resorts to violence in order to bring about a desired change, it is usually necessary for others to be like-minded. For example, if Paul Hill did not have the enthusiastic support of radical anti-abortionists, he probably would not have felt justified in committing murder. People seem to need the validation of others in order to act in violent or morally questionable ways.

The need to belong is a universal human tendency. Often, the groups in which people participate come with their own unique norms and values. These groups then act as powerful sources of moral authority. Although individual members may disagree and criticize one another, the group itself is often regarded as beyond reproach. When a group is seen by its members as unimpeachably good, evil can follow. The type of ethical assessment that is capable of preventing an individual from acting in a morally questionable manner may not take place when actions are group-mandated. The group is good, therefore, its mandates must be in the service of good. In the interest of "team play," some organizations actively promote unilateral thinking among members (Jackall, 1988). In such groups, particularly idealistic ones, apostates are often severely scorned. Therefore, members may be led to remain consistent with the group's values and goals out of fear. In organizations with hierarchical structures, the motivation to comply with the demands of authority figures may be enough to keep members in line with the group's goals.

The power of this motivation was demonstrated in a famous experiment conducted by Stanley Milgram (1963). In this experiment, participants were instructed to deliver powerful electric shocks to another person. The person who was supposedly receiving the shocks was actually a confederate of the researchers. This person would writhe and scream when the shocks were administered by the participants. Despite outward signs of that person's distress, the participants complied with the experimenter's demands, delivering what they thought were harmful and potentially fatal shocks. The participants in this study displayed a strong motivation to obey authority, in this case, the experimenter. This finding should not be surprising given that one of the first moral lessons that parents teach their children is that it is wrong to disobey the instructions of a legitimate authority figure. When people are given such instructions, their default reaction is usually obedience. As Milgram's experiment indicates, this is true even when the instructions are to harm another human being.

In everyday life, people rarely have the time to engage in deliberate analysis of ethical concerns. Even if such analysis were possible, people would often have to choose between a potential wrong and a definite wrong. Disobeying an authority figure is inherently wrong. Obeying a questionable order may or may not be wrong, depending on the relevant factors and the specific situation. Especially in complex organizations, individuals are unlikely to have sufficient information to decide, with any certainty, that a superior's orders are immoral. Obeying authority seems to be the safest option.

Competition with other groups can intensify one's sense of identification with a particular group (Baumeister, 1997). Intergroup rivalries can become extremely intense when each group is convinced of its own goodness and superiority. Evil could be simply defined as: that which opposes good. Accordingly, if one's own group is regarded as supremely good, then any opposing group must be regarded as evil. In intergroup rivalries, both sides often believe that they are competing against evil. People are much less willing to reach a compromise when they believe that they are dealing with the forces of evil. Ordinarily, people might have ethical reservations about treating a competitor in a cruel or hateful manner, but if they believe that they are competing against pure evil, they might ignore such reservations. Another factor relevant to intergroup competition involves the very nature of groups. A consistent finding among researchers is that groups tend to be more extreme and aggressive than their individual constituents. This pattern is known as the discontinuity effect. Part of the explanation for this effect is that people often expect more antagonistic interactions when dealing with groups, in contrast to dealing with individuals. As a result, when dealing with a group, people are more likely to take an aggressive approach.

Even if a group's principles are noble, evil can result if its members regard the group itself as more important than the principles for which the group stands. A group can be a means to an end, or it can be an end itself. When a group is regarded as an end itself, what is best for the group becomes the right course of action. Therefore, violent actions can be condoned if they serve to sustain or advance the group. The Terror in postrevolution France provides a vivid example. The goals of the new republic were liberty, equality, and fraternity. Although these goals are admirable, evil resulted when the leaders of the revolution began to regard the maintenance of group solidarity as more important than those goals. They silenced dissent and maintained the integrity of the group using the threat of the guillotine. Anyone who was suspected of being a traitor was executed. The historian R.R. Palmer (1969) explained that the Terror was used primarily to enforce political allegiance. The suffering of the French people during the revolution was meant to result in harmony; it did not. In the end, in the hope of ensuring group unity, the leaders of the revolution betrayed the principles for which they originally stood.

Although revolutionary leaders had no shortage of external enemies, apostates among their own followers received the most severe treatment. Especially in idealistic groups, this is a common pattern. It may seem reasonable to expect groups to show the greatest hostility toward opposing groups, but those who leave the group represent a greater threat. If other members of the group were to follow the traitor, the group would eventually dissolve. Thus, apostates receive severe treatment because they are seen as threats to group solidarity.

THREATENED EGOTISM

North Koreans were encouraged to worship their Dear Leader, Kim Jong Il, as a god. In addition to the approximately 30,000 monuments to Kim, many North Koreans hung pictures of him in their homes so that they could worship him in private. Despite widespread famine, a large proportion of the country's budget was spent on Kim's deification (Marquand, 2007a). As if he were not exalted enough by his followers, Kim wore 4.7-inch-high platform shoes (Marquand, 2007b). Kim claimed that his bloodline traced back to the very first rulers of Korea. In addition, because of the country's isolation, the leaders believe that North Korea is racially superior because of a pure bloodline that has not been diluted by outsiders (Marquand, 2007a). Another source of pride for North Korea is its military. Despite its economic hardships, the country has invested in a nuclear weapons program and one of the world's largest armies. Banners with slogans such as "revel in the pride of being a country in the Nuclear Club" were displayed after North Korea's controversial weapons testing (Ramstad, 2006). The collective egotism (or high self-esteem) displayed by North Korean leaders fits the model of another root cause of evil.

Think of the most hostile or violent individuals that you have known. How would you describe them? Were these people: humble, self-effacing, full of self-doubt? Or, did these individuals display a completely different pattern: arrogant, self-confident, assertive? A common view among scholars is that low self-esteem is a major cause of violence. A simple version of this argument begins with the premise that violent individuals have an inner sense of worthlessness. These individuals then lash out at the world in an attempt to prove their self-worth and thereby gain recognition. According to this view, teaching these individuals to develop positive feelings about themselves would reduce violence by minimizing their sense of worthlessness. The solution seems simple: To avoid violent behavior, love yourself more. Although scholars have often taken for granted that low self-esteem causes violence and aggression, there has been little supporting evidence for this widely held belief. On the contrary, an interdisciplinary literature review conducted by Baumeister, Smart, and Boden (1996) revealed that violence results from high self-esteem that is called into question by someone or something. Aggression is particularly common when an individual's high self-esteem is unstable or otherwise vulnerable to threats. Thus, "threatened egotism" is a common cause of evil.

In both laboratory studies and a field study, Bushman et al. (2009) found that individuals who demonstrated a high degree of narcissism were particularly vulnerable to threatened egotism. Narcissistic individuals hold very high opinions of themselves, which may or may not be based in reality. These strong feelings of self-superiority can be difficult to maintain. In this study, highly narcissistic individuals were found to be more aggressive than others, but only when faced with criticism. This aggression was specifically aimed at the source of the criticism. Kernis, Grannemann, and Barclay (1989) also investigated the link between self-esteem and aggression. In this study, the researchers analyzed the variability of self-esteem scores for each individual participant. They found that individuals with high, but unstable self-esteem scored the highest on hostility measures. Individuals with stable, high self-esteem were found to be the least hostile. Thus, low self-esteem by itself does not cause violence, but neither does high self-esteem by itself. The evidence suggests that violence ensues when a favorable view of oneself is called into question by someone else. North Korea provides a good example of threatened egotism: fervent nationalism and a deified leader confronted with constant reminders that other countries are more powerful and more successful. It is no wonder that international relations can be exceptionally volatile when it comes to North Korea.

Threatened egotism can also help to explain why poor decisions often go unquestioned in corporations and other large organizations. In his study of corporate managers, Robert Jackall (1988) noted that the need for self-promotion present in corporate life often leads managers to be preoccupied with self-image. According to Jackall, narcissism is a common trait among high-ranking executives. Narcissism makes one highly sensitive to ego threats. For this reason, criticism by colleagues and perhaps especially by subordinates is discouraged by managers. When supervisors who hold high opinions of themselves are presented with information that calls into question their sense of supremacy, they are likely to react defensively. Not only is such information typically ignored but its presentation is often met with hostility. Because public ego threats are harder to ignore, they tend to elicit the strongest reaction. One executive who was interviewed by Jackall advised that, after publicly disagreeing with the boss, it would be appropriate to "put your head between your legs and kiss your ass goodbye" (1988, 20). Therefore, employees might refrain from questioning their managers out of fear of retaliation. Managers and executives are not the only ones who might react with hostility to ego threats. Regardless of their place within an organization's hierarchy, individuals with high opinions of themselves are likely to respond to ego threats with aggression.

REVENGE

In the corporate world, as in many other venues, vengeance is a common response to ego threats. Revenge and egotism overlap consistently as causes of evil. When one's sense of superiority is put in question, the offended individual is likely to try to settle the score or reassert dominance. Although people often seek revenge to restore what they view as the proper hierarchy to their relationships, minor offenses are typically met with disproportionately severe retribution. To help explain why this happens, recall the concept of the magnitude gap: Offenses seem greater to the victim than to the perpetrator. In some instances, the magnitude gap can lead to a spiral of ever-escalating revenge. Suppose that you and I are coworkers and that I overhear you making some disparaging remarks about my job performance in front of our supervisor. The offense is probably rather insignificant in your eyes; you are merely keeping the boss up to date with how our work is progressing. As a victim, however, I see your comments as extremely harmful and worry that your remarks will cost me my reputation and possibly my job. I might feel that retaliation such as vandalizing your car is warranted. If I were to vandalize your car, you would find my response was inappropriate and excessive. Feeling victimized yourself, you might seek to get even by physically injuring me. If you were to injure me, I might feel entitled to further revenge. In this hypothetical situation, you and I might both feel like victims. I was the victim of the original offense, while you could claim to be the victim of excessive retribution. Therefore, you and I both feel that we have a score to settle. This can lead to continued violence. Revenge is more common in some organizations than in others. When victims believe that perpetrators will be dealt with appropriately, they are less likely to take matters into their own hands. Aquino, Tripp, and Bies (2006) analyzed the factors that affect revenge-seeking in organizations and concluded that revenge tends to be less common when an organization's justice system is perceived as fair.

SADISM

Giving someone a promotion, firing someone, making someone smile after a compliment, and making someone cry as a result of admonishment are all examples of how one can affect another person. Power is essentially the ability to exert influence over another. Individuals with a high need for power desire to elicit sincere emotional responses from others. This desire can result in evil if the person seeking power is content to elicit negative emotions from others in order to satisfy his or her desire. Receiving direct pleasure from causing another to suffer is known as "sadism." While the term "sadism" is sometimes used with reference to a pattern of sexual behavior involving dominance over others, that is not its meaning here.

Recall that, in victim accounts, perpetrators are typically portrayed as inflicting either random, senseless harm or harm out of a sadistic desire to cause someone else to suffer. As noted, despite their inaccuracy, victim accounts are the most frequent and trusted sources when it comes to incidences of evil. Because of the primacy of the victim's perspective and the prevalence of the myth of pure evil, a disproportionate amount of evil is attributed to sadism. In reality, sadism is rarely the cause of evil. The most vivid examples of genuinely sadistic evil occur in extreme environments, involve professional torturers, pathological killers, and war criminals and are not of practical importance in the vast majority of organizational life. Nevertheless, the mechanisms behind sadistic evil may be at work in a less extreme fashion in typical organizations.

After collecting information from nearly 1,000 workers over an eight-year period, Harvey Hornstein (1996) identified mild sadism as the primary reason that supervisors bully subordinates. This type of abuse is not motivated by organizational demands; the abuse is an end in itself. The bullying bosses described by Hornstein receive direct pleasure from harming subordinates. Because belittling and intimidating people are effective ways of demonstrating power, having this type of effect on people is validating for power-seeking individuals. In hierarchical organizations, it is often easy for supervisors to bully subordinates, who might endure abuse out of fear of losing their jobs. Bullying is a way for supervisors to demonstrate their power over their subordinates.

In addition to its intrinsic appeal for power-seeking individuals, workplace bullying can, in some circumstances, be advantageous to one's career. The humiliation of colleagues can be used to advance one's relative status within an organization. Interfering with a colleague's work can reduce competition. Similarly, supervisors can bully subordinates in order to discourage any possible rivals (Salin, 2003). Thus, a workplace bully might be motivated by both career-related goals (instrumental evil) and the sheer pleasure of harming others (sadism). Although distinct, the four root causes of evil can and do work together.

THE IMMEDIATE CAUSE

It is clear that people have plenty of reasons to engage in evil behaviors. In this chapter, it has been argued that antecedents of evil include the desire for monetary gain, passionate devotion to a cause, and the desire to maintain a sense of personal pride. Given the ubiquity of these precursors, it may be appropriate to question why there is not more evil in the world. The answer is that self-control enables people to restrain themselves from acting on violent or malevolent impulses. Whatever the root cause of an evil action, the immediate cause is a failure of self-control. This point is crucial. Evil does not need to be actively promoted; all that is required is a weakening or a removal of the forces that restrain it. Let us briefly discuss a few of the major factors that compromise the effectiveness of one's self-restraint.

When faced with conflicting obligations, even a person with strong self-control might find it difficult to do the right thing. Here, the difficulty lies in determining the right course of action. In Milgram's obedience studies, participants were faced with conflicting obligations. Specifically, the obligation to obey authority conflicted with the obligation to refrain from harming others. Participants generally complied with the experimenter's demands, however, many participants displayed outward signs of distress indicative of inner struggle. Disagreement with authority is a common example of conflicting obligations. When your sense of inner morality is in conflict with your superior's orders, you are typically left with two options. One option is to disobey the orders, face the consequences of insubordination, and hope that you were justified in your decision. The other is to obey the orders, suffer from a guilty conscience, and possibly face blame associated with your complicity.

For self-control to be effective, people need to consider the broad implications of their actions. Evil actions must be identified before they can be avoided. In order to determine whether an action is evil, it is necessary to step back and thoughtfully consider its consequences. A narrow, rigid mindset that is only focused on the here and now is not capable of this type of reflection. Attending to the details of a specific procedure forces the mind to engage in low-level thinking, in which broad implications are not considered (Vallacher and Wegner, 1987). Thus, Nazi accounts of the Holocaust tend to focus on specific tasks, ordered lists, and logistics. Concentration on their specific tasks enabled Nazis to perform evil deeds that thoughtful consideration would have prevented. Employees of any organization are at risk of engaging in narrow, rigid thinking. When people are absorbed in their own tasks, they may fail to assess the broad implications of their work. When focusing on *how* to perform a task, one can neglect consideration of the *why* and, especially, the *why not*.

DO ORGANIZATIONS DIRECTLY CAUSE EVIL?

Organizations are continually implicated in human suffering, but are organizations ever the direct cause of human suffering? To answer this question, it will be helpful to review some of the main ways that organizations contribute to the evil in the world.

Inherent characteristics of groups in general can facilitate evil. For example, recall the concept of diffusion of responsibility. When responsibility is shared by members of a group, individuals within the group feel less personally responsible. Consequently, individuals within an organization are unlikely to feel enough pressure to denounce their organization's unethical behavior. This allows an organization's members to transgress without being condemned by others within the organization.

People can purposefully manipulate an organization's structure in ways that facilitate evil. For example, Nazi leaders used a division of labor to make it easier for people to commit atrocities. The task of genocide was divided into many small tasks carried out by different individuals. This allowed Nazi soldiers and even non-Nazi German citizens to complete their tasks without having to acknowledge the true significance of their actions.

People can also take advantage of an already established organizational structure to pursue personal goals at the expense of others. This is how the corporate managers described by Jackall (1988) were able to reap the benefits of their reckless cost-cutting strategies. Because these corporate managers received frequent promotions, they were able to milk facilities and leave before having to deal with the aftermath.

In every example of evil that we have described, people, not organizations, were the actual perpetrators. Nevertheless, organizations can be powerful facilitators of evil. Organizations can permit, coordinate, and even promote evil. However, the ultimate cause of evil is the transgression of individuals.

CONCLUSION

Numerous factors make organizational evil distinct from evil perpetrated by lone individuals. Diffusion of responsibility within an organization reduces the incentive for members to act ethically. When responsibility is shared by members of a large organization, individuals within the organization are less likely to feel personally responsible for the organization's transgressions. Similarly, division of labor within an organization can make it difficult for individual members to realize the greater purpose or meaning of their actions.

Organizations typically function to reach specific goals, but sometimes maintenance of the organization becomes the primary goal. When the organization's survival becomes an end in itself, extreme measures may be tolerated in the interest of that objective.

In addition to the factors that facilitate evil within organizations, other factors can cause evil promoted by organizations to be perceived as more egregious than evil perpetrated by lone individuals. Organizations are often held to high moral standards because of their resource superiority and because of the potential magnitude of harm that can result from organizational evil.

The need to belong is a universal human tendency. Therefore, it is often difficult for people to resist the pressure to conform to the group's standards, even if the group's behavior is morally reprehensible. Organizations have the potential to act as powerful sources of moral authority. Evil can ensue when members unquestioningly subscribe to the norms and values of the organization.

REFERENCES

American Management Association. 2006. The ethical enterprise: Doing the right things in the right ways, today and tomorrow. Study. www.amanet.org/images/HREthicsSurvey06.pdf.

Aquino, K., T.M. Tripp, and R.J. Bies. 2006. Getting even or moving on? Power, procedural justice, and types of offense as predictors of revenge, forgiveness, reconciliation, and avoidance in organizations. *Journal of Applied Psychology*, 91, 3, 653–668.

Bakan, J. 2004. *The Corporation: The Pathological Pursuit of Profit and Power.* New York: Free Press.

Baumeister, R.F. 1991. *Meanings of Life.* New York: Guilford Press.

———. 1997. *Evil: Inside Human Cruelty and Violence.* New York: Freeman.

Baumeister, R.F., L. Smart, and J.M. Boden. 1996. Relation of threatened egotism to violence and aggression: The dark side of high self-esteem. *Psychological Review*, 103, 1, 5–33.

Baumeister, R.F., A. Stillwell, and S.R. Wotman. 1990. Victim and perpetrator accounts of interpersonal conflict: Autobiographical narratives about anger. *Journal of Personality and Social Psychology*, 59, 5, 994–1005.

Bergen, P., and K. Tiedemann. 2010. The almanac of al Qaeda. *Foreign Policy*, 179, 68–71.

Borak, D. 2010. Greenspan takes little blame for financial crisis. *Investment Management Weekly*, 23, 15 (April 12), 27.

Bushman, B.J., R.F. Baumeister, S. Thomaes, E. Ryu, S. Begeer, and W.G. West. 2009. Looking again, and harder, for a link between low self-esteem and aggression. *Journal of Personality*, 77, 2, 427–446.

Campo-Flores, A. 2003. An abortion foe's end. *Newsweek*, September 7, 142, 10, 52.

Cappiello, D. 2002. Metal shops a toxic threat for neighbors/Electroplaters face charges as residential area polluters. *Houston Chronicle*, December 8. www.chron.com/CDA/archives/archive.mpl?id=2002_3606921/.

Dahlburg, J. 2003. Murderous abortion foe awaits death: Paul Hill admits killing a doctor and a clinic escort in 1994. Activists on both sides anticipate more violence if Florida executes him this week. *Los Angeles Times*, September 1, A14.

Darley, J.M., and B. Latané. 1968. Bystander intervention in emergencies: Diffusion of responsibility. *Journal of Personality and Social Psychology*, 8, 377–383.

Dowie, M. 1977. Pinto madness. *Mother Jones,* September/October. http://motherjones.com/politics/1977/09/pinto-madness/.

Fuller, T. 2009. Protesters in Thailand enter grounds of regional meeting. *New York Times,* April 11, A5.

Hans, V.P., and M.D. Ermann. 1989. Responses to corporate versus individual wrongdoing. *Law and Human Behavior,* 13, 151–166.

Hesse, P., and J.E. Mack. 1991. The world is a dangerous place: Images of the enemy on children's television. In *The Psychology of War and Peace: Images of the Enemy*, ed. R. Rieber, 131–153. New York: Plenum.

Hornstein, H.A. 1996. *Brutal Bosses and Their Prey: How to Identify and Overcome Abuse in the Workplace*. New York: Riverhead Books.

Hoyle, R.H., R.L. Pinkley, and C.A. Insko. 1989. Perception of social behavior: Evidence of differing expectations for interpersonal and intergroup interaction. *Personality and Social Psychology Bulletin*, 15, 3, 365–376.

Institute for Global Labour and Human Rights. 2008. The Toyota you don't know: The race to the bottom in the auto industry. Report, June 9. www.globallabourrights.org/reports?id=0503/.

———. 2010. NFL and Reebok fumble: Women paid 10 cents to sew $80 NFL Peyton Manning jerseys. Report, February 4. www.globallabourrights.org/reports?id=0003/.

Jackall, R. 1988. *Moral Mazes: The World of Corporate Managers*. New York: Oxford University Press.

Johnson, K. 2010. Drug cartels uniting rival gangs. *USA Today*, March 16. www.usatoday.com/NEWS/usaedition/2010–03–16–1Arivalgangs16_ST_U.htm?POE=click-refer/.

Kernis, M.H., B.D. Grannemann, and L.C. Barclay. 1989. Stability and level of self-esteem as predictors of anger arousal and hostility. *Journal of Personality and Social Psychology*, 56, 6, 1013–1022.

Lichtblau, E., and S. Shane. 2010. Report faults 2 who wrote terror memos. *New York Times*, February 20, A1.

Lifton, R.J. 1986. *The Nazi Doctors: Medical Killing and the Psychology of Genocide*. New York: Basic Books.

Luhnow, D., and N. Casey. 2010. Killing escalates Mexico drug war. *Wall Street Journal*, June 29, A1.

Lyall, S. 2010. Mindful of image, incensed Icelanders try to sort out debt. *New York Times*, March 6, A4.

Marquand, R. 2007a. N. Korea escalates "cult of Kim" to counter West's influence: In a time of famine and poverty, nearly 40 percent of the country's budget is spent on Kim family deification. *Christian Science Monitor*, January 3. www.csmonitor.com/2007/0103/p01s04-woap.html.

———. 2007b. How Kim Jong Il controls a nation. *Christian Science Monitor*, January 4. www.csmonitor.com/2007/0104/p01s03-woap.html.

Milgram, S. 1963. Behavioral study of obedience. *Journal of Abnormal and Social Psychology*, 67, 371–378.

Palmer, R.R. 1969. *Twelve Who Ruled: The Year of the Terror in the French Revolution*. Princeton: Princeton University Press.

Pawel, M. 2010. To save Salinas: Can its rejuvenated libraries lead the way in the fight against gang violence? *Los Angeles Times*, January 31, A29.

Post, J.M. 1990. Terrorist psycho-logic: Terrorist behavior as a product of psychological forces. In *Origins of Terrorism*, ed. W. Reich, 25–40. Cambridge: Cambridge University Press.

Powell, M., and J. Zeleny. 2008. Obama casts wide blame for financial crisis and proposes homeowner aid. *New York Times*, March 28, A19.

Puzzanghera, J. 2010. Financial crisis: Fannie Mae as villain and victim: The panel looking at the loan mess gets both versions, as all parties deflect blame. *Los Angeles Times*, April 10, B1.

Ramstad, E. 2006. North Korea emphasizes nuclear pride: Propaganda push indicates disarmament discussions could yield little progress. *Wall Street Journal*, December 15, A8.

Salin, D. 2003. Ways of explaining workplace bullying: A review of enabling, motivating and precipitating structures and processes in the work environment. *Human Relations*, 56, 10, 1213–1232.

Saltmarsh, M. 2009. Anger and fear over the financial crisis fuel May Day protests across Europe. *New York Times*, May 2, A6.

Sounder, J. 1995. Gang warfare: Dadz in the hood. *Economist*, November 4, 33.

Urbina, I. 2010. BP officials took a riskier option for well casing. *New York Times*, May 27, A1.

U.S. Chemical Safety Board. 2007. U.S. Chemical Safety Board concludes "organizational and safety deficiencies at all levels of the BP Corporation" caused March 2005 Texas City disaster that killed 15, injured 180. News release, March 20. www.csb.gov/newsroom/detail.aspx?nid=205/.

U.S. Congress. House. House Permanent Select Committee on Intelligence. 2006. Al-Qaeda: The many faces of an Islamist extremist threat. Report, June. www.fas.org/irp/congress/2006_rpt/hpsci0606.pdf.

U.S. Environmental Protection Agency, Office of Transportation and Air Quality. 2006. Fuel economy labeling of motor vehicles: Revisions to improve calculation of fuel economy estimates. Draft technical support document, January. www.epa.gov/fueleconomy/420d06002.pdf.

Vallacher, R.R., and D.M. Wegner. 1987. What do people think they're doing? Action identification and human behavior. *Psychological Review*, 94, 1, 3–15.

Part III

Faces of Organizational Evil

13

The Evil of Utopia

Stewart Clegg, Miguel Pina e Cunha, and Arménio Rego

All countries struggle with being imagined communities (Anderson, 1982). Considerable organizational effort is expended on seeking to fix, and sometimes resist, particular imaginings, through symbols, songs, roles, and relationships to these. Chief among the symbols of nationhood are anthems. Singing anthems is something that everyone can, and is, expected to join in with. The range of such anthems—from the banalities of "God Save the Queen" ("Send her victorious, happy and glorious") or "Advance Australia Fair" ("Our home is girt by sea") to the bloodthirsty, such as "La Marseillaise" ("Entendez-vous dans les campagnes, / Mugir ces féroces soldats? / Ils viennent jusque dans vos bras / Égorger vos fils, vos compagnes! In English translation the lyric states "Do you hear, in the countryside, the roar of those ferocious soldiers? They're coming right into our arms to cut the throats of our sons and women!")—is enormous.

At the most extreme, the imagining expressed in such anthems seeks to close off all other possibilities, all other opportunities for voice or exit other than those that the authorities want to imagine. National anthems are often filled with exhortations to fight and the glorification of death in the name of one's country. Considerable organizational resources can be committed by states to the task of enclosing citizens in the pure ether of their rulers imagining of what these citizens should be. Many cases in recent history come to mind: the German Democratic Republic, North Korea, Myanmar (Burma), . . . and Democratic Kampuchea (Cambodia).

In the case of the national anthem of Democratic Kampuchea led by the Khmer Rouge, these words were more than metaphors or an homage to past war heroes.

> Bright red Blood covers the towns and plains
> Of Kampuchea, our Motherland,
> Sublime Blood of the workers and peasants
> Sublime Blood of the revolutionary men and women fighters!
> The Blood changes into unrelenting hatred
> And resolute struggle,
> [Which] . . . frees us from slavery. (Short, 2004, 248)

In fact, these words expressed the trail of blood left by the revolutionary army in its own "traumatized" country (van der Kroef, 1979), Cambodia, between 1974 and 1979.

One thing that societies such as the German Democratic Republic, North Korea, Myanmar, and Democratic Kampuchea have in common is a quality that, to the Western liberal imagination, is immediately recognizable: being Kafkaesque. The adjective "Kafkaesque" tends to be used in everyday language and by organization theorists as a metaphor for the dark, labyrinthine bureaucracies where nothing can be taken for granted (ten Bos, 2004). In this chapter we move from a metaphorical to a literal interpretation of Franz Kafka's message in some of his classic novels, namely *The Trial* and *The Castle*. In these, Kafka suggests that bureaucracies can confront people with processes that may be both lethal and impossible to understand. In other words, he offered a representation of organizations as "edifices of repression" (Warner, 2007, 1028). There are many analogies between Kafka's view of organizations and Erving Goffman (1961), who chose to study total institutions (such as those represented in *The Trial, The Castle,* and *In the Penal Colony*, a story that takes place on a hot day in a tropical penal colony, where an execution is about to happen) in which organizational extremes render the power dimensions of organizing processes more explicit. According to Goffman, total institutions exist in many different shapes, including schools, monasteries, hospital, prisons, and military units. They can be described as closed spaces where people are expected to change one way or another under the influence of intense surveillance. They are either to conform to a particular imagining, to be made to conform, or, if their deviance makes conformance impossible (by being Jewish, communist, homosexual, etc.), to be dealt with as the Other that makes dominant imaginings possible. As Kafka shows us in *The Trial*, sometimes the otherness that can be attached to one is inscrutable, indecipherable, and terrible.

In this chapter, we analyze the Khmer Rouge revolution with special consideration of the case of the movement's leader, Pol Pot, the man who led the clique that tried to construct a utopian project and decided that all means, including management by terror and murder on a massive scale, could be considered to turn such a project into reality. The result of this utopian vision was, as we now know, a genocide that features high on the list of the crimes against humanity perpetrated in the twentieth century (Jones, 2008). Utopia has remained a peripheral topic in organization studies (for an exception, see Parker, 2002). It should not have, however, if only because of the ways in which some organized/ organizational utopian projects have resulted in totalitarian realities. Thus, organization and utopia have a close connection. In this case, we explore the utopian project devised by Pol Pot and the Khmer Rouge (1974–1979) regime in Cambodia.

The chapter is divided into three major sections: utopia, organization, and terror. In the first we consider the nature of utopia, in general, and the case of the utopian project devised by the Central Committee of the Communist Party of Kampuchea (CPK), in particular. In the second section, we consider one of the most horrible and extreme exemplars of the Kafkaesque organization as reality, in the case of the former S-21 extermination center. In the third section, we focus on the implementation of the revolutionary utopia, fed by Pol Pot's paranoid organization, which created a state based on terror. We also consider how old and new institutional systems were used to enforce the power of the revolutionaries and, especially, how they made use of the old to build the new. Utopias do not materialize out of nothing. We conclude with some possible implications of our analysis for organizational scholars.

As the case of Democratic Kampuchea makes clear, good, bad or, in this case, genocidal leadership does not emerge in a social vacuum (Kellerman, 2004; Vaughan, 1999). On the contrary, it can incubate for long periods in the appropriate favorable social/institutional contexts. Therefore, approaching leadership from an institutional view offers a useful way of understanding the emergence of bad, unethical, criminal, or genocidal leaders and organizations. With this chapter, we contribute to the literature on organizational evil by considering an extreme case that highlights processes that may be less visible in ordinary organizational and institutional contexts and explore some processes, macro, meso, and micro, that have made such events possible.

More specifically, the chapter stresses four points. First, total institutions, especially extreme total institutions, such as Pol Pot's Kampuchea, should be studied by organizational researchers, because such extreme cases expose processes that may be more difficult to track, but are no less relevant in other organizational settings (Goffman, 1961). Second, the way in which forms of totalitarian governance and management are organized should not be ignored by organization theory (Clegg, 2006), as totalitarian regimes are not only political and sociological endeavors but also organizational ones. Third, the study of leadership processes in extreme contexts can expose practices that deviate from the usual optimistic leadership discourses found in the management literature. Fourth, the study of "bad leadership" (Kellerman, 2004) is as important as the study of virtuous leadership, because organizations, even advanced political contexts, are not unfamiliar with these leadership practices.

TOWARD UTOPIA: A CAMBODIAN EXPERIMENT

April 17, 1974, was the day "two thousand years of Cambodian history ended." These were the words of Ieng Sary, one of the top cadres of the Khmer Rouge. From then on, Cambodians would be starting a new society, "more glorious than Angkor." In addition, Sary added, the CPK would lead the nation along roads "no country in history has ever gone before" (in Short 2004, 7). As would soon become apparent, this vision would result in a totalitarian regime—totalitarianism being the process of defining people's happiness for them through an ideology that promises the end of all injustice, to be achieved by subordinating the whole society to the one-party state, using the state's monopoly control of all aspects of individual life, especially through ideological and repressive apparatuses (Althusser, 1971). Less than four years later, on January 1979, this vision ended.

At least 1.7 million people died in between, in the name of an ultraradical ideology, a "Khmer utopia," as Short has put it (2004, 350). The Khmer utopia figures prominently among the major human tragedies of the twentieth century, but utopian projects are not uncommon. As Gray (2007) observed, since the French Revolution political life has been transformed by a succession of utopian movements. If an alternative form of organization is a constitutive element of a definitive statement of utopia (Parker, 2002), organization is at the core of utopia. As Grey and Garsten discussed (2002), there are organized and disorganized utopias, but even the latter have some idea about the (dis)organization of society. Therefore, students of organization should be more alert to the utopian possibilities contained in organizational practice and discourse (Parker, Fournier, and Reedy, 2007).

Democratic Kampuchea provides a radical case study of the organization of utopia: Parts of Sary's speech mentioned above were terribly prescient. No country in history had ever gone so far, in modern history, in the organization of a totalitarian regime that could be described as the first modern slave state in which all citizens became objects to be used by the state's apparatuses in ways idealized by being based in an ultraradical utopian ideology. To explain how that happened, we consider the original vision and its implementation.

A Vision for Cambodia

Pol Pot's vision for Cambodia was "to plunge the country into an inferno of revolutionary change where, certainly, old ideas and those who refused to abandon them would perish in the flames, but from which Cambodia itself would emerge, strengthened and purified, as a paragon of communist virtue" (Short, 2004, 288). In this new form of social organization, the reason for living would no longer be "to have" but "to be"—being in a "society without desire, without vain competition, without fear for the future" (Short, 2004, 314).

The goal of the CPK was the construction of a "clean, honest society" (Short, 2004, 247), freed from every form of exploitation, a society with no classes and no differentiation. The Cambodian utopia of the Khmer Rouge was expressed in various domains of language and everyday life. Change started with the country's name itself. The Kingdom of Cambodia was part of the past. The new nation would be called Democratic Kampuchea (DK), a designation that recovered the original indigenous pronunciation, rather than the Westernized form "Cambodia." The "Khmer" language was now called "Kampuchean." Cambodia was the country of the Khmers, the heirs of Angkor Wat. The new Kampucheans included the Khmers but also the members of other ethnicities in order to avoid the impression of ethnic exclusion. The goal was uniformity, social, economic, even biological, uniformity. Mey Mann, a Khmer Rouge sympathizer, noted when the movement swept to power, that, in the future, "everyone was [to be] exactly 1 m, 60 tall" (Short, 2004, 326). Socially, everything distinctive was unacceptable—for example, wearing spectacles, which was something regarded as bourgeois or intellectual. Interestingly, the same types of measures were taken by the Issarak opposition group, which, twenty years earlier, was the precursor to the Khmer Rouge.

In what follows we elaborate the implications of this suggestion that revolutions can be social irruptions that do not explode out of nothing. The new nation, in summary, would provide a model for the rest of the world, in the political context of the cold war, with communism on the rise as an alternative to U.S. power and the capitalist system. The problems started, as might be expected, with implementation.

Implementing Utopia Through Collectivization and Terror

The Kampuchean project was to design an organizational utopia that would realize a communist society composed of peasants. However, as every organizational student has no doubt read, change may be difficult because old habits die hard. In this case, however, the revolutionary leaders of the CPK accepted that the ends justified every means, including the death of those who held other ideas. Violence and extreme measures were employed to eradicate the feudal and capitalistic aspects of Cambodian society. Members of the classes that were to be abolished were killed in large numbers. Others were "re-educated" as peasants (Pol Pot himself, a schoolteacher, "killed" his own identity and metamorphosed into a rubber plantation worker—see below). In the process, of course, many also died. Money, markets, and property, all emblems of capitalism, were also victims of this vision.

Two major organizational processes were implemented in the country: extreme collectivization and management by terror. One fed the other. Collectivization is core to communist ideology. Private property is viewed with suspicion and should, preferentially, be substituted by common ownership that is administered by the state. In Khmer Rouge Kampuchea, however, the process of collectivization was as radical as any ever attempted. Even Mao Zedong and, later, Deng Xiaoping in China expressed their opinions about what they saw as the radicalism of the measures being adopted in Cambodia under the Khmer Rouge. Money and markets were abolished. Cities—the sites of everything evil according to the Khmer Rouge doctrine—were emptied and citizens force-marched to be collectively re-educated in the countryside. Instead of being re-educated, many ended up being victims of massive state killing campaigns. For the CPK, everything private was undesirable, not only property and goods but also thoughts and emotions. These practices were too radical even for the totalitarian Chinese leaders, whose ideas heavily influenced the Cambodian revolutionaries. However, in the Pol Pot utopian project, this totalitarian enterprise meant freedom. In a speech delivered on September 29, 1977, he argued that 98 to 99 percent of the population had been liberated, felt free, were fully satisfied with the collective system, contributed enthusiastically to the construction of socialism "with all their heart," had become the true masters of the country's destiny, and had complete confidence in the bright future of Kampuchea.

Organizing the New Citizen

In Democratic Kampuchea, people were submitted to a number of tactics that aimed to "destroy their personality." In the villages, local leaders reproduced, line by line, the messages from Angkar, "the organization," the collective name that Sâr and his comrades had called themselves since the mid-1950s, a name that indicates how unclear their affiliations with political parties were at the time (Short, 2004, 121). Not only were the messages the same but the punctuation was repeated with no change. At some point, for example, one nightly message was "to work hard, produce more and love Angkar" (Short, 2004, 323). The repetition was deliberate, as emphasized by the cadres. It was intended to serve as a sort of sermon, in the Buddhist tradition, to "impregnate" people's minds (Short, 2004, 324), in a form of government by incantation. Another Buddhist notion was also appropriated: renunciation. Renunciation, Khmer cadres observed, meant that one should devote oneself totally to the collective without consideration of any form of personal interest. Khmer Rouge discourse aimed to control the mind as well as the body (Short, 2004).

In language, words expressing incorrect ideas were effaced from the vocabulary. For example, "I" should not be used, only "we." Parents should be called "uncle and aunt" by their children. Paradoxically, other adults would be "mother" and "father." Relationships, too, should be viewed as collective. Love was a sign of individual emotions and desires and therefore unacceptable. Marriages were arranged by Angkar, which substituted for the family in this role. Matrimony, of course, was not intended to satisfy the same purposes as marriage in other parts of the world but was entered into with the goal of contributing to the collective good. In this context, it will come as no surprise that, after consummating the marriage, couples often lived apart. In the case of women who still menstruated (and, after a certain point, most did not, due to malnutrition), cadres tracked the dates of their periods so that their husbands could be allowed to sleep with them when they were more fecund, in order to contribute to an increase in the population. The goal was to reach a population of 15 million to 20 million people in ten years, Pol Pot said (at present the population is over 14.8 million; in 1977 it was about 8 million).

Reproductive engineering to achieve the population increase the regime wanted clashed with another radical social experiment in biopolitics: extreme violence used to expunge the collective body of those condemned by the state. A bureaucracy of birth coexisted with a bureaucracy of death in Democratic Kampuchea. Many government initiatives—such as the exodus from the cities, forced labor, famine, torture, and massive executions—led directly to the death of some 1.7 million people in the process of building the new society. Creating new lives that the state could mold took precedence over preserving older lives that were already corrupt and decadent because of their experiences prior to Year Zero.

Violence, the Khmer Rouge assumed, was part of the purification process: Old ideas would die in the flames. A system of organized terror was implemented. As discussed below, Cambodia had a nationwide extermination system, organized around provincial prisons operating at the local level (Chandler, 2000). S-21/Tuol Sleng, the central extermination center in Phnom Penh, was the apex of this execution system. Between 14,000 and 20,000 people were executed there, including about 600 of the 1,700 guards, a fact that suggests that being a "comrade" did not provide much protection (Chandler, 2000; Meng-Try and Sorya, 2001).

Moreover, in what was a first in the annals of communist history, the armed incursions of Cambodian soldiers into Vietnam led to war between two communist states. Even more Cambodians died as a result of this confrontation. When Vietnamese troops invaded Cambodia in retaliation and the Khmer Rouge fled the capital of Phnom Penh, the remaining prisoners incarcerated in S-21 were killed prior to departure: Only seven people survived their stay at this site. "When Tuol Sleng was discovered, the pools of blood were still coagulating beneath their bodies" (Hawk, 1986). The system of extreme violence performed a major function in Kampuchea: It protected the regime from the enemies it created through its obsessions. Some of these enemies were obviously real, but the generalized paranoia pervading the CPK certainly contributed to the historical events as we have come to know them today.

ORGANIZATION AND THE ELIMINATION OF DEVIANCE

In the spring of 1975, the Khmer Rouge (Red Khmers, in opposition to the right wing, the Khmer Bleu, or Blue Khmers) won a five-year civil war against the U.S.-backed Khmer republic led by the self-proclaimed Marshall Lon Nol, which had been in power since the 1970 coup d'état against the People's Socialist Community of Prince Norodom Sihanouk, established in 1955. In their effort to construct a radical Marxist-Leninist state of Democratic Kampuchea, inspired in part by Maoist thinking, the Khmer Rouge initiated a number of deep social changes. The vision of the Khmer Rouge leaders was one of pure socialism, the creation of a society with no traces of feudalism, capitalism, or any other exploitative forms of social organization. In reality, this vision comprised some traits of primitive communism, given the absence of a well-developed class structure. The society was one in which the forces of production were too primitive to generate the surplus necessary to support an elite non-laboring class (Adler, 2009) and simultaneously provide sustenance for the reproduction of the mass of the population.

At the core of the Khmer state sat the "Party Center," composed of a very small group of the limited Cambodian elite that had been educated in Marxism-Leninism in Paris, as well as being influenced by the Communist Party of Indochina, one of two precursors to the Communist Party of Vietnam. The Party Center was a group of people with changing composition depending on the result of purges that could reach even those at the very top of the regime although Pol Pot, Nuon Chea, Son Sen, Ta Mok (Brothers 1 to 4), and Kieu Samphan remained throughout the regime's existence. The influence of French Marxism on the Khmer Rouge is often mentioned as decisive, although Short (2004) gives short shrift to this idea; Pol Pot was simply too minor a figure and too unintellectual to be very involved in the labyrinthine politics of the French left (see Badiou, 2008). In any case, most of what was discussed in French Marxist circles, such as those that the Cambodian nationalists moved in, would be best thought of as dogma rather than theory (Majumdar, 1998). Short sees the ideological influences as far more local and homegrown, rooted in indigenous habits of viciousness that went back at least to the time of the scenes depicted on the twelfth century friezes at Angkor Wat.

The embrace of Marxism was entirely pragmatic, not theoretical. Cambodians wanted to rid the country of the legacy of French colonialists, who had left the feudal society almost entirely untransformed; thus, any Khmer revolution would have to be based on the peasantry. Khmer Rouge ideology developed as a strange mixture of heterodox Marxism and Cambodian nationalism. The nationalism derived in part from the legacy of French colonialism, especially its Vichy ideology, as well as deep-seated Kampuchean hostility to their Vietnamese and Laotian neighbors. Moreover, Khmer Rouge ideology borrowed structural elements from indigenous Theravada Buddhism. In addition, the Khmer Rouge sought to emulate Mao's Great Leap Forward (1957) and Cultural Revolution (1966–1976) in a "super great leap forward": cities were evacuated, schools closed, factories deserted, monasteries emptied, libraries burned down, money and wages abolished, and the freedom to speak out, organize, meet, and eat privately denied. All life was to be collectivized, even weddings and partner selection. In such a situation, in which virtually all civil society was denied, the state became everything (Widyono, 2007).

The key node of the state, as mentioned above, was the Party Center, and at the middle of the Party Center was Saloth Sâr (1925–1998), a former schoolteacher who adopted the pseudonym of Pol Pot, the best known in a series of aliases, including Pouk, Hay Pol, Grand Uncle, Elder Brother, and First Brother. Pol Pot had attended Catholic secondary school in French colonial Cambodia during the semifascist Vichy period between 1935 and 1947 and was exposed to the ideology of the Vichy leader Marshal Philippe Pétain with its stress on the need for a dominant national leader, its bias against cosmopolitan cities, and its fascist cult of violence. He has been described as "elusive, a shadowy figure with a smiling face and a quiet manner, whose trajectory to tyranny remains something of a mystery" (Kellerman, 2004). Under Pol Pot's leadership, the Khmer Rouge caused the death of as many as 2 million people from malnutrition, overwork, disease, and extermination. Their vision of utopia implied the elimination, first, of all class enemies that would be against the revolution. Later, when the anticipated agricultural paradise of abundance was not realized, the interpretation was linear: If the established quotas, three to six times prewar rice yields (Hawk, 1986), were not being achieved, this could only be due to counterrevolutionary activities. As the end of the Khmer Rouge regime neared, the extermination machine was used not only on "classical" enemies but also the peasants in whose name the revolution was justified (Hawk, 1986).

The drive to construct a collectivist nation of peasants in an autarchic economy was so extreme that some of its ideals were not well received even by those whose interests they were intended to serve. For example, the increasing depth of collectivization led to the communalization of eating, which implied the elimination of the most basic form of private property, a family's cooking utensils. As described by Hawk, this measure was "enormously unpopular among peasants, even those who formerly had supported the revolution" (1986, 31). Not surprisingly, economic and social conditions deteriorated.

Building the new society starting in Year Zero, when the Khmer Rouge seized power, meant that the old had to be eliminated. This meant, literally, the annihilation of people. First, at the most basic level, people died because of starvation, exhaustion (from forced marches and forced labor), and disease (modern medicine was reserved for the army and the Khmer Rouge cadres). Second, massacres were conducted against groups labeled as enemies of the revolution. Religious or ethnic reasons, as well as economic, social, or political ones, were invoked. Extrajudicial mass execution was normal. We next focus on the S-21 extermination center.

The Role of S-21 in the Cambodian Genocide

> It is better to arrest ten people by mistake than to let one guilty person go free.
>
> —Democratic Kampuchea adage (Chandler, 2000, 44)

The extermination camp known as office S-21, the Lycée Ponhea Yat, now an interrogation and extermination center, served as the headquarters of the internal security (or secret) police, Santebal (the term comes from the contraction of two Khmer words, *santisuk*, i.e., security, and *norkorbal*, i.e., police. Among the victims, as well as people from all of Cambodia, there were a few foreigners. The site is now a genocide museum ("modeled after Auschwitz" [Peters, 1995, 60]), open to visitors. The camp comprised a compound of four three-story buildings, arranged in a quadrangle and surrounded by tin and barbed wire fences. At the center of the quadrangle was a one-story office where records were kept. The camp became a secret facility, with several annexes, including the large execution site of Cheung Ek, 18 kilometers west of Phnom Penh, to which prisoners were transported and then executed after interrogation (Meng-Try and Sorya, 2001).

Among the ten security regulations governing the organization were the following:

- Don't try to hide the facts by making pretexts about this and that. You are strictly prohibited to contest me;
- While getting lashes or electrification you must not cry at all;
- If you disobey any point to my regulations you shall get either ten lashes or five shocks of electric discharge.

David Chandler, "the doyen of Western historians of Cambodia" (Short, 2004, 290), described this organization as an extreme example of a total institution (2000, 14). S-21 was a total institutional environment for practically all those who found themselves on the inside, not only prisoners, but also guards, including chiefs: "the chief of guard comrades, Him Huy, was afraid because the number of S-21 comrades decreased day by day, not only the comrades but also the chiefs" (Meng-Try and Sorya, 2001, 43). S-21 can be described as a total institution in a totalitarian regime, that is, a regime striving to invade and control every facet of its citizens' lives (Kets de Vries, 2006).

The S-21 facility played a major role in the Cambodian revolution led by the Khmer Rouge. Its mission as part of Santebal was to protect the Party Center, to be carried out by eliminating the enemies of the revolution. Thus, people were interrogated and made to write biographies to confess their "crimes," which inevitably gave grounds to the suspicions of the Party, and then they were killed, usually after severe torture. In short, S-21 combined a number of functions that tend to be separated in a state operating under the rule of law: incarceration, investigation, counterespionage, and judicial functions. All this simulacra of a judicial system was not much more, however, than a façade, as there was no promulgated legal code or system for Democratic Kampuchea under the Khmer Rouge. As Chandler and others have described, S-21 could be better described as an extermination camp than as a prison.

The bureaucratic features of S-21 should not be ignored. A sophisticated bureaucracy was in place in order to help the state in the processes of searching, finding, interrogating, and eliminating enemies. Like any other state bureaucracy, this one, too, kept detailed records, defined procedures, elaborated manuals, and job descriptions of the most relevant tasks and prepared a number of documents to help the Party Center to make decisions. Among the Tuol Sleng archives left behind when the Vietnamese troops conquered Phnom Penh were thirteen different types of documents listed by Hawk (1986), including arrest forms on individual prisoners, photographs taken at the time of arrest, the handwritten or dictated confessions of about five thousand prisoners, and signed execution orders. There was, in summary, a bureaucracy of death that helped to reconstruct the history of the place.

Bureaucracies can serve unplanned, unexpected goals, including a moral dimension that varies from that considered by Perrow (1986). Perrow sees bureaucracy as the bulwark of a civil society. In uncivil society, however, the products of the extensive procedural routines of bureaucracy are testimony to those whom it processed, providing traces of the disappeared. The bureaucratic system designed by the Khmer Rouge, with its impressively detailed recordkeeping, was a corrupt force designed to sustain rather than to prevent autocracy and abuse (Armbruster and Gebert, 2002).

The two men in charge of S-21 were Duch (b. 1942) and Mam Nay (alias Chan), a former school colleague of Duch. The two men have been described as "strict, fastidious, totally dedicated teachers" (Chandler, 2000, 20). They reported directly to the collective leadership of Democratic Kampuchea, known as "the upper organization," "the organization," or "the upper brothers," to outsiders, and the Party Center for the members. The prison's maximum capacity was 1,500, reached in 1977, and the total population that passed through it on the way to their deaths, according to Chandler, was 14,000 between 1975 and 1979 (Peters [1995] refers to 17,000). Tactics to maintain the secrecy of the place, despite the magnitude of the operation, included, of course, killing all the inmates, the lack of reference in official documentation to the site, keeping outsiders away from the compound, and blindfolding prisoners while moving them elsewhere. This secrecy coexisted with the vast documentation about the victims.

In terms of organization, S-21 was structured around three main units: (1) the interrogation unit; (2) the documentation unit (including a photography subunit that produced the mug pictures that became famous as symbols of the atrocities of the regime); and (3) the largest defense unit, including one subunit to guard the prisoners, another one to bring them in and take them to execution, a limited medical service, and the economic support staff. As already observed, the site was directed by Ta Duch, Ta (grandfather) being the most respectful classification, reserved only to those with greater authority. "Grandfather" Duch was a man in his thirties, who established a disciplinary system based on the memorization of rules, the need to induce reverence for the local authorities, and unquestioning loyalty. Terrible punishment could be meted out to those who, for whatever reason, did not follow the rules, as explained by a former guard, Kok Sros: "Duch told me I had done a good job and I felt that he liked me. I was pretty sure from then on that I was going to survive, because I had been admired from above" (Chandler, 2000, 18).

The daily activities at S-21 followed precise routines. They unfolded in disciplinary time strongly reminiscent of the rules of the model prison discussed in *Discipline and Punish* (Foucault, 1979, 3–6). As noted by Balch and Armstrong (2010), predisposition to wrongdoing is reinforced through repetition. Hence, processes were repeated. The day in the prison started at 4:30 A.M., when prisoners stripped for inspection. Interrogation sessions were scheduled at 6:45 A.M., 1:45 P.M., and 6:45 P.M. Interrogation procedures, including torture, were conducted under a prescribed logic. Interrogators followed an eight-point job description and had a forty-two-page Interrogator's Manual. The goal was to extract a written or dictated confession by the prisoner, revealing his/her presumed treason and crimes against the revolution. Usually, as pointed out by authors such as Chandler (2000) and Hawk (1986), treason comprised being an agent for the CIA, the KGB, the Vietnamese, or even a combination of these and could on some occasions be complemented by other personal indicators of treason or disloyalty toward the revolution. These could include pre- or extramarital sex or a minor error interpreted as sabotage.

An important part of the process of interrogation was the extraction from the prisoners of the names of their "coconspirators." The denunciation of "strings of traitors" is normal in Kafkaesque organizations. Consider the beginning of *The Trial* (Kafka 1999a): "Someone must have been telling lies about Joseph K. (for without having done anything wrong, he was arrested one fine morning)." These processes led, unsurprisingly, to a climate of collective paranoia that eventually reached Angkar itself. After suppressing outsiders, the murder machine turned upon itself, under accusations of bad class consciousness or propertyism.

After their interrogators extracted the confession, prisoners were executed. The daily execution schedule was not usually random. Particular groups were executed on particular days: July 1, 1977, was devoted to the murder of the wives, sons, and daughters of husbands and fathers killed earlier; July 22, 1977, was reserved for "smashing" (as killing was described) people from the Ministry of Public Works (Hawk, 1986). Executions were conducted "in secret, en masse and usually at night" (Chandler, 2000, 119).

S-21 as a Kafkaesque Organization

S-21 was a place described as Dantesque, a hellish anteroom to death, as was clearly understood by many of its victims. Only seven prisoners who entered it are said to have escaped. Siet Chhe, a formerly high-status member of the Party understood this only too well: "I have always understood without any firsthand knowledge [of the place] that once entering S-21, very few leave; that is, there's only entering; leaving never happens. Brother, if this is the case, I have no way out" (Chandler, 2000, 66).

What is both terrible and intriguing at S-21 is its similarity to other places in both fact and fiction. Clearly it evokes parallels with Nazi Germany, to Auschwitz and other death camps; such comparisons have been made repeatedly (Chandler, 2000; Short, 2004). But in addition to the inferno of Dante, the place also brings to mind Franz Kafka. The Kafkaesque nature of the Nazi extermination process has been pointed out, for example, by Collins (1974); S-21 is another iteration—prefigured in fiction but exceeded in reality.

The Czech writer Franz Kafka (1883–1924) wrote about strange, monstrous organizations (Thanem, 2006) that turned innocent people into "others" used for the purpose of legitimating the atrocities of the organization. References to Kafka are not uncommon in organization studies, but these are mostly metaphorical. Many bureaucracies have features reminiscent of the inaccessible castles in Kafka where inscrutable technocrats conduct incomprehensible activities (e.g., Scott, 1987, 5) and build the sort of total institutions that we are discussing here: "I who am in the cage . . . not only in the office but anywhere"

(Kafka, quoted by Janouch, 1971, 20). To grasp the Kafkaesque nature of S-21, consider the following quotations from S-21 files: "These accusations are absurd. . . . They are totally incomprehensible to me. I knew and did nothing of this sort" (59); "I am a termite boring from within" (60); "Only the Party knows my biography" (79); "I was a traitor from the day I entered the revolution until the day I was arrested" (82).

Even the guards had no protection against accusations of treason, especially after the "government became increasingly paranoid" (Peters, 1995, 59). As a former guard observed:

> During the livelihood meetings [ordinary meetings in which guards were expected to critique their previous performance, including shortcomings], Sok always talked about how late I was in getting up and how lazy one was. I was very afraid of everyone, especially Sok. I did not trust anyone. Everyone tried their best to search for one another's faults. I was working and living in fear and horror. I kept trying to work harder and harder, and kept my mouth shut all the time. (Meng-Try and Sorya, 2001, 23)

The dialogue that follows, also retrieved from the files at S-21, is pure Kafka (Chandler, 2000, 77):

> "What was the problem that caused them to arrest you?" the interrogator asked.
> I said I didn't know.
> "The organization isn't stupid," he said. "It never catches people who aren't guilty. Now, think again—what did you do wrong?"
> "I don't know," I said again.

This episode is repeated with members of the S-21 staff itself, including the guards. As noted by one Khmer Rouge comrade guard:

> One of my comrades, named Ann, was arrested and killed without any real reason. Another also disappeared after Peng arrested him on accusations of stealing the party's property. (Meng-Try and Sorya, 2001, 42)

As the above episodes indicate, people could become suspect *because* they were arrested. The Organization knew too well what was good and evil. In this sense, the victims of S-21 found themselves in the same situation as Joseph K., the protagonist in *The Trial*. The fact that so many people confessed to belonging to the CIA, or "C" as it was often called, is also emblematic, as many of them had no idea what the CIA was. That, of course, did not temper the zeal of the Santebal. Joseph K. and the S-21 prisoners were all guilty of something that they were not necessarily aware of. Moreover, as in Kafka's fiction, people could be subjected to degradation ceremonies (Garfinkel, 1956) and "metamorphose" into insects (such as termites in the example above) as in *Metamorphosis*.

Kafka's K is an individual existential symbol of bureaucracies' inhumanity. In Cambodia, thousands of people found themselves in K's position. They were suspicious *because* they were arrested, and they were executed *because* they were suspicious *because* they were arrested. In this system, even the highest dignitaries could be targets, at some point, of the system. Another Kafkaesque dimension of S-21 was the need to strictly follow rules that one did not understood. This is, of course, common to most bureaucracies: Subordinates are expected to obey, not to understand (Clegg, Courpasson, and Phillips, 2006; Jacques, 1996). To make sense of it even more unlikely, the requirement of unquestioning obedience was accompanied by a frequent change of rules—as K., the protagonist in *The Castle*, noted: Every time he tries to understand what is expected from him as land surveyor, he is presented with new rules (Kafka, 1999b). The same occurs in the case of penal colony described in another Kafka story (Kafka, 1919/2011; see also Rhodes and Kornberger, 2009): "no one knows what the law is in the Colony" (Deleuze and Guattari, 1986, 43). Some people complained ("if the higher-ups keep modifying things back and forth suddenly like this, those lower down will be unable to keep up," Sau Kang, the former secretary of Sector 37 in the western zone, said [Chandler, 2000, 85]), but most followed without asking questions. That is easy to understand because asking any questions could be viewed as counterrevolutionary behavior.

Even under torture and expectation of execution, most people were afraid to challenge the cleanliness and the perfection of Angkar or Angkar Padevat. As far as we know, only a few dared to be as assertive as Prak Chhean, a low-ranking soldier from Division 310, in saying: "The Organization is shit" (Chandler, 2000, 99).

TERROR AS A TECHNOLOGY OF CHANGE

As ten Bos points out, the development of a new institutional system of organizations designed to enforce the creation of a new society by plan often progresses in ways that do not result from planning: "one of the important features of the bureaucratic labyrinth is that it takes a while before you are going to notice that you are increasingly absorbed by its complexities" (2004, 16). In this section, we discuss how the CPK leadership used the old institutional frameworks to initiate its radical revolution, with results both expected and unexpected.

The emergence of a utopian vision of a communist society of peasants was intended to create an island of purity amid the confusion of the world, as Pol Pot put it (Short, 2004, 341). This utopian pursuit was supported by what may be called a "rule of terror" (Gibbs, 1989), designed for the purpose of radically changing Cambodian society. The 1974 moment of peripety was not, however, a rejection of the past history of Cambodia. On the contrary, it represented the culmination of a long process that started in the 1960s. In the process, old institutions were subjected to gradual changes that eventually resulted in the emergence of a new institutional system, but one strongly anchored in the old institutions. The generative tension between old and new is characteristic of institutional change processes: "revolutions, even as they destroy, build on the model of what has gone before" (Short, 2004, 282; see also Lanzara, 1998). Leaders and leading organizations, such as political parties and governments, have to build their visions on or against something already in place.

Grey and Garsten (2002) observe that the assumption that utopias transcend time and place could not be "further from the truth. Utopias are intimately tied to the historical and social milieu in which they arise." To understand Democratic Kampuchea it is necessary to explore the historical and social milieu in which this particular utopia was imagined and how neighboring utopias influenced this one. To do so, we show how the old institutional order was used to establish a new institutional order.

Institutional Context: The Old and the New

The revolution led by the Khmer Rouge was part of a wider political movement reaching its apogee at the time, the spread of communism. More than forty countries were experimenting with forms of government inspired by Marxism-Leninism. The most radical experiment was arguably the one in Cambodia, whose extremism surprised even Mao, who was not exactly a model of political moderation. Among the institutions that represented the old order, we consider three at the heart of change: religion in the form of Theravada Buddhism, the family, and the monarchy.

Theravada Buddhism

One of the predictable victims of the communist revolution in Cambodia was religion. After victory, the Khmer Rouge declared that the rights of every Cambodian to fulfill his or her material, spiritual, and cultural needs would be respected, except for reactionary forces, which were banned. The new regime viewed Buddhist monks negatively, as an unproductive class. Although their rights were diminished, some Buddhist ideas were usefully appropriated by the new regime. According to Theravada Buddhism, the dominant religion introduced in the area through Sri Lankan monks around the thirteenth century, nirvana—the realm of selflessness—can be attained only after one lets go of worldly and emotional attachments. The search for this form of detachment from worldly interests was so extreme that in some provinces people were forbidden to sing or laugh. The search for nirvana implied suffering and pain, a lesson appropriated by the regime.

Despite the new perception of religion, many dimensions of Buddhist philosophy were still important in revolutionary Cambodia, at least as means for citizens to make sense of the situation. When speaking to public audiences, Pol Pot would carry a fan, a symbol of the monkhood. His behavior was seen as paralleling the monk's progression to enlightenment. Sopheap, a Khmer Rouge cadre, described Pol Pot as follows:

> For a monk, there are different levels. At the first level, you feel joy. And it's good. Then there's a second level. You no longer feel anything for yourself, but you feel the joy of others. And finally, there's a third level. You are completely neutral. Nothing moves you. This is the highest level. Pol Pot situated himself in the tradition of serenity. (Short, 2004, 340)

Pol Pot's place in the order of things could be explained to the public using religion and superstition. A guide in Angkor Wat likened Pol Pot to Yama, the Hindu deity of the underworld (Chandler, 2000, 118). The advent of the Khmer Rouge was also anticipated in the predictions of a key Theravada Buddhist text, the *Puth Tumniay* and equated with the legendary "five hundred thieves," millennial bandits that would rob people of everything, including their material possessions, their families, and eventually their lives. The country could now be considered a sort of Buddhist hell (Short, 2004, 315).

Family

Another victim of the Khmer Rouge was the family. The old bourgeois family was no longer tenable under the new collectivistic paradigm, and the notion of family was redesigned to adhere to the new logic. Children were separated from their families, educated in the regime's schools, and incorporated in the army as comrades, cleansed of the vices of the old order. Mothers were advised not to establish deep emotional bonds with their children—a form of egoistic self-interest. Even eating together as a family, and all the rituals that went along with it, was outlawed in this total collectivization of society. People were dispossessed of their now-unnecessary cooking utensils, and meals were served in collective spaces. Traditional women's roles were now prohibited, and a core family activity was simply erased. Communal eating rapidly became of the most hated aspects of life in the new Cambodia.

Under Pol Pot, the traditional, bourgeois family of the past was to be exchanged for a big collectivist family—the Kampuchean family of equals. The Angkar (in fact the CPK, as recognized in 1977) substituted for the family in arranging marriages as well as taking charge of other "self-centered," traditional family institutional roles. Nothing was outside the interest of this big national family united by the party. Henceforth the obligation of particular families would be to understand and accept the new state and its philosophy of the common good. Meng-Try and Sorya (2001) describe how children were taken from their families to be indoctrinated and made responsible, in some cases, for some of the worst tasks in the Khmer Rouge regime, namely, in the S-21 extermination center. They were, literally, the children of the revolution.

The Monarchy

The monarchy was a symbol of the old Cambodia. Due to the evolution of Cambodian politics, the Khmer Rouge established an alliance with Prince Sihanouk to combat Lon Nol, President of Cambodia in 1970. After the revolutionary army took control of Phnom Penh, Prince Sihanouk reassumed his position as head of state, returning from exile, from which he was received accordingly and managed to keep his palace but he had no contact with the outside world, despite being declared a "great patriot" and being treated with exceptional benevolence (Short, 2004). Before long he was placed under house arrest in what he came to call the "golden cage" of the Royal Palace. An absolutist monarch, Sihanouk would cede power to an equally absolutist ruler, though not one of royal origin. Under Khmer Rouge domination, the monarch resigned as head of state and fled to China, at which point Pol Pot declared that the monarchy and the legacy of feudalism were definitively dismantled. In his youth, he argued: "Monarchy is an unjust doctrine, a malodorous running sore that just people must eliminate" (Chandler, 1999, 37). Malodorous sores were not tolerated in the new society, so one might have expected that the sovereign would lose his head. However, Sihanouk was seen as too important to lose his head in view of the peasants' respect for the country's monarchs as well as the revolutionaries' previous alliance with Sihanouk, who had the support of China and North Korea.

A popular Buddhist text explained to Cambodians that the happiness of the people was proportional to the wisdom of the king. The monarch was now substituted by Angkar, headed by Pol Pot. The "Angkorian model of statecraft, dressed in communist clothes" (Short, 2004, 338) reigned. In the new Kampuchea, Sihanouk's "subjects" gave way to Pol Pot's "masses," but the logic was not much different.

Old rivalries were played out by proxy over Kampuchea. The Khmer Rouge were the beneficiary of Cold War competition. They received Chinese military aid to resist the Soviet-supported Vietnamese occupation as a proxy for the Sino-Soviet conflict. Initially, communist Vietnam was an ally of the Khmer Rouge but on May Day in 1975, Khmer Rouge soldiers killed more than five hundred Vietnamese civilians, sparking subsequent massacres of ethnic Vietnamese that led to informal and sporadic hostilities over the next three years (Kiernan 1985).

In 1978 Pol Pot sought to distract attention from the bloody purges of party deviants. War against Vietnam, some of whose territory in the Mekong delta was claimed by the Khmer, was an easy strategy. In May 1978, Radio Phnom Penh declared the regime's intention of killing the entire Vietnamese population of 50 million in order to recover land regarded as Khmer territory. Ironically, when incidents of aggression against Vietnamese in the frontier region made a Vietnamese invasion seem inevitable and imminent, Pol Pot sought Prince Sihanouk's in legitimation for the war. Old institutions, again, found a new usefulness in the Khmer Rouge revolution. On September 28, 1978, Khieu Samphân, Democratic Kampuchea's ceremonial chief of state, gave a banquet for Prince Sihanouk, who, due to house arrest, had not been seen in public for more than two years. The revolution was coming to an end, but paranoia and executions remained. Vorn Vet and Kong Sophal, two senior cadres, were arrested and taken to S-21, as a sign of how much the politic body of Democratic Kampuchea was rotting from within.

The regime eventually collapsed on January 7, 1979, after an invasion force of Vietnamese 120,000 troops launched a seventeen-day blitzkrieg, and Phnom Penh fell. The war put an end to the Khmer Rouge domination of Democratic Kampuchea. Pol Pot and the Democratic Kampuchean leadership left Phnom Penh in January 1979, with Khmer Rouge cadres burning rice granaries as they retreated, which led to a severe famine. The leadership regrouped in western Cambodia and in the Cardamom mountains, establishing a sort of underground government. Not much is known about him after the defeat. In September 1985 the government announced his retirement from the role of commander of Democratic Kampuchea's "National Army." He was captured in June 1997. Internal conflicts and dissent (Lizée, 1997) within the former Democratic Kampuchean structure led it to split into opposing factions, the largest of which joined the government of Cambodia under Prince Sihanouk. Despite the new government of the People's Republic of

Kampuchea sentencing Pol Pot to death in absentia, soon after they took over power in 1980, Pol Pot was subsequently sentenced to life in prison in July 1997 and died of alleged heart failure on April 15, 1998, as one of the bloodiest leaders of the twentieth century.

CONCLUSIONS

The case of the Khmer Rouge regime can be used to illustrate a number of important aspects that tend to be obscured in mainstream management theory. The adequacy of total institutions as sites for organizational research has been pointed out by Goffman (1961), and in this chapter we consider the case of an extreme total institution, the slave state of Democratic Kampuchea, to explore the conditions under which a leader such as Pol Pot can emerge and an organization such as the CPK evolve. Democratic Kampuchea has attracted significant attention from historians, sociologists, and political scientists—so why the neglect of it by organization scholars?

Although CEOs are routinely expected to have visions these days (Clegg, 2006), such visions can be dark. In this case, one man's vision of purity resulted in genocide. It is easy for the advocates of extreme organizational visions to create a Manichean world of loyalists and enemies (O'Shaughnessy and Baines, 2009). Supposedly positive visions can be used to manipulate people's worst instincts. The desire for revenge among peasants was triggered by the revolution; it presented peasants as exemplary role models in contrast to the viciousness of the urbanites, whose citizens needed re-educating in the hard toil of the countryside. The lack of formal checks and balances may allow a regime to transform a rhetoric of equality and participation into despotism. In the end, the fear instilled by Angkar was so extreme that no one could feel safe.

Ethical leadership does not necessarily result from visions and discourses that emphasize consistent ideologies and coherent values. The case suggests that examples of "ethical" leadership, whose discourses center on virtue and purity, can actually hide perverse practices. Our discussion also indicates that ethical leaders need to understand that they have a responsibility for creating mechanisms for controlling and voluntarily limiting their own power. Self-righteous leaders are potentially dangerous because they come to believe that the goodness of their intentions should lead to more rather than less personal power and discretion.

Some general organization factors were at work in this case. One of the unexpected outcomes of Sihanouk's use of the coercive machinery of the state to annihilate political opponents in 1966–1967 helped the success of the CPK. While abolishing political pluralism, Sihanouk also encouraged the survival of the communist party because it was the only political movement well-prepared to operate clandestinely. According to some students of Cambodia (Jackson, 1989), the Khmer Rouge, a relatively small fighting force (60,000 in a population of 7 million), took power because it was able to step into a political vacuum left by the former republican government. After its demise, in the absence of any pluralistic or democratic politics, the stakes fell to the last organization standing as it emerged from the shadows; thus, this case illustrates the importance of pluralism (Kornberger, Clegg, and Carter, 2006).

Organizations, however, are often less open to a multiplicity of voices than they probably should be, especially in the face of fear and violence (Arendt, 1963). If we aim to discover the reasons why open debate thrives or stifles, we should consider the processes taking place in these extreme case studies rather than discard them as monstrous organizations. A theory of organizations must thus include the monstrous type of organization (Thanem, 2006) rather than seeing the world of organization only through lens of the many good things that they can achieve.

In our case study, the Kampuchean tragedy was produced by an elusive leader with clearly paranoid behavior, animated by a vision of a utopia that would recover the greatness of Angkor. This explanation is not intended to justify the existence or the actions of the Khmer Rouge but, instead, to suggest that some institutional contexts are more likely than others to create bad leadership, which may, in turn, have the power to open a Pandora's box of massive violence. Therefore, organizational researchers and business ethicists should consider not only the usual types of explanations (individual dispositions versus contextual factors) but also the evolution of power dynamics over time in any given institutional context. Understanding Saloth Sâr's transformation into Pol Pot might not be possible without combining individual, organizational, and institutional elements.

There is an interdisciplinary lesson here as well. Although the development of a unified organization theory at business schools has achieved a great deal in terms of professionalization, creating a coherent body of practice and practitioners, it has also narrowed concerns and focus. Although it is desirable to learn positive lessons from practice, this should not come at the expense of overlooking the excesses of organizations. Collaboration with researchers from other areas should be considered: Political scientists, historians, sociologists, social and clinical psychologists, and anthropologists are potential partners in gaining a macroview of how dysfunctional charismatic leadership emerges. Additionally, institutional theory needs to explore how old institutional paradigms can be appropriated by new leaders in their pursuit of institutional entrepreneurship—as we have discussed above.

Our discussion of the case of Pol Pot and the Khmer Rouge offers a number of insights. Leaders and their political regimes should be viewed from an institutional perspective— that is, it is not possible to capture the nature of leadership and followership processes without considering the role that institutions, existing and emerging, play in the process. The old institutions of Cambodia were used to destroy the ancient regime and to leverage the creation of the new one. In other words, the totalitarian regime was possible because of, not in spite of, the old institutions. Utopian projects, organized or disorganized, have many potential implications, desired and undesired. Organization and management scholars have expended much effort on the analysis of utopian projects, but research comparing business and political dark visionaries might shed new light on the topic, so the study of catastrophic leaders should be part of organizational research. Visionary leaders with power and tools can be extremely dangerous for their people and organizations. The study of infernal leaders and their followers can help explain deviations from reason and virtue and explain the persistence and pervasiveness of organizational evil. The explicitness of these processes in Democratic Kampuchea can help highlight variations of the same phenomena in "normal organizations." More time and attention should be paid to leaders such as Pol Pot and to those followers who enabled the reign of terror. Organization studies owe it to humanity.

REFERENCES

Adler, P.S. 2009. Marx and organization studies today. In *The Oxford Handbook of Sociology and Organization Studies,* ed. P.S. Adler, 62–91. New York: Oxford University Press.

Althusser, L. 1971. *For Marx.* London: New Left Review.

Anderson, B. 1982. *Imagined Communities.* London: New Left Review.

Arendt, H. 1963. *On Revolution.* London: Penguin.

Armbruster, T., and D. Gebert. 2002. Uncharted territories of organizational research: The case of Karl Popper's "Open society and its enemies." *Organization Studies*, 23, 169–188.

Badiou, A. 2008. Badiou: On different streams within French Maoism. Kasama: Outlaws in the eyes of America. Interview, November 3. http://mikeely.wordpress.com/2008/11/03/badiou-on-different-streams-within-french-maoism/.

Balch, D.R., and R.W. Armstrong. 2010. Ethical marginality: The Icarus syndrome and banality of wrongdoing. *Journal of Business Ethics*, 92, 2, 291–303.

Chandler, D. 1999. *Brother Number One: A Political Biography of Pol Pot.* Boulder, CO: Westview Press.

———. 2000. *Voices from S-21: Terror and History in Pol Pot's Secret Prison.* Chiang Mai, Thailand: Silkworm Books.

Clegg, S.R. 2006. Why is organization theory so ignorant? *Journal of Management Inquiry*, 15, 426–430.

Clegg, S.R., D. Courpasson, and N. Phillips. 2006. *Power and Organizations.* Thousand Oaks, CA: Sage.

Collins, R. 1974. Three faces of violence: Toward a comparative sociology of violence. *Theory and Society*, 1, 415–440.

Deleuze, G., and F. Guattari. 1986. *Kafka: Toward a Minor Literature.* Minneapolis: University of Minnesota Press.

Foucault, M. 1979. *Discipline and Punish.* Harmondsworth, UK: Penguin.

Fukuyama, F. 1992. *The End of History and the Last Man.* New York: Free Press.

Garfinkel, H. 1956. Conditions of successful degradation ceremonies. *American Journal of Sociology*, 61, 420–424.

Gibbs, J.P. 1989. Conceptualization of terrorism. *American Sociological Review*, 54, 329–340.

Goffman, E. 1961. *Asylums.* Harmondsworth, UK: Penguin.

Gray, J. 2007. *Black Mass: Apocalyptic Religion and the Death of Utopia.* London: Penguin.

Grey, C., and C. Garsten. 2002. Organized and disorganized utopias: An essay on presumption. In *Utopia and Organization*, ed. M. Parker, 9–23. Oxford: Blackwell.

Hawk, D. 1986. Tuol Sleng extermination centre. *Index on Censorship*, 15, 1, 25–31.

Jackson, K.D., ed. 1989. *Cambodia, 1975–1978: Rendezvous with Death.* Princeton: Princeton University Press.

Jacques, R. 1996. *Manufacturing the Employee: Management Knowledge from the 19th to 21st Centuries.* Thousand Oaks, CA: Sage.

Janouch, G. 1971. *Conversations with Kafka.* London: Andre Deutsch.

Jones, A. 2008. *Crimes Against Humanity.* Oxford: Oneworld.

Kafka, F. 1999a. *The Trial.* London: Vintage Books.

———. 1999b. *The Castle.* London: Vintage Books.

———. 1919/2011. *In the Penal Colony.* Harmondsworth, UK: Penguin.

Kellerman, B. 2004. *Bad Leadership.* Boston: Harvard Business School Press.

Kets de Vries, M.F.R. 2006. The spirit of despotism: Understanding the tyrant within. *Human Relations*, 59, 195–220.

Kiernan, Ben, 1985, *How Pol Pot came to power: a History of Communism in Kampuchea*, 1930–1975. London: Verso.

Kornberger, M., S.R. Clegg, and C. Carter. 2006. Rethinking the polyphonic organization: Managing as discursive practice. *Scandinavian Journal of Management*, 22, 3–30.

Lanzara, G.F. 1998. Self-destructive processes in institution building and some modest countervailing mechanisms. *European Journal of Political Research*, 33, 1–39.

Lizée, P.P. 1997. Cambodia in 1996: Of tigers, crocodiles, and doves. *Asian Survey*, 37, 65–71.

Majumdar, M. 1998. Marxism and Marxian thought. In *Encyclopaedia of Contemporary French Culture*, ed. A. Hughes, and K. Reader, 358–361. London: Routledge.

Meng-Try, E., and S. Sorya. 2001. *Victims and Perpetrators? Testimony of Young Khmer Rouge Comrades*. Phnom Penh: Documentation Center of Cambodia.

O'Shaughnessy, N., and P.R. Baines. 2009. Selling terror: The symbolization and positioning of jihad. *Marketing Theory*, 9, 227–241.

Parker, M. 2002. *Utopia and Organization*. Oxford: Blackwell.

Parker, M., V. Fournier, and P. Reedy. 2007. *The Dictionary of Alternatives*. London: Zed.

Perrow, C. 1986. *Complex Organizations: A Critical Essay*, 3d ed. New York: McGraw-Hill.

Peters, H.A. 1995. Cambodian history through Cambodian museums. *Expedition*, 37, 3, 52–62.

Rhodes, C., and M. Kornberger. 2009. Writing in the crowded margin: Transgression, postmodernism and organization studies. In *Bits of Organization*, ed. A. Pullen and C. Rhodes, 99–118. Copenhagen: Copenhagen Business School Press.

Scott, W.R. 1987. *Organizations. Rational, Natural, and Open Systems*, 2d ed. Englewood Cliffs, NJ: Prentice-Hall.

Short, P. 2004. *Pol Pot: The History of a Nightmare*. London: John Murray.

ten Bos, R. 2004. The fear of wolves: Anti-hodological ruminations about organizations and labyrinths. *Culture and Organization*, 10, 7–24.

Thanem, T. 2006. Living on the edge: Toward a monstrous organization theory. *Organization*, 13, 163–193.

van der Kroef, J.M. 1979. Cambodia: From "Democratic Kampuchea" to "People's Republic." *Asian Survey*, 19, 8, 731–750.

Vaughan, D. 1999. The dark side of organizations: Mistake, misconduct, and disaster. *Annual Review of Sociology*, 25, 271–305.

Warner, M. 2007. Kafka, Weber, and organization theory. *Human Relations*, 60, 1019–1038.

Widyono, B. 2007. *Dancing in Shadows: Sihanouk, the Khmer Rouge and the United Nations in Cambodia*. New York: Rowman and Littlefield.

14

Lawyers' Ethics in Decline

Martha Derthick

Lawyers play an important part in the governance of virtually all sizable organizations, whether as in-house counsel or independent individuals (or firms) under contract. It would be comforting to believe that the norms of the legal profession impose ethical constraints on organizational behavior, but it would also be naive. Lawyers today often fail to counsel ethical conduct in their clients and, worse, violate ethical norms and professional canons themselves.

To support this argument, I begin by adducing evidence from the history of lawyers who have served the tobacco industry. Drawing on critiques from within the profession, I then argue that although lawyers' conduct in the tobacco case may be extreme, it is not anomalous.

THE LAWYERS DID IT

Nearly a decade ago, I argued in an academic paper that lying by cigarette company executives about the safety of their product was "a tactic prescribed by lawyers to secure victories in court" (Derthick, 2002, 286–293). Insofar as one credited this argument, I wrote, it became necessary to look for the explanation of the companies' behavior less in the greed and moral turpitude of its executives and more in the incentives created by an adversarial legal system and the culture of the legal profession. It seemed possible that cigarette executives were neither more nor less evil than the rest of us, but, in order to save their businesses, they unblinkingly followed the advice of the country's most prestigious lawyers, to whom they turned when they began to fear the threat of both tort actions (lawsuits) and government regulation (Derthick, 2002).

It was possible to make this argument because legal actions against the companies had made many of their internal documents public. These revelations began on a large scale with discovery proceedings in the case of *Cipollone v. Liggett Group, Philip Morris, and Loews* in a federal district court in New Jersey in the late 1980s and with the related theft of documents by Merrell Williams, a paralegal, from the warehouse of a Louisville law firm, Wyatt, Tarrant, and Combs, counsel to the Brown & Williamson Tobacco Company, also in the late 1980s. They reached a climax in 1998 with massive discovery proceedings in a suit brought by Minnesota against the cigarette companies. As a result of settlement in that case and other cases brought by state attorneys general, millions of tobacco company documents are now stored for public use in a warehouse in Minnesota and are available on the Internet (Drew, 1965). For this chapter, I relied primarily on secondary sources that had made use of the documents rather than attempting to examine them myself.

Lawyers' prominence in the cigarette companies' policymaking with regard to smoking and health dates from the mid-1960s. It was a response to the release in 1964 of *Smoking and Health,* the report of an advisory committee to the U.S. Surgeon General that was the beginning of government efforts to make a scientific case against cigarettes. Within days of the report's release, the Federal Trade Commission (FTC) announced hearings on proposed new regulations of the industry. To mount a defense against this growing threat, the company presidents turned to their lawyers, whom they supposed were skilled in the use of public power.

In addition, the companies added to their staff new lawyers who were known for their Washington connections. Late in 1963 Philip Morris, for example, engaged Arnold, Fortas, and Porter, an eminent Washington firm one of whose principals, Abe Fortas, had connections with Lyndon Johnson, who as president would nominate him to the Supreme Court. The industry formed a committee of lawyers from Washington firms, one representing each of the Big Six cigarette companies—R.J. Reynolds, American Tobacco, Brown & Williamson, Liggett & Myers, P. Lorillard, and Philip Morris—along with one of the industry's defense lawyers who had experience with personal injury suits. The journalist Elizabeth Brenner Drew constructed this contemporaneous account of the committee's activity:

> This committee met almost daily, from the time of formation in early 1964 through completion of congressional action on the labeling bill this year [1965]. It covered every contingency for the companies: it planned the industry argument in the FTC hearings, it planned a court test of the FTC ruling if that became necessary, and it deeply involved itself in the maneuvering in Congress. Once the issue came before Congress, the lawyers' committee wrote testimony, drafted bills and amendments, served as central casting for witnesses most likely to see the industry's point of view, and fed to friendly congressmen statements and questions to be asked of witnesses. (1965, 77)

More or less simultaneously, the general counsels of the companies began meeting as a body, having been constituted by the presidents as a Committee of Counsel. Lawyers from the British American Tobacco (BAT) Company, visiting the United States in the fall of 1964, concluded: "The lawyers are . . . the most powerful group in the smoking and health situation" (Tursi, White, and McQuilkin, 2000, 99). The companies' deepening engagement with government—legislatures, regulatory agencies, and courts—made lawyers the most powerful force in the industry.

On the relationship between smoking and health, the lawyers took a hard line. They would admit nothing. The visiting BAT lawyers wrote in 1964: "their policy, very understandably, in effect is 'Don't take any chances.' It is a situation that does not encourage constructive or bold approaches to smoking and health problems, and it also means that the Policy Committee of lawyers exercises close control over all aspects of the problems" (Tursi et al., 2000, 99–100).

Vis-à-vis the health effects of smoking, lawyers adopted a willfully ignorant stance, an approach designed by specialists in legal contestation to serve legalistic ends. The first wave of tort suits came in the 1950s and 1960s, and the company lawyers concentrated on winning in court, which was the arena that they knew. Their policy of admitting nothing was buttressed by their litigation tactics, which from the start called for fighting every case to the very end. To settle rather than go to trial could have conceded some responsibility for smokers' illness. Without either conceding or denying that there was risk in smoking, the companies built their cases on a showing that smokers assumed the risk.

The ignorance prescribed by lawyers on strategic grounds had effects outside the companies' legal departments and the courts. In particular, it had chilling effects on in-house research. Company scientists who came too close to learning what the companies did not want to know—because it could weaken their position in court if they were shown to know it—found that their laboratory operations could be shut down and their jobs jeopardized.

Lawyers' influence had chilling effects as well on searches for a safer cigarette. At Liggett & Myers, where an organic chemist named James Mold labored for years over a cigarette made safer by the addition of palladium, attorneys "hovered over all aspects of the project, including scientific meetings at which, according to Mold, 'All paper that was generated—research progress reports, memoranda, notebooks, or what-all—were to be directed to the legal department and turned in at the end of the meeting'" (Kluger, 1996, 657). The aim was to cover the whole project with the cloak of a privileged lawyer-client relationship. The palladium cigarette was never marketed, the company said, because improved safety was unproven. Mold thought that it was kept off the market out of fear of liability claims based on the inference that the company's other products were unsafe (Kluger, 1996).

R.J. Reynolds did attempt to bring a safer cigarette, the Premier, to market in the late 1980s. It heated rather than burned tobacco. But customers did not like it, nor did the industry's critics, who thought that the only safe cigarette was no cigarette. And, once again, neither did the lawyers. Soon after Reynolds announced the Premier, William S. Ohlemeyer of Shook, Hardy, and Bacon, a Kansas City firm specializing in tobacco litigation, lamented that the new cigarette could undermine "the tobacco industry's joint defense efforts." He wrote, "The industry position has always been that there is no alternative design for a cigarette as we know them. Unfortunately, the Reynolds announcement . . . seriously undercuts this component of the industry's defense" (Tursi et al., 2000, 295–296).

The lawyers' influence spread also to the Council on Tobacco Research, a consortium of the major manufacturers created in the 1950s allegedly to foster research but in reality primarily a public relations instrument. The council had a category of "special projects" that did not go through the usual scientific review process. They were given preferential treatment because the lawyers anticipated that the results might be useful in buttressing the companies' position in court. In particular, the lawyers sought research results that demonstrated environmental or genetic origins of cancer.

Company scientists, who were under pressure from chief executives to find a scientific solution to the problem of smoking and health—and who were disposed as professional scientists to acknowledge that a problem actually existed—were constantly in tension with the lawyers. A veteran employee of Philip Morris told the author Richard Kluger:

> There was a conflict in the company between science and the law that's never been resolved. . . . [Helmut Wakeham, Philip Morris's research director] was addressing the issue purely as a scientist—lawyers look at the problem in a different way, and so we go through this ritual dance—what's "proven" and what isn't, what's causal and what's just an association—and the lawyers' answer is, "Let's stonewall." . . . If Helmut Wakeham had run things, I think there would have been some admissions. But he was outflanked by the lawyers, led by Paul Smith, who some people felt walked on water. The lawyers were saying, in effect, "My God, you can't make that admission" without risking liability actions against the company. So there was no cohesive plan—when critics of the industry speak of a "conspiracy," they give the companies far too much credit. . . . None of us at that time was sure what we could do, what we should or shouldn't do—or say. (1996, 230–231)

Wakeham himself referred to Smith as the "company czar" on smoking and health, who constantly raised the specter of the company's losing a lawsuit.

Other strategies than the one the industry adopted were at least conceivable, if not realistic. Addison Yeaman, who was general counsel for Brown & Williamson in the early 1960s, made an arresting suggestion for cooperation with the government as publication of the report to the surgeon general drew near.

> One would hope the industry would act affirmatively and not merely react defensively [to the report]. We must, I think, recognize that in defense of the industry and in preservation of its present earnings position, we must either a) disprove the theory of causal relationship or b) discover the carcinogen or carcinogens, co-carcinogens, or whatever, and demonstrate our ability to remove or neutralize them. This means that we must embark—in whatever form of organization—on massive and impressively financed research into the etiology of cancer as it relates to the use of tobacco; what constituents or combination of constituents in cigarette smoke cause or are conducive to cancer of the lung. . . .
>
> The [Council on Tobacco Research] cannot, in my opinion, provide the vehicle for such research. It was conceived as a public relations gesture and (however undefiled the Scientific Advisory Board and its grants may be) it has functioned as a public relations operation. Moreover, its organization, certainly in its present form, does not allow the breadth of research—cancer, emphysema, cardiovascular disorders, etc.—essential to the protection of the tobacco industry. I suggest that for the new research effort we enlist the cooperation of the Surgeon General, the Public Health Service, the American Cancer Society, the American Heart Association, American Medical Association and any and all other responsible health agencies or medical or scientific associations concerned with the question of tobacco and health. The new effort should be conducted by a new organization lavishly financed, autonomous,

self-perpetuating, and uncontrolled save that its efforts be confined to the single problem of the relation of tobacco to human health.

Thus to accept its responsibility would, I suggest, free the industry to take a much more aggressive posture to meet attack. (Yeaman and Brown & Williamson Tobacco Corporation, 1963)

To whom this memorandum was addressed is unclear. It was marked "strictly private and confidential." We do not know whether it was seriously considered within Brown & Williamson, let alone the larger industry. There is no reason to suppose that it would have been well received, nor, given the subsequent history, is there reason to believe that public health organizations would have welcomed such an overture. The assumption that the industry and public health organizations would be adversaries, not collaborators, was widespread and consistent with the customary operation of the American legal system. To depart from it would have required extraordinary acts of trust, imagination, innovation, and acceptance of responsibility on both sides. When searches for a safer cigarette subsequently began by the government in the 1970s, they were not conducted cooperatively, nor were they conducted for long. The thrust of government policy has been to prevent smoking rather than to modify cigarettes (Derthick, 2005).

As the role of industry lawyers became known in the 1980s, and as the industry came under mounting assault from both private litigants and the state attorneys general in the 1990s, some of the lawyers leading the assault wanted to target opposing lawyers in their lawsuits. In particular, they named Shook, Hardy, and Bacon, whose deceased leader, David Hardy, had been the principal "outside" architect of the industry's strategies. Of the firm's four hundred lawyers, fifty were in its tobacco unit. Ron Motley of the Charleston firm of Ness, Motley, which was in the vanguard of the fight against the industry, elected to include in Florida's suit the charge that Shook, Hardy had abetted a civil conspiracy. However, the case settled without going to trial, and then the same thing happened in Texas (Zegart, 2000).

Michael Ciresi in Minnesota, who was collaborating with Attorney General Hubert Humphrey, was another lawyer who wished to expose the industry lawyers' role. His approach was to obtain damning documents, including 39,000 documents that industry lawyers had tried to shield with a claim of attorney-client privilege. Ciresi succeeded in having a judge rule that those disputed documents should go into the public archive in Minnesota (Derthick, 2005).

Government lawsuits against the tobacco industry reached a climax with *United States v. Philip Morris et al.,* which was brought by the administration of Bill Clinton in 1999 and continued by the administration of George W. Bush. The charge was that cigarette manufacturers had conspired since the 1950s to defraud and mislead the American public and to conceal information about the effects of smoking. The suit went forward under the Racketeer Influenced and Corrupt Organizations (RICO) Act, which was passed in 1970 to combat organized crime. It has since been employed by federal prosecutors much more widely, but this was the first time it had been used against an entire industry.

The suit progressed slowly through years of pretrial proceedings and discovery, the exchange of millions of documents, a trial of nine months with live testimony from 84 witnesses and written testimony from another 162, and millions of dollars in billable hours for lawyers. In 2006 District Court Judge Gladys Kessler found the companies guilty and excoriated them in an opinion of nearly 1,700 pages. Reaching the same conclusion I had in 2002, but with far more examination of the evidence and far more credibility, she singled out the industry's lawyers for condemnation:

> a word must be said about the role of lawyers in this fifty-year history of deceiving smokers, potential smokers, and the American public about the hazards of smoking and second hand smoke, and the addictiveness of nicotine. At every stage, lawyers played an absolutely central role in the creation and perpetuation of the Enterprise and the implementation of its fraudulent schemes. They devised and coordinated both national and international strategy; they directed scientists as to what research they should and should not undertake; they vetted scientific research papers and reports as well as public relations materials to ensure that the interests of the Enterprise would be protected; they identified "friendly" scientific witnesses, subsidized them with grants from the Center for Tobacco Research and the Center for Indoor Air Research, paid them enormous fees, and often hid the relationship between these witnesses and the industry; and they devised and carried out document destruction policies and took shelter behind baseless assertions of the attorney client privilege. What a sad and disquieting chapter in the history of an honorable and often courageous profession. (Kessler, 2006)

HONOR AND COURAGE IN THE LEGAL PROFESSION

Judge Kessler's observation apropos one dramatic and well-publicized case is consistent with what eminent critics of the legal profession have been saying generally. The lament for what has been lost can be found, among other places, in books by a Yale Law School dean (Kronman, 1993), a Harvard Law School professor (Glendon, 1994), and a respected corporation executive and public servant who was trained as a lawyer (Linowitz with Mayer, 1994). These critiques have in common a concern over three late twentieth-century developments: lawyers' intensified commitment to serving clients rather than courts or the society at large, an unbridled acquisitiveness, and a choice for combat over compromise.

How to reconcile an obligation to clients with the often-competing obligation to courts and society has long bedeviled the legal profession. This is not an easy question, though the British Lord Henry Brougham in 1820 was prepared to treat it as such. Speaking on the floor of the House of Lords, he said:

> [A]n advocate, in the discharge of his duty, knows but one person in all the world, and that person is his client. To save that client by all means and expedients, and at all hazards and costs to other persons, and, amongst them, to himself, is his first and only duty; and in performing this duty he must not regard the alarm, the torments, the destruction which he may bring upon others. Separating the duty of a patriot from

that of an advocate, he must go on reckless of the consequences, though it should be his unhappy fate to involve his country in confusion. (Wilkins, 2009, 302)

The initial canons of the American Bar Association (ABA), adopted in 1908, went to the opposite extreme and proclaimed that a lawyer "advances the honor of his profession and the best interests of his client when he renders service or gives advice tending to impress upon the client and his undertaking exact compliance with the strictest principles of moral law" (Glendon, 1994, 80).

Late in the twentieth century, the ABA's guidance was very much watered down. Terms like "honor" and "principles of moral law" disappeared. By 1983, the ABA merely said: "In rendering advice, a lawyer may refer not only to law but to other considerations such as moral, economic, social and political factors, that may be relevant to a client's situation." According to Mary Ann Glendon, the most hotly debated issue in connection with the 1983 rules was whether a lawyer should be required, rather than merely permitted, to disclose information he "has reason to believe is necessary to prevent a client from causing death or serious bodily harm to another person." The proponents of mandatory disclosure lost out to the advocates of ironclad client confidentiality (Glendon, 1994, 80–81).

The firm of Shook, Hardy, and Bacon, it would seem, was either showing the way or drifting with the tide. Either way, in single-mindedly serving their client, the tobacco industry, they were not at odds with the evolving profession. Nor were the tort lawyers who mounted an attack on tobacco in the late 1990s at odds with the profession in making huge profits.

Traditional ethics of the profession discouraged both self-promotion and self-enrichment. Advertising was prohibited; extravagant fees were discouraged. The ABA's canon of 1908 on the subject of advertising was a quintessential statement of the profession's lofty conception of itself:

> The most worthy and effective advertisement possible, even for a young lawyer, is the establishment of a well-merited reputation for professional capacity and fidelity to trust. This cannot be forced, but must be the outcome of character and conduct. . . . [S]olicitation of business by circulars or advertisements, or by personal communications, or interviews not warranted by personal relations, is unprofessional. . . . Indirect advertisement for business by furnishing or inspiring newspaper comments concerning causes in which the lawyer has been or is engaged, . . . the importance of the lawyer's positions, and all other like self-laudation, defy the traditions and lower the tone of our high calling, and are intolerable. (Hazard, Koniak, and Cramton, 1994, 957)

Courts joined with the ABA in enforcing the prohibition on advertising. As late as the mid-1970s, San Francisco's Melvin Belli, the "King of Torts," was suspended in California for thirty days for sending to *Time* and *Newsweek* a news release promoting the twentieth anniversary of his annual seminar for trial lawyers and for appearing in a *New York Times* advertisement endorsing Glenfiddich Scotch whiskey (Hazard et al., 1994, 959–960).

By the 1960s, however, critics both inside and outside the profession were objecting to the prohibition on advertising, and they were supported, crucially, by the U.S. Supreme Court. In 1976 the Court accorded First Amendment protection to commercial speech (*Virginia State Bd. of Pharmacy vs. Virginia Citizens Consumer Council Inc.*) and in 1977 began extending that protection specifically to advertising by lawyers (*Bates vs. State Bar of Arizona*, 433 U.S. 350). Justice Sandra Day O'Connor dissented in terms reminiscent of the ABA's original canon. Lawyers' professionalism "entails an ethical obligation to temper one's selfish pursuit of economic success," she wrote (Hazard et al., 1994, 976–977). She feared that advertising would diminish the profession's public service orientation. The ABA, which had persisted with prohibitions on advertising even while modifying the moralistic tone of its canons, had to abandon its position. It changed its rules to stress merely that advertising should not be misleading (American Bar Association, 1982).

The ABA's rules on fees were unchanged even as the practices of law firms flouted their spirit. As of 1980, the Model Code of Professional Responsibility (Disciplinary Rule 2-106) said: "A lawyer shall not enter into an agreement for, charge, or collect an illegal or clearly excessive fee" (American Bar Association, 1982, 13). At about this time, according to Glendon, the billable hour, which was introduced in the 1950s as a sensible tool of office management, turned into a frenetic way of life that dominated law firms. Billing of clients had become their overriding goal, with members under intense pressure to log long hours—even absurd hours, as in the case of members who managed to bill 27 hours in one day by flying from the East to the West Coast. Trade publications reported on earnings and profiled the winners in what had become a contest to see who could make the most money (Glendon, 1994). Lawyers became millionaires. The *Wall Street Journal* reported early in 2011 that top partners at big law firms in Los Angeles, Washington, and Chicago were earning $10 million or more a year while the average partner at a U.S. firm earned $811,000, figures notable for both their absolute size and the gap between the peak and the average (Koppel and O'Connell, 2011). As an industry, lawyers became the biggest contributors to political campaigns. According to the Center for Responsive Politics, which compiles contributions by industry and interest group from records of the Federal Election Commission, lawyers and law firms led all contributors in all nine election cycles between 1990 and 2006, though in 2008 they dropped to second place, having been topped by retirees (Center for Responsive Politics, 2010).

The all-time winners in this unseemly competition were the tort lawyers who collaborated with the attorneys general of state governments in the 1990s to sue tobacco companies for the recovery of Medicaid expenses incurred on behalf of smokers. The companies ultimately entered into a settlement with the suing states, in which private tort lawyers were very big winners. The attorneys general had hired roughly a hundred law firms, most of which worked with contingency-fee contracts that promised them as much as 33 percent of the proceeds. Firms in general expected to realize millions of dollars, while some, such as those of Mississippi's Richard Scruggs and South Carolina's Ron Motley—both of whom had contracts with twenty to thirty states—realistically aspired to a billion dollars or more. Florida's lawyers received $3.43 billion; Mississippi's, $1.43

billion; and those of Texas, $3.3 billion. A precise total was never revealed, but it was probably around $15 billion (Derthick, 2005).

The size of these fees, both in total and in individual cases, astounded observers with knowledge of the legal profession. Professor John Langbein of the Yale Law School put it sardonically:

> Mr. Scruggs is a historic figure. His picture is going to go into the legal history books, along with Justinian and Lord Coke. He's going to be there for having had the unbelievable nerve to demand billions upon billions of dollars and then actually to get it, or at least come very close. The idea of charging this kind of money in connection with a legal system is unheard of, not only in our own legal tradition, but anywhere else. When Europeans hear these numbers, their jaws hit their desks. No well-run polity needs to pay $8 billion or $40 billion to facilitate the ordinary functions of government. To pay this kind of money to private entrepreneurs for what is basically a public function is extraordinary, unprecedented, and deeply unprincipled. (Derthick, 2005, 194)

As lawyers grew richer in the United States of the late twentieth century, they also grew more numerous and powerful, deriving power from their role as expert practitioners of adversarial legalism. This is what Robert Kagan has called the distinctive American practice of making public policy through legal contestation. The style of such contestation, according to Kagan, is litigant activism, "in which the assertion of claims, the search for controlling legal arguments, and the gathering and submission of evidence are dominated not by judges or government officials but by disputing parties or interests, acting primarily through lawyers" (Kagan, 2001, 9).

Beginning in the mid-1960s the United States experienced an explosion of both litigation and the legal profession. Always legalistic, the society now became more adversarially so. Always disproportionately led and influenced by lawyers, the society abruptly ceded vastly more weight to them. Whereas the United States had just under three hundred thousand lawyers in 1960, it had more than a million in 2000. It had 1 lawyer for every 695 persons in 1951 but 1 for every 264 persons in 2000 (Carson, 2004). The dean of Harvard Law School calculated in 1992 that if lawyers continued their recent rate of increase, by 2023 the country would have more lawyers than people (Clark, 1992).

As a result of the litigation explosion, lawyers were cast less and less in the role of disinterested statesmen, the historic ideal, and more in the role of embattled warriors, a change deplored by the profession's critics. No longer consensus builders, problem solvers, troubleshooters, dispute avoiders, and dispute settlers, they had, instead, become fomenters of conflict (Glendon, 1994).

Whether the profession should be held responsible for this change is doubtful. On the one hand, Kagan argues that American lawyers and law professors, "in sharp contrast to their counterparts in other democratic nations, have created and defended a body of legal ethics that exalts adversarial legalism." Far more in the United States than elsewhere, lawyers' codes of ethics "endorse zealous advocacy of clients' causes . . . without regard to the interests of justice in the particular case or broader societal concerns." Moreover, "American lawyers' professional culture is unique in permitting and implicitly encouraging them to advance unprecedented legal claims, coach witnesses, and attempt to wear down their opponents through burdensome pretrial discovery. In the hands of some practitioners—not all, but not merely a few—entrepreneurial, manipulative, and superaggressive modes of getting clients and litigating push the limits of adversarial legalism even further" (Kagan, 2001, 55–56). In no other country are lawyers so entrepreneurial in seeking new kinds of business or so quick to propose new legal theories to expand liability.

Yet Kagan declines to characterize lawyers as the primary cause of the expanding domain of adversarial legalism. He argues that broad political currents and interest groups have been the sorcerers that conjured adversarial legalism, "thereby generating demands for more legally trained apprentices." More fundamentally, he argues that adversarial legalism arises from the tension between a political culture that demands comprehensive government protection from harm and injustice but is juxtaposed with government structures that fragment authority, making action difficult. Adversarial legalism helps resolve the tension. In a structurally fragmented government, lawsuits and courts provide "nonpolitical" mechanisms through which individual litigants can demand high standards of justice (Kagan, 2001, 15–16, 55). An army of lawyers is required to make this "alternative" system work. The army developed as political culture changed to foster expectations of "total justice," in Lawrence Friedman's (1985) phrase. This was a change grounded in transformative social movements of the 1960s and succeeding decades, beginning with the civil rights movement and followed quickly by the environmental movement, with consequences that spread throughout the making and implementation of public policy.

Virtually every significant domestic domain of public policy in the United States has been affected by the spreading litigiousness, but tobacco offers a particularly vivid and compelling example. Before the mid-1990s, tort litigation against cigarette companies proceeded independently of legislative policymaking and in no way substituted for it. The plaintiffs were individuals, and the case outcomes applied to them alone. But then two new kinds of lawsuits appeared, in contrast to those brought previously on behalf of individual plaintiffs. One type of new suit was the class action, which consolidated the claims of individuals. Courts proved unreceptive to class actions in tobacco. The other new category of suits, much more important than the class actions, were those brought beginning in 1994 by the attorneys general of state governments who sought indemnification for the governments' medical expenditures on behalf of smokers. These suits culminated in 1998 in a Master Settlement Agreement that constructed a new nationwide regime of tobacco regulation and required cigarette manufacturers to pay billions of dollars annually to state governments, in addition to yielding huge profits for the private tort lawyers who collaborated with the attorneys general (Derthick, 2005).

This extraordinary outcome, without precedent in the history of American public policymaking, vividly illustrates the enlarged role of litigation and enlarged power of lawyers. The ferocity of tobacco litigation illustrates the intensity of today's legal contests, in which lawyers are cast as warriors, far removed from the dignified problem solvers, trouble shooters, and dispute avoiders recalled with admiration by Glendon.

The tort lawyers who challenged the tobacco industry loathed their opponent. This was in part a response to the industry lawyers' aggressiveness. From the earliest days of tobacco litigation, the industry's lawyers would pay any price, go any distance, and use any litigating tactic to win. For the most part, they won by exhausting their opponents, who had far less money than they did. Their litigating philosophy was summed up by an official of R.J. Reynolds, maker of Camels: "To paraphrase General [George] Patton, the way we won these cases was not by spending all of [Reynolds's money], but by making that other son of a bitch spend all of his" (Derthick, 2005, 28). In addition to hating the industry's lawyers, the tort lawyers hated the industry, which at least some of them came to see not just as one more courtroom adversary but as an evil monster, comparable to the great killers of the twentieth century—Hitler, Stalin, and the Khmer Rouge (Derthick, 2005, 72).

For their part, the industry lawyers, of course, lost none of their intensity as the battle raged through the late 1990s and into the next decade. The state governments' lawsuits against cigarette companies were followed by a federal lawsuit—the one that reached a climax with Judge Kessler's 1,700-page opinion in 2006. Allan Brandt, a historian of public health at Harvard and author of a tome on cigarette smoking, appeared for the government as an expert witness. When he told the lead prosecutor that he understood that the companies' lawyers would try to undermine his credibility, she replied: "No. That's not it. They want to destroy you and leave you in a pool of blood" (Brandt, 2007, 500–501).

CONCLUSION

Many law professors and members of the legal profession are concerned about the decline in its integrity. They prepare casebooks and teach courses about professional responsibility. They serve as ethics officers in law firms. Such activities are presumably helpful in reinforcing what survives of the profession's exalted sense of public responsibility, but with regard to law schools, one has to pay attention to what they do as well as to what their faculty members say in courses on professional responsibility. This observation is prompted by a story in the *New York Times* in the summer of 2010 reporting that some law schools were retroactively inflating grades or deliberately changing grading systems to make them more lenient in an effort to help their graduates find jobs in a difficult economic climate. (Leading law schools—Harvard, Yale, Stanford, University of California at Berkeley—had abolished letter grades in favor of a pass/fail system.) In a different approach to helping students get jobs, Southern Methodist's law school had begun paying profit-making law firms to hire its students as interns (Rampell, 2010).

People who act immorally are at risk sooner or later of getting caught breaking the law, so that the last line of defense against an amoral rogue lawyer is the legal system itself. Following scandals in the 1980s in which savings and loan institutions defrauded their clients, the Securities and Exchange Commission began treating lawyers who helped clients lie on registration statements as unprivileged co-conspirators. Lawyers were made to pay fines to the government and compensation to victims of fraud because they had given what they knew or should have known to be false testimony before banking regulators (Linowitz with Mayer, 1994).

In 2008 Richard Scruggs, the superrich tobacco tort lawyer, was found guilty of attempting to bribe a judge, fined $250,000, sentenced to five years in prison, and deprived of his license to practice law. (The offense was unrelated to tobacco litigation.) Scruggs asked to be sent to a minimum security federal prison in Pensacola, Florida, where another Mississippi attorney and former Scruggs associate was serving an eleven-year sentence for bribing two state court judges (Boyer, 2008; Mohr, 2008).

Four members of the New York firm of Milberg Weiss, including partner Melvyn I. Weiss, served sentences of six months to two and a half years beginning in 2008 after having been found guilty of paying clients to pursue shareholder class action cases. Milberg Weiss was a specialist in such cases. "It's no fun being in prison," partner William S. Lerach told a reporter. "You are away from your family, your loved ones, and your dogs" (Kolker, 2010; Strassel, 2010, A21).

This short list of lawyer lawbreakers could, of course, go on. Its purpose is not to incriminate the profession, which presumably contains no higher a proportion of flawed individuals than the population as a whole. The point is, rather, that it no longer deserves to be thought of as a moral exemplar, still less as a bulwark against immoral behavior within organizations.

REFERENCES

American Bar Association. 1982. *Model Code of Professional Responsibility and Code of Judicial Conduct.* Chicago: National Center for Professional Responsibility.

Boyer, P.J. 2008. The bribe: How the Mississippi lawyer who brought down Big Tobacco overstepped. *New Yorker,* May 19, 45.

Brandt, A.M. 2007. *The Cigarette Century.* New York: Basic Books.

Carson, C.N. 2004. The Lawyer statistical report: The U.S. legal profession in 2000. In *Problems in Professional Responsibility for a Changing Profession,* 5th ed., ed. A.L. Kaufman and D.B. Wilkins, pp. 732–733. Durham, NC: Carolina Academic Press.

Center for Responsive Politics. 2010. Lawyers/Law firms: Long-term contribution trends. OpenSecrets. org. www.opensecrets.org/industries/totals.php?cycle=2010&ind=K01/.

Clark, R.C. 1992. Why so many lawyers? Are they good or bad? In *Problems in Professional Responsibility for a Changing Profession,* 5th ed., ed. A.L. Kaufman and D.B. Wilkins, 734–736. Durham, NC: Carolina Academic Press.

Derthick, M. 2002. The lawyers did it: The cigarette manufacturers' policy toward smoking and health. In *Legality and Community: On the Intellectual Legacy of Philip Selznick,* ed. R.A. Kagan, M. Krygier, and K. Winston, 281–293. Lanham, MD: Rowman & Littlefield.

———. 2005. *Up in Smoke: From Legislation to Litigation in Tobacco Politics,* 2d ed. Washington, DC: CQ Press.

Drew, E.B. 1965. The quiet victory of the cigarette lobby. *Atlantic Monthly,* 216 (September), 76–80.

Friedman, L.M. 1985. *Total Justice: What Americans Want from the Legal System and Why.* New York: Russell Sage Foundation.

Glendon, M.A. 1994. *A Nation Under Lawyers: How the Crisis in the Legal Profession Is Transforming American Society.* New York: Farrar, Straus and Giroux.

Hazard, G.C., Jr., S.P. Koniak, and R.C. Cramton. 1994. *The Law and Ethics of Lawyering,* 2d ed. Westbury, NY: Foundation Press.

Kagan, R.A. 2001. *Adversarial Legalism: The American Way of Law*. Cambridge: Harvard University Press.

Kessler, G. 2006. Final Opinion, Civil Action No. 99-2496 (GK), *United States v. Philip Morris USA et al.* www.tobaccofreekids.org/content/what_we_do/industry_watch/doj/FinalOpinion.pdf.

Kluger, R. 1996. *Ashes to Ashes*. New York: Alfred A. Knopf.

Kolker, C. 2010. Milberg lawyers leave jail, hit links, slopes; reflect on life. Bloomberg, March 20. www.bloomberg.com/apps/news?pid=newsarchive&sid=awQckBIC.AiQ/.

Koppel, N., and V. O'Connell. 2011. Pay gap widens at big law firms as partners chase star attorneys. *Wall Street Journal*, February 8, A1.

Kronman, A.T. 1993. *The Lost Lawyer: Failing Ideals of the Legal Profession*. Cambridge, MA: Belknap Press of Harvard University.

Linowitz, S.M., with M. Mayer. 1994. *The Betrayed Profession: Lawyering at the End of the Twentieth Century*. New York: Charles Scribner's Sons.

Mohr, H. 2008. Famed litigator gets 5-year term for conspiracy to bribe judge. *Washington Post,* June 28, A3.

Rampell, C. 2010. In law schools, grades go up, just like that. *New York Times,* June 22, A1.

Strassel, K.A. 2010. From bully to felon. *Wall Street Journal*, March 2, A21.

Tursi, F.V., S.E. White, and S. McQuilkin. 2000. *Lost Empire: The Fall of R.J. Reynolds Tobacco Company.* Winston-Salem, NC: Winston-Salem Journal.

Wilkins, D.B. 2009. Team of rivals? Toward a model of the corporate attorney/client relationship. In *Problems in Professional Responsibility for a Changing Profession*, 5th ed., ed. A.L. Kaufman and D.B. Wilkins, 302–310.

Yeaman, A., and Brown & Williamson Tobacco Corporation. 1963. U.S. Exhibit 56, 986, Report: Implications of Battelle Hippo I and II and the Griffith Filter. http://legacy.library.ucsf.edu/tid/ncw36b00/pdf.

Zegart, D. 2000. *Civil Warriors: The Legal Siege on the Tobacco Industry.* New York: Delacorte Press.

15

The Moral Dimension of Security Outsourcing

Frank Anechiarico and John Dehn

> Few men have virtue enough to withstand the highest bidder.
>
> —George Washington, letter, August 17, 1779

PUBLIC/PRIVATE GOVERNANCE AND NATIONAL DEFENSE

Over the past fifteen years, the U.S. government has increased the outsourcing of national defense functions to the point that it is now routine. Unfortunately, the shift in defense outsourcing from a matter of cost or convenience to one of necessity was largely unguided by law or democratic values. During this period, security outsourcing to private military contractors (PMCs) has become a signal example of what Adams and Balfour call "administrative evil" (2004). This chapter examines the origins and evidence of this phenomenon.

Virtue, it may be argued, inheres neither in free markets nor in structures of governance. Beginning with Adam Smith's treatise on the topic (1767), the debate over the morality of markets is ongoing. And, while Smith's "impartial spectator theory" recognizes the need for good intentions, he does not find much evidence for their influence in the marketplace (1767, 1330). Likewise, the inherent virtue in public-private governance (also known as New Public Management, or NPM) remains a point of contention. Steven Cohen's "strategic framework" for public-private governance is typical of the way that scholars approach the need to recognize "social context" (and social values) in public-private governance:

> It is critical that government managers resist bias and easy assumptions in making the outsourcing decision. Data should be collected about operations, and the political and social context of the program area must be well understood before making the "make-or-buy decision." (2001, 440)

Thus "political and social context" aims to guide one to the "right" outsourcing decision. Its use in this context should include an assessment of the likelihood of maintaining social virtues or values, including justice.

This chapter does not reflect the views of the U.S. Army, the U.S. Department of Defense, or the U.S. government.

It may be argued further that the principles underlying justice in a constitutional democracy are found neither in the operational parameters of modern government nor in the bargain between producers and consumers. Instead, citizens of the modern state rely on the rule of law to measure the justness of a government policy or action. Thus faithful administration of the law is a proper place to evaluate the moral status of public-private governance in security outsourcing.

Fundamentally, public administration operates to translate law into action. This chapter presents a critical view of the contemporary public administration of the laws and politics establishing and supporting security outsourcing in the United States. The view here is based on four, related contentions:

1. the *exigent reinterpretation of the law* (in reaction to bureaucratic dysfunction and a widespread demand for measurable performance),
2. in furtherance of a *constructed notion of the public good* (which in this context features often-mythical financial and other benefits of outsourcing combat zone security),
3. results in the *derogation of public morals* (failure to assess the consequences of outsourcing, in this case, and
4. a *loss of democratic accountability* (resulting from a lack of broad public participation in militarized national defense).

Adams and Balfour provide evidence supporting these contentions in case studies of Germany during World War II, the National Aeronautics and Space Administration (NASA) in the 1980s, the establishment of relocation camps in United States in the 1940s, and the treatment of detainees in American custody in the past decade. The organizational imperative to launch the *Challenger* space shuttle as quickly as possible was the exigent circumstance that led to a reinterpretation of NASA's mission. The reinterpretation led NASA's leaders to compromise on their moral responsibility for safety (Adams and Balfour, 2004, 95). In Nazi Germany, fervid nationalism became the exigency that lead to the bureaucratic routine of the Holocaust (2004, 62). And the fear of an invasion of the West Coast in 1942 led to exigent reinterpretation of the equal protection guarantee in the U.S. Constitution and the internment of thousands of Japanese Americans (2004, 138). More recently, the exigency of terrorism, as interpreted by high officials of the administration of George W. Bush led to the torture of detainees held by U.S. forces at the Abu Ghraib prison in Iraq, at the detention facility at Guantánamo Bay, and at a variety of foreign sites to which detainees were sent in process known as "extraordinary rendition" (Adams, Balfour, and Reed, 2006).

Adams and Balfour identify administrative evil and distinguish it from other forms of evil in three ways:

- "One is our modern inclination to unname evil, an old concept that does not lend itself well to the scientific mind-analytic mindset." The language of outsourced national security is fraught with euphemisms. The odious aura of "mercenaries" or "soldiers of fortune" does not readily attach to "private security contractors."

- "The second difference is found in the structure of the modern, complex organization, which diffuses individual responsibility and requires the compartmentalized accomplishment of role expectations in order to perform work on a daily basis." Diffuse authority is a well-established pathology of bureaucratic organization . . . and often a common feature of modern war. Outsourcing war-zone security exacerbates the problem by delegating already fractionalized governmental war-making authority to nongovernmental actors.
- "The third difference is the way in which the culture of technical rationality has analytically narrowed the processes by which public policy is formulated and implemented, so that moral inversions are now more likely." Weber's notion of routinization explains how processes developed under norms of technical rationality dominate public policy and replace democratic values with supposed imperatives of cost savings and market profitability. (2004, 5)

The tragic consequences of administrative routine noted above are reminders of how administration of the law can be inverted in purpose and effect. However, it is also important to examine routines that may not have tragic consequences but nevertheless result in erosion of a polity's moral basis. The erosion continues over time because the constructed idea of the public good becomes what Adams and Balfour call a "mask," shielding administrators from awareness of evil. Outsourcing conflict-zone security, based on the redefinitions of the public good in the theory and practice of public-private governance, has become routine. Exigent need and broad acceptance of public-private governance have masked or walled off the consequences of routine security contracting. The most significant consequence, as the next section explains, is bureaucratic acceptance of the loss of innocent life without accountability.

OUTSOURCING AS A PENTAGON ROUTINE

By the time defense policymakers studied it in the 1990s, public-private governance had already become a well-accepted routine at all levels of the U.S. government. A landmark study by the Defense Science Board (DSB) recommended that "all DOD *support* functions should be contracted out to private vendors" (1996, 1; emphasis added). The DSB, which advises the undersecretary of defense for acquisition and technology, exempted "inherently governmental functions" and operations "directly involved in war-fighting" (1996, 1). Overall, the DSB's study found that $7 billion to $12 billion could be saved by outsourcing (DSB Task Force, 1996, 77).

The DSB accepted the model of early adopters of public-private management like Indianapolis-Marion County. Indianapolis-Marion County's outsourcing of sixty municipal service functions in the early 1990s is featured in the DSB's report as an example of budget reductions made possible by "aggressive" contracting (DSB Task Force, 1996, 27A). To support its sweeping endorsement of outsourcing, the DSB references other municipal examples and cities, specifically, the manifesto of NPM, *Reinventing Government,* by Osborne and Gaebler (DSB Task Force, 1996, 27A, 68A; Osborne and Gaebler, 1992).

The idea that more aspects of national security could be provided by the private sector advanced after the (first) Persian Gulf War with increased use of PMCs in training, advisory, and logistics roles in the Balkans and then Iraq and Afghanistan. Security functions were then added. The Center for Public Integrity reports that between 1994 and 2002 "the U.S. Defense Department has entered into 3,061 contracts with 12 of the 24 U.S.-based PMCs" (Peterson, 2002). In the four years after the 2003 U.S. invasion of Iraq, State Department spending on private armed security contracts grew from $1 billion to $4 billion (Broder and Rohde, 2007). In February 2009, 8,380 Defense Department security contractors were in Iraq (Schwartz and Swain, 2011). By the following March, the number had grown to 11,610.

Another approximately 2,000 PMCs in Iraq are under contract with the State Department's Bureau of Diplomatic Security, which adopted the Pentagon's approach (Pincus, 2010). The trend persists in spite of the drawdown of U.S. troops in Iraq to a baseline 50,000 by August 2010. As noted by a Congressional Research Service report in August 2010, "Since June, 2008, as troop levels dropped by 57,000 (37%) . . . the number of contractors providing security actually increased by 26%" (Belasco, 2010, 2).

REPLACING TRADITIONAL MILITARY FUNCTIONS

The security services of PMCs revolve around the following functions:

- static security—protecting fixed or static sites, such as housing areas, reconstruction work sites, or government buildings;
- convoy security—protecting convoys traveling in Iraq;
- security escorts—protecting individuals traveling in unsecured areas in Iraq; and
- personal security details—providing protective security to high-ranking individuals. (Elsea, Schwartz, and Nakamura, 2008, 3)

The December 2007 contract between the State Department and three PMCs—Blackwater, Triple Canopy, and DynCorp International—makes apparent the high degree of discretion given to PMCs in performing these functions. Among the "goals of this acquisition," the contract lists the following:

- high contractor leadership of PRS [protective services] details,
- high quality personal protective services details,
- high quality instant, situational decision making, e.g., response to threats. (U.S. Department of State, 2005, 4U)

These goals are the *sine qua non* of conflict zone security, and its annotation in the contract indicates the traditional, military nature of the fractionalized and compartmentalized function that is being outsourced. Not coincidentally, the three elements together resonate with what the U.S. Army calls the "protection warfighting function," which includes

protecting personnel (combatants and noncombatants), physical assets, and information of the United States and multinational military and civilian partners. The protection warfighting function facilitates the commander's ability to maintain the force's integrity and combat power. Protection determines the degree to which potential threats can disrupt operations and counters or mitigates those threats. . . . Protection is a continuing activity; it integrates all protection capabilities to safeguard bases, secure routes, and protect forces. (U.S. Army, 2008, 4–6)

COMMODIFYING NATIONAL SECURITY

The shift from reliance on the military for certain national security functions to reliance on contractors follows the technical rationality of market-based solutions to public problems. The primary effect of security outsourcing is to transform defense from an element of national sovereign identity into a market commodity. Conflict-zone security, like other market commodities, is specified in contracts, measured by the quarter, and adjusted to the express demands of the buyer.

David Harvey has developed a theoretical approach to the influence of capital exchange on sovereign identity and popular participation in governance. Harvey (2004) argues that the common property of a society—of which control and direction of national security and defense is one part—is being increasingly commoditized and sold. This process shifts the commons to the capital sector, where the imperative is to reap greater profits by increasing business. Harvey considers outsourcing and privatization part of the dispossession of sovereign rights and assets:

> Accumulation by dispossession is about dispossessing somebody of their assets or their rights. Traditionally there have been rights which have been common property, and one of the ways in which you take these away is by privatizing them. (2004, 4)

In the decade in which the United States has been at war in Iraq and Afghanistan, the use of PMCs has become routine. More contracts are let, which reinforces a fundamental change in war zone security from an inherently governmental function to a commodity. In this way, the calculus of providing security is governed by the same market dynamics that are found in the market for any other commodity. The buyer pursues efficiency and effectiveness in the purchase agreement, and the seller pursues profit. The profit orientation drives sellers to find more work and to both encourage and exploit the occasions that might provide growth opportunities.

The catchphrase justification for government outsourcing, that government should "steer, not row" (Savas, 1982), reserves the managerial steering function to public officials. However, as proponents of public-private governance point out, markets are nonhierarchical (Lane, 2006). The buyer does not steer but meets the seller at the equilibrium point, where demand and supply intersect. Inevitably and in short order, the official contracting party changes from an executive manager into a consumer.

A promise was made to citizens in the formative period of public-private governance: "The results are greater efficiency, enhanced responsiveness, and an environment that rewards innovation" (Osborne and Gaebler, 1992, 81). Thus the Defense Department and the State Department become purchasing agents with the means and motive to obtain the highest-quality service for the money spent. A key element of public-private governance is the use of market competition either to goad inefficient government agencies to better performance or to replace them through privatization.

However, some evidence suggests that outsourcing does not necessarily produce cost savings or efficiency. For example, a 2007 cost assessment by the House Committee on Oversight and Reform found that the cost of hiring a typical Blackwater security contractor was "four to ten times higher" than the cost of recruiting, training, and providing for an equivalent U.S. soldier at the rank of sergeant (Schwartz and Swain, 2011). The assessment noted that Blackwater was billing the U.S. government in the hundreds of millions of dollars a year, yet despite the cost there were no plans—and still are none—to replace PMC guards with service members (ibid.).

THE WAGES OF COMMODIFICATION

National defense and war-zone security have become market commodities incrementally. This gradual change yields a second, significant effect of security outsourcing: a deficit in democratic accountability that has grown as PMCs have become indispensable and those relying on them have become increasingly unwilling to hold them to account for their conduct and thereby risk losing their services.

The first step in commodifying national security and defense was the abolition of the draft in 1973. Military service is no longer either an inherent feature of U.S. sovereignty or an obligation of citizens. The all-volunteer force is but one of many options in the labor market available to young people. (In bad economic times, however, options are fewer.) Fifteen years after the abolition of the draft, historic cuts in force structure were made as the cold war wound down. These cuts led to further reliance by defense policymakers on the marketplace to obtain national security-related goods and services.

The combination of these factors—the all-volunteer force, force structure and personnel reductions, and the use of contractors for a range of services—made it less controversial for the Executive Branch to gain congressional and popular acceptance for or acquiescence in an increasing variety of military operations around the world. Because of these factors, the military now comprises volunteers who reflect a small proportion of the population and security contractors are often staffed with foreign nationals. Thus the taxpayers have become increasingly estranged from those who provide their national security and defense.

Evidence of this can be seen in the degree to which casualties among the contractors substitute for military casualties, thus reducing the political costs of war. The majority of the approximately 1,000 contractors killed in Iraq from 2003 to 2007 were employees of PMCs (Isenberg, 2009). One suspects that the number would be lower if the jobs they were performing had been done by the members of the armed forces. If not, the number of U.S. armed forces killed in action in Iraq during that period (3,496) would be larger by almost a third. The fact that the number of military casualties is lower because of the contractors reduces and alters the narrative in which American families and communities have sacrificed their sons and daughters. The media have paid virtually no attention to the number of contractor casualties, thus omitting it from the public's notion of the human cost of military engagement. For all intents and purposes, the use of PMCs and other frontline contractors allowed the U.S. government to obscure more than 20 percent of the operational deaths in Iraq. This masking of the human cost of the conflicts in Iraq and Afghanistan has moral implications for the way that armed conflict is entered into, conducted, and assessed.

INDISPENSABILITY, INCREASED DEFICITS, AND THE LACK OF ACCOUNTABILITY

The moral implications of outsourcing security stem from these democracy deficits. These deficits have grown because PMCs are increasingly indispensable to those employing them. This dependence results in having government official "consumers" who are increasingly willing to accept what is available in the market and unwilling or unable to hold PMCs to account for their conduct for fear of further increasing costs or losing PMC services.

The governments of both Iraq and Afghanistan have demanded the withdrawal of some or all security contractors from their territory in the past few years. The well-known responses of the U.S. government to these demands are a clear indication of extraordinary degree to which security has become an indispensable private function. They have thereby acquired the political prerogatives that indispensability implies.

If diplomats and other U.S. officials cannot freely travel in Baghdad, much less the rest of the country, without protection from PMCs, who in reality is "steering" conflict-zone security? The answer might be found in events subsequent to an incident in Baghdad's Nisour Square on September 16, 2007.

While guarding a State Department convoy that was crossing Baghdad outside the bounds of the heavily guarded Green Zone, the chief of Blackwater security for the convoy—a man known as Hoss—noticed a car speeding toward the convoy. After warnings, the extent of which are contested, Blackwater employees opened fire on the car with machine guns, stopping it, preventing any loss of life in the convoy, and killing seventeen Iraqis. Blackwater contends that some of the Iraqis who were killed had opened fire on the convoy (von Zielbauer and Glanz, 2007, A1).

Reports of investigations of the Nisour Square shootings by the U.S. Army and the Federal Bureau of Investigation (FBI) found Blackwater responsible for the deaths and injuries. The Army report labeled the behavior of Blackwater personnel "criminal." The *Washington Post* reported on observations of Army officers at the scene.

> "It appeared to me they [Iraqis] were fleeing the scene when they were engaged. It had every indication of an excessive shooting," said Lt. Col. Mike Tarsa, whose soldiers reached Nisour Square 20 to 25 minutes after the gunfire subsided.
>
> His soldiers' report—based upon their observations at the scene, eyewitness interviews and discussions with Iraqi police—concluded that there was "no enemy

activity involved" and described the shootings as a "criminal event." Their conclusions mirrored those reached by the Iraqi government, which has said the Blackwater guards killed 17 people. (Raghavan and White, 2007, A01)

The State Department contract with Blackwater and two other PMCs includes a provision about the use of force:

> Deadly force will only be used after all non-violent efforts are exhausted to stop a life threatening disturbance at any post manned by guards. . . . The use of Deadly Force represents the last resort by a guard for the restoration of order. (U.S. Department of State, 2005, 73)

This provision covers possible disturbances the gates of U.S. embassies or consulates, where hired guards might be better employed. Convoys are not mentioned in the contract, even though protecting them was a major part of Blackwater's job in Iraq. Convoys through Baghdad pass thousands of people who might appear dangerous or imminently threatening to guards lacking knowledge of the local area. It was only after the Nisour Square shootings and a State Department review by a panel of outside experts that notice was taken of the challenges of convoy security.

The effect of the Nisour Square shootings on the State Department's security contracts was minimal. Richard Griffin, the assistant secretary of state for diplomatic security, resigned shortly after the event, but the contract with Blackwater and other PMCs operating in Iraq stayed in place, unmodified (von Zielbauer and Glanz, 2007, A1). The State Department's passivity was opposed by the Iraqi government, which demanded local prosecution of those responsible for the shooting and the immediate withdrawal of Blackwater from Iraqi territory. The State Department issued carefully phrased condemnations of "attacks on innocent Iraqi civilians," without referring specifically to the behavior of Blackwater at Nisour Square (Crowley, 2010). The State Department had decided to retain Blackwater, which continued to guard convoys for another year. In the course of the year after the Nisour Square shootings, according to Human Rights First (2008), Blackwater was involved in dozens of incidents involving the loss of civilian lives.

In a public appearance in November 2010, Condoleezza Rice, who served as secretary of state during this period, was asked to explain why Blackwater's contract was not cancelled. Her reply is a clear example of the way in which assertion of exigency in conflict zones resulted in the reconstruction of the public good of security.

> We really had no choice. My responsibility was to protect our people in Iraq—a job the U.S. military could not do—so we relied on contractors. I would point out that sanctions against Blackwater were pursued by the Justice Department and that Blackwater did lose the contract. (Rice, 2010)

As it turned out, the pursuit of Blackwater by the Justice Department was unavailing. Bringing PMCs to justice for misconduct is a problem that began in the first months of the U.S. occupation of Iraq and continues to this day. In June 2004, L. Paul Bremer, the then-head of the Coalition Provisional Authority (CPA), issued CPA Order 17 the day before the CPA went out of business and the Iraqi government regained a measure of sovereign authority. "Contractors," the order read, "shall not be subject to Iraqi laws or regulations in matters relating to the terms and conditions of their contracts." It was left to U.S. prosecutors to bring charges, in late 2008, against six Blackwater guards for voluntary manslaughter. A year later, a federal district court judge dismissed the case for a lack of admissible evidence.

On December 31, 2008, a status of forces agreement between the United States and Iraq went into effect. The agreement provides that "Iraq shall have the primary right to exercise jurisdiction over United States contractors and United States contractor employees" (U.S.-Iraq SOFA, 2008, 10). Five weeks later, Iraq's Interior Ministry refused to give Blackwater a license to continue operating in Iraq. Even though other PMCs operate in Iraq and its government had issued demands for Blackwater's expulsion since the Nisour Square incident, the United States did not replace Blackwater. As a *New York Times* report put it:

> The Iraqi government has sought in the past to expel Blackwater, but American officials in Iraq who rely on the company's heavily armed guards for security have said they have no alternative but to continue using the security contractor. (Williams, 2009, A1)

In September 2009, the State Department announced that it had agreed to an extension of its contract with Blackwater for, in particular, helicopter lift and air transport security services in Iraq, until a replacement contractor could be found. The contract extension was for an indeterminate period, though a Bureau of Diplomatic Security spokesman said it was "limited" (Radia, 2009).

Much the same reaction came from U.S. officials in the wake of a demand for the removal of PMCs in Afghanistan from President Hamid Karzai on August 19, 2010 (Filkins and Shane, 2010). As the assessment by Sean Naylor in the *Army Times* (2009) put it:

> Ill-disciplined private security guards escorting supply convoys to coalition bases are wreaking havoc as they pass through western Kandahar province, undermining the coalition's counterinsurgency strategy here and leading to at least one confrontation with U.S. forces, say U.S. Army officers and Afghan government officials.
>
> The security guards are responsible for killing and wounding more than 30 innocent civilians during the past four years in Maywand district alone, said Mohammad Zareef, the senior representative in the district for Afghanistan's intelligence service, the National Directorate of Security.

Apart from the behavior of these PMCs, which indicate most clearly the moral dimensions of conflict-zone contracting, contracts for other services in Iraq and Afghanistan also demonstrate that U.S. government officials had become accustomed to and tolerant of misconduct by major contractors. One example is the award by U.S. Central Command in March 2007 of $508 million to IAP Worldwide for construction of electricity generating and transmission facilities in Iraq. Building power plants for civilian populations does not fit the definition of outsourcing; it is not an activity that had been or could reasonably be expected to be carried out by government employees. However, at the same time, the House Committee on Oversight and Reform was holding hearings on an emerging scandal over the way that IAP was running the Army's Walter Reed Medical Center in Maryland. The *Washington Post* ran a series of articles detailing the long delays for ultimately inadequate treatment of wounded soldiers sent to the hospital from battlefields in Iraq and Afghanistan (Vogel and Merle, 2007, A1).

The investigation resulted in the resignation or firing of three general officers, including Major General George Weightman, the Walter Reed commander (Cloud, 2007, A1). IAD's removal for cause from a highly sensitive, high visibility contract was noted in press reports, yet Defense Department procedures did not prevent awarding the firm a second contract.

These examples demonstrate the high level of agency dependence on PMCs and other conflict-zone contractors. This dependence reshapes the nature of market exchange for conflict-zone security. Contracting agencies pay PMCs a premium for their services and accept or tolerate malfeasance. In return, contractors use whatever measures they deem necessary to protect agency personnel and absorb casualties that might detract from public or congressional support for the mission.

THE ACCOUNTABILITY DEFICIT

In a report on PMCs in Iraq, the Congressional Research Service considered the consequences of the State Department's relationship to Blackwater.

> [T]he State Department's alleged protection of Blackwater, as its employees act as if they are above Iraqi law and kill Iraqis with impunity, makes it difficult to advocate for such issues as the importance of the rule of law and human rights as U.S. Foreign policy objectives. (Elsea et al., 2008)

Whether the State Department actively protected Blackwater's misconduct and illegality or just tolerated it, the result is the same: a lack of accountability for the conduct of contractors wielding deadly force in the name of the United States. This was the case in Nisour Square and the U.S. embassy in Kabul, and it was the case in the State Department's response to demands by the governments of Iraq for removal of Blackwater and by the government of Afghanistan for the removal of all PMCs. It is also the case with IAD's status with the Defense Department in spite of the Walter Reed scandals.

The commodification of armed security functions further increases, or at least perpetuates, these accountability deficits. In spite of media attention, congressional investigation, and academic discussion, one strains (ultimately unsuccessfully) to hear a broad public call for establishing accountability over PMCs or their employees for the means by which they provide security. It may only be through the conflict of these methods with the ultimate goals of the public agencies procuring them—meaning the extent to which they win the hearts and minds necessary to prevail in a counterinsurgency (Thurnher, 2008)—that may ultimately lead to the establishment of some modicum of accountability.

Accountability Supply and Demand

The routine of security outsourcing appears to have breached the DSB's exemption of "inherently governmental" and "war-fighting" functions. In recognition of the problem posed by PMCs under Federal Acquisition Regulations, the Defense Department issued a rule establishing procedures to ensure that security contractors are in compliance with Federal Acquisition Regulations (FARs). The rule holds that:

> It is the responsibility of the combatant commander to ensure that the private security contract mission statements do not authorize the performance of any inherently Governmental military functions, such as preemptive attacks, or any other types of attacks. Otherwise, civilians who accompany the U.S. Armed Forces lose their law of war protections from direct attack if and for such time as they take a direct part in hostilities. (U.S. DoD, 2006)

This rule, however, begs the question of whether PMC *operations* involve performance of inherently governmental functions. The focus on mission statements would ensure that contract officials avoid only the most obvious indications of illegality.

Robert Behn poses a basic question regarding public-private governance that applies particularly well to private armed security personnel, "How will we hold whom accountable for what?" He reports that public-private governance advocates respond: "Don't hold us accountable for process; hold us accountable for results" (Behn, 2001, 62). However, it is the "process" by which PMCs attempt to provide security that raises serious questions of accountability.

It has been noted that, in general, public-private governance's shift of public functions to the private sector "limits the degree to which citizens can meaningfully affect policy and administration" (Box et al. 2001, 613). In the case of PMCs, opportunities for public participation appear to be even more attenuated. Outsourcing combat-zone security to PMCs virtually eliminates citizen oversight and accountability because citizens are not the direct consumers or beneficiaries of the service being provided. Furthermore, their location outside the traditional command structure of the U.S. military leaves oversight to the agencies and officials that signed the contract. The operational and political position of PMCs insulates them from effective public monitoring and review.

The governance challenges to creating and effectively implementing accountability for PMCs and their individual employees involve issues that can be called "supply" and "demand" accountability problems. The supply problem involves complex legal and practical challenges to creating and implementing effective accountability systems. The demand problem refers to a lack of the democratic impetus necessary to fully understand, analyze, and resolve accountability supply problems related to PMC misconduct.

The complexity of modern armed conflict and the inherent challenges to the (almost exclusively extraterritorial) governance of those participating in them require political commitment to creating and effectively implementing a system or "supply" of account-ability. As shown, however, privatizing combatant functions perpetuates a decrease in democratic participation regarding the use and governance of militarized armed force. This increasing democratic deficit results in a corresponding accountability "demand" deficit. The less accountable PMCs are, the more it appears that the formal profession of arms has been replaced by commoditized and ultimately unaccountable surrogates.

Accountability and Private Warriors

Singer's detailed account of the dependency of governments through the seventeenth century on mercenary armies provides informative background for the modern role of PMCs. The 1989 UN Convention on Mercenaries is based on the following definition.

A mercenary is any person who:
- (a) Is specially recruited locally or abroad in order to fight in an armed con-flict;
- (b) Is motivated to take part in the hostilities essentially by the desire for private gain and, in fact, is promised, by or on behalf of a party to the conflict, material compensation substantially in excess of that promised or paid to combatants of similar rank and functions in the armed forces of that party;
- (c) Is neither a national of a party to the conflict nor a resident of territory con-trolled by a party to the conflict;
- (d) Is not a member of the armed forces of a party to the conflict; and
- (e) Has not been sent by a State which is not a party to the conflict on official duty as a member of its armed forces. (United Nations 1989, Article I)

Because most employees of Blackwater and other PMCs were U.S. or Iraqi nationals, the UN definition does not fit. However, the fit of the other four elements of the defini-tion is instructive given the development of sanctions related to the hiring of for-profit soldiers in international conflict.

The solidification of the nation-state in the seventeenth century as the primary unit of governance and its relative monopoly on military force produced a body of international law on armed conflict and the status of combatants. From this point on, a soldier would need to be willing to become subject to state-created international law to be a participant in war, or perhaps we should say an "acceptable" or "legal" participant in warfare. Indeed, the very definition of a lawful belligerent was tied to an individual's formal association with a national army in both Hague and Geneva law. The 1977 protocols to the Geneva Conventions deny mercenaries the right to participate in hostilities by denying them the protections afforded members of national armed forces. This should not be surprising considering that states seeking to preserve or further enhance their monopoly on the use of force were the source of these laws.

Weak Governance, the Persistence of Mercenaries, and the General Problem of Accountability

In spite of these changes in the law, it is now clear that mercenaries have effectively survived into the modern era of nation-states and the laws they have created to govern conflict. As recounted by Singer, individual mercenaries in the 1950s and 1960s thrived in decolonization (2008, 37), where weak states meant weak enforcement of the law, particularly the laws governing armed conflict.

Likewise, Singer's analysis of the current uses of mercenaries leads one to the inescapable conclusion that areas of weak national or international governance are what create both the need for and the impunity of mercenaries. Businesses and aid groups hire PMCs to protect their resources, goods, and transportation systems in countries unable to do so with available public agencies and resources. Weak governments with weak armies have hired them to defeat insurgents. Sometimes, rebel or insurgent groups have hired them to combat governments (2008, 3–18).

These situations might be generally described as accountability supply deficits. Governance is weak because the governing body, national or international, lacks the capacity to enforce applicable international or domestic legal norms. This leads to conflict and the displacement or ineffectiveness of national governance. The demand for accountability is sometimes present, but for various reasons, the structure for providing it is weak.

There is, however, another facet to the modern use of mercenaries and PMCs: their use by powerful governments, such as that of the United States, to assist in accomplishing foreign policy objectives in areas of weak governance, such as combat zones and areas of postconflict reconstruction. The provision of even a small portion of a country's collective security for its policy instruments in combat zones falls squarely within what became the traditional realm of national armed forces. In other words, PMCs that might not fully subscribe to the laws governing professional soldiers now carry out the task of those soldiers.

PMCS AND THE SUPPLY OF ACCOUNTABILITY

Historically, mercenaries were only held to account for results, as Behn says public-private governance advocates would have it for all government outsourcing. The means or methods by which PMCs delivered their services, whether armed combat or security, have not traditionally been a real concern of those who procure their services. Only effectiveness matters; defeating a threat equals success. There is little or no incentive for PMCs or the governments employing them to "supply" accountability for the means used to achieve victory. This is especially the case when PMCs are indispensable and there are only a few from which to choose.

In addition to reducing the number of government employees and associated costs, public-private governance purportedly lowers cost through bidder competition. However, the bidding process for the defense and security services is often quite different from the examples of municipal procurement used as models by the DSB. For security-related contracts, major constraints on the number of bidders are the location of the work and the risk to contract personnel. When these factors are combined, the contracting agencies are often left with just one company that is ready to fulfill the terms of the contract immediately. The contract regulations of governments conventionally allow exceptions to the lowest responsible bidder rule for situations in which a "sole source" must be given the job, indicating that there are no other sources that can supply the equipment, expertise, positioning, and readiness. Nevertheless, the belief in these cost savings perpetuates the use of PMCs in spite of accountability shortcomings.

Sole-Source Contracts: Cost and Accountability

Sole-source contracts, common in the Iraq and Afghanistan theaters, result in both higher prices and less accountability. Clear evidence of fraud, waste, or abuse by sole-source contractors has little impact on contracting decisions, because there is literally no alternative to keeping offending companies in place. This was the case with evidence of contract fraud in Iraq by Halliburton, as reported to the Defense Department and Congress by William Bowen, special inspector general for Iraqi reconstruction. Bowen's report is summarized in testimony before the Senate Appropriations Committee by the head of the Government Accountability Office, Comptroller General David Walker:

> U.S. efforts in Iraq have relied extensively on contractors to undertake reconstruction projects and provide support to U.S. forces. However, a lack of well-defined requirements, poor business arrangements, and inadequate oversight and accountability has negatively affected reconstruction and support efforts. (2008, 2)

Accountability and the Uniform Code of Military Justice

These varied accountability deficits and their causes are further demonstrated by the lack of a clearly feasible method for holding PMCs or their employees criminally responsible for their conduct. It is highly doubtful that the Uniform Code of Military Justice (UCMJ), the statutory code that governs U.S. soldiers and military tribunals known as courts-martial, could have been used to charge Blackwater personnel for either incident described above. Even if it were clear that UCMJ jurisdiction, including as later modified, extended to these contractors at the time of these incidents or similarly situated contractors today—and it is not—there are potential constitutional problems with the assertion of UCMJ jurisdiction over civilians.

The Fifth Amendment requires indictment by a grand jury before trial "for a capital, or otherwise infamous crime . . . except in cases arising in the land or naval forces" or federalized state militia. The UCMJ does not provide for a grand jury, though it has a more thorough preliminary hearing under its Article 32. Whether cases involving State Department contractors might be considered to "arise in" the land or naval forces is unclear but doubtful.

There are also Sixth Amendment questions regarding the right to a jury trial. Courts-martial are tried before a panel of military members, not a jury. At least one scholar has thoughtfully argued that these are not necessarily insurmountable obstacles to military jurisdiction, given the necessities of war and the broad historical understanding of a military commander's authority. However, this conclusion was related to civilians who clearly accompanied the armed forces (Peters, 2006). Contractors working for the State Department do not necessarily meet these historical criteria.

The Military Extraterritorial Jurisdiction Act (MEJA) of 2000 extends nonmilitary federal court jurisdiction, but only to "persons employed by or accompanying the Armed Forces outside the United States" for crimes punishable by more than one year in prison (Military Extraterritorial Jurisdiction Act, 2000). It was originally designed for those residing or working at military bases overseas. Hence, there were no law enforcement assets added to aid in implementing it. It relied on investigations by existing military investigators, local law enforcement authorities, or both.

Security contractors that provide services to other government departments do not necessarily fall within this jurisdiction, even if those agencies are working with the Department of Defense. Furthermore, it is not clear whether security personnel subcontracted by other contractors, even if those other contractors work for or with the Department of Defense, fall within this grant unless they are "accompanying the Armed Forces."

Beginning in 2004, MEJA also applies to "contractors of any other U.S. agency to the extent that the contractor employee's employment relates to supporting the mission of the DOD overseas" (Military Extraterritorial Jurisdiction Act, 2000). However, MEJA has been successfully applied to contractors in only a few cases in Iraq and Afghanistan and to none of the security contractors involved in the incidents discussed here (Tiefler, 2009).

PMC Accountability in the Absence of Military Command Oversight

In addition to these significant legal issues, there are substantial practical hurdles to enforcing the law in a combat zone. Armed conflict often renders normal modes of governance ineffective. For this reason, the UCMJ vests military commanders with disciplinary powers that include powers to investigate and punish. The laws governing war also place an affirmative obligation on these commanders to punish or prevent war crimes of which they are or become aware. In addition, the U.S. Army has detachments of criminal investigators who deploy to war zones with military units to aid commanders in these functions.

Contractors have no true "commanders" and carry with them no internal law enforcement because they are nongovernmental. They have no authority to prosecute and punish, only to hire and fire. If they do not fall within the military's legal or practical ability to investigate, law enforcement agents who do not routinely operate in combat zones must be sent to conduct the investigation. The problems that they face have been reported in relation to the Nisour Square shooting.

> Even the total number of fatalities remains uncertain because of the difficulty of piecing together what happened in a chaotic half-hour in a busy square in a war zone. Moreover, investigators could not rely on videotapes or photographs of the scene, because they were unsure whether bodies or vehicles might have been moved. . . . In addition, investigators did not have access to statements taken from Blackwater employees, who had given statements to State Department investigators on the condition that their statements would not be used in any criminal investigation like the one being conducted by the F.B.I. (Johnston and Broder, 2007)

As this account makes clear, what is often called the "fog of war" is an apt metaphor for the issues surrounding the establishment of criminal legal accountability for security contractors. Establishing guilt beyond a reasonable doubt, as is necessary for criminal conviction, is not an easy matter in the best of circumstances. In war, the challenges to doing so are exponentially magnified. The more isolated the wartime incident, the fewer the victims, the more difficult it becomes to establish important facts, such as an individual suspect's subjective knowledge or intent. Such details are often lost or undiscoverable in the chaos and violence of combat.

Finally, even if these obstacles are overcome, it is understandable that one might be inclined to excuse or mitigate actions taken in the heat of battle and in a dangerous environment. As explained by one scholar considering why contractors might prefer to be subject to prosecution under the UCMJ:

> Though military exigencies may never serve as a defense to war crimes, it would undoubtedly prove helpful for any jury hearing a case to fully appreciate any mitigating or extenuating circumstances. To put the issue differently, were a contractor accused of abusing a battlefield detainee in the rough and tumble of a wartime environment, who might the contractor truly prefer on his jury: courts-martial service members on site who have shared a common purpose and mission or twelve civilians thousands of miles away from the battle zone, drawn from the safety and comfort of suburban America, who cannot possibly understand "ground truth" and may not even support the goals of the underlying military campaign? (Peters, 2006, 411)

RELIANCE ON INTERNAL CONTROLS

Ronald Reagan's guideline for relations with nuclear adversaries, "Trust, but verify," should also apply to agency relations with security contractors. However, as the preceding section unfortunately demonstrates, legal, political, and administrative verification all failed. That leaves trust and a reliance on whatever internal controls are discernable in the structure and operations of PMCs. The investigation of Blackwater's internal administration by the House Oversight and Reform Committee in 2007 revealed a remarkably loose command structure for an organization with a military mission. Blackwater personnel, the committee discovered, were not employees of the truncated corporation, but independent contractors hired for the term of the mission for which the State Department or another agency had hired the corporation. Blackwater security guards, including those involved in the Nisour Square shooting, were, in essence, subcontractors. Therefore, the corporation argued that it was not responsible for withholding federal income tax, Social Security, or Medicare contributions from their pay.

The committee found that this independent contractor arrangement with its guards was known to State and Defense Department officials. The awareness of government officials of the loose connection between corporate officials and armed guards became especially troubling when the committee discovered that Blackwater, as a condition of its contract with each guard, "prohibited the guard from disclosing any information about Blackwater to 'any politician' or 'public official'" (Simmons, 2007).

Loosely linked employment relationships are not uncommon among companies that rely for nearly all their business on government contracts. The flexibility and low-cost for which the private sector is valued as an option for the provision of public services comes at the price of less than adequate internal controls of the use of armed force in the volatile environment of a conflict zone.

CONCLUSION

The Constitution provides the legal framework for establishing accountability over the national military. The UCMJ establishes processes to ensure individual accountability of military members. However, the routines of public-private governance have allowed PMCs to perform military functions while circumventing structures designed to ensure military accountability. These routines are buttressed by sole sourcing, combat-zone exigency, the fog of war, and the ethos of "steering, not rowing."

A solution to the problems presented by security contracting begins with the understanding that the accountability deficit described here is not just a failure of administrative oversight but a moral failing in controlling the use of deadly force by those wielding government authority. If the moral significance of the consequences of these activities is not recognized, the events described here become merely one more cost of doing business. The next step is to map the interlocking routines that construct the public good (security as a commodity) in response to perceived exigency (the absence of alternatives). The principal routines can be ordered from the general to the specific:

- identification of government functions as fungible products,
- distinction between military service, responsibility for national defense, and the obligations of citizenship,
- congressional acceptance of the indispensability of PMCs,
- separation of conflict-zone contracting from military command,
- broad reliance on PMCs for protective services in Iraq in Afghanistan by the State and Defense departments,

- treatment of PMC conduct as a procurement, not a law enforcement issue,
- protection of PMCs from prosecution and removal by host governments.

That these elements have become routine should raise questions about reliance on public-private governance in the United States. Although the narrative here appears pessimistic, it is not intended to imply the inevitability of moral failure in the procurement of conflict-zone security or other public services. Crucial to preventing such failure, however, is the need to revive "inherently governmental functions," a term that has been neglected or ignored in the rush to outsource. If agencies are required to specify these functions to the Office of Management and Budget or, more appropriately, in the testimony before Congress—outsourcing will become a matter of appropriate deliberation and debate, rather than a bureaucratic routine with troubling moral consequences.

REFERENCES

Adams, G.B., and D.L. Balfour. 2004. *Unmasking Administrative Evil,* rev. ed. Armonk, NY: M.E. Sharpe.

Adams, G.B., D.L. Balfour, and G.E. Reed. 2006. Abu Ghraib, administrative evil, and moral inversion: The value of "putting cruelty first." *Public Administration Review,* 66, 5, 680–693.

Behn, R.D. 2001. *Rethinking Democratic Accountability.* Washington, DC: Brookings Institution Press.

Belasco, A. 2010. The Cost of Iraq, Afghanistan, and Other Global War on Terror Operations Since 9/11. CRS Report for Congress 7–5700, September 2. Congressional Research Service, Washington, DC.

Box, R.C. 2009. *Public Administration and Society Critical Issues in American Governance.* Armonk, NY: M.E. Sharpe.

Box, R. C., G. Marshall, B.J. Reed, C. Reed. 2001. New public management and substantive democracy. *Public Administration Review*, 61, 5, 608–619.

Broder, J.M., and D. Rohde. 2007. State department use of contractors leaps in 4 years. *New York Times*, October 24, A1.

Cloud, D.S. 2007. General is fired over conditions at Walter Reed. *New York Times,* March 1, A1.

Cohen, S. 2001. A strategic framework for devolving responsibility and functions from government to the private sector. *Public Administration Review*, 61, 4, 432–440.

Crowley, P.J. 2010. Federal District Court Dismissal of Indictment Against Blackwater Contractors. Press release, January 8. U.S. Department of State.

Defense Science Board (DSB) Task Force. 1996. Report of the Defense Science Board Task Force on Outsourcing and Privatization. August.

Elsea, J.K., M. Schwartz, and K.H. Nakamura. 2008. Private Security Contractors in Iraq: Background, Legal Status, and Other Issues. CRS Report for Congress, August 25. Congressional Research Service, Washington, DC. www.fas.org/sgp/crs/natsec/RL32419.pdf.

Filkins, D., and S. Shane. 2010. Afghan leader sees plan to ban private guards. *New York Times*, August 16, A1.

Harvey, D. 2004. Interview. *Conversations with History*. Institute of International Studies, University of California, Berkeley, March 2.

Human Rights First. 2008. Private Security Contractors at War: Ending the Culture of Impunity. Report. New York. www.humanrightsfirst.org/wp-content/uploads/pdf/08115-usls-psc-final.pdf.

Isenberg, D. 2009. Shadow force: Private security contractors in Iraq. Cato Institute, February 16. www.cato.org/pub_display.php?pub_id=9979/.

Johnston, D., and J.M. Broder. 2007. FBI says guards killed 14 Iraqis without cause. *New York Times,* November 14.

Lane, D. 2006. Hierarchy, complexity, society. In *Hierarchy in Natural and Social Sciences,* ed. Denise Pumain, 81–119. Dordrecht: Springer.

Military Extraterritorial Jurisdiction Act. 2000. 18 U.S.C. §3261.

Naylor, S. 2009. Trigger-happy security complicates convoys. *Army Times*, November 29. www.army-times.com/news/2009/11/army_convoy_security_112909w/.

Osborne, D., and T. Gaebler. 1992. *Reinventing Government: How the Entrepreneurial Spirit Is Transforming the Public Sector.* Reading, MA: Addison-Wesley.

Peters, W.C. 2006. On law, wars, and mercenaries: The case for courts-martial jurisdiction over civilian contractor misconduct in Iraq. *Brigham Young University Law Review*, 2, 367–414.

Peterson, L. 2002. Privatizing combat, the new world order. Center for Public Integrity, October 28. http://projects.publicintegrity.org/bow/report.aspx?aid=148/.

Pincus, Walter. 2010. The cost of security for Americans who stay in Iraq when troops leave will be high. *Washington Post*, November 29, A19.

Radia, K. 2009. Controversial Blackwater security firm gets Iraq contract extended by State Department. *ABC News.com*, September 1. http://abcnews.go.com/Blotter/Blackwater/Story?id=8466369.

Raghavan, S., and J. White. 2007. Blackwater guards fired at fleeing cars, soldiers say. *Washington Post*, October 12, A01.

Rice, C. 2010. Address delivered at Hamilton College. Clinton, New York, November 1.

Savas, E.S. 1982. *Privatizing the Public Sector.* Chatham, NJ: Chatham House.

Schwartz, Moshe and Joyprada Swain. 2011. Department of Defense contractors in Afghanistan and Iraq: Background and Analysis. CRS Report for Congress, 7–5700, R40764, Congressional Research Service, May 13.

Simmons, G. 2007. Rep. Henry Waxman levels tax fraud allegations against Blackwater. Fox News, October 23. www.foxnews.com/story/0,2933,304221,00.html.

Singer, P.W. 2008. *Corporate Warriors: The Rise of the Privatized Military Industry.* Ithaca: Cornell University Press.

Smith, Adam. 1767. *The Theory of Moral Sentiments*, 3d ed. London: Millar, Kincaid, and Bell.

Thurnher, J. S. 2008. Drowning in Blackwater: how weak accountability over private security contractors significantly undermines counterinsurgency efforts. *Army Lawyer*, July, at 64.

Tiefler, C. 2009. No More Nisour Squares: Legal Control of Private Security Contractors in Iraq and After. *Oregon Law Review*, 88, 3, 745–775.

United Nations. 1989. *International Convention Against the Recruitment, Use, Financing, and Training of Mercenaries*. December 4. Article I, §1, (c)–(e).

U.S. Army. 2008. *Field Manual 3–0: Operations*. February. http://downloads.army.mil/fm3–0/FM3–0. pdf.

U.S. Department of Defense (DoD). 2006. Defense Federal Acquisition Regulation Supplement; Contractor Personnel Authorized to Accompany U.S. Armed Forces (DFARS Case 2005–D013). *Federal Register*, 71, 116 (June 16).

U.S. Department of State. 2005. Contract for Security Services: Blackwater, DynCorp, and Triple Canopy. Bureau of Diplomatic Security, Worldwide Personal Protective Services (WPPS) Program II, July.

U.S.-Iraq Status of Forces Agreement (SOFA). 2008. Article 12, Section 2, p. 10. November 17. http://graphics8.nytimes.com/packages/pdf/world/20081119_SOFA_FINAL_AGREED_TEXT.pdf.

Vogel, S., and R. Merle. 2007. Privatized Walter Reed workforce gets scrutiny. *Washington Post*, March 20, A3.

von Zielbauer, P., and J. Glanz. 2007. Under siege, Blackwater takes on air of bunker. *New York Times*, October 24, A1.

Walker, D. 2008. Stabilizing and Rebuilding Iraq: Actions Needed to Address Inadequate Accountability over U.S. Efforts and Investments. Testimony Before the Senate Committee on Appropriations, March 11.

Williams, T. 2009. U.S. won't renew Blackwater's contract in Iraq. *New York Times,* February 9, A1.

16

Devolution

Larry M. Zwain

It's not an unfamiliar story. A strong organizational concept developed in conjunction with unique cultural attributes promises not only profit but a change in the way business is done. Yet in revolutionizing the modern business model, greeted with fanfare and acclaim in the media, the expectations of phenomenal performance can exceed reality. Whether with whole or partial intent or as an incremental slide beyond unethical to evil, some organizations are unable to maintain the entrepreneurial zeal with which they began and resort to tactics of financial "impression" management. Such tactics, which unethical and might be illegal, create and sustain a culture of evil that decimates careers, fortunes, reputations, and lives. The case presented here is a real-world example of how this occurred in a company that readers might know well. The discussion that follows is based on published reports and contacts with an executive who had a firsthand view of the entire operation. It is a useful study in how an organization in whom investors and employees alike had high hopes devolved into an exemplar of evil.

BACKGROUND

In the mid-1980s, Boston Chicken (BCI, later changed to Boston Market) offered a new way of eating home-style meals in a fast food environment: dine in or take out. The owners had a vision of creating a whole new segment in the highly competitive fast-food restaurant industry: take-out food that tasted as if it were cooked at home, or what they called "Home Meal Replacement." By basing their menu on rotisserie chicken and offering take out, they would have several existing, large-scale restaurant chain competitors, such as KFC, as well as supermarkets seeking to expand their ready-to-eat offerings. The success of Boston Chicken after its acquisition by two ex-Blockbuster senior execs depended on its ability to expand rapidly, develop name recognition, and essentially engage in three businesses: operating restaurants, selling and supporting franchises, and financing area development. They built a solid and innovative operating organization with strong support from the headquarters and somewhat unique franchising and accounting systems.

Boston Market achieved many of its early goals and expanded to number more than eleven hundred restaurants more rapidly than any other restaurant chain in history. To do so, it underwrote "financed area developers" (FADs), backed by systems support from the Support Center (HQ), including a unique program of sizable loans from the company to help developers finance new restaurants. The business was applauded by Wall Street investors for its rapid expansion from thirty-four stores in June 1992, when it was acquired (the IPO in November 1993 listed at $20 per share, went to $54 per share and closing at $48 per share for the third largest IPO in history, yielding over $130 million), to one thousand stores in November 1996. The firm reported increasing revenues and earnings through 1996, with reported $0.63 EPS in 1995 and $0.90 in 1996. Yet in October 1998 the company filed for voluntary bankruptcy, with over $900 million in debt. Soon, two senior company executives were alleged to have violated certain federal and state securities laws. The executives were alleged to have issued "false and misleading public statements relating to [Boston Chicken's] business position and future prospects" (Boston Chicken, Inc. Securities Litigation).

The following is a description of how questionable practices developed to create a seemingly progressive and inventive organization, while at the same time orchestrating a scheme that many investors believe bilked out of them over $1 billion and simultaneously funding a few senior executives' personal goals. Investors claimed that BCI execs devised/executed a scheme/expansion plan to take a business (fast-food restaurants) and structure it in a fashion that permitted them to hide losses while retaining revenues to lure in more investors by reporting sensational profits as the expansion plan unfolded at an exceptional rate. The result was a class action lawsuit filed on behalf of all persons who purchased or otherwise acquired BCI stock or debt securities.

HISTORY

BCI's impetus was, on the one hand, to provide customers with an alternative to existing fast food choices and, on the other, to offer them a way to have a meal close in quality to what they could have at home without the time and effort of doing it themselves after a long day at work. It began in 1985 with marinated chicken roasted in brick-fired ovens accompanied by a choice of side dishes, such as mashed potatoes, vegetables, and corn bread. The first small store opened in Newton, Massachusetts, and it did not take long before people were lining up to get in. The *Boston Globe* raved that it attracted customers from all over the Boston area. By 1992, thirty-three stores were in operation, with sales exceeding $22 million.

Scott Beck and Saad Nadhir were young "chain-store capitalists" who saw Boston Chicken as a way to transform their prior learning into their very own gold rush. Beck saw his father co-found the waste and environmental services company which became Waste Management, Inc. (WMI) by aggressively purchasing many smaller garbage collection services across the United States to become one of the leading companies in its sector. Beck later became an early franchisee of Blockbuster Video (1985), and then, learning from his father's examples, rapidly built, acquired and converted more units until becoming Vice Chairman/COO of the entire chain by 1989. Nadhir was Blockbuster's SVP-International Development.

FRANCHISING AND GROWTH

The WMI and Blockbuster experiences inculcated in Beck and Nadhir a realization of the truly transformative power of profitable growth: new jobs in the communities and wealth for shareholders. They believed that their efforts could take a company "beyond the ordinary." Rather running than a company where employees would work only to collect paychecks, they envisioned a more stimulating environment, in which employees would find a higher purpose in their work. They wanted to provide an environment where both the company and the individual would thrive and their collective and personal energies would contribute to an overarching sense of purpose. They both believed in the intoxicating experience of being on a winning team and believed that growing companies would attract the best talent.

Rapid growth would be their most compelling case for going beyond the ordinary. Having had hands-on experiences as franchisees and franchisors, they learned the reasons for the success of franchising, which provides a "turnkey" package for entrepreneurial dreams:

1. brand recognition: professionally produced marketing materials, consumer, research, new product development, promotions, merchandising, etc.;
2. proven business models: the success of existing stores (as expressed in uniform franchise operating circulars), consistent operating, purchasing, and distribution systems;
3. training and ongoing support; and
4. occupancy standards: building prototypes, equipment standards, known capital costs, real estate packages, etc.

In short, Beck and Nadhir saw for themselves how the theory of franchising can work in practice, in which franchisees have higher success rates than nonfranchise business owners who have to start their business "from the ground up." Aside from more rapid growth, the franchisor could also expect:

1. After building the concept, infrastructure, and support systems, franchisors save on general and administrative overhead costs (G&A) and capital by selling franchises, collecting fees (per store), royalties, and marketing funds—and the franchisees add the overhead and raise their own capital.
2. A new and critical difference: To encourage franchise "partners" who have a wealth of retail or food service experience and keep the franchisees focused on operations, by allowing them to rely on the Company to raise the capital (instead of the individual "partner" as was the conventional practice) so the "partners" (franchisees) could spend time opening and operating stores.
3. Franchising—but in a different way—"Financed Area Developers" (FADs):
   - Large exclusive territories to attract more experienced operators with bigger visions than ordinary "mom and pop" or single-unit operators of most of the existing, heavily franchised retail brands (e.g., McDonald's, Subway, Dairy Queen)

- All FADs partially financed by the company:
  - Company raises money and lends back to FADs in the form of a convertible loan
  - Company owns much of the real estate
  - FADs pay royalties, new store fees, marketing, interest, and accounting fees to keep a strong "growth culture"
- Company financing convertible into two-thirds ownership of FAD organizations
- "Support Center" run by the Company to support FADs, to "free them up" so they can run the stores

As they built the organization, Mark Stephens, an executive with investment banking expertise, recognized immediately that he could use this unique financing method to raise easy money and profit handsomely from it. (Later, Mark would become chief financial officer and vice chairman.)

GROWTH STRATEGY

In 1991 Boston Chicken had fifteen to seventeen stores in second-rate locations that maintained fairly substandard operational quality and systems. Yet even with these drawbacks each of the individual stores averaged from $900,000 to $1 million a year in sales, a very respectable performance at the time. Beck and Nadhir sought to gain control of the company and to realize their transformative power of growth theory. They organized an investment group, acquired Boston Chicken—which had grown to thirty-four stores by the time they gained control—and followed Beck's notion of *fast, good, cheap* as their growth strategy (Prewitt, 1995).

In developing a "brand strategy," they polled Boston Chicken customers, who stated that what they liked was the quality of "casual dining" with the convenience of fast food—"quick, quality meals." When asked, "Where would you have eaten dinner if not at Boston Chicken?" respondents predominantly mentioned "mom." Many customers responded that they would usually get takeout from grocery stores, deli counters, Chinese restaurants, or pizza parlors, but now found that Boston Chicken gave them the kind of quality and convenience of "home cooking" that they could not find anywhere else. Realizing that success requires constant adaptation, Beck and Nadhir first decided to change the name from Boston Chicken to Boston Market to indicate their larger vision. After the acquisition, a newly recruited inventive team surveyed customers and talked with potential franchisees, who expressed the view that to avoid having potential customers in three- or four-person families decide to go elsewhere because the restaurant offered only one main protein—rotisserie chicken—more choices should be available. Thus they added new entrees—turkey, ham, and meatloaf—and renaming the store would showcase the new expanded offerings. To further broaden its appeal beyond the usual fast food menu, they would also increase the number of side dishes (e.g., steamed vegetables, zucchini marinara, mashed potatoes, creamed spinach), which had the additional benefit of addressing the needs of more health-conscious customers.

- According to Beck, *fast* growth was important to gain critical mass and to achieve efficiencies in such areas as advertising, recruiting, distribution, and operations. *Good:* he believed that tasty food was critical in developing a loyal customer base and ensuring continued success. *Cheap* referred to the need to be able to be profitable on a per-store basis without sacrificing quality.

CORPORATE CULTURE

Boston Market's headquarters, or "the Support Center" as it was called, employed almost six hundred people in Golden, Colorado. Beck and Nadir defined the culture as one of "trust, loyalty and hard work, goals that go beyond money, which allows each of us to focus on different things at the same time in order to accelerate value creation. We don't have to worry about the others' ability to get things done." Yet, according to *Nation's Restaurant News*, "despite those attributes, Beck and Nadhir do indeed work from a motive common to many other executive leaders—profit. But it is a unique focus on shareholder value and ways to generate profit that shapes the organization" (Howard, 1996, 156). Senior executives sat at open work stations rather than in offices, coffee areas had couches and memo boards for spontaneous brainstorming sessions, and conference rooms had floor-to-ceiling glass walls. In addition to the physical setting, the atmosphere at the Support Center was casual: The dress code did not require suits, the office phone directory was alphabetized by first names rather than last, and framed pictures of every full- and part-time Support Center employee hung on the walls of the building's entrance. Furthermore, amenities such as a children's playroom (called "Chickasic Park") for parents who needed to bring children to work after day care ended and a "quiet room" for employees to relax in were part of Boston Market's employee-focused culture.

Employees at the Support Center were enthusiastic about working for Boston Market. Pride stemmed from not only believing in the company's well-publicized statements and in the quality of the products provided but also from the company's belief in hard work and having fun. For example, a position was created for a director of community and culture, and the person who filled it was also seen as the "class president." Her role was to help people enjoy working by encouraging participation in company-sponsored activities and charitable and philanthropic events and to produce a company yearbook, including a picture of each person in the company, news clips, stories about ongoing projects, and company picnic photos. The idea was to help generate excitement and pride in working together for Boston Market. Beck believed that having a strong company culture was important: Happy employees generate satisfied customers. Boston Market's strong culture was also reflected in the compensation structure, which included both bonuses and stock options for everyone. Bonuses were tied to preroyalty cash flow as a short-term incentive, while stock options were used as a long-term "golden handcuff" to keep individuals at the company. "Golden handcuff" is a slang term to describe incentives given (often to senior executives) to discourage resignation and ensure long-term "loyalty" after departure. It was unusual to use stock options as liberally as BCI did with stock options for everyone.

Beck believed that giving employees equity resulted in an organization where everyone was motivated to achieve the same goal.

Technology was also integral to the culture. In fact, the company received a Smithsonian Award in 1995 for technological innovations. Instead of a lagging information system, which inhibited the growth of many businesses, Boston Market utilized technology to fuel growth. Data management capabilities were shared with employees and managers. For example, store operators could compare their results with those at other stores, and if an operator noticed an area where another store had managed to achieve greater savings, then that individual could contact that store manager directly for help:

- Intellistore: a software package to allow sales and cost data (and customer comments) to be downloaded from stores. Can be used to analyze information and assist managers in scheduling labor, tracking inventory, and managing production.
- Boston Notes: an adaptation of Lotus Notes, can be used in the day-to-day business; for example, allows area developers access to most of the marketing and operations projects in their developmental stages. Can also schedule all recurring meetings on the system with automatic notifications to each participant for new day, time or location, eliminating too much call time or secretary time.
- Point-of-Sale Systems (POS): includes communications, accounting and office automation software. Proprietary technology developed in 1992 to eliminate a large paper trail used to manage the stores. Saves managers hours of time each week.

In 1993, Mark Stephens joined the team, having already proven himself successful in raising capital to fund Boston Chicken's growth. The attractiveness of Boston Chicken's organizational model, combined with Stephens's creativity in raising funds, created market expectations that excited investors. But the combination of a spectacular initial public offering (IPO), glowing public offering documents, and unique structure concealed FADs' financial results from public view, and the concealment had corrupted the people inside the Support Center whose enthusiastically spun stories turned out to be more like fairytales.

STRUCTURED REPORTING AND ACCOUNTING SYSTEMS

A key operating rule and technology-simplification standard at Boston Market was a "performance measurement system," whose purpose was to monitor information and provide real-time feedback from every aspect of the company (Support Center employees, operating partners, store employees, customers, shareholders, and competitive information). It was thought that by providing store managers, FADs, and executive decision-makers with systems and processes for fixing problems before they affected the bottom line, Boston Market's ability to satisfy shareholders would be enhanced (Howard, 1996).

One example of Boston Market's use of technology and infrastructure systems is the implementation process of the company's accounting system. The idea was to create a system that was concept independent and multiunit, with cost per store to be no more than $250 per period (in five years or less). A full-service accounting system was created for each FAD and its outlet that included all general-ledger activities, sales accounting, accounts payable, fixed assets, payroll, and treasury. They leveraged the buying power of the combined FADs to deliver benefits, property and liability insurance, and other programs with service coverage and cost savings that would greatly exceed what the FADs could individually negotiate. The rationale for creating such a system was that Boston Market's FADs were designed to be operators rather than builders of systems and accounting infrastructures. In effect, the Boston Market FADs would be outsourcing their accounting function to the Support Center so that they and their store managers could concentrate on more value-added activities.

FINANCED AREA DEVELOPERS

By 1996 franchise chains accounted for roughly 25 percent of U.S. restaurant outlets and 43 percent of industry sales. There were about 110,000 franchised chain outlets in the United States, including McDonald's, Burger King, Wendy's, KFC, and Pizza Hut. As discussed, the benefit of franchising is that participating stores have the ability to rapidly expand brand-name recognition without the parent company's bearing the full cost of acquiring land, buildings, or equipment. The franchisee typically bears these costs and pays the parent company a royalty fee of between 3 percent and 6 percent of sales. Franchisees also typically contribute 4 percent of sales to advertising. In return, the parent company usually provides training, marketing support, and so forth. Boston Market, rather than using the typical individual and small multi-unit sales operators, instead utilized an "area developer" strategy. The idea of area developers had been used before, but Boston Market applied the strategy to achieve what was then unprecedented growth (see Table 16.1 for number of stores and sales by year). While most restaurant franchisers typically sold a maximum of twenty units to an individual operator, each Boston Market developer was required to commit to between thirty-five and a hundred units over a three- to five-year period (minimum thirty-five to forty stores) (Steinberg, 1994).

Boston Market used strict criteria in choosing area developers. Each had to have at least fifteen years of experience in multi-unit retail/restaurant operation or local real estate. In addition to providing evidence that the local area developer could assemble a qualified team to work in the territory, becoming an area developer also required raising between $2 million to $5 million in equity capital (see Table 16.2 for summary of store operation cost).

Selling the selection idea to eventual franchisees was like recruiting for an elite college: as many as a hundred applicants might vie for only ten or so spots. When asked, "How do you open so many stores in a year?" they answered: "no one is—all of the partners are!" There were approximately fourteen core partners, and fifteen to twenty stores opened each year for each partner. The Support Center would assist them, but the FAD was where the action really took place. The partners had the wealth of retail and food service experience—Boston Chicken would raise the capital so that the partners could spend time opening and operating stores. The vision was a $5

Table 16.1

Boston Market Sales, 1990–1996

Year	Stores	System Retail Sales ($)
1990	13	8.2 million
1991	29	20.8 million
1992	82	42.7 million
1993	217	154 million
1994	534	383.7 million
1995	829	729.9 million
1996	1,075	1.25 billion

Table 16.2

Individual Boston Market Store Operation Costs

Development Cost	$700–$750k w/out land $1.2–$1.5 million w/ land
Typical Sales	$1 million (annually)
Operating Income	$135,200 (~13% of sales)
Typical Size	3,000 sq ft (retail)
Staff Required	20–60 people
Number of Seats	50–70
Franchise Fees	$35k per store 5% royalty 2% national adv fee 4% local adv fee $16.5k per store accounting/software fees

Source: Romeo, 1994, 100.

billion brand providing outstanding service and value to the customer, employees, and shareholders.

The economics of the FADs were as follows (Smith Barney 1996, 21):

1. Each FAD puts up 25 percent of the required capital, and Boston Market supplies the remaining 75 percent in the form of a note bearing an interest rate typically 1 percent above the company's cost of borrowing (with the option to convert the note into a two-thirds equity interest in the FAD stores after two years).
2. The conversion price is typically at a 12 percent to 15 percent premium over the equity investment made by the FAD.
3. If the conversion occurs, the FAD may or may not continue to operate and develop the restaurants, depending on the agreement that is reached.
4. Individually, the FADs benefit by contributing no more than 25 percent of the original capital while retaining a 33 percent equity interest if they are converted.

5. Once converted, the stores' operating results are consolidated on Boston Market's financial statements and the FAD's equity interest is reflected as a minority interest.

STORE ECONOMICS

In the restaurant industry, store economics are dominated by high fixed costs such as land, building, utilities, equipment, and interest expenses. Due to the service nature of the business, labor is largely a fixed cost as well. Store payroll expenses, including benefits, combined with cost-of-goods (COGS) such as food, beverage, and paper costs, typically account for about 60 percent of gross sales. After subtracting other costs including utilities, advertising, occupancy, and maintenance expenses, as well as royalties and franchise services fees, the restaurant industry average pretax profit is approximately 7 percent of sales. As a result, the key determinant of profitability is the sales level in the store. Because Boston Market concentrated on *fast* growth and *good* food *cheap* during the early growth stages, Beck's overarching strategy of "fast, good, cheap" may have come at a high price (see Table 16.3) (Brown, 1996, 4).

Boston Market had stores profitable at $1.265m annual unit volume as shown in Table 16.3 level of sales, and several franchisee stores exceeded this level. Boston Chicken's fast growth received an enviable amount of free media plugs from hit TV shows as well as in popular novels. For example, in an episode of a popular NBC sitcom of the time, "The Single Guy," the star's father says he had few regrets in life: "not spending more time with his son and not investing in Boston Chicken stock." With the positive focus on their company, BCI leadership wanted to expand beyond Boston Market. In August 1996, Boston Market publicly announced goals to triple the number of stores to 3,600 within seven years. Beck, Nadhir, and Stephens also wanted to replicate Boston Market's rapid expansion and FAD strategy by starting up "Progressive Bagel Concepts." By combining three very successful regional bagel companies (Offerdahl's, Bagel & Bagel, Brackman Brothers), buying two more (Baltimore Bagel, Bagel Shop), and creating an "instantly" consolidated national chain named "Einstein Brothers Bagel Company," they quickly became one of the top two leading chains in the "bagel sector" of the restaurant business. Using Boston Chicken to make a convertible loan to help the bagel company get started and vowing to expand Einstein's just as quickly as Boston Market—with a similar culture, Support Center, structured reporting, accounting, and FADs—Beck said, "I believe in investing to create a future." Investors, employees, and partners had watched Beck do it before—and they believed he could do it again. In fact, by 1999, BCI predicted that it would be a $3 billion giant with an 18 percent margin. Investors bought into the ideas, pouring $1.4 billion in equity financing into the firm. A finicky market sent BCI's stock plummeting by about 30 percent from its March 1996 high of $37 a share, but with news of the expansion plans as well as the Einstein's IPO boosted the shares to regain $34 a share by August.

The BCI system's retail sales grew from $42.7 million at the time of the 1992 acquisition to over $1 billion by the end of 1996 (see Table 16.1). The stock price soared as the company reported high earnings, and many investors favored the FAD concept. Despite

Table 16.3

Boston Market Potential Unit Economics ($000)

Average Unit Volume	$1,265	
Expenses		
Food & Paper	443	35%
Payroll	304	24%
Other Operating	164	13%
Ops Margin (pre-occupancy)	354	28%
Rent Expense	76	6%
Depreciation	63	5%
Ops Margin (after occupancy)	215	17%
Total Unit Investment (including land)	$1,150	
Operating Return on Investment		30.8%

its somewhat novel financial structure and aggressive accounting practices, the company showed reported earnings growing from $1.6 million in 1993 to over $34 million in 1995 on $159 million in revenues. Of course, there are no sure things in the stock market—but the case was being made by BCI and some investors that "if you're not in the stock now, you're going to miss the move."

Yet by 1996, some on Wall Street had their doubts. Some analysts suggested that the volume of loans Boston Market was making to the FADs was excessive and being used to cover losses at the operating level. In addition, these analysts believed that the profitability of the company was dependent on the revenue generated from the loans to the FADs. They noted that the 1995 loans to franchisees generated 21 percent of BCI's revenue—including $33.25 million in interest income—while royalty fees generated another 22 percent of revenue (or $35 million) and franchise fees totaled $13.7 million. In summary, a prominent restaurant research industry analyst, Roger Lipton, said the financial reports from BCI "have substantially subverted their story; I've never seen a company come as close to lying. They've got a cash-flow sinkhole" (Schine, 1996). He and other analysts argued that Boston Market's FADs constantly needed more cash because costs were too high and sales were too low.

As shown in Table 16.3, the stores that averaged about $24,000 per week in sales did quite well. But with the rapid growth, fewer of the stores operated by the FADs were "mature" enough to achieve the $24,000 per week level of sales. In fact, of the stores that appeared to approach the ideal level, numbers were inflated by including free-meal coupons for employees, promotions, and other discounts, which other restaurant chains include as "gross sales"—but deduct the "promotions and allowances" to report "net sales." If reported this way, Boston Market's net sales fell to roughly $21,500 per week. The company was also selective in the way that its numbers were disclosed. Being organized around fourteen regional franchise companies, rather than hundreds of small franchisees that other chains typically have, BCI did not report clear, systemwide numbers that showed sales and operating results at existing stores.

In reality, franchisees suffered significant operating losses. Their rapid pace growth resulted in soaring operating losses. The FADs, supported by "loans" from BCI, paid back huge royalties and fees, causing operating losses that were hidden by BCI. Such operating losses jumped from $51.3 million in 1994 to more than $158.5 million in 1996 and $325 million in 1997, while BCI was retaining the revenues long enough to lure investor monies with reports of sensational profits. BCI reported $800 million in revenue for 1996, but kept the losses to themselves, essentially displaying "a charade of profits" (Corrigan, 1998). Average annual losses for each store jumped from $54,750 to $180,400, totaling over $200 million in just three years. The company took the position that it had no obligation to report the operating losses from "independent area developers" (FADs). With the rapid growth and rising operating losses BCI's loans to FADs also ballooned. Loans jumped from $200 million in early 1995 to $550 million by July 1996. Many of the FADs had exhausted their original equity capital. BCI was covering the growing operating losses by piling on loan after loan, "basically recirculating money raised from . . . shareholders . . . and claiming it as profit" (Corrigan, 1998). Beck made the argument that the losses were nothing more than expected start-up costs tied to rushing out a new national restaurant brand with a new kind of speed. Individual "mature" stores were said to making "buckets of money," but rapid expansion required big capital outlays, pushing some area developers into the red.

By 1998, the impact of the big loans, combined with store operating losses, caused the company to crash. Proper reporting had been sidestepped for a long time through the alchemy of BCI accounting systems. Even senior executives at the Boston Market brand and FADs could not see all the hidden numbers. The securities litigation that grew out of these schemes alleged that Stephens and Nadhir had "devised and executed a scheme to take a business—fast food stores—and structure it in a fashion that permitted them to" (Boston Chicken, Inc., Securities Litigation) hide the losses described above. The FAD system of "purportedly independent marketing affiliates" was viewed as a key mechanism of the scheme. As stated in *The Motley Fool* (Corrigan, 1998), BCI was more like a finance company than a restaurant chain. Shareholders lost their money, employees lost jobs at headquarters as well as at the restaurants that were closed, debt was refinanced, and thousands were negatively affected. A court-appointed trustee filed a financial malpractice and negligence lawsuit accusing the company of defrauding bondholders and creditors. The investors were left with $900 million in losses when the company filed for bankruptcy in 1998, making it one of the decade's greatest financial disasters (Corrigan, 1998). An amended version of the original complaint was filed that added damage claims for alleged violations of Colorado's racketeering laws.

The 180-page complaint filed against BCI details, with striking similarities to the Enron saga and many other prominent cases of investor bilking, the $1 billion financial implosion of the once-high-flying company before its remaining 750 stores were sold to McDonald's for $176 million in May 2000. Defendants included Arthur Andersen—the same Big Five accounting firm that handled Enron's questionable accounting and auditing practices. Unusually blurry accounting, recklessly rapid growth, and a culture built on the pride of its own inventiveness devolved into showing profit at all costs, with the expectation that some day a good story might be told.

REFERENCES

Boston Chicken, Inc. Securities Litigation. U.S. District Court re District of Colorado Civil Action No. 97-CV-1308-WDM "Claims of Plaintiffs."

Brown, Alex. 1996. Analyst's report: Boston Market. January 4, 4. Internal publication.

Corrigan, L. 1998. Fool on the Hill: An investment opinion—A chicken autopsy. *Motley Fool*, October 7. www.fool.com/EveningNews/foth/1998/foth981007.htm.

Howard, T. 1996. Scott Beck and Saad Nadhir: Entrepreneurial partners balance each other as they glide along the cutting edge. *Nation's Restaurant News*, October 9, 156.

Prewitt, M. 1995. Scott Beck: Chairman, chief executive, Boston Chicken, Golden, Colorado. *Nation's Restaurant News*, January 1. http://findarticles.com/p/articles/mi_m3190/is_nSPEISS_v29/ai_16376493/.

Romeo, Peter. 1994. What's so special about Boston Chicken? *Restaurant Business*, April 10, 100.

Schine, E. 1996. The squawk over Boston Chicken. *Business Week*, October 21. www.businessweek.com/1996/43/b3498139.htm.

Serwer, A.E. 1994. Lessons from America's fastest-growing companies. *Fortune*, August 8, 45. http://money.cnn.com/magazines/fortune/fortune_archive/1994/08/08/79610/index.htm.

Smith Barney. 1996. Analyst's Report. February 9. Internal publication.

Steinberg, C. 1994. A chicken in every pot: Boston Chicken's strategy for lightning growth. *Success*, April, 66.

17

Organizational Systemic Factors of Evil in an Academic University Culture

Geri Miller

We must all learn to live together as brothers or we will perish together as fools.

—Martin Luther King Jr.

This chapter provides a theoretical framework of the expression of evil in academic culture. Specifically, it offers the reader: (a) a definition of organizational evil within the context of academia, (b) a framework that names and describes the factors of organizational evil in a university setting, and (c) based on this framework, possible actions that can be taken by faculty in response to such evil.

RATIONALE FOR DEVELOPMENT OF A FRAMEWORK

Before defining organizational evil, it is necessary to discuss the rationale for writing such a chapter and the dangers in doing so. The goal is to provide the faculty member reading this chapter with a framework for understanding what has happened to him/her, to his/her loved ones or colleagues in an academic setting, or what may occur to a faculty member in an academic environment. This is not meant to be a venue of personal vendettas, in which individuals, departments, or institutions are named as inherently evil. Rather, it is meant to assist the reader in understanding the dynamics of organizational evil so that a basis for healing from such evil can be consciously formed.

Writing on this topic can have three dangers. First, the reader might say, "What happened to the author to cause such an interest in this topic?" The author, who has more than twenty years of experience as a faculty member, has heard stories from other faculty members both nationally and internationally that reflect a lack of humanity in academic settings—stories in which faculty have been bruised, wounded, and, unfortunately, in some cases even psychologically/spiritually destroyed by the culture of academia. Although such organizational evil cannot be eliminated, one can prevent it, inhibit it, or at least heal from it, by understanding its occurrence, formation, and expression. There is power in naming (Branch and Miller, 2006). In addition, the author tired of reading anecdotal stories of harmful experiences (some of which were full of blaming, venting, and "finger-pointing") and found some common themes in the stories that, if identified, could be helpful to faculty in facing and responding to organizational evil.

Second, the reader, upon initial exposure to this topic, might state, "This does *not* happen at my university (college/department)." The reader is encouraged to remain open-minded because: (a) an expression of evil may have occurred, but the reader might be unaware of it; or (b) if it has not occurred, its dynamics can be understood so that it may be prevented.

Third, there seems to be a tendency to view evil and violence as extremes. This chapter encourages both the discussion and examination of organizational evil, and the violence through which it is expressed, on a continuum. The discussion and examination occurs through the presentation of a framework through which to view the academic setting for such dynamics.

DEFINITIONS

Organizational evil is defined here as the evil that occurs within an organization.

What, then, is evil? Miller and Hood describe "evil" as:

> behavior that causes suffering in others whether it is intended, motivated, or accidental, and the perpetrator of the evil action has lost the sense of humanness in oneself and others. This reflects the perspective, then, that all humans have the capacity for evil action and does not attempt to label the person, but rather label the act, as evil. (2006, 357)

Evil is a possible outcome of fear. When we experience fear, the action that we choose to protect ourselves has the potential to be evil, the potential to act inhumanely toward others.

In academic circles, there may be a hesitation in naming evil because it is not a neutral term but, rather, reflects the view of the definer (Miller and Hood, 2006). Evil exists in a context, and the word may be necessary to explain the unexplainable experience of evil (Miller and Hood, 2006). Russell (1988) describes three types of evil (metaphysical, natural, moral), one of which, moral, is described in this chapter. Moral evil is evil in which one person knowingly inflicts suffering on others.

"Organizational evil," then, is moral evil that occurs within an organization. The organization discussed here is academia. The organizational evil in academia is explored as expressed in academic violence. Although violence can be experienced by administrators, faculty, and staff in a university setting, its impact on faculty is explored here. "Academic violence" is a combination of personal behaviors and systemic practices deriving from power and influence that are misused and experienced by the faculty member as demeaning (Lee and Leonard, 2001). Miller et al. (2009) define academic violence as a degree of "meanness" in order to encourage the view of it on a continuum. The authors also describe it as behavior that violates someone else's human rights. The personal behaviors and systemic practices of academic violence are explored within the factors of the framework following the presentation of the overall theoretical framework.

ORGANIZATIONAL EVIL AS EXPRESSED IN ACADEMIC VIOLENCE

Monahan and Steadman (1996) presented a risk assessment of violence using the analogy of a weather pattern. A summary of this analogy is presented here within the context of organizational evil as expressed through academic violence.

Predicting the weather has temporal specificity, meaning that it is short term and requires frequent assessments. It is also context specific in that it predicts behaviors. In order for hazards related to the weather to be predicted, information is needed on the variables and emergency managers are needed to suggest public precautions. The main goal is to maximize chances for people to get out of harm's way. Organizational evil in academia is proposed to have the same dynamics of temporal specificity and context specificity and the need for information on variables in order to prevent harm.

Weather forecasts can be similar to organizational evil in that they can occur for a specific time period, in a specific area, and with a degree of hazard certainty. Forecasts come in three possible levels: (a) no message, (b) watch, and (c) warning. In a *watch*, the situation is closely monitored and one prepares for action, while a *warning* recommends that immediate action is taken to prevent harm from occurring. The latter two levels have both a descriptive aspect (the forecast is time, area, and certainty specific) and a prescriptive aspect (additional information is needed and risk management strategies are presented).

This chapter details factors that can be explored for the additional information needed to predict the weather pattern of organizational evil as expressed in academic violence as well as proposed risk management strategies that can be taken to maximize the chances for individual faculty to get out of harm's way. Within this framework, a *watch* describes a situation with a lower risk that organizational evil will be expressed in academic violence, and a *warning* describes a situation in which there is high risk of the expression of organizational evil in academic violence. A *watch* and a *warning* include the same contributing factors and risk management strategies but to different degrees. The difference in degree creates a continuum of contributing factors and risk management strategies.

CONTRIBUTING FACTORS

Three areas of contributing factors are examined here: individual categories (bullies, victims, witnesses, leaders), organizational tendencies, and academic tendencies. According to the weather analogy, these contributing factors require the garnering of additional information in order to determine whether a *watch* or *warning* forecast will be given and, therefore, the action that needs to be taken.

Individual

Buber (1970) discusses the "I-It" interaction: The perpetrator of violence views the other person as an object, thereby legitimizing disrespectful and hurtful treatment of them as nonhuman.

Three roles are viewed from this perspective: bullies, victims, and witnesses. Academic violence, focusing on individual components, is anchored in a bullying perspective because of the similarities in the dynamics. For example, a participant in a presentation on academic violence relayed a story about his young son's response to an academic experience he had as a faculty member:

> At the end of a work day, his child asked him, "What are you upset about?" He shared a brief sketch of a painful work experience that happened that day. His son replied, "Sounds like the meanness I face from the bullies at school." That simple response, that simple definition, helped him name the violence that he might have otherwise dismissed and assisted in breaking his denial about the violence he was experiencing. (Miller et al., 2009)

Hixon summarizes the research on bullying. Bullies have high status and power while victims have low status and power. Bullying tactics used are "making threats, insulting, becoming violent, and ridiculing" (2009, 262). Bullies use aggression to save face or increase self-esteem, status, or power. Bullying behavior and tactics that are autocratic in nature are used by individuals who have a high degree of power or social status. Witnesses share group-level psychological relationships and view victims as members of out-groups, thereby legitimizing the bullies' attacks on victims.

Leaders also have the potential to be bullies. Those who encourage chaos and conditions conducive to bullying make decisions that are capricious, based on limited facts, have a specific focus, and apply rules to a targeted group/individual (Herbst, 1999).

In this framework, individuals should examine themselves and colleagues to determine which of the roles they fit: bullies, victims, witnesses, or leaders. Each role is necessary for organizational evil as expressed in academic violence to occur. Systems need a check and balance to monitor for power differentials for faculty in academia and to monitor for ineffective leaders. At the same time, employees in the organization should avoid being "seduced" into viewing individuals from a stereotypical perspective, for example, blaming the victim. Power differentials are sometimes demonstrated in obvious ways, such as tenured and nontenured status, but having this status does not guarantee that someone has a specific level of power or status. For example, a tenured professor may have job security, but have low status and power within the system from a relational perspective. Perhaps additional information should be gathered whenever there is obvious conflict between faculty members or administrators regarding these four roles. Additional information on status, power, autocracy, and belonging can assist in predicting the level of academic violence.

Organizational Tendencies

Resnicow and Page (2008) describe some organizations as complex and adaptive, involving multiple components—meaning that the whole is greater than the sum of its parts. Within such organizations, the authors state that changes are not linear and predictable because the change process is sensitive to the initial conditions and is highly variable and hard to predict—that is, these organizations operate like the weather. Other organizational factors that lend themselves to the expression of violence are the lack of mutual respect, shared responsibility, and social inclusion (Ahmed, 2008), which invites aggressive, violent behaviors between members of academia. Finally, an environment characterized by chaotic decisions, arbitrary application of rules, and the absence of independent reviews and enforcement can lend itself to the expression of organizational evil (Herbst, 1999).

To determine the risk level for the expression of evil, information should be gathered on: (a) the degree of complexity, adaptability, and multiple components of the system; (b) the amount of mutual respect, shared responsibility, and social inclusion; and (c) how decisions are made, how rules are applied and enforced as well as the inherent checks and balances of the system.

Academic Tendencies

Academia has been described by some authors as organized anarchy (Cohen and March, 1974). It has a tendency for high individual achievement and discipline to exist alongside increasingly diminished resources (Spratlen, 1995). Additional contributing factors to the organized anarchy are ambiguous and conflicting institutional or individual goals, loose coupling (degree of individual bonding to the institution), and fluid participation (amount of involvement by the individual with the institution) (Cohen and March, 1974; Weick, 1979). It might have a lack of policies and consequences regarding inappropriate behavior (Hawke, 2003). It can be a system fertile for the expression of evil through violence because it: (a) tends to be complex and adaptable and have multiple components; (b) may lack respect, responsibility, and social inclusion; and (c) may encourage chaotic decision with preferential treatment in terms of applying and enforcing "laws" within an environment that lacks checks and balances.

In addition, Nelson and Lambert (2001) describe three normalization techniques used in academia to minimize the evidence of aggressive behavior. The first is "appropriation and inversion," in which the bullies claim to be victims. The second is "evidentiary solipsism," in which bullies portray themselves as uniquely able to define the "true" meaning of events. In the third one, "emotional obfuscation," bullies use symbols and images to elicit an emotional response in the academic audience.

Again, as in the section on organizational tendencies, additional information should be gathered to determine the risk level for the expression of evil that focuses on: (a) the complexity, adaptability, and multiple components of the system; (b) the amount of mutual respect, shared responsibility, and social inclusion; and (c) how decisions are made, laws are applied and enforced as well as the inherent checks and balances of the system. However, in addition to this general organizational assessment, a special aspect of academia requires the examination of the presence of the three normalization techniques unique to academia that minimize the evidence of aggressive behavior (see Figure 17.1).

Figure 17.1   **A Framework for Organizational Systemic Factors of Evil in an Academic University Culture**

Contributing Factors

Individual
- Bullies
- Victims
- Witnesses
- Leaders

Organizational
- Chaotic decisions
- Arbitrary law application
- Absence of independent reviews and enforcement

Academic
- Three normalization techniques of violence

Risk Management Strategies

Individual
- "I-thou"
- Resiliency
- Spiritual life
- Academic peer support

Organizational/Academic
- Policies on academic violence (modeled and with consequences)
- Independent reviews of academic violence
- Awareness of the use of the three normalization techniques for violence

RISK MANAGEMENT STRATEGIES

Individual

Risk management strategies vary, depending on the individual faculty member's professional descriptors (tenure, status, power, etc.) and personal orientation and values. In spite of these variables, some common suggestions can be made. An important caution here, however, is that each faculty member needs to make a respectful individual decision in response to the violence experienced. Such a process may require time and dialogue with trusted others to find the path(s) that seem to best fit that individual in that context at that developmental stage of his/her life.

First, the faculty member can take a nonviolent approach that invites Buber's (1970) concept of the "I-Thou" relationship (Miller et al., 2009). By refusing to "bully back," over time the faculty member might extinguish the aggressive behavior. This can also be a way of keeping one's spirit "alive," refusing to act like an "it" despite being treated like one.

Second, the faculty member may want to focus in on and develop the following resilient factors (Discovery Health Channel and APA, 2002):

- make connections;
- avoid seeing crises as insurmountable;
- accept change as a part of living;
- move toward one's goals;
- take decisive actions;
- look for self-discovery opportunities;
- nurture positive view of oneself;
- keep things in perspective;
- maintain hopeful outlook; and
- take care of oneself.

Third, the faculty member might want to focus on a spiritual life. Spirituality is broadly defined here as the answer to the question "What keeps one's spirit alive?" (Miller, 2003). This question can be used as a guide to help the faculty member ensure that he/she reads, practices his/her life philosophy, takes part in activities, and spends time with loving people in order to continue to live with the violence and oppression experienced from the academic evil. It is critical that the faculty member continue to believe in his/her own decency and goodness and be with others who affirm that belief.

Finally, it might help the faculty member to find academic peer support—to talk with trusted others in different departments and at other universities who can mentor or support them through the difficult "weather." This can be facilitated through discussions in which the faculty member discusses general themes and emotions experienced, but no specific names. Such dialogue can invite the sharing of others' stories of academic life that are validating and encouraging. Such dialogue can assist us in seeing ourselves as interdependent, encouraging us to be less likely to take both our failings and the difficulties we are experiencing as personal (Neff, 2008).

Organizational/Academic

Academic settings have three risk management strategies available to them:

1. develop policies on academic violence, model them, and impose consequences for such behaviors;
2. conduct independent reviews of incidences of academic violence;
3. spread awareness of the use of the three normalization techniques for violence that minimize the expression of evil through violence.

The development of such strategies is necessary for an academic setting in order to prevent the expression of evil through violence. Educational institutions must be a safe place, where individuals are respected and cared for. Policies to ensure such safety must be enforced by administrators who refuse to allow the expression of evil to spread at their institutions.

A DEDICATION TO UNIVERSITY PROFESSORS

For all the times of:

- being kind to a student after being treated unkindly by the system of academia;
- spending time with a student instead of working on that journal article, grant, committee work calling to be done;
- responding to the less than adequate work of a student with both compassion and accountability;
- doing all the "extras" that no one sees or recognizes on a larger scale—reading and grading papers carefully, coming early and staying late, writing recommendation letters, redesigning syllabi, finding ways to support and care for students that are more kind than necessary.

This is to acknowledge your good teaching.

REFERENCES

Ahmed, E. 2008. "Stop it, that's enough": Bystander intervention and its relationship to school connectedness and shame management. *Vulnerable Children and Youth Studies*, 3, 203–213.

Branch, V., and G. Miller. 2006. From micro-inequities to murder: Confronting hurtful workplace behaviors. Paper presented at the Association of American Colleges and Universities Conference, Chicago, November 9–11.

Buber, M. 1970. *I and Thou*, trans. W. Kaufmann. New York: Scribner's.

Cohen, M.D., and J.G. March. 1974. *Leadership and Ambiguity: The American College President.* New York: McGraw-Hill.

Discovery Health Channel and American Psychological Association (APA). 2002. *Aftermath: The Road to Resilience.* Washington, DC: American Psychological Association.

Hawke, M. 2003. Practice information: Fostering a humane workplace. *Virginia Nurses Today,* 11: 10.

Herbst, L. 1999. Decoupled force: Chaos theory and interpretations of the Nazi system of power. *Tel Aviver Jahrbuch für Deutsche Geschichte,* 28, 117–158.

Hixon, S. 2009. Psychosocial processes associated with bullying and victimization. *Humanistic Psychologist,* 37, 257–270.

Lee, L.J., and C.A. Leonard. 2001. Violence in predominantly white institutions of higher education: Tenure and victim blaming. *Journal of Human Behavior in the Social Environment,* 4, 167–186.

Miller, G. 2003. *Incorporating Spirituality in Counseling and Psychotherapy.* Hoboken, NJ: Wiley.

Miller, G., and R. Hood. 2006. Hope in the face of evil. In *Forensic Psychiatry: Influences of Evil,* ed. T. Mason, 355–366. Totowa, NJ: Humana Press.

Miller, G., C. Clark, V. Branch, H. Ersever, and J. Leonard. 2009. Using resilience to cope with academic workplace violence. *North Carolina Perspectives,* 3, 26–37.

Monahan, J., and H.J. Steadman. 1996. Violent storms and violent people. *American Psychologist,* 51, 931–938.

Neff, K.D. 2008. Self-compassion: Moving beyond the pitfalls of a separate self-concept. In *Transcending Self-Interest: Psychological Explorations of the Quiet Ego*, ed. H.A. Wayment and J.J. Bauer, 95–105. Washington, DC: American Psychological Association.

Nelson, E.D., and R.D. Lambert. 2001. Sticks, stones, and semantics: The ivory tower bully's vocabulary of motives. *Qualitative Sociology,* 24, 83–106.

Resnicow, K., and S.E. Page. 2008. Embracing chaos and complexity: A quantum change for public health. *American Journal of Public Health*, 98, 1382–1389.

Russell, J.B. 1988. *The Prince of Darkness: Radical Evil and the Power of Good in History.* Ithaca: Cornell University Press.

Spratlen, L.P. 1995. Interpersonal conflict which includes mistreatment in a university workplace. *Violence and Victims*, 10, 285–297.

Weick, K.E. 1979. *The Social Psychology of Organizing.* Reading, MA: Addison-Wesley.

About the Editor and Contributors

Guy B. Adams is a professor of public affairs in the Harry S Truman School of Public Affairs at the University of Missouri. He is co-editor in chief of the *American Review of Public Administration*. His research interests are in the areas of public administration history and theory, public service ethics, and organization studies. He has more than seventy scholarly publications, including books, book chapters, and articles in the top national and international public administration journals. He earned his Ph.D. in public administration from the George Washington University in Washington, DC, in 1977.

Frank Anechiarico is the Maynard-Knox Professor of Government and Law at Hamilton College. His research interests include integrity enforcement and public procurement. With L.W.J.C. Huberts and Frederique Six, he edited *Local Integrity Systems: World Cities Fighting Corruption and Protecting Integrity* (Bju, 2008) and is co-author of "Who Is the Inspector General?" (with Rose Gill Hearn) and "Public Integrity Networks" (with Lydia Segal), which were published in the Fall 2010 issue of *Public Integrity*.

Danny L. Balfour is a professor of public administration in the School of Public and Nonprofit Administration at Grand Valley State University in Grand Rapids, Michigan. He was the founding managing editor of the *Journal of Public Affairs Education* and serves on the editorial boards of several public affairs journals. He is co-author (with Adams) of *Unmasking Administrative Evil* (3d ed., M.E. Sharpe, 2009) and has more than forty scholarly publications, including book chapters and articles in the top national and international public administration journals. He earned his Ph.D. in public administration from the Florida State University in 1990.

Roy F. Baumeister is a social and personality psychologist interested in many aspects of the human condition, including the causes of evil. He received his Ph.D. in Psychology from Princeton in 1978 and is now head of the social psychology program and Eppes Eminent Scholar at Florida State University. He has written more 450 publications, including 28 books.

Domonic A. Bearfield is an assistant professor of public service and administration in the Bush School of Government and Public Service at Texas A&M University. His research focuses on improving the understanding of public sector human resources, ethics, and public management. He describes his work as the examination of race, representation, and reform. The author of several articles and book chapters, he has published articles in a variety of journals including *Public Administration Review, Public Performance and Management Review, International Journal of Public Administration,* and *Administrative Theory and Praxis.* He also serves on the editorial board of *Public Administration Review.*

Stewart Clegg is a research professor in Management and director of the Centre for Management and Organization Studies Research at the University of Technology, Sydney. A prolific publisher in leading academic journals in social science, management, and organization theory, he is also the author and editor of many books, including recently, *Strategy: Theory and Practice* (with Carter, Kornberger, and Schweitzer; Sage 2011).

Miguel Pina e Cunha is a professor in organization theory at the Nova School of Business and Economics, in Lisbon, Portugal. He has published articles in journals such as the *Academy of Management Review, Human Relations, Journal of Management Studies, Journal of World Business, Organization,* and *Organization Studies.* His research deals with positive and negative organizing and emergent processes in organizations, such as improvisation, surprise, and serendipity.

John Dehn is a Senior Fellow in West Point's Center for the Rule of Law, a member of the editorial committee of Oxford's Journal of International Criminal Justice and a J.S.D. candidate at Columbia University Law School. He is formerly an Assistant Professor at the United States Military Academy, where he taught international, constitutional, and military law.

Martha Derthick is an Emerita Professor of government and foreign affairs at the University of Virginia, where she taught American political institutions and public policy. Previously she was a member of the Governmental Studies Program at the Brookings Institution. Among her books are *Policymaking for Social Security* (Brookings Institution Press, 1979), *The Politics of Deregulation* (with Paul J. Quirk, Brookings Institution Press, 1985), and *Up in Smoke: From Legislation to Litigation in Tobacco Politics* (3d ed., CQ Press, 2011).

J. Patrick Dobel is the John and Marguerite Corbally Chair in Public Service at the University of Washington. He teaches strategy, leadership, and public ethics. He has consulted with numerous public and nonprofit organizations and worked on several ethics commissions. Recently he oversaw the academic and compliance integrity of the University of Washington athletic programs. He writes the blog *Point of the Game*, pointofthegame.net.

Melvin J. Dubnick is Professor of Political Science at the University of New Hampshire, Professor Emeritus at Rutgers University–Newark, and a Fellow of the National

Academy of Public Administration. He has written on issues related to accountability and is particularly interested in the development and use of accountability strategies to deal with perceived instances of social and organizational evil.

Michael R. Ent is a graduate student in social psychology at Florida State University. His research interests include guilt, revenge, and self-control.

Gerald R. Ferris is the Francis Eppes Professor of Management and professor of psychology at Florida State University. He received a Ph.D. in business administration from the University of Illinois at Urbana-Champaign. Ferris has research interests in the areas of social influence and effectiveness processes in organizations and the role of reputation in organizations, and he is the author of articles published in such journals as the *Journal of Applied Psychology, Organizational Behavior and Human Decision Processes, Personnel Psychology, Academy of Management Journal, Academy of Management Review, Journal of Management,* and the *Journal of Organizational Behavior.* He served as editor of the annual research series Research in Personnel and Human Resources Management from its inception in 1983 until 2003. Ferris was the recipient of the Heneman Career Achievement Award and the Thomas A. Mahoney Mentoring Award, from the Human Resource Division of the Academy of Management, in 2001 and 2010, respectively.

H. George Frederickson is the Edwin O. Stene Distinguished Professor of Public Administration at the University of Kansas. He is President Emeritus of Eastern Washington University. Frederickson is the author or co-author of *The New Public Administration; The Spirit of Public Administration; The Public Administration Theory Primer;* and *Measuring the Performance of the Hollow State.* His most recent book, *Social Equity and Public Administration,* was published in January 2010. Frederickson is a fellow of the National Academy of Public Administration and serves on the Academy Board of Directors. He is editor-in-chief of the *Journal of Public Administration Research and Theory.* Frederickson has received the Dwight Waldo Award, the Charles Levine Award, the John Gaus Lecture Award, and the Distinguished Research in Public Administration Award. The Lifetime Award for Contributions to Public Administration Research of the Public Management Research Association is named in his honor, as is the *PA Times* Best Article Award.

Dave Grossman is a former West Point psychology professor, professor of military science, and an Army Ranger, who is the author of *On Killing* (which was nominated for a Pulitzer Prize), *On Combat,* and *Stop Teaching Our Kids to Kill.* He is currently the director of the Killology Research Group. Since the terrorist attacks of 2001, he has written and spoken extensively on the terrorist threat, with articles published in the *Harvard Law Review* and *Civil Policy* and many leading law enforcement journals.

Michael Harvey is Distinguished Chair of Global Business in the School of Business Administration at the University of Mississippi and has a joint appointment at both

Bond University (Australia) and the University of Mississippi. He received his Ph.D. in Marketing and Management from the University of Arizona. Harvey has been an active researcher and consultant for global organizations for the past thirty years. His areas of research interest include global human resource management and global strategy.

Carole L. Jurkiewicz is the Woman's Hospital Distinguished Professor of Healthcare Management and the John W. Dupuy Endowed Professor in the Public Administration Institute of the E.J. Ourso College of Business at Louisiana State University. Her work focuses upon organizational performance as a function of employee ethicality and organizational structure. She has published widely in the areas of organizational and individual performance, ethics, power, and leadership, adding to her academic career many years of experience as an executive in private and nonprofit organizations and a consultant to governments.

Jonathan B. Justice is an associate professor in the School of Public Policy and Administration, University of Delaware, where he teaches courses in public budgeting and finance, and policy analysis. His areas of research activity include public budgeting and finance, accountability and stewardship, and local economic development. Before becoming an academic, he worked for local government and nonprofit organizations in and around New York City.

David R. Mandel is a senior defense scientist at DRDC Toronto and an adjunct associate professor of psychology at the University of Toronto. He received a Ph.D. in psychology from the University of British Columbia. His research largely focuses on human judgment and decision making in the realm of defense and security. His two co-edited books include *The Psychology of Counterfactual Thinking* (Routledge, 2005) and *Neuroscience of Decision Making* (Psychology Press, 2011).

Arthur D. Martinez is assistant professor of management in the College of Business at Illinois State University. He received a Ph.D. in management from Florida State University. His main area of research interest is power in organizations, with particular reference to power differentials in dyadic interactions in organizations. He has published articles in such journals as *Journal of Labor Research, Organizational Dynamics, Human Resource Management Review,* and the *Journal of Leadership and Organizational Studies.* In addition, he has presented his research at both national and regional professional conferences. Before pursuing his Ph.D., Martinez worked in both industrial engineering and business planning at Intel Corporation and as a management analyst at United Airlines.

Geri Miller is a professor in the Department of Human Development and Psychological Counseling (Clinical Mental Health Counseling Track) at Appalachian State University. She holds a Ph.D. and is a Diplomate in Counseling Psychiatry, American Board of Professional Psychiatry. Dr. Miller is a licensed psychologist, a licensed professional counselor, a licensed clinical addictions specialist, and a substance abuse professional practice board certified clinical supervisor.

Miriam Moeller is assistant professor of international business in the UQ Business School at the University of Queensland. She received a Ph.D. in management from the School of Business Administration at the University of Mississippi. Her research has appeared in the *Journal of International Human Resource Management, Organizational Dynamics, Journal of World Business, Journal of Management History, Journal of Applied Social Psychology,* and *Human Resource Development Quarterly,* among others.

Gerson Moreno-Riaño is dean of Regent University's School of Undergraduate Studies as well as an associate professor of government there. He received his Ph.D. in Political Science at the University of Cincinnati, class of 1999. Moreno-Riaño's areas of expertise include the history of political philosophy, with a special emphasis on early modern political ideas, democratic theory, and political theology and ethics. His publications include five authored/edited books as well as numerous chapters and articles in scholarly books and academic journals. His latest publications include the edited *The World of Marsilius of Padua* (Brepols, 2006) and the co-authored *The Prospect of Internet Democracy* (Ashgate, 2009).

Joseph Nowinski has held positions as assistant professor of psychiatry at the University of California San Francisco and associate professor of psychology at the University of Connecticut. He received his Ph.D. in clinical psychology from the University of Connecticut and completed a post-doctoral fellowship at the State University of New York at Stony Brook. He currently has a clinical and consulting practice in Tolland, Connecticut.

Barbara Oakley is an associate professor of engineering at Oakland University in Rochester, Michigan, and a former vice president of the Institute of Electrical and Electronics Engineers' (IEEE) Engineering in Medicine and Biology Society—the world's largest bioengineering society. She earned a B.A. in Slavic Languages and Literature and a B.S. in Electrical Engineering from the University of Washington in Seattle. She received a M.S. in Electrical and Computer Engineering, and a Ph.D. in Systems Engineering, both from Oakland University. Her work focuses on the complex relationship between neurocircuitry and social behavior. Oakley is a recipient of the National Science Foundation's (NSF) Frontiers in Engineering New Faculty Fellow Award, John D. and Dortha J. Withrow Teaching Award, Naim and Ferial Kheir Teaching Award, and she was designated as NSF New Century Scholar. She has also received the NSF Antarctic Service Medal following her work as a communications expert at the South Pole Station. Prior to her academic career, Oakley also rose from the ranks of Private to Captain in the U.S. Army, during which time she was recognized as a Distinguished Military Scholar. Oakley is an elected fellow of the American Institute for Medical and Biological Engineering and the author of *Hair of the Dog* (WSU Press, 1996), *Evil Genes* (Prometheus Press, 2007) and *Coldblooded Kindness* (Prometheus Press, 2011). She is also a co-editor of *Career Development in Bioengineering and Biotechnology* (Springer, 2008) and *Pathological Altruism* (Oxford University Press, 2012).

Arménio Rego is an assistant professor of Organizational Behavior and Human Resources Management at the Universidade de Aveiro, Portugal. He received a Ph.D. in Management from ISCTE–Lisbon University Institute and has published articles in journals such as *Applied Psychology: An International Review, Journal of Business Ethics, Journal of Business Research*, and *Journal of Occupational Health Psychology*. He is also author or co-author of more than thirty books on topics such as leadership, organizational behavior, organizational justice, human resources management, coaching, and corporate social responsibility. His research deals with positive organizational scholarship.

Dan J. Stein is a professor of psychiatry and chair of the Department of Psychiatry at the University of Cape Town and visiting professor of psychiatry at the Mount Sinai School of Medicine in New York City. He received his medical degree from the University of Cape Town and his Ph.D.s in clinical neuroscience and in philosophy from the University of Stellenbosch. His psychiatry residency and post-doctoral fellowship were completed at Columbia University. He has a particular interest in anxiety disorders, in which his work ranges from basic neuroscience to epidemiological research.

Edith van't Hof is a researcher and Ph.D. candidate at the University of Cape Town and VU University Amsterdam. She completed much of her training in the Netherlands, obtaining degrees in both clinical psychology and medical anthropology. She has a strong interest in cross-cultural research and is currently completing her doctoral research on minimal psychological intervention for psychological distress implemented in townships in South Africa.

Margaret H. Vickers is Professor of Management in the School of Business, University of Western Sydney. She received an MBA and Ph.D. She has significant research expertise in workplace adversity and associated health and equity issues including workers with disability and chronic illness; bullying in the workplace; resilience in workers; worker layoffs; caring for a child with disability while working full time; living and working with Multiple Sclerosis (MS); emotions and grief in the workplace; and living with mental illness. She is an experienced qualitative researcher and author of more than 130 international refereed articles and two books, *Work and Unseen Chronic Illness: Silent Voices* (Routledge, 2001) and *Working and Caring for a Child with Chronic Illness: Disconnected and Doing It All* (Palgrave Macmillan, 2006). She is the recipient of numerous competitive Australian government research grants and is currently an international editorial board member of eight international journals, including: *Employee Responsibilities and Rights Journal; Journal of Management and Organization; Qualitative Research in Organizations and Management: An International Journal; Administrative Theory & Praxis;* the *International Journal of Action Research; First Person*, a Subsection of the *Journal Organizational Management Journal;* the *Review of Disability Studies: An International Journal;* and the *Asia Pacific Journal of Business Administration*.

Larry M. Zwain is Managing Director of National Retail Concept Partners, LLC, and serves on the Board of Directors of several national corporations. He received an MBA from Dartmouth. . He has more than thirty years of domestic and international experience in the restaurant industry, including key senior executive positions with PepsiCo, Boston Market, and McDonald's as well as being a franchisee of Papa John's Pizza. He was an Edward Tuck Scholar at Dartmouth's Amos Tuck School of Business and member of the Tuck School Board of Advisors as well as guest lecturer there and at the University of Colorado.

Index

Borich, G., 117
Bosnia, 195
Boston Chicken/Boston Market (BCI), 277–87
  potential unit economics, 286t
  sales totals, 284t
  store operation costs, 284t
bounded evil, 4
Bouraine, A., 180
Bowen, William, 271
Box, R.C., 268
Boyd, R., 48
Boyer, P.J., 256
Boyett, J., 119
BP-Transocean Deepwater Horizon oil rig explosion
  (2010), 97, 211
BPD Central, 43
Brackman Brothers, 285
Braier, G., 181
Branch, V., 289
Branch Davidians, 60
Brandt, Allan M., 255
Brannigan, A., 32
Breitbart, Andrew, 150
Bremer, L. Paul, 266
Brenner, M., 33, 59, 60
Brief, A.P., 149
Brin, Sergey, 99, 100
Briner, R.B., 172
British American Tobacco (BAT) Company, 246
British Petroleum (BP), 211
Broder, J.M., 261, 273
Bromley, D.B., 154
Brooks, David, 194
Brouer, R.L., 105
Brougham, Henry, 250–51
Brown, A., 116
Brown, J.D., 51
Brown, P., 128, 129
Brown, R.G., 11
Brown & Williamson Tobacco Company, 245, 246,
  248, 249
Browning, Christopher, 27, 146
Bruce, V., 52
Brüne, M., 48
Buber, M., 291, 294
Buckley, M.R., 105, 108
Buddha, 128
Buddhism, 229, 231, 238–39
Buffalo, M.D., 158n.12
Buffett, Warren, 36, 37, 58, 80
bullying
  academic violence and, 292, 293, 294
  sadism and, 217–18
  sanctionability of, 154, 155
  workplace, 163, 164, 170–74, 176
Bundy, Ted, 96
Bunge, M., 147, 158n.6
Bupp, Chip, 59–60
Bureau of Alcohol, Tobacco, and Firearms (BATF), 60
Bureau of Diplomatic Security, 261, 266

bureaucracy, 83, 233–34, 259, 260
  Kafkaesque, 226, 235–37
Burger King, 283
Burma. *See* Myanmar
burnout, workers and, 164
Bush, George W., 20, 21, 77, 88, 90, 249, 259
Bushman, B.J., 215
Buss, D.M., 90–91, 93, 96, 98
Byrne, C.C., 185
Byrne, J.A., 105
Byron, Christopher, 49, 55, 57, 60, 68n.6, 68n.7
bystanders, of evil, 89, 180–82, 185, 207

Cahn, S.M., 32
Calhoun, L., 196
Calvinism, 137
Cambodia, 183, 225–43
  See also Khmer Rouge; Pol Pot
Campbell, Alastair, 192
Campbell, W.K., 7, 8, 10, 12
Campione, J., 116
Campo-Flores, A., 213
canons, 130, 131, 132
Cappiello, D., 205
Card, Claudia, 16, 105
Card, R.F., 175
Carey, B., 35
Carlat, D., 32, 36, 58
Carnegie family, 80
Carson, C.N., 253
Carter, C., 241
Casey, E.S., 129
Casey, N., 210
Cassidy, C., 181
Castle, The (Kafka), 226, 237
Castro, Fidel, 59
casualties, military, 263–64
Cather, W., 62, 63
Catholic Church. *See* Roman Catholic Church
Ceausescu, Nicolae, 10
Cebula, R., 36
Center for Public Integrity, 23, 261
Center for Responsive Politics, 252
Central Intelligence Agency (CIA), 21, 22, 24, 25
Challenger space shuttle, 259
Chamberlain, P., 118
Chandler, David P., 55, 183, 230, 232, 233, 234,
  235, 236, 237, 238, 240
character, 82, 193–94
charismatic figures, 146
checks and balances, 65, 66, 67, 292, 293
Chelmno, 145
Cheney, Dick, 21
Chi Fung factory, 207
child abuse, 154
child labor, 79–80
child pornography, 3
children
  borderlines, 53
  in Cambodia, 239

children *(continued)*
  media's impact on, 12
  torture of, 88, 89
China, 31, 99, 229, 231, 240
Chomsky, Noam, 6, 35
Christian Science, 61–64
Christianity, 131, 192
  extremist violence, 212–13
Christie, R., 44, 45, 46, 48
Church of Scientology, 56
Cienfugos, A.J., 185
*Cipollone v. Liggett Group, Philip Morris, and
    Loews*, 245
Ciresi, Michael, 249
Clark, R.C., 253
class action lawsuits, 254, 278
Clegg, Stewart R., 166, 167, 174, 175, 176, 225–43
Cleghorn, Sarah, 79
clerics, 124, 130, 134, 136–38, 139, 140
client confidentiality, 251
Clinton, Bill, 249
Cloud, D.S., 267
Coalition Provisional Authority (CPA), 266
Cochran, B., 35
codes of behavior, 4
codes of conduct, corporate, 99
Cohen, L., 116
Cohen, M.D., 293
Cohen, Stanley, 148, 150
Cohen, Steven, 258
Cole, J., 130, 131, 137
Cole, S., 32, 58
Coleman, Daniel, 21
collective unconscious, 109
collectivization, 228–29, 231–32, 239
Collins, James C., 138, 139
Collins, R., 235
collusion, 19
colonialism, 78, 80, 231
Comer, D., 169, 172, 176
commerce, 80–81
commercialization, 12
commons, the (concept), 84
Communist Party of Indochina, 231
Communist Party of Kampuchea (CPK), 226, 227,
    228–30, 237, 239, 241
Communist Party of Vietnam, 231
communist regimes, 35, 64, 65, 238
  Cambodia, 227, 228–32, 237, 240, 241
  See also China; Soviet Union
compartmentalization, 66
compensation, survivors and, 183
competition, groups and, 214
concern for others, 5
condemnation, 148
Confessions (Augustine), 195
Congress, U.S., 36, 246, 271, 275
Congressional Research Service, 261, 267
Conquest, R., 35
consciousness, 197–98

consent of the governed, 200
Consideration (supervisory dimension), 109–15
Constitution, U.S., 259, 274
constitutional government, 200, 259
control, 44f
  borderlines and, 48, 49
  Machiavellians and, 38, 44, 56–58
conversion, religious, 135–36
Conway, N., 172
Cooke, D.J., 35, 44
Coombs, C.K., 36
Coons, A., 110, 111
Cooper, K.J., 158n.1
Cops, Teachers, and Councilors (Maynard-Moody
    and Mushno), 85
Corinthians, 127
corporate culture, 281–82
corporate evil, 87, 94–98
corporate psychopaths, 57
*Corporation, The: The Pathological Pursuit of Profit
    and Power* (Bakan), 34, 209
corporations, 36, 80–81, 87, 94–98, 208–9
  Bakan's view of, 34–37
  codes of conduct, 99
  organizational evil roots and, 216
  as "persons," 145
Corrigan, L., 287
corruption, 36, 37, 83, 164
Cortina, L.M., 149
Cosby, Bill, 68n.5
Cosmides, Leda, 47, 48, 51, 57–58
Council on Tobacco Research, 247, 248
Courpasson, D., 237
courts-martial, 271, 272
cover-ups, 19
Craig, William, 191–92
Cramer, J., 36
Cramer, V., 39
Cramton, R.C., 251
crime, 204, 210
  See also specific types of
criminalization, 154–55
Critcher, C., 148
Crocker, David, 183
Cromwell, Oliver, 137
Cross, R., 89
Crowell, S.E., 40
Crowley, P.J., 265
cult killings, 11
cults, 32
cultural distance, 9
Cultural Revolution (China), 231
culture
  academic, 289–96
  corporate, 281–82
  industrial crafting of, 7
culture, organizational
  evil development and, 3, 4, 5, 8–9, 12
  holiness and, 138–39
  psychopathology and, 5–6, 6f, 10